"*The Carbon-[...]* [...] g our carbon impact on th[...] to give us all the head start we need to move towards a sustainable lifestyle. If you're willing to do the work, this book will inspire you to squeeze every molecule out of your carbon budget."

—Paul Scheckel, author of *The Home Energy Diet*

"Stephen and Rebekah Hren have grasped the nettle and implemented simple and ingenious do-it-yourself technologies to achieve the goal of zero-carbon living. Their book offers a rich selection of options for all who desire to reduce their carbon footprint."

—John Terborgh, Director of the Duke University Center for Tropical Conservation and author of *Requiem for Nature*

"This is an excellent resource for people committed to reducing their energy consumption and global carbon emissions."

—Joe Loper, Vice President for Policy and Research, Alliance to Save Energy

"The Hren's book provides an meaningful pathway to a carbon-free lifestyle— including everything from the latest in high-tech equipment to homemade solutions that will satisfy the earthiest of back-to-landers."

—Michael Welch, Redwood Alliance

"We can't pontificate our way out of the awful mess we have, and we can't whine our way out either. We have to design our way out, and *The Carbon-Free Home* explains in plain language how to start designing-out in our own crawlspaces and attics. The measures we take now for our individual independence will soon enough be required for our collective survival."

—Stan Goff, author of *Hideous Dream* and *Full Spectrum Disorder*

THE CARBON-FREE HOME

36 Remodeling Projects to Help
Kick the Fossil-Fuel Habit

THE CARBON-FREE HOME

36 Remodeling Projects to Help
Kick the Fossil-Fuel Habit

Stephen and Rebekah Hren

Chelsea Green Publishing | White River Junction, Vermont

Project Manager: Emily Foote
Copy Editor: Susan Barnett
Proofreader: Nancy Ringer
Indexer: Christy Stroud
Designer: Peter Holm, Sterling Hill Productions

Printed in 2008
First printing, May 2008
10 9 8 7 6 5 4 3 2 1   08 09 10 11 12

Our Commitment to Green Publishing

Chelsea Green sees publishing as a tool for cultural change and ecological stewardship. We strive to align our book manufacturing practices with our editorial mission and to reduce the impact of our business enterprise on the environment. We print our books and catalogs on chlorine-free recycled paper, using soy-based inks whenever possible. This book may cost slightly more because we use recycled paper, and we hope you'll agree that it's worth it. Chelsea Green is a member of the Green Press Initiative (www .greenpressinitiative.org), a nonprofit coalition of publishers, manufacturers, and authors working to protect the world's endangered forests and conserve natural resources.

   The Carbon-Free Home was printed on 60# Joy White, a 30-percent post-consumer-waste recycled, old-growth-forest–free paper supplied by Thomson-Shore.

Library of Congress Cataloging-in-Publication Data
Hren, Stephen, 1974-
   The carbon-free home : 36 remodeling projects to help kick the fossil-fuel habit / Stephen and Rebekah Hren.
      p. cm.
   Includes bibliographical references and index.
   ISBN 978-1-933392-62-2
1. Ecological houses. 2. Dwellings--Energy conservation. 3. Sustainable living. I. Hren, Rebekah, 1975- II. Title.

TH4860.H84 2008
644--dc22

                            2008006287

Chelsea Green Publishing Company
Post Office Box 428
White River Junction, VT 05001
(802) 295-6300
www.chelseagreen.com

Contents

We dedicate this book to our parents,
Joyce and John Hren and Linda and Lane Wharton,
who never failed to support us during even
our most outrageous adventures

ACKNOWLEDGMENTS

We are very indebted and extremely grateful to the following authors, organizations, and friends, whose excellent work has greatly improved the information we are able to present to our readers:

Solar Energy International. For their great work promoting renewable energy and teaching Rebekah all about photovoltaics. "To provide education and technical assistance so that others will be empowered to use renewable energy technologies."

Solar Cookers International. We present two of their solar-cooker plans that are taken from the 10th edition of *Solar Cookers: How to Make, Use and Enjoy*, which is available on the Internet at http://solarcook ing.org/plans/Plans.pdf. This is an excellent resource for further information about solar cooking, including recipes and the history of solar cooking. "SCI is a nonprofit, nongovernmental organization spreading solar cooking for the benefit of people and the environment."

The Kerr-Cole Sustainable Living Center. We have presented an edited version of their Solar Wall Oven installation instructions. The instructions in their entirety can be found at the Web site: http://www .solarcooking.org/bkerr/DoItYourself.htm. "Educating individuals and families to integrate sustainable living practices and technologies into their lives, with focus on technologies and practices relating to the home environment."

Aprovecho Research Center. Many of Aprovecho's great articles helped us understand the fundamentals of heating and cooking with wood, especially *Designing Improved Wood Burning Heating Stoves* (2006) by Bryden, Still, Ogle, and MacCarty. "To research, develop, and disseminate technological solutions for meeting the basic human needs of low income and impoverished people and communities in third world countries, in order to help relieve their suffering, improve their health, enhance their safety, and reduce their adverse impacts on their environment."

Patricia MacComber, the College of Tropical Agriculture and Human Resources, and the Texas Water Development Board. Their excellent public documents explain whole-house rainwater collection systems. See "Guidelines on Rainwater Catchment Systems for Hawaii" and "The Texas Manual on Rainwater Harvesting."

Oasis Design and Art Ludwig. For their groundbreaking work with rainwater collection and graywater reuse, especially *The New Create an Oasis with Greywater*.

Joseph Jenkins. We excerpt the composting toilet system that Mr. Jenkins outlines in the third edition of his book, *The Humanure Handbook*. This book is an excellent read on a neglected but vital topic and we hope that you'll pick up a copy.

Bob Crosby. During our research into biogas and anaerobic digesters, we had the pleasure of several long conversations and many e-mails with Bob Crosby of Biorealis Systems, Inc. (www.biorealis.com), on the feasibility of constructing home-scale humanure biodigesters. Bob has created several working prototypes for humanure biodigesters and maintains an awesome Web forum on the subject that we highly recommend. He has graciously allowed us to reprint the designs for his original prototype and bench-scale digester.

Lee Reich. Reich's excellent *Uncommon Fruits for Every Garden* helped us tremendously as we planned our edible landscape and provided us with detailed information on many of the species we summarize. It's a great book for anyone with even just a small piece of dirt.

Eric Toensmeier. Generally for his work with Dave Jacke on *Edible Forest Gardens*, but specifically for his garden guide *Perennial Vegetables*, which greatly bene-fited our garden, our stomachs, and especially this book.

We also wish to thank our friends and families who have joined us for work parties and labor trades and suffered through many a long evening's discussion of energy issues. To name just a few and risk leaving many out: Matt Bua, Rachel Burton, Kelly and Ryan Dimock, Tom Honey, Jon Kirschten, Mimi Logothetis, Kyra Moore, Brian Quast, Elizabeth and Noah Read, Pat Schell, Keith Shaljian, Dan Stern, Kevin Svara, Rachel Wharton, and all the folks in NC Powerdown.

"Man's capacities have never been measured; nor are we to judge what we can do by any precedents, so little has been tried. What people say you cannot do, you try and find you can."
HENRY DAVID THOREAU

"Sentiment without action is the ruin of the soul."
EDWARD ABBEY

Table of Projects

Project Title	Time	Cost	Energy Saved	Renter Friendly	Skills	Page
Batch Solar Water Heater	Three to Four Days	Variable ($500–3,000)	High	No	Intermediate Carpentry	110
Bench-Scale Biogas Digester	Afternoon	Inexpensive ($50)	Low	Yes	Basic Plumbing, Basic Carpentry	189
Building a Horizontal Trellis for Shading	Afternoon	Inexpensive ($50–200)	High	Yes	Basic Carpentry	220
Building a Vertical Wall Trellis for a Windbreak	Afternoon	Inexpensive ($50–100)	High	No	Basic Carpentry	222
Building an Active Solar Air Heater	Several Weekends	Variable ($10–30/sq. ft.)	High	No	Advanced Carpentry	140
Closed-Loop Pressurized Solar Water Heater	Three to Four Days	Expensive ($3,000–7,000)	High	No	Intermediate Carpentry, Advanced Plumbing, Intermediate Electrical	105
Earth Plaster an Existing Wall	Weekend	Inexpensive ($5–50)	Low	No	Basic Masonry	136
Electrical Consumption Analysis	One Hour	Free	Varies	Yes	None	23
Energy Diary	One Week	Free	High	Yes	None	36
Evaporative Cooling Box	Afternoon	Inexpensive ($5–50)	High	Yes	Basic Carpentry	84
Haybox Cooker	One Hour	Free	Low	Yes	None	77
Humanure Toilet and Hacienda	Weekend	Inexpensive ($50–200)	High	No	Moderate Carpentry	184
Inoculating Logs with Mycelium	Afternoon	Inexpensive ($20–100)	Low	Yes	None	209
Install a 5-V Metal Roof	Several Weekends	Expensive ($1–2/sq. ft.)	High	No	Advanced Carpentry	163
Insulating a Hot-Water Tank and Hot-Water Pipes	Three Hours	Inexpensive ($50–100)	Medium	Yes	Basic Carpentry	100
Insulation of Existing Fridge	Weekend	Inexpensive ($50–100)	High	Yes	Moderate Carpentry	83
Laundry Graywater to Catchment Container	Afternoon	Inexpensive ($5–100)	Low	Yes	Moderate Carpentry, Moderate Plumbing	176
Making and Applying Slip Straw and Clay Slip	One Weekend or more	Inexpensive ($5–50)	High	No	Basic Carpentry	125
Making Cob	Several Weekends	Variable ($0–500)	Medium	No	Moderate Carpentry, Basic Masonry	134
Northern Window Conversion to Cold Box	Weekend	Inexpensive ($50–100)	High	Yes	Moderate Carpentry	86
Outdoor Cob Oven	Several Weekends	Inexpensive ($50–100)	Low	Yes	Moderate Carpentry	72
Outdoor Solar Shower	One Day	Inexpensive ($5–100)	Medium to High	Yes	Basic Plumbing, Basic Carpentry	101
Panel Cooker	Afternoon	Inexpensive ($5–20)	Low	Yes	Basic Carpentry	55
Planting Edible Perennials	One Hour	Inexpensive ($5–50)	Low to Medium	No	None	202
Potato Barrel	One Hour	Inexpensive ($5–10)	High	Yes	None	224
Rain Barrel	Afternoon	Inexpensive ($20–100)	Low	Yes	Basic Carpentry, Basic Plumbing	152
Renewable Electric System Site Analysis	Afternoon	Free	N/A	No	None	25
Resetting a Water-Heater Thermostat	One Hour	Free	Medium	Yes	Basic Electrical	99
Sealing Drafts	Weekend	Inexpensive ($5–50)	High	Yes	Basic Carpentry	121
Sealing Unused Windows	One Hour	Inexpensive ($10–100)	Medium	Yes	Basic Carpentry	117
Sheet Mulching and Polycultures	Afternoon	Inexpensive ($5–20)	Low	Yes	None	198
Simple Box Cooker	Afternoon	Inexpensive ($5–20)	Low	Yes	Basic Carpentry	52
Solar Wall Oven	Several Weekends	Inexpensive ($50–100)	Low	No	Advanced Carpentry	58
Storm Windows	One Hour	Variable ($~70/window)	High	No	Basic Carpentry	118
Wood Cookstove	Several Weekends	Expensive ($2,000–4,000)	Varies	No	Advanced Carpentry	71
Woodstove Installation	Several Weekends	Expensive ($1,000–5,000)	Medium	No	Advanced Carpentry, Moderate Masonry	144

HOW TO USE THIS BOOK

This book is designed as a guide for the owner of an existing home who is motivated to reduce and eventually eliminate his or her use of nonrenewable fossil energy and its accompanying carbon dioxide emissions. The book is arranged into chapters by specific household needs that are commonly provided by fossil energy, such as refrigeration and hot water. For each chapter, we first describe ways in which a typical home's existing infrastructure can be made more efficient. We then list alternative options and how to achieve them. At the beginning of each section, you'll find information on approximately how long each project will take and how much it will cost. In addition, you'll find a general description of the project, the energy it saves, its ease of daily use, its long-term level of maintenance, and the skills, tools, and materials you'll need to move forward.

Some chapters provide more hands-on projects than others. In particular, the chapter on renewable electric systems limits itself to site evaluation and system overviews due to the complexity and danger of homeowner installation of these systems. It's certainly possible for the dedicated and skilled homeowner to install them, but detailed books on installing renewable electric systems already exist. Instead, this book presents DIY alternatives for basic household-energy needs. For those of you embarking on building your own home, we hope there is also much here in theory and practice that will help you design and build a carbon-free home, although that is not our focus. For renters, there are quite a few projects, including many conservation measures, that can help you greatly reduce your energy use.

The book can be perused at random, but if you decide to kick the fossil-fuel habit altogether, it's best to spend some time drawing up a plan and budget and to proceed in a somewhat orderly manner. This is because doing some things first could make doing other things harder later on. For instance, installing a solar hot-water heater on your roof and then deciding you want to replace your asphalt shingles with a metal roof for rainwater catchment and passive cooling can mean a substantial disassembly of your solar hot-water panels.

If you're just starting out on your journey away from fossil fuels, we encourage you to flip through and accomplish some of the easier tasks. The table at left includes 36 projects, listed by cost, difficulty, renter-friendliness, and other criteria. Many of these projects can easily and dramatically reduce your energy use. For those of you who are already aware of what's possible and want to get down to brass tacks, read the section in the first chapter on how to plan for a whole-house conversion.

Near the beginning of each chapter, in the "Our Story" section, we'll discuss what choices we made and why. We hope that by reading our story you will better understand how differences in climate, free time, money, and skill shaped the decisions we made about what systems we chose and that you will find our example both illuminating and inspiring. It is most important not to become overwhelmed. Remember that any little bit helps, and, most likely, achieving a carbon-free home will be a long hike up a steep road. But that doesn't mean you won't get there or that you won't find the journey very satisfying. Good luck!

Introduction

WHY CARBON FREE?

Since the industrial revolution began, we have depended on what seemed to be a limitless supply of fossil energy hidden just beneath our feet. First coal, then oil, then natural gas were discovered and exploited, the earth scoured for their deposits; control of these fuels became the subject of political maneuverings and even war.

The accumulated harm from two centuries of burning fossil fuels has become overwhelming. Carbon dioxide in our atmosphere has accumulated to levels not seen for more than 650,000 years. Our globalized economy is dependent on continuous access to dwindling supplies of these fossil fuels, leading to partnerships with rogue states and an unhealthy interest in the impossible goal of controlling the volatile Middle East.

The impetus for our destructive behavior is unarguably our ever-increasing demand for energy. What at first seemed like a blessing has turned into a curse. We take for granted the fabulous things that fossil energy makes available to us, such as heated and cooled homes, refrigeration, constant electricity, washing machines, dryers, and long daily commutes. But the earth, the source of this luxurious lifestyle and the repository of its pollutants, is showing undeniable signs of stress on every level. The specific incident that might make history as marking the beginning of the end of the fossil-fuel era is not terribly important, whether it's the peaking of the mighty oil fields in Saudi Arabia or the ice sheets of Greenland slipping into the sea. What is important is that we need to act now, in our own homes and lives, and get ready for the renewable energy revolution.

The good news is that a small group of folks back in the day saw the end of the fossil-energy era approaching and began to embrace renewable energy from the sun, wind, earth, and sea. Why their message did not inspire more converts before now is the subject for someone else's book; nevertheless, research into living a sustainable life has been gaining momentum for over four decades, and we can harvest the fruit of that hard work. It is now possible to live a very good life, not much different from the one many of us are living right now, using only renewable energy and free of accumulating carbon emissions.

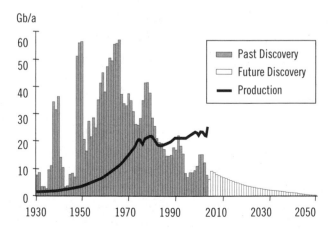

Oil accounts for roughly 40 percent of all energy used worldwide, and nearly 95 percent of all transportation fuel. The world now consumes roughly 4 barrels of oil for every new barrel discovered. Source: Association for the Study of Peak Oil, 2002

Fall 2000. Putting the first few rafters into our hand-built cob home. We lived out here for six years until the endless driving drove us nuts.

This book is a guide for those interested in the path to getting all of their own energy from renewable sources and living a life free of fossil fuels. It shows you how to reduce personal energy consumption as much as possible and how to retrofit an existing home so as to obtain all heating and cooling, all cooking and refrigeration, and all hot water and electricity from renewable sources, discussing in detail as many options as possible for each category. It also covers sustainable transportation options as well as garden and landscaping ideas, as poor choices about these issues can negate hard-won gains in other parts of the home.

The motivation for this book was our own determination to take responsibility for our actions and wean ourselves completely from fossil fuels. On a personal level, we felt compelled to do this because of our growing understanding of fossil energy depletion and the reality that these fuels are going to be less available and more expensive as time goes on. At least as important, we felt we had a moral obligation to act to mitigate our contribution to the ravages of pollution, most significantly global climate disruption, that are the inevitable and accumulating result of our use of fossil fuels. For so many reasons, and especially for the energy independence it provides, we hope you will join us in the journey to carbon-free lives.

WHAT WE MEAN BY *CARBON FREE*

Throughout this book, you'll hear us refer to the terms *carbon free*, and, almost as frequently, *fossil-fuel free*. Carbon is the basis for all life forms, so the phrase *carbon free* may seem odd. However, over the last year or two, awareness has increased dramatically of the imminent deleterious effects of global climate disruption caused primarily by carbon dioxide emissions from burning fossil fuels. Sustainable alternatives to fossil-

Our first attempt: the passive and active solar home we built together, made of cob and a 30-mile drive from the nearest urban area.

fuel-based and carbon-dioxide-emitting activities are commonly referred to as carbon neutral or carbon free, and that is how we are using the term. Burning plant-based fuels such as wood or biodiesel also emits carbon dioxide. But two considerations lead us to consider these plant-based fuels carbon free: Because these fuels can be used in equal amounts to what can be reproduced in a comparable time frame and because plants capture carbon during their lives in an amount equal to that which is given off during their use as fuel, they are "carbon neutral" by design.

Fossil fuels permeate every aspect of modern civilization, of which we're a part. We cannot claim that none are ever burned for our specific benefit. However, we have managed to eliminate their use from nearly 100 percent of our daily activities in our home, our transportation, and much of our food. We believe such a carbon-free life is possible for every person on the planet.

OUR STORY

Energy issues have always been a mild obsession for both of us. Early on, it seemed strange to us that our lives failed to make use of the obviously prodigious solar resources that were available. We couldn't understand why the homes we lived in were not designed to take advantage of the sun in winter, why there were so few clotheslines hanging in our neighbors' yards, or why there were zillions of acres of grass where there could be fruit trees or vegetable gardens.

What started out as a passing interest led to more research and study. The deeper we dug, the more serious the issue of energy seemed to become. As we went about our daily lives—eating, driving, working, shopping—it started to become clear that everything we did only made things worse. Everything we did required more and more energy, and every day this did more damage to the natural beauty we saw around us. The weather got hotter and weirder, we had to give money to oil companies like Exxon-Mobil that refused to pay for their oil spills and denied global climate disruption, and our government initiated a preemptive war in our name, with all the murder and torture that the word *war* implies, to try to control the last reserves of dwindling crude oil.

Our initial reaction was to buy a chunk of land in the country and try to become "independent." We built our own passive-solar house out of cob (a traditional mix of clay, sand, and straw), went off-grid, and tried to grow our own food and raise poultry. Meanwhile, we still had jobs back in town and often wanted to socialize there, which meant frequent 40-minute drives. Not long after the elation of successfully installing our photovoltaic panels, getting our cob home past its final inspection, and legally moving into our new home, we learned that an automobile uses as much energy while it's running as 350 100-watt bulbs! Driving an hour to town and back used the equivalent amount of energy as running our home's electrical needs for over a month.

How ironic! We had been criticizing our friends who refused to replace their incandescent bulbs with compact fluorescents, yet here we were, driving all the time, the worst offenders of all! On top of that, the idea that we could live self-sufficiently out in the woods turned out to be a cruel joke. Although neither of us had much of a green thumb, we had assumed it would be easy to grow most of our own food organically and with minimal petroleum inputs. Instead we spent a great deal of time doing a halfway job and getting meager returns. The garden became our enemy, and we were shackled to it, every evening, picking bugs and pulling weeds in the blistering heat.

It became obvious we had made a mistake. We'd tried to start from scratch and throw everything out, including the established communities and the infrastructure of towns and cities, and do it all ourselves. Running away to live in the woods isn't an option for most people, and if everyone tried to do it, it would become even more futile. We were and are convinced that as day turns to dusk for fossil fuels, we must take a good look at our surroundings and learn to live with what we have already built, what we've spent our free fossil currency on: the infrastructure, especially the housing, that already exists in our towns and cities. For us, it was time to learn from our mistakes and move back to the city, a city that had oodles of existing and abandoned houses just waiting for a good retrofit, a good farmer's market filled with local organic produce, and friends, jobs, and entertainment. It was time to do things in a way that others could see and emulate. It was time to do it right.

RESOURCES

Books
Check your local library!

Flannery, Tim. 2005. *The Weather Makers: How Man Is Changing the Climate and What It Means for Life on Earth.* New York: Atlantic Monthly Press. Mr. Flannery goes beyond a convincing argument for the severity of climate change and offers a range of personal and policy changes for dealing with the problem.

Heinberg, Richard. 2005. *The Party's Over: Oil, War, and the Fate of Industrial Societies*, Revised and Expanded Edition. Gabriola Island, BC: New Society Publishers. Mr. Heinberg's understanding of energy is spot-on. A must-read.

Meadows, Donella H. 2004. *The Limits to Growth: 30-Year Update.* White River Junction, VT: Chelsea Green Publishing. Shows how all resources, not just energy, have natural geological limits.

Monbiot, George. 2006. *Heat: How to Stop the Planet Burning.* London and New York: Allen Lane. Ideas for how to reduce our energy consumption by 90 percent by 2030.

DVDs
A Crude Awakening. 2007. An excellent introduction to peak oil.

The End of Suburbia. 2004. Examines oil depletion's likely impact on America's sprawling suburbs.

An Inconvenient Truth. 2006. If you still haven't seen Al Gore's convincing summation of the fact of human-made global climate disruption, see it soon with as many folks as you can round up.

What a Way to Go: Life at the End of Empire. 2007. Not only takes a broad look at global climate disruption and peak oil but also exposes fundamental fallacies that lead to these destructive behaviors. (For more information visit www.whatawaytogomovie.com.)

Incentive Programs

Some of your carbon-reducing projects may qualify for subsidies or rebates, depending on where you live. DSIRE (Database of State Incentives for Renewables & Efficiency) is a comprehensive source of information on state, local, utility, and federal incentives that promote renewable energy and energy efficiency; see www.dsireusa.org.

Internet

Energy Bulletin. Excellent all-around energy and global-warming coverage. www.energybulletin.net

Oil Drum. Thorough and groundbreaking articles on peak oil, including message boards. www.theoildrum.com

CHAPTER 1

Understanding Home Energy Use

Your Household Energy Budget • What Is Heat? • Planning a Whole-House Conversion • The Solar Window • Special Considerations for Retrofitting • Resources

Energy provides us with the necessities, comforts, and luxuries that make a home a personal place of refuge from the world. By almost any measure, we're consuming more energy in our homes than is sustainable, but this fact alone doesn't mean that a combination of conservation and renewable energy will result in our homes being any less comfortable. Beyond converting to renewable sources of energy, much of what we need to do is learn how to use all energy more wisely in the first place. In order to do this, we need to know how much energy we use now, how much is available from renewable sources, and how energy is captured and deployed.

YOUR HOUSEHOLD ENERGY BUDGET

We Americans use a prodigious quantity of energy, 95 percent of it nonrenewable. Let's familiarize ourselves with the numbers so we can better understand where we get that energy and where it goes.

A Btu is the amount of energy required to raise the temperature of one pound of water by one degree Fahrenheit. On average, the typical home in the United States uses just around 100 million Btus of energy per year. This number includes all fuels used for all purposes except transportation. However, the production of these 100 million Btus requires, on average, 172 million Btus. The remaining 72 million Btus are lost to inefficiencies in transmission and refining.[1]

To extricate ourselves from fossil-fuel dependence means we must learn to live on our annual income of energy from the sun, no longer depending on the

TABLE 1.1 Fossil and Renewable Fuels and Their Energy Content	
Fuel	Btu/Unit
Gasoline	115,000/gallon
Diesel/Heating Oil	130,500/gallon
Ethanol	75,700/gallon
Biodiesel	110,000/gallon
Propane	92,000/gallon
Natural Gas	1,027/ft³
Solar Energy	317/ft2/hour
Hydrogen	333/ft³
Coal (bituminous)	11,500/lb
Coal (sub-bituminous)	8,200/lb
Coal (lignite)	6,500/lb
Firewood (unseasoned)	1,600/lb
Firewood (air dry)	6,400/lb
Firewood (oven dry)	8,600/lb
Source: Oak Ridge National Laboratory	

limited accumulated residue of past solar energy. Is it possible? The average annual *insolation* (energy from the sun) hitting 100 square feet is around 58 million Btus. If we were able to convert every bit of energy received from the sun into usable power, we could power the average home with less than 300 square feet of sunny space—an area smaller than a quarter of the average roof.

Unfortunately, we also drive a lot, typically over 12,000 miles a year.[2] This adds about another 148 million Btus per household, since there are generally two vehicles per household, with average fuel consumption of 21 miles per gallon of gasoline. Still, this would require only approximately an additional 300 square feet of insolation space, if we could use all the solar energy striking that area.

Of course, we're nowhere near collecting 100 percent of the solar energy that hits our homes. Most homes don't collect any, except by accident. But considering that plants, which have been at it for billions of year, are capable of capturing only around 5 percent of the solar energy that falls on their leaves (which they do through photosynthesis), it bodes well for our cleverness as humans that we are capable of capturing around 15 percent in photovoltaic (PV) panels and 70 percent or more in heating applications.

The easiest and most efficient way to exploit the abundance of solar energy striking the earth each day is by heating things up. This is good, because heating things such as water and indoor air is a large part of what we want from our energy in the colder climes of the northern hemisphere. Together, space heating, water heating, and cooking are half of our energy budget, so capturing solar energy at 70 percent efficiency for these purposes is fairly straightforward and highly effective.

We use a lot of energy to keep things hot or cold. Heating or cooling our homes, cooking or storing our food, and heating water all require the capture and control of heat. Having a better understanding of the fundamentals of heat will help in the effective design and installation of any renewable-energy systems in your home.

TABLE 1.2 A Typical Home's Energy Budget Allotment	
32 percent	Space Heating
13 percent	Water Heating
12 percent	Lighting
11 percent	Air Conditioning
8 percent	Refrigeration
6 percent	Computers and Electronics
5 percent	Washer/Dryer/Dishwasher
4 percent	Cooking
9 percent	Miscellaneous

Source: U.S. Department of Energy, *Buildings Energy Data Book*, September 2006

WHAT IS HEAT?

Since capturing and retaining heat without burning fossil fuels is vital to achieving a carbon-free home, it's worthwhile to expand your understanding of what heat is and how it moves. Heat is nothing more than the transfer of energy between matter. This always occurs from warmer bodies to cooler ones, in accord with the Second Law of Thermodynamics, which states that in a given system differences in temperature, pressure, and density even out, leading to a state of *entropy.* Heat transfer cannot be stopped, only slowed.

Methods of heat transfer. Large sources of heat are created in one of four ways: chemical reactions such as burning, nuclear reactions (fusion in the sun or fission in a nuclear reactor), electromagnetic dissipation (or turbulence resulting from conflicting magnetic fields) as in an electric stove, and mechanical dissipation (or turbulence resulting from physical contact), also called friction. After its creation, heat moves in one of three ways: radiation, conduction, and convection.

1. *Radiation* is the electromagnetic movement of energy through space. This occurs in straight lines in all directions.
2. *Conduction* is the movement of energy through physical contact. This happens within a body and between bodies wherever they touch. Dense materials conduct energy more easily than porous materials do. Generally, this means metals are highly conductive, masonry and earth less so, and light, fluffy materials like straw and feathers much less so.
3. *Convection* is the movement of energy into or out of a body through fluids, both liquid and gas, flowing around it. Convective heat loss generally happens upward because of gravity. As the fluid becomes heated, it becomes less dense and thus lighter. As it moves up, it is replaced by denser, cooler fluid, and the heat transfer continues.

Slowing heat transfer. Often in our homes we wish to build up heat in some places and keep it from entering other places. For instance, we want to keep heat out during hot summer days but concentrate it in any food we are cooking. Whether we're trying to build heat up or keep it out, we want to regulate the transfer of heat as much as possible by using the appropriate materials.

It is often the case that heat is being transferred by several means simultaneously, and this makes complete heat regulation all but impossible. One method of heat transfer usually predominates, however, so if we address the predominant method we'll make our heat regulation as effective as possible.

The best way to slow *radiation* is by means of a **radiant barrier**. Effective radiant barriers are reflective, such as mirrors, sheets of metal, or white paint. *Conduction* is slowed by **limiting the contact of the material with other objects**, especially those that are denser and hence more highly conductive. The ideal way to stop conduction would be to suspend an object in a vacuum. *Convection* is slowed by **stopping the flow of air** around an object. This can be done by wrapping the object.

To complicate matters, a tactic that slows one type of heat loss may speed up another. For example, trying to slow heat transfer from conduction runs counter to trying to slow it from convection. To stop conduction we might have the object floating in air. But air is a great medium for the transfer of heat through convection. So it becomes necessary to compromise between stopping heat loss from convection and from conduction. This is usually done by using materials that are light and fluffy. This minimizes direct-contact losses through conduction while restricting the flow of air around the object and hence losses from convection. The larger the air pockets, however, the greater the amount of convection, even within an air pocket.

The ideal method of stopping convection is a vacuum—the absence of all fluids. Yet radiation can move uninhibited through a vacuum. And radiant barriers are often extremely conductive. So even though heat trapping will necessarily be less than perfect, it can still be extremely effective if you keep

in mind the nature of the materials you are using and what you are trying to accomplish.

Storing heat. Within a given volume of space, the amount of energy that a given material can store—often referred to as the thermal mass of the object—varies tremendously depending on its density. Air, which holds very little matter, also holds very little heat. Denser materials like stone hold much more heat, and metals, the densest common materials, hold even more. This is the same general relationship that a material has to conductivity. Materials with very high thermal mass are often very conductive, because denser material has molecules closer together and thus can transfer energy faster. If you add an equal amount of heat to both a chunk of iron and a fluffy feather pillow, the iron will release that heat and reach room temperature well before the pillow does. Refer to Table 7.2 for the relative thermal conductivity of various common building materials. These facts, somewhat counterintuitive, are important to keep in mind when we start to think about storing additional warmth. This will be discussed in greater detail in chapter 17.

Heat bridges. *Heat*, or *thermal*, *bridges* are zones of higher conductivity that can suck much of the heat out of an otherwise well-insulated space. Since metal is denser than wood, the metal handle and hinges in a wood door can wick through much of the heat that is lost through the door. But in a wall, wood becomes the wick: Wood studs can wick through much more heat than the surrounding insulated wall cavities. It's important to keep heat bridges in mind and minimize their presence without compromising structural integrity or function.

Now that we're familiar with the basics of home energy use and heat storage and transfer, it's time to take a look at how all these things relate to the real world of the home you're living in. Even if your house may not be the ideal candidate for a quick conversion to carbon freedom, there are almost certainly many things you can do to use fossil energy more wisely and to start taking advantage of the solar energy reaching your home.

PLANNING A WHOLE-HOUSE CONVERSION

Puttering around your own home, you may think the possibility of freeing it from fossil fuels to be somewhat remote. As our culture has progressed down the route of enslavement to fossil energy, a massive amount of infrastructure has been cumulatively built all around us to tap into its high energy flows. You're probably wondering, "Is it really possible to live a life without fossil fuels that doesn't resemble the squalid existence of a peasant in the Middle Ages?"

The answer, of course, is a resounding "Yes!" We do not have to abandon civilization and live in a cave or tiny cabin to retrofit our lives for fossil-energy independence. It will take dedication and, yes, initially, much time, effort, and money. As a reward it brings freedom from the polluters and the war machine, the shifty politicians and their moral compromises to "preserve our American way of life," a life, in fact, of utter hopeless dependence. And as the price of fossil fuels climbs steadily upward, instead of being dragged into poverty you'll save more money year after year. With every step it brings a lifting of the shame that haunts us, the shame of being a member of one of the most intelligent species on earth but seemingly unconcerned with the health of the planet or its other residents. Once you've made up your mind and planned out your strategy, you can once again hold your head up high as you hike through the woods, knowing you respect each plant and animal you see and are acting accordingly to stop the world from burning. As your home sheds its fossil-energy shackles, you will know that as the last great oil fields descend into senescence and the mad addicts' scramble for the dwindling supplies of crude becomes ever fiercer, your own home and life will stand as a beacon of hope to all those around you being dragged down into the quagmire. Instead of despair they will see a lifeboat to salvation.

Everyone who picks up this book will have a different style of house in a different climate and setting, and a different set of skills. Nevertheless, some general guidelines will be helpful.

If you are a homeowner, you must assess whether your home is worth converting. You are considering venturing out on a long-term commitment that will cumulatively require a lot of time and money. If you worked hard, two or three weekends a month, say, it will probably take two to three years. Working a more leisurely weekend every month or so it could take five or more years to retrofit a home. Even if you do a lot of the work yourself, you will probably still spend a rather large quantity of money. To make our home carbon free, we spent $40,000 on materials, and we did the work ourselves. If you hire out a lot of the work, the cost could easily be twice that, although you will greatly speed up how fast the work is accomplished.

How well built is your residence? If you live in a deteriorating trailer, it's not going to be worth it to spend this kind of energy and money on retrofitting it, since trailers and many other prefab homes typically don't last more than a quarter century. But if you live in a prefabricated home or are just renting your home, don't panic. Although you won't want to launch a full-scale conversion to carbon freedom, there are plenty of simple steps you can take to reduce your use of fossil energy, as we'll explain later in this chapter.

If you live in a solidly built home that is way out in the boondocks, then you probably have to drive almost everywhere. Making your home fossil-fuel free when you have to fill up your car twice a week with gasoline isn't ideal, but it's still a huge improvement. Suburban and exurban development poses special problems because by its nature it requires vast inflows of energy, mainly because where folks live has been segregated from where they work, shop, and play. We'll talk about some broad solutions to this dilemma in chapter 11, but don't forget that any reduction in fossil-energy use benefits both you and the planet. Of course, if you live in a suburban or rural setting because you're near your means of employment, then that's a different story.

Ideally, then, you own a well-built home that is as near as possible to where you work, shop, and play. This first step is quite a large one! It could easily take a few years to save up the down payment and to find such a home. But part of the motivation for us in writing this book is the hope that we can teach others from our own mistakes, like building an energy-conserving home in the middle of nowhere. If you do not start out with a home that meets these criteria, you will undoubtedly get stuck partway down the path to fossil-energy independence. Then to make it all the way could likely mean starting over from scratch.

If you are renting or not yet in the home of your choice, there are still quite a few projects that can be done. Building a solar cooker or an evaporative cooler for your food, for example, can be a great introduction to many of the fundamental principles of heat and renewable energy, and you can take them with you when you move! Peruse the list of renter-friendly projects in the "Table of Projects."

Conservation comes first. For homeowners and renters alike, unless you have already been extremely conscientious in your energy use, the first step toward a carbon-free home is conservation. There is a lot of low-hanging fruit in this area, including many simple behavioral adjustments that can dramatically lower your energy use. The energy diary described in chapter 3 is a great way to familiarize yourself with your own specific energy budget. In the same chapter we also discuss installing a whole-house minute-to-minute electricity meter, which is another great way to learn where all that energy is going.

Familiarize yourself with your energy and water bills. How does your consumption compare to the average in your area and to that of your neighbors? Before you seriously undertake any of the larger renewable systems described in this book, your own household's consumption should be at least a third less than the average. We have met and read about lots of folks who live on less than a kilowatt-hour of electricity a day per person, about one-tenth of the American average of 800 kWh per month per household.[3] Once you get your own consumption down low enough, solar electricity and other renewable systems suddenly become much more affordable, because you'll be able to get by with smaller systems and the price will come down accordingly.

Finding time and money. A carbon-free home may seem desirable, but you may be wondering how on earth you'll find the time and money to do it. It's more than likely that the reader of this book is not average, but on average a two-adult household owns two cars and each adult watches four hours of television a day. A recent study[4] found that if a two-adult household could eliminate one of those cars and instead bike and use public transportation the annual savings would be over $6,200! So if car and television use were cut in half, the average two-adult household would have 28 hours of extra time a week and over six grand a year for retrofits.

Many of the projects described in this book start saving you money as soon as they're installed. Insulation and window and door sealing are very inexpensive and can save tremendous amounts of heating and cooling energy. Solar hot-water heaters have higher up-front costs, but once you install one, you see a $20 to $40 monthly savings on your utility bills. Every time you spend money on an energy-saving device, you pay a moderate up-front fee but then have much lower monthly energy costs. The average household spent $2,100 on energy bills in 2007,[5] much of which you will eventually eliminate. For example, we spend less than $50 a year on our energy bills, primarily on ethanol (grain alcohol) for our cookstove. We have only one car, and that runs on waste veggie oil, so we save the $2,700 of average vehicle fuel costs as well. Combined, this amounts to $11,000 of annual savings ($6,200 plus $2,100 plus $2,700). And as energy costs rise, this savings will only increase.

Another financing option is your local bank. Investing in energy-saving devices that will actually pay for themselves is a no-brainer for many lenders. Utility companies are also surprisingly liberal with loans for energy-saving devices. These financing methods can allow you to install renewable energy systems while still paying roughly the same monthly bills as before—except now there is actually an end date to when you have to stop paying! And don't forget to look up the numerous federal and state tax breaks available (see the resources section of this chapter for tax information online databases).

Beyond these options, quitting the fossil-fuel habit requires reorganizing your life to match your new priorities. While many of the projects listed in this book are hard work, there is often an element of creativity in hands-on construction that produces a sense of satisfaction once completed. There are hobbies that are productive and enhance your quality of life, and there are hobbies that are a drain on your finances and time. Reconfiguring one's life, hobbies, and priorities to go with the energy flows of nature rather than being opposed to them is, we believe, inherently self-rewarding and consciousness-expanding, and can save you a bundle of loot to boot.

Making an action plan. From a practical standpoint, devising a broad plan of how to proceed, along with an estimated budget and timetable, will help ensure your eventual success. We highly recommend labor trades as part of your plan. Labor trades with others working along similar lines not only save money but also will greatly expand your knowledge. It's often the case with many of the larger projects that twice as many hands makes things go more than twice as fast. In most cities and towns, there are several environmental groups meeting regularly. These are great places to start looking for potential labor trades. A few nationwide groups are listed in the resources section.

As you draw up a plan, you'll likely need to address landscaping issues. Do you have access to enough sunlight? You cannot live off your annual income of solar energy in the shade. It is a sad fact that if large trees block most of your sunlight, chances are you will forever be dependent on fossil fuels to run your home. A landscaping strategy that harvests some of the larger trees for timber, firewood, and mulch and replaces them with shorter edibles like fruit trees should be adopted. Other landscaping issues can provide quick

energy relief for very little effort, such as trellising vines for shading. These are discussed in chapter 10.

Part of the planning process is to evaluate your skills in various fields. Where certain skills are lacking, stick with the simpler projects. For instance, if you have very few plumbing skills, then you could start out with something like installing a rain barrel or some simple graywater diversion. If your carpentry skills are wanting, then you could try starting out with an evaporation cooler or insulating your fridge. For each activity, we've listed the general skill level required, so you'll know if it's something you should be trying to tackle or not. Almost every library and used bookstore has loads of how-to books on things like plumbing and carpentry that cover the basics of these trades. Picking up a few of these and perusing them will teach you a lot very quickly, and probably pay for the effort involved in obtaining them in a few minutes by preventing common mistakes.

Broadly speaking, it's better to do some things before others. Some activities have a higher return on energy saved per cost and time, while doing certain things first will hinder other activities. You probably don't want to spend a great deal of effort on biogas production for a relatively small amount of cooking gas when you have not yet reaped the much more substantial energy rewards from installing a solar hot-water heater, for instance. Likewise, putting up photovoltaic panels on your roof and then deciding you want to have a metal roof for rainwater-collection purposes would mean having to redo much of the PV installation.

In very general terms, here are some thoughts on what we think should be addressed sooner rather than later:

- Behavioral changes: These are simple and reap immediate rewards. They include steps such as replacing incandescent lightbulbs with compact fluorescents, air-drying clothes, and lowering the temperature setting on your water heater.
- Adding insulation: Almost every house could use more insulation. Generally speaking, the older your home, the more poorly insulated it

was initially. Priority should be given to attics, where heat escapes, and to northern walls, where lots of cold comes in. Unless you live in a very warm climate, Zone 8 or higher, you must have insulated walls to ever hope to achieve fossil-energy independence. Of course, what you're trying to keep warm or cool is your body, and insulating should start here, as should cooling. An extra sweater, wool socks, and some thermal underwear when it's cold and fans and cold showers when it's hot are amazingly effective.

- Reducing the use of electric-resistance heat: Wherever you can eliminate electric-resistance heat (turning electricity into heat), the energy savings will be substantial, even if you have to replace this source of heat with another fossil fuel. Burning coal, turning it into electricity, transmitting it hundreds of miles, and then turning this energy back into heat, whether it's for your toaster, your heat pump, your dryer, or your water heater, results in inefficiencies that waste more than three-quarters of the original energy.[6] Address these electricity-to-heat activities first, preferably replacing them with behavioral changes or renewable energy systems. If you can't live without them, replacing these appliances with gas-fired versions can still significantly reduce your use of fossil fuels.

Installing active renewable energy systems such as solar electricity should be one of the last things you tackle, even though they are undoubtedly some of the coolest things on earth and you'll be champing at the bit to get to them. Active systems are distinct from passive solar designs that collect solar energy and turn it into heat without any moving parts. As you reduce and/or eliminate superfluous electrical appliances from your home, you may even find your need for any electricity to be not worth the trouble. More than likely, you'll want a few photovoltaic panels (or, if your situation is right, a wind or water turbine), but making this the last priority will ensure that you have to spend as little money as possible on these very expen-

sive items. The energy return on solar electric panels, while undoubtedly positive, is relatively low compared to lots of simple conservation strategies. The energy return is definitely much lower for solar electric panels than for solar hot-water panels. Between the two, we strongly recommend you direct limited funds to solar hot water first.

THE SOLAR WINDOW

Determining your home's solar window is another first step toward living a life powered by the sun. The solar window describes how accessible the sun is based on your home's geographical location, surrounding obstructions, and climate. The path of the sun changes every day, as does your home's access to it. The solar window describes the totality of these individual daily paths. The precise spot where you live is different from where everyone else lives in several fundamental ways. These all have a direct impact on your home's solar window and include:

1. Existing vegetation and its potential growth
2. Average seasonal *insolation* (hours of cloudless sun per day) and climate extremes
3. Position on earth (latitude) relative to the sun
4. Orientation of your home, its roof, and other existing structures relative to solar south
5. Terrain such as mountains and other potential obstructions such as complicated roof designs and power lines

To get started, if you haven't already, take stock of where your home is in relation to the sun at various times of the day and the year. Beginning when you get up in the morning, watch where sunlight falls on your property throughout the day. Pay special attention to where it is in midmorning, midday, and midafternoon through the seasons. Which exterior walls of your house are shaded? When does the roof get sun in the morning and when does it stop in the evening? What surrounding structures cast shadows on which part of your home, and at what times of the day? Additionally, which parts of your house, such as dormer windows and chimneys, shade other parts?

As the seasons change, many of these sun and shade patterns will gradually change with them. When the sun sinks into the sky during winter, the number of obstructions to sunlight on your property will likely increase. However, deciduous trees will lose their leaves over the course of the autumn. Consider how these changes would affect efforts at heating your home with solar energy. You can use a horizontal level to cast shadows on east- and west-facing walls during the solstices and equinoxes. By marking these shadow lines in chalk on your home, you can have empirical measurement of these angles. The solstices will give you the entire range of angles at which the southern sun will strike your home. The equinox angles should be the same and correspond to your home's latitude. The solar path in midsummer is the most complex, so

pay extra attention as the sun makes its way over your property. The sun starts to the northeast at dawn, is high up overhead and a little to the south at midday, and sets in the northwest at dusk. Each time you watch the path of the sun over the course of a day, remember that it will follow this exact same path on the other side of solstice, so that May 21st will be the same as July 21st, April 21st the same as Aug 21st, and so on. By watching the solar path from one solstice to the next, you will have seen the entire range of sunlight on your property.

Much of what you discover about the position of the sun over the course of the year may be counterintuitive. Since the earth's axis is at a fairly steep incline (around 23 degrees), and in addition to spinning like a top the earth is also circumnavigating the sun, your relative position to the sun is constantly changing. Studying this intricate dance before engaging in it will decrease the likelihood of missteps.

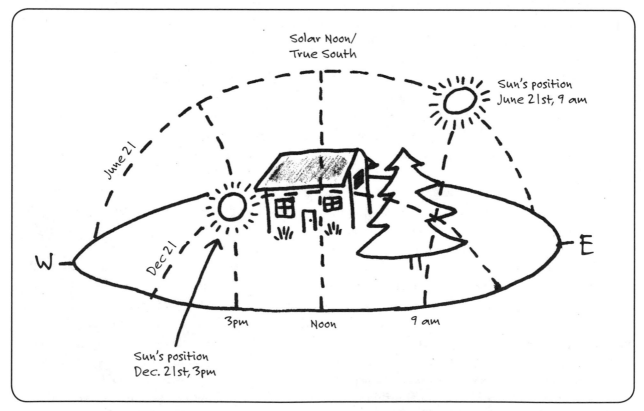

FIG. 1.1. **Obstructions can limit solar access and vary according to time of day and season. Identifying solar availability should be paramount in accessing your home's renewable-energy potential.**

One important aspect of the solar window is *solar south*, also called *true south*, which can vary substantially from the magnetic south that a compass reading will give you. Determining which direction is solar south is simple. First, you need to determine when sunrise and sunset are for any particular day. This information is available from local newspapers and news channels. Add up the total number of hours in the day, and then cut this number in half. Add this number to sunrise and you'll have solar noon. When solar noon arrives, hang a plumb bob (a string with a weight attached) and record in which direction the shadow falls. This will point along the solar north/south axis. You can also find this information on the Internet, or by using a magnetic declination chart and adjusting your compass, but becoming familiar with your home's orientation to the sun is a critical component of fossil-fuel-free living.

An amazing and effective tool has been invented to take a snapshot of the solar window for any particular location for the entire year. This nifty little device is called the Solar Pathfinder (the Solmetric suneye is a digital version, but it's much more expensive). The Solar Pathfinder works by positioning a half-globe over an outline of the path of the sun for each month of the year. By leveling this half-globe and pointing it toward true south, the reflection of any potential obstructions at any time of day for any month of the year can be outlined on the provided sun-path chart. This will then allow you to tally up your solar potential for any specific site on your property. See sidebar for examples of the Solar Pathfinder at work.

By studying your solar window, you'll discover what substantial obstructions are lying between you and your goal of relying on solar energy. Depending on

FIG. 1.2. **The large willow oak, trimmed by the power company to lean toward our house, was at the end of its life span and rotted out at the bottom (a fact we did not discover until we had the tree cut down). This tree blocked 80 percent of our solar energy many months of the year.**

Cutting the Tree to Save the Forest

After the willow oak was removed from the front of our property (see figure 1.2, page 9), we did some calculations to figure out how much potential solar energy it had blocked. The amount of energy coming from the sun changes over the course of the day, because the closer the sun is to perpendicular to an object, the more energy that object receives. By outlining what obstructions block the sun during what month and at what time of day and combining this number with the average insolation for our region (determining average insolation is discussed in more detail in chapter 2), the average amount of solar energy for a typical day of each month can be roughly calculated.

In the winter Durham, North Carolina, averages about four hours of sunlight per day, with the oak blocking about 75 percent of our home's sun, or three hours. We combined that information with the amount of solar collector area we will have installed once our carbon-free conversion is completed to figure out the overall lost potential.

168 square feet	Passive Solar Heating
64 square feet	Solar Hot Water
1.2 kWh	Photovoltaics

Using the standard insolation measurement of 317 Btus/square feet/hour, our potential lost solar income for our home is thus:

$$168 \text{ ft}^2 + 64 \text{ ft}^2 = 232 \text{ft}^2 \times 317 \text{Btu/ft}^2/\text{hr} = 73{,}544$$
Btu/hr × 3 hrs/day = 220,632 Btu/day, which at 70 percent efficiency leaves us with **154,442 Btus per day.**

In addition, since 3,412 Btus equals 1 kWh, including our 1.2 kWh photovoltaic system adds 3,412 Btus/kWh × 1.2 kWh × 3hrs = **12,283 Btus/day.**

Total = 166,725 Btus/day of lost potential.

FIG. 1.3. **Our solar window prior to tree removal. The white lines correspond to the path of the sun during different months (the white line at the top represents the path of the sun during the month of December, the line at the bottom to the month of June). The numbers along the bottom correspond to the time of day. For almost the entire year, the oak shaded our home from early in the morning until early afternoon.**

FIG. 1.4. **Solar access after tree removal. Only December and January are at all obstructed during midday, in this case by another oak across the street. The open space where the oak had been was planted with pears, cherries, peaches, plums, gooseberries, and wildflowers. This area has quickly become a haven for a variety of birds and butterflies not found in the willow oak monoculture surrounding the rest of the street.**

This gets us to a total of 25,008,780 Btus of lost solar energy over the 150 days of winter.

To calculate lost potential solar energy for summer we'll add only the photovoltaic, as our hot summers would produce enough hot water with just a few hours of sun and we don't need any passive solar-heating gain.

However, the shading problem is much worse from our willow oak for the remaining seven months as the sun is lower in the sky, averaging 85 percent blockage of the potential solar energy. For the six hours of average summer sun per day this totals:

6 hr/day × 0.85 (loss factor) × 3,412 Btus/hr = **17,401 Btus/day of lost potential energy.**

So for the remaining 215 days of the year (summer) this totals

215 × 17,401 = **3,741,215 Btus of lost solar energy in the summer.**

Note that these particular Btus are actually very clever electrons that can do things like run lights and computers, but for simplicity's sake we'll leave them as Btus.

The grand total comes to **28,749,995 Btus/yr**

blocked by the willow oak that we are now able to capture.

Just to make a comparison, let's say we had decided we wanted to preserve the willow oak and find another way to supply our energy needs without using fossil fuels. The most readily available source of stored solar energy in our area is wood, so that would be our next-best choice after solar power.

Average-quality wood will produce about 20 million Btus/cord. It takes about three and a half 12-inch-diameter trees to make a cord of firewood. Generally speaking, wood-burning efficiencies are around 70 percent. So to generate 28,749,995 Btus (the solar energy equivalent blocked by our willow oak) would require about 41,071,421 gross Btus. This is about two cords, or about seven full-grown trees, *every year*! If we lived in this home another 40 years and this tree remained in place, we would have cut down about 280 full-grown trees to make up for our missing solar access. This would truly have been a case of clear-cutting the forest to save the tree.

In addition, removing the oak opened up to the sun several thousand square feet of orchard and garden space and provided more than five years' worth of firewood as well as organic material for the inoculation of five different varieties of mushroom. How we dealt with the additional cooling requirements created by the tree removal is detailed in the "Our Story" section of chapter 17.

where you live, there's a pretty good chance that at least one of these obstacles will be a big tree.

Opening up your solar window. Older homes, especially in the eastern half of the country, are often surrounded by stately older trees. While these trees provide shade in the summertime and are beautiful to boot, their presence becomes problematic as we move toward lives powered by our annual income of solar energy. Their haphazard placement is a relic of the days of energy decadence. Often placed along streets or in front of homes, their position relative to our solar needs is at best random. It is an unfortunate reality that one of the first steps on your road to becoming carbon free might very well be to have one or more trees pruned or taken down. While our solar resource is potentially large and we are capable of living quite comfortably on it, when this resource is cut in half or more by existing trees this task becomes much more difficult.

"Is it really necessary to cut down some of my trees?" you're probably asking. We often think of the trees surrounding our home as our companions, friends on our journey around the sun. Maybe for you it won't be, but we'll share our example to help illustrate how necessary it could be.

Our home had a large willow oak directly in front of the house in between the sidewalk and the street. Power lines ran above it, and the villainous Duke Power had repeatedly clipped the tree so that almost the entire canopy was leaning toward the house. Oaks are notorious for retaining their leaves well into winter. While many trees would allow around 50 percent of the available energy through their canopy, willow oaks let through almost none. Also willow oaks grow fast for oaks, and their life span is only about 70 to 80 years. The ones lining our street are around this age.

For all these reasons, we knew that we needed to remove the tree. After much negotiating with the city arborist, explaining our intentions to become fossil-energy independent, and assuaging the concerns of the neighborhood association, we were given permission to have the tree taken down.

There can be no doubt that cutting down healthy trees is a painful and emotionally draining endeavor. We are not happy about having to advocate cutting some down. The good news is that you can then plant multiple shorter trees, which can be a variety of flowering and/or fruiting trees that will add beauty and diversity to your yard. There's an old saying that it takes a wise man to plant a tree when he knows he is too old to see it full grown. Farsightedness in reworking our landscapes to provide solar access and plant diversity will go a long way toward correcting the shortsightedness that got us into the current mess.

Of course sometimes the tree that is blocking your solar access is your neighbor's. Approach this subject with delicacy. Bake some cookies, explain your solar aspirations, and offer to replace the tree with shorter varieties in addition to paying the cost of the removal. In some states, especially California, solar access is enshrined in law. This prohibits very tall construction that would block solar access as well as offering a mechanism for negotiations with neighbors when their trees block a property owner's access to the sun.

SPECIAL CONSIDERATIONS FOR RETROFITTING

Even if your home has an open solar window with plenty of access to the sun, there are still likely to be issues with your home's orientation, roofline, and even type of construction that could make it a challenge to complete its conversion to carbon freedom. Primary among these is its orientation to true south. It is a sad fact that even though the fundamentals of passive solar design have been well known for decades, most houses built up to now do not take solar orientation into consideration.

The ideal orientation for a house is with its broadest side facing true south. As it happens, though, most houses face the road, no matter in what direction it lies (or how ugly that road may be). Fortunately, even a home that is as much as 30 off true south still gets nearly 90 percent of the potential solar gain. Beyond 30, the percentage drops off (see table 1.3). There's a good chance that some aspect of your home will fall within this solar-ideal 60 degrees (30 to SE or 30 to SW of true south), meaning many of the solar strategies detailed in this book should work well with the variety of potential retrofits available. Beyond this 60 degrees, meaningful solar gain, especially for heating purposes, is still achievable in structures facing southeast to due west.

If the narrow rather than the broad side of your home falls within this 60 degrees, a long-term strategy might be to expand your home, via an attached greenhouse for example, along its southern exposure. The north side of the home could potentially be retrofitted for an alternative use. It could be opened up as a screened-in porch, for instance, moving the functions of the existing room into the now passively solar-warmed addition. The porch, being on the north side, would stay comfortable in the summertime. In the winter, it would make a good windbreak. It could potentially be closed in during winter as an unheated entranceway.

Another potential use for the northern room would be for water storage. In colder climates, this room could have a window-box fridge built into its interior for keeping food cold (see the "Northern Window Conversion to Cold Box" project in chapter 5). The entire room could be used as a kind of root cellar, the large mass of the water maintaining a constant cool temperature. During summer, the thermal mass of the stored water could be a potential source of daytime cooling. Opening the door and blowing a fan over and around the cistern could provide a great degree of cooling during the daytime. Windows could be opened up at night to cool it all back down again. A long-term strategy of reconfiguring your home's orientation to expand the southern exposure and limit its northern exposure by renovations like these can solve the problem of improper orientation.

Such renovations could potentially lead to a large-scale rearrangement of your home. It's another example of why it's important to plan out a long-term strategy before you tackle any major projects. Opening up a northern room as a screened-in porch when you recently blew insulation in the walls, for instance, would make a big mess and cost extra money.

The pitch of your roof can also play a large role in accessing the solar energy that falls on your home. Steeper roofs suffer more from being oriented away from true south. Table 1.3 describes this in detail.

Multifamily dwellings can also present difficulties for solar retrofitting. Generally speaking, such housing uses less energy than stand-alone single-family housing. The greatly reduced exterior wall space, where much of the home's heat transfer to the outside takes place, is a big plus. However, it may not be feasible, for political or structural reasons, to retrofit one part of the home in isolation. Don't assume that your neighbors aren't like-minded and give up prematurely. Throw a potluck dinner to discuss the idea of installing solar systems. Be sure to prepare your argument in advance, and if your neighbors agree, figure out what you need to do next to make it happen. Since multi-family dwellings are primarily in much more energy-efficient urban areas, this is housing stock that needs to be saved. So we need to figure out the best way to move forward in converting it to fossil-fuel freedom.

One of the advantages of retrofitting a home rather than trying to build from scratch is that you have a place to live while you work. It's probably not the ideal place, of course, due to the ignorance and/or greed of the original builder/architect. But beyond the incredible amounts of savings in time, money, and energy from using an existing building and its surrounding infrastructure, a retrofitted home saves many thousands of dollars in the years of rent that could potentially be spent when building a new home, however well designed and "earth-friendly." The fact is that nothing is more earth-friendly than using what you've already got, except in the worst of scenarios (McMansions out in the boondocks, for instance). Accept your home's imperfections, but also consider the fact that, with much less work than building something from scratch, it can be an entirely different home, rearranged and retrofitted to live off its annual supply of solar energy.

TABLE 1.3 Tilt Angle vs. Building Orientation						
Degrees from South/Tilt	0 (FLAT)	18	30	45	60	90 (VERTICAL)
0 (SOUTH)	0.89	0.97	1.00	0.97	0.89	0.58
23	0.89	0.97	0.99	0.96	0.88	0.59
45 (SE or SW)	0.89	0.95	0.96	0.93	0.85	0.60
68	0.89	0.92	0.91	087	0.79	0.57
90 (E or W)	0.89	0.88	0.84	0.78	0.70	0.52

Two factors affect the amount of insolation a given surface receives: the tilt of the surface and how far off true south it is. The above chart is based on a latitude of 30. Hence, at a 30-degree tilt and 0 degrees off south, the surface gets 100 percent of available sunlight. At 90 degrees off south and 30-degree tilt, it still gets 84 percent of available sunlight, while a vertical wall (90-degree tilt) facing east or west gets just about half (52 percent) of the available solar energy. If the spot is sunny, even this lesser amount can provide meaningful solar energy for air or water heating. Source: "A Guide to Photovoltaic (PV) System Design and Installation," California Energy Commission, June 2001

RESOURCES

Books
Venolia, Carol, and Kelly Lerner. 2006. *Natural Remodeling for the Not-So-Green House: Bringing Your Home into Harmony with Nature*. New York: Lark Books. Not focused on energy per se, but has great remodeling ideas for doing more with less space.

Internet
California's solar access laws. Great examples of solar easement laws. www.gosolarnow.com/images/pdf%20Files/CASolarAccessLaws.pdf

Embodied Energy Calculator. Btu calculations show the embodied energy of the construction of your home. www.thegreenestbuilding.org

Meetup. Has a variety of groups where like-minded individuals can be found. Topics include the environment, green homes, permaculture, alternative energy, peak oil, global warming, and natural building. www.meetup.com

National Geophysical Data Center. The easy way to find magnetic declination and true south. www.ngdc.noaa.gov/seg/geomag/jsp/struts/calcDeclination

Post Carbon Network. Groups dedicated to weaning their towns and cities off fossil fuels. www.relocalize.net

Products
Solar Pathfinder. At around $250, these puppies are expensive. See about sharing the cost with some like-minded folks in your area, or check with local solar installers about renting one. They can also be rented at www.gaiam.com for $25/week. www.solarpathfinder.com

Endnotes
1. "World Consumption of Primary Energy by Energy Type and Selected Country Groups, 1980–2004." Energy Information Administration (July 31, 2006).
2. American Automobile Association.
3. Energy Information Administration (www.eia.doe.gov).
4. American Public Transportation Board.
5. Alliance to Save Energy.
6. U.S. Department of Energy—Energy Efficiency and Renewable Energy: "A Consumer's Guide to Energy Efficiency and Renewable Energy," and the Office of Electricity Delivery and Energy Reliability "Overview of the Electric Grid."

CHAPTER 2

Renewable Electric Systems

What Is Renewable Electricity? • The Renewable Energy Paradigm Shift • Our Story • Systems Overview • Demand and Site (Production) Analysis • System Components • Resources

WHAT IS RENEWABLE ELECTRICITY?

What counts as renewable electricity? We're really not interested in tesla coils and flywheels, solar towers, or nanotechnology, at least for homeowner applications! What we're talking about here is tried and true, and available to the average homeowner. In addition, testing has proven these technologies give a positive return on the embodied energy invested in the materials, thus breaking through to actual renewability. These parameters leave us three basic options for residential-scale renewable electricity production: photovoltaics (PV), microhydro, and wind turbines. Although there is an argument to be made that biofuel generators, biomass, or fuel cells can also produce renewable home-scale electricity, they won't be the focus of this chapter for a few reasons—because we aren't yet convinced that the energy return is greater than the energy invested, the technologies needed to implement them aren't available on a large scale yet, or perhaps just because it is unpleasant and impractical to run your whole house off a noisy fuel-hungry generator. One other thing we are not discussing in this chapter is solar thermal equating to solar hot water or hot air, because those are separate and technologically distinct from these electrical systems (and covered in chapters 6 and 7, respectively).

Renewable energy systems are expensive, no way around it. But are they worth it? As an installer of renewable electric systems, Rebekah has sold and designed systems for many different types of homes and people and has noticed that homeowners have generally the following four different reasons—and often some combination of the four—for deciding to move to renewable electricity:

1. To offset some or all fossil electric consumption in order to reduce environmental footprint and carbon emissions.
2. To secure a source of backup power during grid failures (or for power where the grid is unavailable or extremely expensive to access).
3. For cost: to stabilize the price of household electricity at a set level, receive rebates and tax credits, and avoid future fossil-fuel-price-driven increases (looking for the nebulous payback).
4. For prestige (early-adopter syndrome): solar panels on the roof function like a new car in the driveway or a new computer gadget—cost is no object!

It is a worthwhile exercise to see which of these four reasons fit your situation, as it will affect your installation decisions. Our first priority by far was to reduce our carbon emissions to as close to zero as possible. However, we also wanted backup nonfossil power for grid failures, which meant we decided to install a more expensive battery backup photovoltaic system, as opposed to a straight grid-tied system that would shut itself off when the grid failed (these systems are discussed in more detail under the PV system overview below). The third reason—payback—is a strange dilemma. While it sounds great and some companies provide complicated charts showing accelerated depreciation schemes

Solar Thermal vs. Solar Electricity

Solar thermal is more efficient and cost effective than solar electricity.

In October 2007, Rebekah had the opportunity to tour the California solar thermal manufacturing plant of SunEarth, Inc., where solar hot-water panels are made. The electrical consumption of the plant is currently offset by a beautiful 175-kilowatt photovoltaic (solar electric) array on the roof of the plant, where SunEarth also tests various solar thermal (hot-water) technologies. The photo at right centers on one section of the PV array (more modules can be seen to the far left, flat on the roof surface), and that's Cully Judd, the owner of SunEarth, posing with his two lovely daughters. This particular section of the roof visually demonstrates the comparable efficiency and energy output of solar thermal (solar hot-water) collectors versus photovoltaics (solar electric modules). Amazingly, because of their greater efficiency at converting the sun's energy directly to heat and thus to hot water, those *two* flat-plate solar thermal collectors (SunEarth's Empire series) down at the left side of the photo produce

FIG. 2.1. **Solar thermal and photovoltaic technologies work side-by-side on the roof of the SunEarth, Inc. manufacturing plant.**

slightly more energy (as measured in Btus) per day than the 32 PV (solar electric) modules (Sharp 165-watt modules) stretching out to the right. Yet the photovoltaics cost seven times as much as the solar thermal and take up 5.6 times the space! Hard to believe, but for skeptics, we show the watt-by-watt comparison below, using industry-tested energy outputs and average installation costs.

Of course, electricity is a magical thing, and we know the value in PV doesn't always manifest itself via cost-benefit analysis, but the bang for your buck clearly lies with solar thermal.

TABLE 2.1 Solar Thermal Photovoltaics

SRCC Rating (warm climate) = 984 Btus/square foot/day	Module STC Rating @ 1,000watts/m^2 = 165 watts (Shell SQ 165)
Area (80 ft^2) x 984 = 78,720 Btu/day 78,720 Btus @ 3.414 Btus per watt = **23 kWh/day**	165 watts x 32 modules = 5,280 watts Avg. daily energy output (AC) = **21 kWh/day***
Total Area = **80 square feet**	Total Area = **449 square feet** **5.6 TIMES THE SURFACE AREA NEEDED FOR PV; LOWER ENERGY OUTPUT**
COST ANALYSIS Solar Thermal: 80 ft^2 x \$85/ft^2 = **\$6,800**	Photovoltaics: Avg. \$9/watt x 5,280 watts = **\$47,520** 7 TIMES MORE EXPENSIVE FOR THE PV!

*Calculations with standard deratings from the National Renewable Energy Laboratories PVWatt Calculator; available online at http://rredc.nrel.gov/solar/codes_algs/PVWATTS/

and things we can't even pretend to understand, the reality is complicated. Rebekah shies away from talking about payback with customers. Some states, like California and New Jersey, have such good incentives available that short payback times are a reality. But we can't predict the future price of electricity, when your battery bank and inverter will fail, or what decisions Congress or your state will make on tax incentives. PV modules we buy with 25-year warranties come from businesses only three years old, and who's to say that those manufacturers will be in business even five years from now? Unknowable variables aside, we do fully expect our PV modules to last at least 25 years, possibly more. An investment in renewable electricity might be the best financial investment you've ever made. We wouldn't bet the house on that, but we would bet it will be a moral and thoroughly unregretted investment, and that's enough payback for us.

Tangentially, what else do you demand a payback on that you purchase? Cars, furniture, clothes, food, even fossil electricity? Of course not! You pay and pay and never expect a cent back. The only other things we can think of that bring up the dreaded "P" word are *other* household energy-efficiency investments, of which this book is full. Why should energy efficiency alone require a payback? Perhaps because capitalist society has so devalued efficiency itself in the drive for growth. Each step you take to efficiency limits the amount of fuel you'll need to purchase, limits the growth for fuel providers, limits the expense of environmental cleanup, and so on. What impetus is there for efficiency besides morality and frugality?

As for prestige, we're all for it: renewable energy *should* be prestigious! We've seen installations where if one house has 4,000 watts of PV power, the neighbor has to get 5,000 watts. As far as competing with the Joneses goes, we can't think of a better subject for competition. It is analogous to a disintegrating inner-city neighborhood, where if one family starts working on a house and yard, it can set off a chain reaction of investments in renovations up and down the block. We've all heard of Hollywood actors driving hybrids, so why not use your own roof as an advertisement for

renewability and stake a claim as the owners of the first renewable energy system in the neighborhood?

THE RENEWABLE ENERGY PARADIGM SHIFT

Often when we think of fossil-fuel-free electricity we picture giant wind turbines in remote locations, or snow-covered cabins tucked away in the woods with a few solar panels in the yard. But it doesn't have to be that way. You don't have to live off-grid to live off renewable energy.

There has been a paradigm shift, a quiet revolution, in renewable electricity in the past 10 years from off-grid systems to utility interactivity. Utility interactivity means that any electrical production created by systems on or at a house (or office building, farm, etc.) that is not consumed by the homeowner can actually spin the utility meter "backward" and sell power back to the grid. ("The grid" is shorthand for a private or cooperative utility provider that maintains and supplies the local electric grid, which is interconnected with and inseparable from the national and international grid.) The details of interconnection and sales vary from place to place and utility to utility. However, the true import of interconnection lies in two important facts: First, houses tied to the grid need not worry about limited production; as long as the grid is up, it will cover any consumption demands over and above what the household-based systems are producing. Second, the flip side is that there will rarely if ever be any wasted renewable production! This second fact is to us the more fascinating and valuable part of interconnectivity—that whatever excess production you create above what you are using feeds the grid with clean energy and will effortlessly be used by your neighbors, directly displacing fossil sources of electricity.

Compare this to off-grid-system owners who often find themselves with more available clean renewable power than they or their batteries need or can use productively. The nature of off-grid systems is that they should be sized for worst-case-scenario demand and production, in order to keep users out of the dark when the sun isn't shining or the wind isn't blowing. The standby power (the excess) in times with lots of sun or wind in off-grid systems is truly clean energy wasted, as the system would be happy to provide it, if a place can be found for it to be used.

Ninety-five percent or more of the installations that Rebekah does as a professional solar installer are grid-tied, and the same is true for many other installers around the country, especially in places like California that lead the country in utility-interactive systems. And while there will always be places and people in need of off-grid systems, we believe the future in this country for renewable electricity lies with utility interaction, and similarly with micro-grid local production networks that can be separated from the national grid.

Does this paradigm shift mean the same do-it-yourself ethic that created so many off-grid systems in the past can continue as before? We're all for home-owner installations, but only within reason. As an electrician, Rebekah believes the danger and complexity of tying a renewable electricity system to the grid means calling in the professionals can often be a wise decision. Utility-interactive systems absolutely must be inspected. There isn't an alternative, unless you want to be liable for unlimited damages to the utility. Whenever an inspector gets involved, it means permits and licenses must be obtained. While many jurisdictions allow homeowners to pull (obtain) electrical permits, sometimes requiring a homeowner exam, we ask that you proceed with caution. Utility-interactive systems operate under completely different rules than off-grid systems, meaning dangerously high DC voltage, and interconnection guidelines that are progressively more difficult to understand. It takes years of study and practice to get a thorough grip on safety parameters and good installation practices, and we realize that while some homeowners have the skills to do it, many do not and it would be unsafe for them to try. So with those caveats in mind, this chapter is going to focus on how to make a sound decision about what specific type of renewable electricity will work best for you and your home, as opposed to laying out instruc-

tions for physical installation. There exist well-written, detailed installation handbooks for homeowners who prefer to go it alone, referenced and listed at the end of the chapter in the resources section. We recommend the Web site www.findsolar.com for those wishing to hire an experienced installer.

OUR STORY

Since we live in an urban, indeed downtown, environment, microhydro and wind were immediately out of the question for us, for all the reasons discussed below in the site-analysis section. We knew we wanted a photovoltaic system that could offset all our energy usage, and we also knew we wanted battery backup, since we often experience hurricanes in the summer and ice storms in the winter. The utility grid here in Durham, North Carolina, is fairly unreliable, as we have thousands of willow oaks, planted en masse by an urban gardening group in the 1930s, that are all aging out simultaneously, with large limbs falling frequently during storms.

To size our PV system, we used an off-grid sizing worksheet that Rebekah created, tallying all our daily loads and looking at peak-sun hours and climatic data, although we eventually plan to tie the system to the grid. By using an off-grid instead of grid-tied worksheet, we made sure that we produced enough power every day to cover our consumption, instead of averaging out for the year (offsetting all consumption with production over the longer term). Offsetting means that perhaps you produce more than you use in one month, but the extra production is "banked" against future months when you might consume more electricity than your PV system creates. Sizing our system to cover everyday consumption isn't a question of taking the moral high ground. In fact, sizing a PV array to offset consumption might in fact be preferable to sizing a system to cover all daily loads, because in all likelihood it could be a smaller system. But since we are currently off-grid, we had to size our system for days of clouds and rain that might or might not occur.

Since we haven't yet tied our house to the grid and are living off our daily PV system production, we had no choice but to size the system to meet daily demand, and thus occasionally we have extra power that we can't export to our neighbors.

There are a few reasons we have not yet tied to the grid, although we definitely plan to eventually and don't recommend living off-grid where the grid is available. Primarily, our utility, Duke Power, charges high administrative rates to feed PV power back via a secondary production meter into its grid. Second, we are waiting to see what happens with the institution of Renewable Energy Portfolio Standards (REPS) in our state, which mandates that the utilities must supply a percentage of their electricity with renewable resources. The legislature here in North Carolina passed a REPS package (12.5 percent by 2020). With the new REPS, it is possible that the utilities here will start to offer nonproduction credits, paying a rebate, $4/installed watt for example, for the rights to say they own your "green" energy for a set period of time. Under such a system we could get a one-time check for signing away "green" rights for say, 20 years. Many states have slightly different versions of the renewables rebate right now. The Web site www.dsireusa.org lists these rebates.

Right now North Carolina does have a great (and highly replicable) production-based incentive through a program called NCGreenpower. NCGreenpower is a nongovernmental organization that collects dollars through the utilities, allowing regular customers to "buy" renewable energy as a portion of their regular electric bill, and then distributes those dollars, on a cents-per-kilowatt-hour-of-production basis, to renewable energy providers who are tied to the grid and "sell" power (spin the meter backward). It is a great system, but right now the base rate and administrative fees Duke Power charges can't be met with our NCGreenpower payments, since we have a relatively small PV system. So we would in effect be paying Duke Power to take our PV power, sell it, and use the proceeds to build more coal-burning power plants. But we are sure this is a temporary phenomenon, growing

pains of the new utility interconnection rules that are being developed around the country and change at lightning speed.

The third reason we didn't tie to the grid is that we are just fixated on controlling our consumption; it became a fascinating game at some point, and we know that living off-grid makes us incredibly aware of how we use electricity. Fourth, since our house is a duplex, we are able to create a small "mini-grid," letting our housemates use much of our extra power.

To return to system sizing, we knew basically what our loads would be: lights, our off-the-shelf (AC) 14-cubic-foot refrigerator, one desktop computer (albeit a small one with flat-panel LCD screen), a stereo, a washing machine, fans, and the occasional power tool. After running the numbers, we discovered we could get by with a 1,200-watt PV array. We chose six 200-watt Kyocera modules, because the price per watt was low and Kyocera is a reliable manufacturer (Rebekah will install pretty much any module, as long as it comes from a reliable manufacturer). We don't have a backup generator, and have in fact never used one despite years of living off-grid. If the supply gets tight, we conserve, doing things like skipping the movie or turning down the fan. The array has been doing a great job of keeping us in power (Rebekah's constant monitoring of production and consumption also helps). We have an 800-amp hour battery bank, with lead acid deep-cycle batteries (eight 6-volt 400-amp hour batteries). Ironically, the worst time of year for living off-grid in North Carolina is midsummer because of the heat and haze (in most places the longest days of the year are the best for PV). Plus our refrigerator and fans have to run double-time in the heat while the array output is low. Our 1,200 watts is small when compared to many other residential PV systems, but it is completely sufficient to cover our consumption.

The rest of this chapter is dedicated to helping you figure out what renewable electricity can work in your specific location, and how to meet and understand your demand. First, we'll go through an overview of photovoltaics, wind turbines, and microhydro, so you understand the different technology and system structures. Second, we'll look at your specific household consumption, as you have to know what your consumption is before you can design a system to meet it. Third, we'll discuss how to do a site analysis at your home, as the three types of renewable energy systems we are discussing have very different environmental requirements. Finally, we'll look at the various components that make up the different systems.

SYSTEMS OVERVIEW

Photovoltaics

The term *photovoltaic* (PV) relates to the production of electric current at the junction of two substances exposed to light. PV modules are made up of solar cells, most commonly made of silicon doped (chemically bonded) with boron and phosphorous, then lined with metal conductors that act as pathways for the electricity. The cells are excited by photons from the sun, creating voltage and current. The number of cells in a panel dictates the voltage of the module as a whole, and the size of each cell dictates the current the module can supply.

A photovoltaic cell functions by capturing a portion of the available energy of photons from the sun, which is approximately 1,000 watts/square meter (92 watts/square foot) in good sun conditions. The efficiency of a particular photovoltaic module is the percentage of that available 1,000 watts/square meter the module is able to convert to electricity. For example, a manufacturer might claim 20 percent efficiency, meaning if you buy a one-square-meter module, you should see 200 watts of power (20 percent of 1,000 is 200) produced by the module if it is placed perpendicular to the sun's rays in optimal sun and temperature conditions. People often complain about low module efficiency, and approximately 20 percent is the high end of what is available on the market now for PV. But 20 percent of free and nonpolluting is a heck of a lot better than 10 or 15 percent of dirty and expensive, the corresponding efficiencies of coal-powered electricity and gas-powered cars![1] People often ask us

if it is a good idea to wait to purchase PV modules until they improve in efficiency or cost. We absolutely don't think so. The modules on the market now work great and will produce dependable electricity at a fair price for a generation or more. We don't expect to see the price per watt falling dramatically anytime soon (it hasn't budged since 2004, in fact quite the opposite: it increased through most of 2005 and 2006), nor do we think efficiencies will improve quickly, although they are slowly rising, but often at increased cost per watt. Breakthroughs are possible, but the lag between discovery and product availability could be upward of a decade.

It's important to note that photovoltaic cells are unique in that they produce direct current (DC) power, as opposed to the alternating current (AC) that the normal house uses. Hence, to use PV electricity in a house, it is almost always necessary to convert a large chunk of the PV power production from DC to AC, which is the job of an inverter.

There are three basic types of PV systems available. The first is a **straight grid-tied** (or **utility-interactive**) system, meaning your PV production is sent back to the grid through an inverter and then through your regular electric panel (or through a second production meter), and there are no batteries to provide backup power. Because of the way utility-interactive PV inverters work, they shut down when the grid shuts down, meaning you get no power from the sun, not even just a little bit, until the utility is back up. That you might not have power even with PV panels on your roof can be a hard concept to grasp. To have PV power when the grid is down, you must opt for the second type of system—**grid-tied with battery backup.** A grid-tied with battery backup system entails installing an electrical "backed-up-loads panel" that powers house loads like refrigerators and lights when the utility is down. In power outages, the chosen loads are isolated from the grid, powered by PV and batteries via the inverter, and continue to function normally until the power is back on. The third type of PV system, an **off-grid system,** is more commonly found in rural areas. It is not tied to the grid at all and is dependent on a

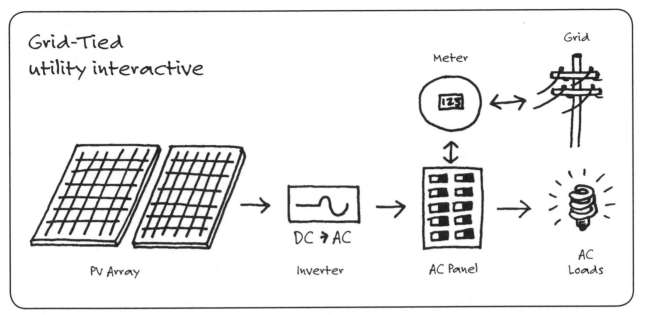

FIG. 2.2. **The main components of a utility-interactive photovoltaic system.**

battery bank to function properly. There is no reason that an off-grid system can't function perfectly well in an urban area.

So what type of system do you want? Having a utility-interactive system means that you won't ever run out of power, as can happen after days of cloudy weather off-grid, because the grid is acting as your battery. In addition, it means that you won't ever be producing PV power with no place to go ("wasted power"), as can happen off-grid when batteries are full and loads are light. The grid will take all the power you can give it, and this has significant implications; in a world that desperately needs each and every possible reduction in fossil-fuel consumption, it seems wrong to let any PV power go unused if it could offset coal power. But the distance from your house to the available grid might make an off-grid system more economically feasible than paying for power lines to be run to your house. Or you might live where there is no grid!

For grid-tied systems, the next question is, batteries or no batteries? Utility-interactive PV systems without batteries will under no circumstances work when the grid is down. This is a National Electric Code requirement, and because of the design of inverters, there is no way around it (yes, that's right, it is absolutely 100

percent impossible to hot-wire that inverter to get any power when the grid is down). Well, ask yourself, how often does your power go out? Once every five years? If so, maybe you should look at a break from electricity as a luxury to be enjoyed. Battery-based systems are more expensive, require more maintenance, and take up more space. But if you live in a region plagued by ice storms, hurricanes, and frequent weeklong blackouts, as we do, then you might prefer battery backup. Another option is to install a biodiesel generator for renewable energy backup when the grid is down, and go straight grid-tied. System cost analyses have shown it to be cheaper to install a diesel generator along with utility-interactive PV than a battery-based PV system.

Energy production

PV arrays are referred to by the amount of wattage the modules they contain are rated at. A 2,000-watt (2kW) array contains some number of modules that add up to 2,000 watts (perhaps 10 200-watt modules or 20 100-watt modules). What that wattage number means is that in optimal sun conditions, a clear day at noon with panels perpendicular to the sun, your array should be capable of delivering close to 2,000 watts of power instantaneously. In optimal sun conditions for an hour, the array will produce 2 kilowatt-hours (kWhs) of energy. The energy, in kWhs/month, an array will produce depends on the shading on the array, the angle and azimuth of the array, and the number of sun hours the system receives, which in turn depends on the weather and the average peak-sun hours per day in your locale.

Wind Generators

A wind turbine is a generator—a permanent magnet alternator. A rotor with blades captures the energy from the wind as it is spun by the wind. The power output is usually referred to as "wild" AC, which is rectified (transformed and converted) to DC power, to feed batteries and a stand-alone or grid-tied inverter. Installing a wind-turbine system entails making many of the same decisions as for a PV system, such as whether it should be utility interactive or not, and whether to have battery backup if it is utility interactive. It is only relatively recently that residential wind turbines have been installed as utility interactive. One reason is that they are most often found in remote areas. Wind turbines can work well in conjunction with PV arrays, because when the wind is blowing the sun might not be shining, and vice versa. Due to the intermittent characteristics of wind, off-grid wind systems must have battery banks to ensure constant power availability.

Energy production

How much power will a turbine produce? Well, it's complicated. Factors include the height of the turbine (which relates to turbulence), the wind velocity, the air density, and the size of the area swept by the blades. Wind power is a function of air density, instantaneous wind speed (the "velocity"), and the area intercepting the wind (the blade length or the square of the rotor diameter).

The actual equation is: Power = ½ air density (or 0.00508 at sea level) times area in square feet times wind speed in miles per hour cubed. Note the cube on the wind speed. What that means is that the power available varies with the cube of the wind speed, hence

small increases in wind speed, even for short times, can mean big increases in power. There is a lot of math involved in calculating potential outputs. Fortunately manufacturers publish charts detailing the relationship among turbine size, wind speed, and production values. Table 2.3 is an example of a chart from Bergey WindPower. These manufacturers' charts should be taken with a grain of salt, though, since they come from the manufacturer and not an independent test facility, but are a good starting point.

Microhydro Turbines

Microhydro turbines produce power much as wind turbines do—they are basically generators. Water pressure and flow cause runner blades to turn, just as wind causes blades to turn on a wind turbine. Electricity is produced by the rotation of the generator via electromagnetic induction. The power produced by a microhydro turbine depends on the same factors as with wind: density of water (as opposed to air), the size of the turbine, and the pressure of the water (analogous to the velocity of the wind). The power produced can be wild AC power rectified (transformed and converted) to DC power, or it can be regulated AC power, depending on the turbine design. The power output is fed to a battery bank or straight to an electrical panel, which can be utility interactive or off-grid.

Energy production

The power in water is greater than the power in air, because water has a much higher density than air. This allows small microhydro turbines to create as much power as large wind turbines. How much power a turbine will provide is best understood by looking at a turbine manufacturer's chart. Because every potential site has a different combination of head (elevational drop) and flow, and every turbine has different power outputs for various levels of head and flow, it is impossible to generalize. Table 2.3 shows an example chart. If you are going to build your own turbine, you can get an idea of production by looking at a similarly sized mass-produced turbine.

DEMAND AND SITE (PRODUCTION) ANALYSIS

So which of these systems will work for you? To answer that question, we will first examine your electric consumption (the demand side of the equation) and then move to satisfying the supply side via site analysis. Site analysis means assessing what will work best in different locales to meet demand with the current feasible renewable electric supply mechanisms.

Electrical Consumption Analysis

Renter friendly.

Project Time: 1 hour over the course of a month.

Cost: Free.

Energy Saved: Varies.

Ease of Use: N/A.

Maintenance Level: N/A.

Skill Levels: None.

Materials: None.

Tools: Calculator.

Utility-Grid-Connected Houses

The first step to investigating installing renewable electricity is to gauge your own level of electricity consumption. You may have gotten an idea of yours if you started an energy diary (see chapter 3). For households that are connected to the grid, the best place to start is your current electric bill. How many kilowatt-hours (kWh) a month of electricity are you consuming? All you need to do to find out is read your bill, which states monthly usage. Consumption obviously varies throughout the year, with lows usually coming in fall and spring and highs in summer and winter. Another good source of information is the electric utility meter on your house. Most people ignore their meter, but you should take a moment to find it, learn to read it, and pay attention to what it tells you. Perhaps you can even prove the utility bills incorrect!

Reading a utility meter

Utility meters are either analog or digital. Digital meters are quite easy to read as your cumulative consumption is in bold digital numbers on the front. You can easily calculate daily, weekly, or monthly usage in kWh by writing down the number you see with a date attached, waiting, and then subtracting it from a future number and date. Analog meters are also readable, with usually five dials with numbers 0 through 9 and a needle or marker resting on a number. If the marker is between two numbers, choose the lower number, unless it is between 0 and 9, in which case you should write down 9. Write down the dial numbers from left to right, and the complete number will correspond with your cumulative kWh usage. Mark this down, come back in a week, write down the new number, subtract the first, and you have the number in kWhs of how much energy you consumed during the past week! You can calculate usage for any period of time as long as you keep good records.

Finding average daily consumption

It is quite simple to analyze daily grid-tied electrical demand. It is best to start with an average of monthly consumption, as months will vary throughout the year. To get an estimate of average monthly kilowatt-hour consumption, you can add up 12 electric bills, and divide that number by 12 for the monthly average. Or, if you don't have 12 bills, take a high bill and a low bill and use the average. To find average daily consumption, take your average kWh monthly consumption, and divide by 30 for the average days in a month. That average daily kWh tells you how much renewable electricity you will need to create or purchase on a daily basis to meet your demand.

Understanding what a kilowatt-hour is

To understand what the kWh number means, it is useful to look at the examples of hot-water heaters and PV panels. First, let's look at a consumption example. Say your electric hot-water heater draws 4,500 watts of power (for typical household appliance draws see table 2.2). For electricity, power is an instantaneous quantity measured in watts, while energy has a cumulative time component and is measured in watt-hours. Each hour your heater is on, it uses 4,500 watts times

TABLE 2.2 Some typical appliance draws	
Appliance	Draw (watt/hr)
Small Radio	15
TV 13"	70
Ceiling Fan	100
Furnace—Gas	750
Vacuum	800
Coffeemaker	900
Toaster	1,000
Dishwasher	1,500
Hair Dryer	1,600
Window AC Unit	2,000
Household AC 2 Ton	3,000
Heat Pump	5,000
Electric Clothes Dryer	6,000

1 hour, or 4,500 watt-hours of energy, or 4.5 kWh. So if it heats for two hours a day, it will consume 2 hours × 4.5 kW = 9 kilowatt-*hours* of electricity. On the flip side—production—of the equation, look at a 2,000-watt or 2-kilowatt PV array. A 2-kilowatt PV array, which could be made up of 10 200-watt panels, produces approximately 2 kilowatts of power when the sun shines on it. So if you have five sunny hours, your array could produce 2 kW × 5 hours, or 10 kWh of electricity in a day. Just because the water heater draws 4,500 watts and the PV array produces only 2,000 watts doesn't mean the PV can't produce enough energy for the water heater over the course of a day, but the time element is crucial to understand. In this example the hot-water heater draws 4.5 kWh and consumes 9 kWh in a day, while the 2-kilowatt PV array can produce 10 kWh in five hours of constant sun (see figure 2.3 for an illustration of a 2.4-kilowatt array).

Rebekah has found that there exists much confusion in the general public over the habit of the solar industry to refer to PV arrays by their cumulative wattage. Many homeowners she has encountered believe that a 2-kilowatt array will produce 2,000 kWh per month. As mentioned above, what the 2-kilowatt name means is that the array simply produces 2,000 watts of power in perfect sunlight conditions. A closer generic

monthly estimate would be 300 kWh (assuming an average of 5 peak hours of sunlight a day and 30 days in a month means 2,000 watts times 5 hours times 30 days equals 300 kWh per month). Inefficiencies must then be taken into account, which will reduce this 300 kWh by approximately 20%.

Calculating a PV array's output

The easiest way to find out what an array will produce in your environment prior to installation is to visit the PVWatts Calculator provided by the National Renewable Energy Laboratory (http://rredc.nrel.gov/solar/codes_algs/PVWATTS/). The program very accurately uses historical climatic data to estimate monthly and annual production for varying system sizes. There are several variables that the user can change to get a very accurate estimate. The calculator can derate (estimate subtracted production) for system inefficiencies, like less-than-optimum tilt angle or azimuth, dirt, shade, and so on. It can also estimate added production for enhancements like arrays mounted on trackers that follow the sun.

It is possible to use the program to size an array to match your entire household consumption. Enter 1.0 as the DC rating (kW) system into the calculator, then divide your house's yearly kWh consumption by the yearly kWh production value for a 1 kW array that the calculator gives you. The answer will be the size (in kW) of PV array you would need to install to completely offset your consumption.

Of course, with a grid-tied system you don't need to offset your entire consumption! You can install a very small PV system, and the rest of your consumption will be met with utility-provided power. PV systems are quite modular, so if you have a limited budget it can be a workable solution to install perhaps 1,000 watts this year, and 1,000 watts again in a few years. Of course, keep in mind that your current demand may not be constrained by any variable except the heavily subsidized cost of electricity and your own conservation habits. Once you decide to consume only renewable energy, you might find your demand sharply dropping!

Off-Grid House

Off-grid households have a harder task ahead of them to figure out demand. Instead of offsetting yearly consumption, off-grid renewable energy systems must be able to meet peak demand at any time of the year, just as the national grid must, or face blackouts. However, we are not focusing on off-grid houses, as this book is about renovating preexisting houses, which we assume already have a power source, most often the grid, and we are not advocating abandoning the grid. There are several Web sites with great off-grid-system-sizing calculators. One of our favorites is at the Alternative Energy Store—see http://store.altenergystore.com/calculators/off_grid_calculator/. Of course, this is an online store that also sells photovoltaic components, so caveat emptor, and try a few sizing programs to get a feel for the technicalities and to compare results. Rebekah has also designed a spreadsheet program for off-grid sizing that can be found at Chelsea Green's Web site.

Renewable Electric Systems Site Analysis

Project Time: Afternoon.

Cost: Free.

Energy Saved: N/A.

Ease of Use: N/A.

Maintenance Level: N/A.

Skill Level: None.

Materials: None.

Tools: Solar Pathfinder or equivalent, ruler, protractor, tape measure, bucket, Internet access.

The flip side of consumption is production. It is necessary to understand the limitations of your site and the requirements of the different renewable-electricity systems to be able to figure out what can work for you to produce the electricity needed to meet your demand. We will look at the environmental requirements for PV, wind turbines, and microhydro turbines. For urban sites, it is rare to be able to incorporate renewable electricity in a form other than photovoltaics. Residential-size wind towers generally have to be at minimum 30 feet higher than anything within a 300-foot radius, a particularly hard arrangement within the confines of a

FIG. 2.3. **These two pole-mounted arrays contain PV modules whose cumulative power is rated at 2,400 watts (2.4 kW). This moderately sized PV array is capable of meeting the electrical needs of an energy-conscious household.**

Courtesy Honey Electric Solar

city. Even if a good spot could be found, to erect one in a city is sure to raise the ire of neighbors and city managers and possibly encourage litigious activity, although we applaud test cases!

Microhydro sites need either a lot of water flow or a lot of elevational drop (head). Good microhydro systems need a stream or other water supply that provides a steady combination of both head and flow. For one example, check the Energy Systems and Design Stream Engine microhydro turbine wattage output chart in table 2.4. The left column shows head in feet and meters, and the top row shows flow in gallons/liters per minute. You can see the changing power output as a relationship between head and flow. If you installed this turbine where there is a flow of 20 gallons/minute at a head of 20 feet, you would see 40 watts of continuous power, and 40 watt-hours of energy per hour. This is not a lot of energy output for what is certainly an unusual confluence of water and elevation to find within a city. Although it isn't beyond the realm of possibility to find a suitable watercourse within the city, it certainly isn't common, especially since the water must be diverted to the turbine from the source stream and then returned, which raises water-rights issues as well.

To reiterate, urban renewable electric systems are nearly always going to be photovoltaic (PV) systems.

Rural systems can be much more flexible, including hybrid combinations of wind, microhydro, and PV, and maybe even a biodiesel generator thrown in to boot.

Siting Photovoltaics

Where can a solar electric array be installed? The best PV site has at least five and preferably more hours of completely unshaded solar access every day of the year (including holidays!). PV can go on roofs, ground mounts, sheds, garages, porch awnings, a car roof, backpacks, boat decks . . . use your imagination and PV can go just about anywhere that the sun shines! A good rule of thumb for space requirements is that you can fit approximately 1,000 watts of PV modules in 100 square feet. If you figured out using the PVWatts calculator that you need a 2,000-watt array to cover your consumption, you are looking for a sunny area of about 200 square feet. In the Northern Hemisphere, photovoltaics are best installed facing in a southerly direction, but east, west, flat, or vertical installations can still capture a surprisingly large percentage of the available energy. If your roof has a low slope (not a steep pitch), then an array that faces east or west can still function quite well.

The best and least expensive way we've found to check solar access (your solar window) in an instant is to buy or rent a Solar Pathfinder. The Solar Pathfinder can reliably tell you via reflections on a globe if the spot you are standing on will be shaded at any time of day, any day of the year. Chapter 1 includes Solar Pathfinder photos from our house. It's not only good for PV array locations; it is also a great tool for picking out the perfect garden spot. Without a tool like the Solar Pathfinder, it can be very hard to tell if that pine tree or chimney is just tall enough to shade your roof at noon in December, unless it is noon in December! One way to guesstimate shading is to stand facing south and spread your arms wide from east to west. If there is any shadow-casting object in front of you within the semicircle span created by your arms, it could shade the spot in which you are standing, depending on the height of the object and how far it is

from you. Don't forget that the sun is much lower in the sky in winter, thus creating longer shadows from shorter objects. If you have the lead time, another good way to check solar access is to take a morning picture and an afternoon picture of the most likely spots, once every month or two for a year. Review the pictures and check for shading patterns.

Don't forget that chimneys, plumbing vents, dormer windows, and other rooftop objects create shade as well! Often homeowners with a clear yard forget to look on the roof itself for shade creators.

One last method to check for solar blockage is to determine how low the sun will be at the winter solstice. By adding your latitude to 23 degrees (the tilt of the earth), you will know how far the sun dips down in the sky off perpendicular (straight overhead). Subtract this number from 90 (the perpendicular) to determine the horizontal angle of the sun in the winter. Use some angle-finding device (such as a carpenter's square or protractor) to mimic this angle and sight along a straightedge to see any potential obstructions.

Something else to check is your neighborhood and town/city covenants; if they do exist and inhibit renewable energy installations, work to change them.

What if you live in the city and your roof is completely shaded? Well, we had to cut down an aging oak tree in front of our house, and it was well worth it—it had shaded 80 percent of our solar window during winter months. We're not advocating a tree-killing free-for-all, but you should carefully weigh the pros and cons of large trees on city lots. Don't forget that sometimes you cut one tree down and another lurks just behind it! Just because one tree casts a shadow on your roof doesn't mean that another won't take its place if the first is removed. Also, trees grow, including your neighbor's that you might have no control over.

Where else can you put PV besides on the roof? Pole mounts can go on a sunny spot in the yard, or you could build a shed with a south-facing roof at the best year-round angle for your region (which corresponds approximately to your latitude, or perhaps slightly less than latitude with utility-interactive systems to take advantage of longer summer days). Other ideas include patio covers, awnings on the side of the house, and greenhouse windows (PV modules now exist that let light through between the solar cells). Vertically hung modules, if south facing, can capture a large percentage of the available solar energy.

What other options are there if you don't have a sunny enough spot, or if the summer shade of a tree outweighs any solar benefits you might receive from cutting it down? Perhaps you could start a micro-grid with neighbors who do have good solar access, paying for part of the array on their roof in exchange for part of the electricity. By purchasing part or all of a system to be installed on a neighbor or friend's house, even without tapping the electricity generated, you would be entitled to renewable-energy tax credits, possible rebates, or greenpower payments. Although the system wouldn't be on your own roof, you would still have the thrill of indirectly offsetting your own fossil-fuel consumption. States, utilities, and some nationwide programs have different schemes for paying producers of renewable energy, some on a per-watt cost basis, some as per-kilowatt payments for power that feeds back to the grid, and some as pure carbon-emission-offset payments. Check out what your state has to offer (see www.dsireusa.org), and think outside the box. It may be that in the end the best decision is to offset your personal fossil-fuel consumption by purchasing renewable energy credits (RECs or greentags) from a nationwide provider. The U.S. Department of Energy maintains an Energy Efficiency and Renewable Energy Web site that compiles lists of REC providers. See the resources section at the end of this chapter.

Siting a Wind Turbine

When looking for a good site for a wind turbine, there are two main factors in the equation: average wind speed and open-area availability.

Basically, you cannot put even a small wind turbine on the roof of a house. They create too much noise and vibration. Also, wind turbulence is detrimental to a turbine and its electrical production; such turbulence can be a problem when a turbine is located less than 30 feet above a roof structure or any other objects

less than 300 feet away (a full 50 feet of height above objects within 500 feet is recommended). You can use a building to stay a turbine tower, but it should be an unoccupied building because of the above-mentioned noise and vibration. To reiterate—the turbine is not just 30 feet or more above ground level; it should be at the very least 30 feet above any object within 300 feet, such as a tree or house, to avoid wind turbulence. So the options are necessarily very limited in urban areas, unless you happen to have a large lot, few neighbors, and easygoing city administration. In rural areas, the choices are greater: guyed mast towers, freestanding truss or lattice towers, or tapered tubular towers can be built and placed in open areas to hold turbines. Towers built to hold turbines are now available in specially built and relatively inexpensive kits.

So, how much wind do you need? Nine to 11 miles per hour average wind speed is the amount that small residential wind turbines are designed to accommodate. Note that this is an average wind speed and not gusting. Different turbine manufacturers have charts available that list expected output as related to average wind speed. As an example of expected power output for a specific turbine, table 2.3 is an output chart for a Bergey Wind Power XL.1 2.5-meter-diameter wind turbine. Note the average wind speed across the top of the chart; as average wind speed increases, output increases. Wind turbines are peculiar in that the instantaneous power output is extremely variable, as the power available in wind increases dramatically with wind speed. This chart uses average wind speed to calculate daily, monthly, and annual energy production.

The National Renewable Energy Laboratory accumulates data on average annual wind resources throughout the United States. You can go to www.nrel.gov/wind and look through the resource section to see how the lab rates wind resources on state maps. Also, the National Climatic Data Center (www.ncdc.noaa.gov), part of the National Oceanic and Atmospheric Administration, has data on average wind speed by city. Where we live, near Raleigh, North Carolina, the NCDC estimates our monthly average wind speed varies between 6 and 8 miles per hour. Not a prime

TABLE 2.3 Bergey WindPower Co. BWC XL.1 Wind Turbine Predicted Energy Production

Wind Speeds Taken at Top of Tower (no wind shear)									
Annual Average Wind Speed (m/s)			3.5	4	4.5	5	5.5	6	6.5
Annual Average Wind Speed (mph)			7.8	8.9	10.1	11.2	12.3	13.4	14.5
Production in kWh (24VDC)		Daily	1.9	2.8	3.9	5.1	6.4	7.7	8.9
		Monthly	55	85	115	155	195	235	270
		Annually	680	1,010	1,410	1,850	2,320	2,790	3,260
Wind Speeds Taken at 10 Meters (per standard wind resource maps)									
US-DOE Wind Power Class			1	2	3	4	5	6	7
Annual Average Wind Speed (m/s)			~8.9	~10.7	~12.1	~13.0	~13.9	~15.0	~18.8
Annual Average Wind Speed (mph)			~4.0	~4.8	~5.4	~5.8	~6.2	~6.7	~8.4
Production in kWh (24VDC)	30 ft (9m) Tower	Daily	2.6	4.3	5.8	6.8	7.8	9.1	12.7
		Monthly	80	130	175	205	240	275	385
	64 ft (20m) Tower	Daily	4.1	6.4	8.2	9.3	10.4	11.7	14.7
		Monthly	125	195	250	285	320	355	445
	104 ft (32m) Tower	Daily	5.2	7.8	9.7	10.9	12	13.1	15.4
		Monthly	160	235	295	330	365	400	465

Assumptions: Inland site, Rayleigh wind distribution, shear exponent = 0.20, altitude = 1000 ft (300 m)
Note: Battery charge regulation (batteries full) and wire run losses will reduce actual XL.1 performance. PERFORMANCE MAY VARY

Output charts can be found for most manufactured wind turbines, and are helpful in analyzing your site for production possibilities. Courtesy Bergey Windpower Co.

site for a small wind turbine. But we didn't have to look at a data chart to figure that out. The wind here is notoriously uneven, kicking up violently before thunderstorms and dying out for weeks at a time in the hot summer. If you can afford to spend some time studying your site in different seasons, perhaps installing an anemometer (a device to measure wind speed), you can get a good idea of whether a small wind turbine might work for you. You don't need constant wind all the time, but if you don't have daily wind, you will need to think about hybrid systems or grid backup. Some areas in the mountains have great nighttime thermal winds; other areas have wind only in the winter. Situations such as these are ideal for a hybrid system with photovoltaics.

Siting a Microhydro Turbine

Where can a microhydro turbine be installed? Good sites have either a lot of water flow, a lot of elevational drop (head), or a workable balance of the two. To be practical, microhydro systems need a combination of head and flow somewhere between these extremes: 2 feet of drop (the head) and 500 gallons per minute, or 2 gallons of water per minute and 500 feet of drop.

How do you assess your site? You must try to estimate the available flow (gallons per minute) and head separately. Measuring flow and head can be a tricky business, involving buckets, gauges, levels, water lines, and measuring tapes. If you have access to a stream that you think might work, then a more thorough analysis than we detail here could be worthwhile. For a quick easy guess at flow in gallons per minute, if you have an accessible spot such as a small waterfall you can stick a 5-gallon bucket in the flow and measure how fast it fills—for example, filling in 30 seconds means 10 gallons per minute. If there isn't an accessible spot, the other way to measure flow is to build a weir, a labor-intensive project that involves basically building a small dam with a hole in the middle that the water has to flow through, enabling you to catch the flow and measure it. If you have a watercourse where flow is obviously huge, then you probably need to worry only about the second part of the equation—head.

Approximating head is tricky. Head is measured as the vertical distance between the start of the captured water line and the input of the turbine. You can make a guesstimate, perhaps with an altimeter watch read at the intake spot and the turbine location, but before investing in a system you should get an accurate measurement.

To measure head you need to start at the bottom of the potential penstock route (where the turbine would sit) and, working with a friend, try to estimate the rise to a possible point of intake (where the water enters the route to the turbine). This can be done with a level and a stick of known height (5 feet in this example). Start at the lowest elevation and work your way toward the highest spot—the intake. Using your 5-foot-tall measuring stick, sight along the top of the stick with your level to a reference point at ground level, such as the base of a tree or a rock or your friend's feet. Instead of sighting along the stick, you could instead use a string level or water level from the top of the stick to the reference point for more accuracy. The height (head) between you and the reference point will be 5 feet. Your friend can mark the reference spot, and you can start over again at the reference spot and work your way to the intake point. Keep track of the number of times it takes you to make it from the lowest spot—the turbine's future home—to the highest spot, the intake, and multiply that times five. If it takes three different markings and movements to get to the top, you have a 15-foot head. Voilà: a slightly inaccurate but very good ballpark guess at your head!

Another good measurement to make at this point is the horizontal distance from turbine to intake. This will tell you how much pipe you would need to build the system. If you are looking at 50 feet of drop over 600 feet of horizontal distance, for example, that's a lot of distance; it's certainly doable, but it will add expense to the system. Friction losses vary by pipe diameter and distance. Longer distances mean more friction losses, which can be offset with larger pipe. Larger pipe entails lower friction losses but adds expense and trouble to a system design.

Once you have a ballpark notion of your head and flow, take some time to peruse different turbine manufacturers' Web sites. Microhydro turbine manufacturers print data charts, such as in table 2.4, that show power output at different combinations of flow and head. Examining these charts can give you a good idea of which turbine might fit your site and how much power you could expect it to produce.

You not only need a good amount of water and head for microhydro but also must provide a screened

TABLE 2.4 Energy Systems and Design Stream Engine Microhydro Turbine Output in Watts								
Net Head		Flow Rate in Gallons/min (Liters/sec)						
		10	20	40	75	100	112	150
Meters	Feet	(0.67)	(1.33)	(2.5)	(5.00)	(6.67)	(7.5)	(9.50)
3	10	–	20	50	90	120	130	150
6	20	15	40	100	180	230	250	350
15	49	45	110	230	450	600	650	800
30	98	80	200	500	940	1100	*	*
60	197	150	400	900	1500	*	*	*
90	295	200	550	1200	*	*	*	*
120	394	300	700	1500	*	*	*	*
150	492	400	850	1900	*	*	*	*

A good microhydro site is hard to come by, but when you do find one it is often the most reliable, least expensive, provider of 24-hour-a-day renewable electricity. Courtesy Energy Systems and Design intake, a route (usually piped) for the captured water to flow out of the source and into the turbine and back to the stream, a safe (often enclosed) location for the turbine, a transmission route for the electricity, and a protected space for the electrical components. That's a lot of infrastructure, which can be exposed to freezing temperatures depending on location. Freezing temperatures aren't as much of a concern for wind or PV (batteries excepted, which can be sensitive to temperature swings) but make microhydro that much harder to install, as frozen pipes mean zero power and reconstruction expenses.

You must also make sure there aren't restrictions on water access: remember these systems almost always remove some percentage of the water from a stream or creek to get it to the turbine, sometimes for hundreds of feet. Questions to ask yourself include: How will the removal of water affect wildlife in the creek? Do you own the entire watercourse? Will you need county or jurisdictional permission?

What if you live in an off-grid home with a seasonally dependent water supply, so that your microhydro site provides power for only certain times of the year? This can be overcome as long as you plan a hybrid system that relies on other power sources to provide electricity in the downtime when little water is available.

SYSTEM COMPONENTS

PV System Components

PV modules. A single PV panel or module can be rated from less than 1 watt to well over 200 watts. Size is related to wattage; bigger panels are usually higher wattage, but this varies with efficiency factors. The nameplate wattage rating comes from STC or standard test condition ratings. This rating is calculated under optimal lab conditions: 1,000 watts/square meter of sunlight, no excess heat (heat causes efficiency loss due to voltage drop in cells), the panel set perpendicular to the light source, and so on. Therefore, STC ratings are often a bit higher than what is found in the field, but they can also be exceeded, albeit less frequently, at high elevations and

cool temperatures. Module voltage also varies; the usual range is 12 volts DC to 48 volts DC, nominal (open-circuit and operating voltage will be higher than nominal voltage, from approximately 20 to 60 volts DC). There is no such thing as a PV module that produces alternating current (unless it has a microinverter attached); they all produce direct current (DC).

PV array. PV modules make up an array that produces direct current at varying voltages, depending on the wiring design. An array can be any quantity of modules wired together in series and/or parallel. Series connections between modules increase system voltage, whereas parallel connections increase current. Inverters will specify the input voltage they need, which can be a very specific number for battery-based systems or a wide range for straight grid-tied systems. The benefit of higher voltage is lower current, which in turn means that smaller, less expensive wire with lower current carrying capability can be used.

Charge controllers (regulator). Used only on systems with a battery bank, the charge controller regulates battery charging and voltage, ensuring batteries aren't overcharged. Optional features can include stepping voltage down from the array voltage to match the battery-bank voltage (for example, a 48-volt array can feed a 24-volt battery bank); maximum powerpoint tracking, which optimizes the voltage and current point at which the PV array operates to increase power output; and battery temperature sensing, which leads to more effective battery charging, as batteries are temperature sensitive.

Batteries. Off-grid PV systems supplying residences must have a battery bank. Batteries supply enough power for surges like refrigerator or pump start-up and are the only source of power when the sun goes down or a cloud floats by. Battery banks are categorized by amp/hour capacity and voltage and can be small or large, depending on how many days of backup power you desire. Batteries are wired in series and/or parallel to match the system voltage and amp/hour capacity necessary. As with modules, series connections increase voltage, while parallel connections increase amp/hour capacity. For example, two 100-amp/hour

12-volt batteries connected in parallel results in a 12-volt battery bank with 200-amp/hour capacity. Two 100-amp/hour 12-volt batteries connected in series results in a 24-volt battery bank with 100-amp/hour capacity. Is one better than the other? Not really; you still get the same power output, as watts (or power) equals volts times amps. Most household PV systems now go for higher-voltage battery banks for efficiency reasons. You can use smaller-gauge wire with higher voltage and lower current, and copper is expensive!

Inverter. Converts direct current as produced by a PV array into alternating current as used in houses and the electric grid. It is the brain that "sells" power to the grid (and feeds the house) in utility-interactive systems. Other features include maximum power-point tracking (this is default with straight grid-tied inverters), battery charging, and data monitoring.

Misc. PV systems will incorporate racking (rails to mount the array on), DC and AC disconnects, combiner boxes, lightening arrestors, and various other electrical materials.

Cost

Photovoltaics are considered the most expensive renewable electric systems, averaging close to $10/watt when professionally installed for a straight grid-tied system with no batteries, meaning even a relatively small 2,000-watt system without backup power will cost nearly $20,000. A system with batteries averages $12/watt when professionally installed. Homeowner installation would cut approximately 20 to 30 percent of the cost. There are definitely economies of scale—5,000-watt systems can be professionally installed for between $7 and $8/watt.

Life expectancy

Photovoltaic panels are commonly warrantied for 20 to 25 years at 80 percent power output, although industry insiders expect them to produce power for much longer, perhaps 50 years or more at a relatively high percentage power output. As they have no moving parts, the most common cause of failure is weather infiltration and degradation of the electrical connections between cells.

Maintenance

For straight grid-tied systems without batteries, maintenance is almost nonexistent on a daily basis. Inverters are expected to last at least 10 years, so at some point they will need replacement. For off-grid systems, daily checks of system voltage and monthly battery maintenance are required. PV arrays are remarkably maintenance free; rain usually washes the array clean, and grid-tied inverters just hang on the wall happily inverting, turning off and on as the grid demands.

Wind-System Components

Wind turbine. The machine that literally spins in the wind to create power. Available in a dizzying array of sizes and styles, rated by wattage.

Tower. Holds the turbine. In general it must be 30 feet taller (at minimum) than anything within 300 feet. More reliable towers are 50 feet taller than anything within 500 feet. The tower must allow access for servicing the turbine and be built to withstand high winds and bad weather and can be guyed or free-standing. Off-the-shelf tower kits are becoming more common, at lower cost.

Controller. The charge controller regulates battery charging and voltage, as with a PV system, and must be able to operate a dump load to get rid of excess production.

Dump load. For use when the batteries are full or when the grid is down. This can be a simple heating element that is turned on by the controller. Without a dump load the turbine can overheat.

Batteries. Battery banks are categorized by amp/hour capacity and can be of any size, depending on how many days of backup power you desire. Batteries are wired in series and/or parallel to match the system voltage and amp/hour capacity necessary.

Inverter. Converts direct current (DC), as supplied by the turbine after rectification, into alternating current (AC), as used in houses and the electric grid. In utility-interactive systems, it is the inverter that handles the grid interaction.

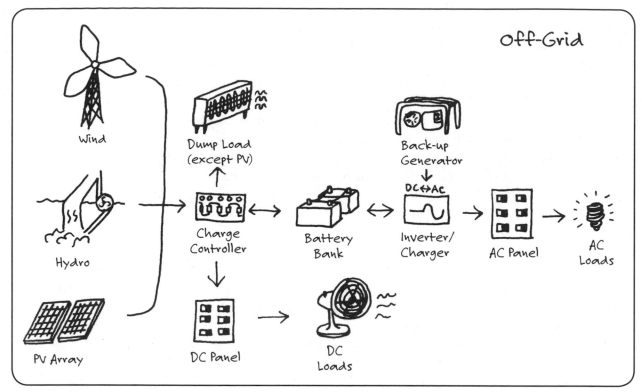

FIG. 2.4. **Some common components of off-grid renewable electricity systems. Not every off-grid system is alike, and there are many possibilities for hybrid systems with different configurations.**

Cost

Wind can be installed for as little as $5/watt, but much depends on the location, height, and construction of the tower.

Life expectancy

Wind turbines carry shorter warranties than photo-voltaic panels, varying by model. According to the American Wind Energy Association, most residential wind turbines have a design life of up to 20 years. Generally speaking, life expectancy for a turbine with regular maintenance should be at least 10 years, and possibly as much as 50 years. The inverter should last 10 years, as should the controller and battery bank.

Maintenance

For off-grid systems, maintenance involves daily voltage checks and monthly maintenance of batter-ies. All generators need twice-yearly inspections and maintenance (greasing and detangling wrapped

wires), which means either climbing the genera-tor tower or bringing the generator to the ground, neither of which is particularly easy.

Microhydro System Components

Microhydro turbine. The machine that spins as water flows over it to create power. Available in vari-ous sizes, rated by wattage and output voltage. Wild AC output may need to be rectified to DC power or constant AC voltage (an alternator can be used).

Pipeline, penstock, flume, or ditch. The water's route to the turbine: water is extracted from an upstream source, routed through the turbine after being filtered for debris, and rerouted downstream to the source return. Most commonly polyethylene or PVC pipe.

Intake. Where the water enters the pipeline or penstock. Screened and protected in some manner.

Batteries. A microhydro system is the only renew-able electric system that may not need batteries in an off-grid situation, as water flows in some places can be so consistent that with a turbine sized large enough to meet peak demand a battery would never be necessary. However, batteries can be used to store microhydro power to meet demand peaks that exceed production, as with wind and PV.

Diversion controller or charge controller. The controller regulates battery charging and voltage, as with a PV system. Optional features include stepping voltage down from the array to match the battery bank voltage. A diversion controller is used to switch on a dump load.

Diversion or dump load. A load (device) that uses power not needed for other loads or battery charging, protecting the turbine from overheating when batteries are full or loads are light.

Inverter. Converts direct current (DC), from either batteries or a rectifier, into alternating current (AC) as used in houses and the electric grid. In utility-interactive systems, it is the inverter that handles the grid interaction.

Misc. Pressure gauge, vacuum breaker, valves, disconnects. The more shutoff valves you install initially, the easier the system will be to maintain later!

Cost

While microhydro is considered the least expensive renewable electricity, and for good reason, the cost is hard to quantify, given huge site differences. A roof is basically a roof and solar energy is relatively constant, but streams vary wildly and can be hundreds of feet from the turbine itself, creating expensive penstocks. Expect to spend anywhere from $1,000 to $20,000.

Life expectancy

Variable—from 10 to 50 years, depending on the durability of the turbine and penstock. Warranties vary, but new turbines should include at least a five-year warranty. The more routine maintenance you do on your turbine, the longer it will last.

Maintenance

Turbines and penstocks need visual inspection frequently. Voltage and power output should be checked regularly. Remove debris from the penstock and intake filter monthly. Turbines need yearly maintenance according to manufacturer's specifications. The more shutoff valves you put in a system, the easier maintenance will be.

RESOURCES

Books

Davis, Scott. 2003. *Microhydro: Clean Power from Water*. Gabriola Island, BC: New Society Publishers.

Dunlop, Jim, with the National Joint Apprenticeship and Training Committee. 2007. *Photovoltaic Systems*. Hertforshire, England: American Technical Publications.

Gipe, Paul. 2003. *Wind Power: Renewable Energy for Home, Farm, and Business*. White River Junction, VT: Chelsea Green Publishing.

Solar Energy International. 2004. *Photovoltaics: Design & Installation Manual*. Gabriola Island, BC: New Society Publishers.

Internet

American Solar Energy Society (ASES). www.ases.org

American Wind Energy Association (AWEA). www.awea.org

Database of State Incentives for Renewables & Efficiency. www.dsireusa.org

Energy Efficiency and Renewable Energy. The U.S. Department of Energy maintains a Web site that compiles lists of renewable energy credit (REC) providers. www.eere.energy.gov/greenpower /buying/buying_power.shtml

Find Solar. Database of solar installers, by geographical area, with customer references and ratings. www.findsolar.com

Interstate Renewable Energy Council (IREC). Nonprofit that supports market-oriented services targeted at education, coordination, procurement, the adoption and implementation of uniform guidelines and standards, workforce development, and consumer protection. www. irecusa.org

Microhydro Web Portal. www.microhydropower.net

National Renewable Energy Laboratory (NREL) *Solar Program.* www.nrel.gov/solar/

North American Board of Certified Energy Practitioners (NAPCEP). Develops and implements credentialing and certification programs for photovoltaic installers. www.nabcep.org

PVWatts. NREL's performance calculator for grid-tied PV systems. http://rredc.nrel.gov/solar /codes_algs/PVWATTS/

Solar Energy Industries Association (SEIA). www.seia.org

Solar Energy International (SEI). Nonprofit renewable energy education classes, including ones on photovoltaics. http://solarenergy.org/workshops /index.html

Magazines

Home Power Magazine. P.O. Box 520, Ashland, OR 97520; (916) 475–3179; www.homepower.com

Photon International, Solar Verlag GmbH, Jülicher Str. 37652070 Aachen, Germany; phone +49/241/4003–0; fax +49/241/4003–300; www.photon-magazine.com

Solar Today, 2400 Central Avenue, Suite A, Boulder, CO 80301; phone (303) 443-3130; fax (303) 443-3212; www.solartoday.org

Endnote

1. U.S. Department of Energy (http://www.fuel economy.gov/feg/atv.shtml).

CHAPTER 3

Appliances and Lighting

Introduction • Our Story • Electric-Resistance Heat and Lighting •The Bogeyman of Phantom Draws • Electric Lighting • Other Lighting Alternatives • Energy-Sipping Appliances and Their Efficient Use • Conclusion • Resources

INTRODUCTION

Human ingenuity has produced an endless supply of gadgets and gizmos that are supposed to make our lives easier. With some, such as the lightbulb, there can be no doubt of their utility. With others, such as the vast array of flashing, beeping children's toys, and many such adult toys as well, the gain in quality of life is not quite so obvious.

Somewhere along the way the "more is always better" credo became etched in stone. The fact that the earth is a floating island of limited resources and limited dumping capabilities got lost among the Jet Skis, blenders, video games, power tools, hair dryers, DVD players, massage chairs, whirlpools, and treadmills. But the facts remain the same, only more so with each passing day.

As you start out anew on your path to fossil-fuel freedom, the first step should be to take a long, hard look at all the baggage you're carrying around. The more electronic stuff you have and need to operate, the more of a burden you are to the planet and the rest of your fellow humans. It's time to grab a notebook, take a stroll around your abode, and take stock of what appliances you have and which ones you need.

We've read a lot about eco-remodeling and going "green" over the last few years, and we've been a little dismayed by how much stuff folks want you to *buy* to try and solve the problem. Energy Star appliances, a hybrid car, a geothermal heat pump, double-paned windows—the list goes on and on. We're more inclined to believe that buying a bunch of stuff is a lot of what got us into this mess in the first place. We think you should start by looking at what you've got and seeing what you can get *rid* of (into the recycling bin or reuse center, of course). Then you can take a look at what you have left, how to use it wisely, and, when the time arises, replace it with something better.

One reason we don't advocate an all-at-once switch from old appliances to new is the embedded energy cost of a new appliance. We'll say it again a few more times later, because it bears repeating: the embedded energy cost in the manufacture of most appliances is, on average, about the same as the appliance will use over its median life span. Therefore, in order to justify replacing a working appliance with a new model it needs to be *more than twice* as efficient as the existing model. Otherwise, you should continue to use the current model until it expires. A great example of this rule is if you own a 10-year-old fridge that could be four or five times less energy efficient than a new model (and, of course, you don't just stick the old fridge out in the garage to keep beer cold). One exception is if you are going off-grid and can't have any gluttonous appliances. Beyond this exception, if you stick with this general rule, however, you will save both money and energy, and by the time you do actually buy a replacement appliance, there may very well be an even more efficient model for you to buy.

OUR STORY

Having lived in an off-grid home before our move to the city, we were already quite conscious of our energy use. We're not Luddites, though. We have our power tools and our computer and food processor and stereo and sundry other occasionally used electronics. We rein in our energy use from appliances by studiously avoiding any that turn electricity into heat, such as hair dryers and space heaters. The electronics we do use are on power strips and we turn these off when we're not using the electronics, also making sure to unplug battery chargers when we're finished charging. Of course, all of our lightbulbs are compact fluorescents, and our washing machine is an Energy Star–rated front-loader, but we truly never feel like we're missing anything vital.

ELECTRIC-RESISTANCE HEAT AND LIGHTING

The rule of half of an appliance's energy being embedded in its manufacture has a large group of exceptions. Plug-in items whose main purpose is to generate heat (such as drip coffeepots and hair dryers) consume way more energy in their use than in their manufacture. Burning tons of coal to heat water to turn a turbine to generate electricity just to be transmitted to your outlet and get turned back into heat is *a major waste of energy*! Oftentimes in this scenario your appliance is accessing just 25 percent of the original heat produced by burning the coal.[1] So as you begin your own energy audit, take special note of appliances whose main purpose is to heat things up. We'll come back to some of them later and discuss alternatives, but eliminating their use altogether should be uppermost in your mind.

Incandescent lightbulbs fall into this category of major energy wasters. Between 90 and 95 percent of the energy that makes it to an incandescent bulb (and, as mentioned, most of it doesn't) turns back into heat instead of producing useful light. Therefore, it's better to think of these things as small heaters than as generators of light.

The Energy Diary

Renter friendly.

Project Time: One week.

Cost: Free.

Energy Saved: Very high. Research has shown that increased consciousness about energy use will bring down consumption an average of 15 percent.

Ease of Use: Medium; requires frequent note-taking.

Maintenance Level: N/A.

Skill Levels: None.

Materials: Notebook, pencil.

Getting a grip on how much energy you use in your home can be difficult. As you go about your day, you don't pay much attention to when you flip on switches, pop things in the oven, open the fridge, leave the computer on, and so on. Because these actions are so entrenched in habit, they slip from consciousness. Spending a week keeping an energy diary will go a long way toward informing yourself of where you're currently spending your fossil-fuel budget.

Before you start any serious conservation measures, set aside a week that's not too hectic for your own energy audit. If possible, get the other members of your household to participate. Depending on how much time you have, you may want to include trips in the car and what food you eat (especially its origin and method of farming) for a comprehensive energy analysis. Don't overwhelm yourself, though. These can always be done separately later.

Inventory all appliances. Before you begin, go from room to room and make a list of *all* of your appliances, including power tools and kitchen gadgets, and their energy requirements. Even if it's unlikely that you'll use many of these over the course of the week, remember that this is a consciousness-raising exercise and it'll be good to know how much juice those things suck up when you do use them. This information can be found on a required label that is usually found next to where the plug exits the appliance. The important numbers to look for are the volts and amps. Typically, you'll see something like "120V 10A." This means the appliance draws the U.S. standard 120 volts and operates at 10 amps. Occasionally you'll see watts or volt-amps on the label. Watts can be estimated as volts times amps, and we talk more about this in chapter 2, but in this example, the estimate comes to 1,200 watts, 120V times 10A. Using this appliance for one hour will use about 1,200 watts, which is the same as 1.2 kilowatts. Another way to measure the power draw of a 120V appliance is with a Kill-A-Watt meter (see the resources section); you plug it into an outlet and then plug the device to be measured in the meter's outlet. The meter shows instantaneous watts, amps, and volts, and it can be left to record watt-hour data for an extended period of time, which is useful for appliances like refrigerators.

Everything that plugs into a standard outlet in an American home uses 120 volts. Appliances with larger draws, such as electric dryers or ranges, often use 240 volts and have different plugs. Eventually, you'll need to figure out how to phase 240-volt appliances out of your life altogether or be willing to dedicate a large percentage of your renewable electricity to power them. There may be other numbers on the label, such as Hz (Hertz, a frequency, standardized at 60 in the United States) or RPM (rotations per minute), but these aren't relevant to your energy diary. For now, don't worry about your refrigerator or heating system, although you may want to get the numbers for them.

Start taking notes. At the beginning of your week, say, Sunday at noon, start keeping tabs, writing down every time you turn on a light or use an appliance. You may be thinking, "Wow, that would take too much time!" If that's the case, you're probably using way too many appliances and your need for an energy diary is that much greater! Stick with it.

Write down when you turn on an appliance and then note when you turn it back off. Precision isn't terribly important; you just want to get a rough idea of how much you're using different appliances and how much energy these are taking. If the rest of the members of your household refuse to participate, you can either try to note down their appliance use or restrict the diary to yourself.

Tally the numbers. At the end of the week, make a tally of the numbers, multiplying the amount of time you used appliances in hours times their watts numbers. This will give you the total watt-hours you used that week, and you can divide it by seven to get a daily number.

Make note of the big draws. What were they? Was the use of that light or appliance necessary? If so, was it necessary for that long? Can you think of any obvious ways of reducing your dependence on those appliances with large draws? Look back over your weekly energy use and make a mental note of any egregious waste. Oftentimes trimming this excess fat can be quite simple and very rewarding.

THE BOGEYMAN OF PHANTOM DRAWS

Unfortunately, that's not all the electricity you're likely using in your home. There's the refrigerator and, probably, some kind of heat pump and/or air conditioner, and perhaps a water heater. An HVAC (heating, venting, and air conditioning) unit may run on something other than electricity, like natural gas, but it still takes electricity to run the pumps and fans.

And then there's the most egregious waste of all: These are appliances that are always partly on in a standby function, so that just in case you are about to turn them on they won't need to charge up and will come on in one second instead of five. Saving you from waiting these trivial few seconds can often mean that several thousand additional watts are expended each day in your home and lost to the world forever. This is equivalent to leaving a faucet or a shower running all day just in case you might happen to want to use it at any moment.

If it were that obvious, of course, it wouldn't happen. But the wasted electricity is invisible, slowly dissipating into the room as heat. Televisions, stereos, DVD players, computers, video game consoles, and many other electronics engage in this antisocial behavior. Any device, like a printer or router, with a black box instead of a plug definitely carries a phantom load. The black boxes are small converters changing AC power to DC power and generating waste heat as they

FIG. 3.1. **Full or abandoned battery chargers continue to suck electricity out of the wall.**

do so. The best method for controlling this outrageous waste is by using power strips, outlets that turn off at a wall switch, or motion-activated outlets. By turning on appliances like these only when you need them (which can be done automatically by motion detector outlets), you will save loads of energy.

The other major phantom draw is battery chargers left plugged in for too long or even left plugged in with the battery removed. Cell phone chargers, laptop chargers, power-tool chargers—all these things will just sit there and continue to suck up energy, dissipating it into the room as heat, for as long as you leave them plugged in. Put your hand next to one of these and you can feel the heat! This is just a simple behavioral change that you need to be conscious of. Learn how long it takes for an appliance's battery to become fully

charged—many have gauges or flashing lights—and try not to leave its charger plugged in much longer than that. And of course, always dispose of spent batteries at a recycling center.

ELECTRIC LIGHTING

One of the easiest ways to greatly reduce your energy use is to switch out incandescent lights with compact fluorescent lights, often referred to simply as CFLs. CFLs can even be substituted for floodlights or grow lights. This is without a doubt a case of the replacement being more than twice as efficient as what is being replaced. Compact fluorescents are four to five times better at converting electricity into usable light and last about 10 times as long. It's true they cost more upfront, but because they are so much more efficient, (1 compact flourescent is equivalent to 4 incandescents) and because they last up to ten times as long, they are a much better value. These things just flat-out save you money. Each compact fluorescent you install will save you between $50 and $60 over its lifetime compared with purchasing additional incandescents and paying for the extra electricity. CFLs can now be purchased that work with dimmers and three-way switches, but you will need to check the label to make sure they are compatible. They are also available in many sizes, shapes, and color temperatures.

Compact fluorescents may not be right for every application. They tend to burn out quickly if turned on and off frequently. One of the very few non-CFLs in our house is the refrigerator light, a 7-watt incandescent that stays on for only a few seconds at a time. Some folks find tasks that require close concentration, such as reading or cooking, to be more difficult with CFLs. Most people don't have problems, but even if you do, CFLs can still be used for much of your general lighting needs. We use them nearly everywhere, and after a very short period of adjustment, we didn't even notice the difference.

There's one other drawback, and that is the fact that compact fluorescents contain 4–5 mg of elemental mercury. Handling the bulbs appropriately will eliminate any potential risk, but be cognizant of the fact that their use entails an additional responsibility to dispose of them properly. Store all bulbs, including burned-out ones, away from the reach of children. Burned-out bulbs should be stored separately until they can be taken to a hazardous-waste-collection facility. Some municipalities have certain dates when they collect this type of garbage from homes. Call and check. If not, you'll have to get them to a disposal facility yourself. Since you're making the trip, you may want to check in with the neighbors to see if they have any CFLs that need to be disposed of.

If you break one, here's the procedure:

1. Don't touch any of the glass with your hands or let anyone else touch it.

2. Open all the windows in the room. Elemental mercury evaporates at room temperature, and breathing it can be harmful. The concentration levels will be quite low, but it's still a worthwhile precaution.

3. Sweep up the broken glass with a broom and dustpan. Don't use your hands or a vacuum cleaner (unless some of the shards landed on carpet). Put the shards in a sealable plastic bag. Wipe the area with a wet paper towel. Throw the used paper towel in with the shards of glass and seal the bag, storing and disposing of it as you would a spent CFL bulb.

Beyond incandescents and fluorescents a new wave of lighting appears to dawning. These are home applications of light-emitting diodes, or LEDs. The potential lies in their steady-state nature, meaning they have a very long life if not bumped around, 5 to 10 times as long as that of CFLs (somewhere in the 50,000 to 100,000-hour range). While there is also the potential for energy savings, on a lumen-by-lumen comparison (lumens are one way to measure the intensity of light), LEDs currently use about the same watts per lumen as a CFL. Since their development and commercialization are relatively recent phenomena, it's not inconceivable that they might overtake CFLs in efficiency in the near future. This potential won't have any effect for at least a few years of this writing, but keep your ears pricked in case there's a breakthrough. At the moment, although they are available, LEDs are quite expensive and relatively hard to find. You might want to consider them for lighting specific areas ("spotlighting"), which they do well, or for halls or passageways where only a little light is needed, as very-low-watt versions are sometimes available.

OTHER LIGHTING ALTERNATIVES

Stopping to think about it, it's no wonder that the taming of electricity was inspired by humanity's desire for lighting. Being in the dark on a cold winter night is miserable. In fact, the first oil well, drilled by Colonel Drake in Titusville, Pennsylvania, in 1859, was done in the hopes that the gooey black stuff would replace dwindling supplies of whale oil, used for lighting. It did that and a whole lot more. Just the fact that a major part of the economy in the first half of the nineteenth century revolved around sending young boys out on ships to slaughter whales and boil down their blubber, the resulting oil being used almost exclusively for lighting, shows what a desirable and sought-after amenity home lighting is.

The alternatives to on-demand lighting are slim pickings. Whale hunting is a serious chore, and highly illegal to boot. All of the alternatives to electric lighting, besides increasing natural daylighting, involve burning something, either fossil fuels such as propane or kerosene or natural oils or waxes. The former are dirty and foul whatever room they're burned in; the latter are expensive and difficult to accumulate in quantity. Both are horribly inefficient, converting just a minuscule fraction, much less than 1 percent, into usable light. The only reason to consider using these alternatives as your main source of lighting is if lighting is your only electrical need and you can thereby sever your ties to electrons altogether. If that is the case, we congratulate you. Be sure to make the best use of these inefficient lighting devices by using reflectors. Aluminum foil and/or mirrors work great and can triple the available light by directing it where you need it. Make sure you purchase nonradioactive mantles if you're using a kerosene lantern, and please, be very, very careful around any flame and do not leave it unattended.

Natural Daylighting

Increasing the natural daylight in your home is something to take into consideration if you find from your energy diary that you need to turn lights on during the daytime. We are fortunate that our house, designed in the 1930s, has no issues with dark rooms. Every bathroom has a window and every hall has natural light. But some condominiums, apartments, and split-level or ranch houses we've seen have a serious lack of daylight.

FIG. 3.2. **Solatube Daylighting System.** Courtesy Solatube International, Inc.

Sunlight pipes (also called tubular daylighting devices) are low-tech devices that work wonders in dark hallways or bathrooms that have an accessible roof to penetrate. Be careful: every time you make a hole in the roof there is a chance for water penetration and damage. Solar tubes must be carefully installed and the flashing and caulking checked regularly.

Skylights require a large hole in a roof. Besides the potential for water infiltration (we've seen a majestic Victorian home whose ultimate ruin was an unmaintained skylight), skylights can allow substantial heat loss in winter and oftentimes direct solar gain in summer. Skylighting in new homes is simply bad design. For retrofits, solar tubes are much cheaper and easier to install than skylights (no heading off roof or ceiling joists) and much less of an energy liability.

Turning part of your south wall into passive solar glazing (large south-facing windows that allow in lots of warming sunshine in winter) can do wonders for brightening a dark home. The pros and cons of various solar-heating strategies are discussed in chapter 7.

There are some cool new technologies on the horizon for natural daylighting for areas where a window or solar tube through the roof won't work. Fiber-optic cables with collectors can be snaked through a house from a roof to reach an area that couldn't otherwise be naturally lighted. These are extremely costly, but prices could soon come down. Parans is a Swedish company that is now offering these for sale.

Biogas Lighting

If you live out in the country and have animals, then you have the potential to create large quantities of biogas (this will be discussed in greater detail in chapter 9). In many areas, gas lighting preceded electric lighting, and new and used gas fixtures are still available. They are popular with the Amish, many of whom avoid the use of any utility-tied electricity (although not fossil fuels in general). Many of these lighting fixtures are very Victorian and quite fancy looking, and they would certainly make great conversation pieces for any visitors.

ENERGY-SIPPING APPLIANCES
AND THEIR EFFICIENT USE

The first wave of appliances were created to do jobs that people didn't want to do or didn't have the time to do. These are the laborsaving appliances such as washing machines. We think it's worthwhile to draw a distinction between this set of appliances and the second wave of amusement appliances. Is there ever such a thing as an efficient use of a video game console, or does it always represent a failure of the imagination? But first, let's talk about the laborsavers.

Once you've completed your energy diary, you'll probably be wondering what you can do with your appliances to wring more work from them for less pay, so you can start saving up and get some cool solar electric panels on your roof. We'll cover stoves in chapter 4 and refrigerators in chapter 5. This is a brief discussion of the rest of the household "necessities."

Clothes Washing

The majority of energy used in washing clothes, up to 90 percent, goes to heating the water that is used. Since front-loading machines use much less (about a quarter) hot water than top-loaders use, they save a great deal of energy. But there's more. All washing machines wash by agitation, but not all agitation is the same. Front-loaders can easily produce agitation by spinning the clothes up so that they then fall down again. Top-loaders require a much more complicated system of forward and backward motion that is not only much harder on your clothing but also uses more energy and is more prone to breaking down. Furthermore, top-loaders are incapable of spinning as much water out during the final spin as front-loaders, meaning your clothing requires much longer drying times. If you then stick that wet clothing in an electric-resistance heat-powered dryer, it's all over. You're an energy glutton, no two ways about it.

So, do the deficiencies of the top-loader qualify it for immediate replacement? In some ways, it depends on how often you use it and how you use it. If you're using cold water to wash your clothes, then it's probably not that big of a deal. As high-quality new front-loaders can cost more than $600, you might want to put off purchasing one as long as possible. However, if you find it necessary to use warm or hot water to wash your clothes, and especially if you ever have to use a dryer, then the priority level goes up a few notches. We've found that clothing from our front-loader comes out cleaner than that washed in our old top-loader, without the need for using warm water very often (in the summertime our solar water heater provides a surplus, so we use hot water to wash clothes). Either way, the improvement is quite substantial, and we would put replacement of top-loaders high up on the priority list. Look at the energy labels when you shop for a front-loader to find the most efficient models, check the Energy Star Web site for ratings, and don't forget that washers have different cubic-foot capacities.

Are there options for washing clothes without using electricity at all? Yes, because folks had been looking to take some of the chore out of clothes washing for quite some time before electricity came on the scene. There's the old-fashioned washboard, of course, although its relegation to musical instrument is not without good reason. Scrubbing on one of these things is a serious workout! Using a laundry plunger is a much more effective option for general agitation. This is a great, time-honored method of washing clothes. Presoaking for several hours in warm soapy water in a large (at least 10-gallon) tub is fundamental to this washing method. The clothes are then plunged until clean. A washboard can be used for especially dirty clothing, and a wringer can be used to squeeze out most of the water. Generally, this is an inefficient method for washing clothes because it can require lots of hot water. If the hot water is solar heated (in a black basin in the sun, for instance), then this is not an issue.

For those looking for an easier, albeit more expensive (around $600 with wringer), nonelectric option, the James Washer has been around for a century and works well. It's basically a tub with a built-in agitator

FIG. 3.3. **Together with a washboard, the laundry plunger is an effective way to get some exercise. And clean your clothes, too, of course.** Courtesy Wise Men Trading & Supply

that is cranked back and forth by means of a handle that sticks out from it. We've never had a chance to use one, but they look like fun. Most come with a clothes wringer for faster drying.

Clothes Dryers

Electric clothes dryers are a colossal waste of energy. They often draw around 6,000 watts. Six thousand! This is more than a typical heat pump or electric water heater, usually thought of as the hogs of the household. Simply put, you should not use this appliance. Gas dryers are more efficient because they use no electric-resistance heat, but they still can draw around 720 watts. That's a lot, equivalent to about 60 compact fluorescents (not to mention the energy of the gas). You should plan on getting rid of electric heat dryers and hopefully gas-fired dryers as well if your climate allows.

Solar clothes drying shows this energy source at its finest. It's a great example of simplicity combined with effectiveness. Hang up something wet in the sun, come back in a few hours, and, voilà, it's dry, clean, and fresh-smelling. Like everything, having the proper tools to access this resource goes a very long way in making sure it's effective and easy to do. Some of this depends on your climate and your own personal habits. We realize some parts of the country have very little sun in the winter, but if you set aside a bit of room, even in a closet or spare bedroom, clothes hung on racks inside will dry fairly quickly in a heated house.

Some or all of the following will make air-drying clothes much more effective and much less of a chore.

Retractable clothesline. An excellent tool for the space-constrained. These come in a variety of lengths and are very simple to install indoors or out. Consider putting these inside near a passive solar wall. The sun will dry the clothes and raise the humidity of the room in wintertime, making it more comfortable inside.

Indoor drying rack. Avoid the cheaper models, as they can fall apart rather quickly. These are generally collapsible and can stand alone or be wall-mounted. We recommend having at least two. Being able to

FIG. 3.4. **Our solar-powered clothes dryer in action, keeping our flowers and herbs company up on our green roof.**

place these in the sun or near a woodstove will greatly speed up drying time in the winter.

Outdoor drying rack. If you've got the room outdoors, a permanent outdoor rack is a very effective method for drying clothes, even when the temperatures barely get above freezing. It requires some time to mount properly, but it should function well for decades.

Clothespins. These are a necessity and come in two varieties: split or spring. Determine your preference and make sure you have plenty. Hanging clothes from pins rather than folding them over the line greatly speeds drying time and greatly reduces the odds that any clothing will fall off and get dirty. Folding clothes generally means two sides of the clothing are not exposed to the air at all. This more than doubles drying times.

Clothespin apron. Using an apron will greatly facilitate hanging up your clothes and make it much less likely you leave the pins on the line to suffer in the elements, thereby greatly decreasing their life span.

Laundry baskets. You need at least two heavy-duty laundry baskets, if you don't already have them. This makes taking clothing to the drying line or rack much easier.

Please, do not skimp on these items. Doing so will only discourage you and before you know it you'll be pining for a fossil-fuel dryer, rather than enjoying your fresh-smelling solar-dried clothes. A complete drying system, including retractable clotheslines, pins, baskets, and indoor racks, should set you back only about a hundred dollars or so. After that, the solar energy is there for the taking!

Computers

Computers have made great strides in efficiency over the past decade. Not surprisingly, smaller computers draw less juice than larger ones (down to 60W for the smallest desktops, and 250W or more for the larger ones). Laptops are sippers in this regard, drawing around 30W of power on average, whereas desktops require additional power for the monitor: 70W or so for the boxy CRT monitors, around 30W for the flatter LCD screens.

We've been dismayed by the exceptionally high turnover rate of computers. Lots of folks seem to keep new ones for only two or three years, and this has resulted in most of the lifetime energy use of a computer going into its manufacture, far more than the typical appliance ratio of 50-50. While laptops are indeed more energy efficient, the fact that they are carried around all over the place (and frequently banged around) greatly reduces their life span. The best-case scenario for lowered lifetime energy inputs would be a laptop (or small desktop with LCD screen) that stayed put in a relatively permanent location.

Perhaps the most important point with computers is to put them to sleep (hibernation mode is closer to a full shutdown) when they are temporarily not in use (half hour or less), or shut them down altogether for longer periods. Most or all computers have "energy" settings that you can change. For example, Microsoft operating systems can be set to hibernate the computer after any length of time unattended. Don't forget that the screensaver function is absolutely not an energy saver and that is not its intended purpose. Set your computer to go to sleep when it is not in use rather than have it waste energy making pictures no one will see.

Dishwashers

Dishwashers can be part of an energy-efficient household. If you're in the market for one, look for the most efficient one, most likely one with the Energy Star label. We've become used to washing our dishes by hand, but we've read recent reports that *if the dishwasher is used properly*, washing dishes in a dishwasher can be significantly more efficient (but none of these studies takes into account the energy in the manufacture of the dishwashers, which on average last about a decade, so we think the jury is still out).

If you are using a dishwasher, follow these standard commonsense directions for efficient use:

1. Make sure the washer is full, but not overloaded, before you run it.

2. Scrape, don't rinse, all food off your dishes. Presoak only if food is burned on.

3. Make sure your water heater is set at 120 degrees F or below (see chapter 6).

4. Avoid using the RINSE HOLD function unless dishes are very dirty; this function uses 3 to 7 additional gallons of hot water.

5. Air-dry dishes. If your washer doesn't have this function, turn it off after the last rinse and prop open the door to avoid electrically heated drying.

Electric-Resistance Appliances

This won't be the last time we'll say it: *Appliances that use electric-resistance heat must go!* Those scheming technophiles are constantly coming up with more all the time, but table 3.1 offers a basic list and some alternatives.

Kitchen Tools

There are more electric kitchen tools than we can name (or that we're aware of). Although many of these have high draws, they are usually used only for a fraction of an hour and therefore do not ultimately use a lot of electricity. We love our food processor for making things like hummus and pesto, and we would be insincere if we expected you not to enjoy your laborsaving kitchen gadgets. Keep in mind that many of these appliances are derived from hand-operated predeces-

TABLE 3.1 Common Appliances That Use Electric-Resistance Heat and Some Alternatives	
Appliance	Alternative
Hair Dryer	Get a less maintenance-intensive haircut, shower in the evening, or dry hair with a towel or in sunshine
Electric Heater, Electric Baseboard Radiator	Passive solar retrofit (see chapter 7)
Electric Coffeemaker	French press and thermos, or cold-drip coffee and heat
Electric Stove	Solar oven, etc. (see chapter 4)
Heating Pad	Warm water bottle
Electric Towel Rack	Sunshine

The Great Pacific Trash Vortex

Fossil fuels aren't just burned for their energy. Broken down into basic polymers and then reformed in myriad different ways, natural gas and oil can be reconstituted into an astounding array of products from plastic bags to medicines to thousands of chemicals of known and unknown toxicity. Having been around for tens of millions of years in many cases, hydrocarbons are obviously very stable materials that are impervious to biodegrading. Instead, most plastics only photodegrade, or break down into ever smaller particles from exposure to sunlight. Many of these tiny pieces then mix with plankton floating in the water and are scooped up by fish unawares. Once they've accumulated inside the fishes' bodies, the plastic particles' similarities to compounds like estrogen make them a potent hormone disruptor, causing sterility, hermaphrodism, and even death.[2]

Perhaps the most alarming example of plastic's longevity is the Great Pacific Trash Vortex. Swirling around in the ocean north of Hawaii where prevailing currents converge is a Texas-sized mass of discarded old toothbrushes, Happy Meal toys, Styrofoam containers, broken pieces of electronics, and, of course, *trillions* of plastic bags. If it didn't make it to the dump (or blew out of the truck on the way there), it'll probably end up here. Unless, of course, it ends up in one of the other seven trash vortices in other parts of the world's oceans. The best thing you can do to stop the growth of these monsters is use cloth bags, reuse and recycle plastic bags when you do end up with them, limit your purchase of new plastic products and use alternatives where available, and of course recycle any other plastic that ends up in your possession.

FIG. 3.5. **All that stuff you buy eventually has to go somewhere. If some part of it is made of fossil fuel–based plastic and it's improperly disposed of, there's a good chance it will eventually make its way to the Pacific Trash Vortex, a swirling pile of half-submerged garbage in the Pacific Ocean that's the size of Texas. This confused albatross probably had a fatal dose of this refuse.** Photo by Cynthia Vanderlip for Algalita Marine Research Foundation.

sors, many of which are still available. There are lots of hand-cranked mills, grinders (including for coffee), and shredders if you want them. Generally, these seem less susceptible to breaking down (and are easier to fix), and, of course, you can still use them even when the power goes out.

Power Tools

Being tradespeople, we understand the need for power tools. Again, many of these are used intermittently and therefore do not use large quantities of power, even though the instantaneous draws are high. Like kitchen tools, many are derived from nonelectric predecessors that are simpler to use and maintain, as well as safer. We've never seen anyone hospitalized from operating a handsaw, but we can't say the same for an electric circular saw. But if you need 'em, use 'em, just be safe.

Entertainment Appliances

Yeah, being entertained is great, even necessary. While trying not to be too preachy, we do want to take a moment to point out the unintended consequences of these appliances. Time being finite, when it's spent watching television or playing video games you are not spending it doing any of the following: gardening, hiking, walking the dog, biking, talking to friends and family, building a solar oven, eating good food, sitting in the sunshine, picking flowers for your honey, or playing ball with your kid. If you're watching TV, then you are being subtlety cajoled into buying things you don't really need while your body slowly deteriorates.

So what is energy-efficient entertainment? How about exploring the infinitely complex and fascinating intricacies of nature? Or the wonders of human architecture and ingenuity just outside your door? Or the marvelous depths of the human soul revealed only by long talks with neighbors, friends, and family or in the ever-expanding wealth of world literature?

So far as the television, we admit that it's not all bad. We watch our fair share of movies and documentaries, many of which are great. Generally, televisions do not have big electric draws, the exception being the new wave of high-definition televisions (HDTVs) that come with plasma displays. These use 5 to 10 times as much as an LCD television of similar size. That's a huge expenditure of energy just to see the pimples on your favorite star's pretty mug! These things are the SUVs of the television world. Forget about 'em, and if one of your friends buys one, make fun of it relentlessly.

CONCLUSION

If it's not using electric-resistance heat, chances are that a particular appliance is not using a whole lot of electricity. Of course, it's always good to check the label and be conscious of the energy requirements of any new appliance you're considering inviting into your home. Electricity is extremely intelligent: you can't run your computer by burning a lump of coal under it, or your coffee grinder or stereo for that matter. Use electricity where it works best, and use other energy sources (preferably solar, biomass, or biogas, in that order, but even natural gas or oil if necessary in the interim) for applications that require heating things up. Radios, stereos, and most other entertainment appliances don't use very much electricity. Don't leave them on when you're not using them, keep them plugged into a power strip if they have a standby function (turn off the powerstrip when the electronics are not in use), and make sure you have a range of hobbies and get outdoors in the garden or woods every now and then.

If you systematically eliminate all the electric-resistance heat from your house (including most incandescent lightbulbs), then you will be well on your way toward powering down to a level of electricity use that can be affordably powered with renewables. The difference between most appliances and electric-resistance heat is one or more orders of magnitude. For example, one hour of drying clothes in an electric dryer is equivalent to about 1,000 hours of listening to a handheld radio, 100 hours of watching television, or 10 hours of running a microwave oven. Be a part of the renewable energy revolution: Hang up your clothes to dry in the sun!

Don't forget that we humans are amazingly adaptable. Once we go a week or two without some item that seemed utterly necessary, a hair dryer, say, we tend to just forget about it and get along without it. It may seem like a hardship at first, but once the new routine is established we just go through our day taking care of business. Despite being generally optimists as a species, we constantly underestimate our ability to adapt to new circumstances or do without what is not vital. There's only one way to see if life will actually be "awful" or "terrible" after forgoing some "necessary" appliance. Give it up for a spell and see how it goes!

RESOURCES

Books

Dean, Tamara. 2008. *The Human-Powered Home: Choosing Muscles Over Motors*. Gabriola, BC: New Society Press. How to run your appliances free of electricity and capitalism's planned obsolescence.

Internet

Ask Mr. Electricity. Michael does a great job of getting down to the nitty-gritty of miserly household energy use. http://michaelbluejay.com/electricity/general.html#phantom

Energy Hog. Great facts and resources for learning about home energy use from the Alliance to Save Energy. www.energyhog.org

How Can I Save Money On My Electric Bill? Watt usage breakdown for typical appliances. http://members.tripod.com/~masterslic/FAQ-2/14.html

Wise Men Trading and Supply. Purveyor of low-tech and appropriate-tech household necessities. www.wisementrading.com

Products

Kill-A-Watt. Tells you how much energy an individual appliance uses while you have it plugged in.

Lehman's Non-Electric Catalog. Started in 1955 to serve the Amish community in Ohio, and still going strong. www.lehmans.com

Power Cost Monitor and *The Energy Detective*. Both give an aggregate amount for how much energy your house is consuming at that moment.

Watt Stopper and *Sensor Plug*. Outlets turn on when someone enters the room and stays on for a set amount of time.

Endnotes

1. U.S. Department of Energy—Energy Efficiency and Renewable Energy: "A Consumer's Guide to Energy Efficiency and Renewable Energy," and the Office of Electricity Delivery and Energy Reliability "Overview of the Electric Grid."

2. Trankina, Michele. "The Hazards of Environmental Estrogen." *World and I* magazine, October, 2001.

CHAPTER 4

Cooking

Introduction • Our Story • Solar Cooking • Our Solar Oven • Premanufactured Solar Ovens • Cooking with Biomass • Cooking with Biomass-Derived Liquid Fuels • Cooking with Biogas • Resources

INTRODUCTION

Because of the high temperatures required, cooking food without burning fossil fuels is one of the more challenging conversions to make. And as it is an activity that generally uses a smaller percentage of a home's energy (4 percent on average) than, say, lighting (12 percent) or refrigeration (8 percent), it may be one you want to tackle after working on larger-gain projects.

That said, cooking food using renewable energy, whether it's from the sun, biogas, wood heat, or plant oil, is highly rewarding and gives a great sense of independence for this most vital of activities. For many folks, one of the greatest fears related to failure of the energy grid or depletion of fossil energy is that they won't be able to cook food. A house without a means of cooking isn't habitable for long.

In pioneer times, wood was plentiful and was the sole heat source for cooking food. This worked fine indoors during the winter and outside in a detached kitchen the rest of the year. But many cooks had to work outside even in bad weather or inside in fireplaces or on cookstoves during hot weather, making the house uninhabitable for most of the evening. Only the wealthy had access to detached kitchens. Fortunately, today a great deal has been learned about capturing solar energy for cooking, using wood heat efficiently, converting biomass to liquid fuels, and small-scale methane production (referred to as *biogas* to distinguish it from fossil accumulations of natural gas, both of which are predominantly methane). By using a variety of methods for cooking when conditions are most suitable, it is quite possible with little hardship to cook all of one's food using renewable energy in a sustainable way.

Familiarizing yourself with the pros and cons of different methods may help show the way toward what configuration you want in your home. If you're lucky enough to have livestock nearby, you may be able to produce enough biogas for all your cooking needs. If you live in the sunny West, you may be able to do most of your cooking with a solar cooker. And if you live in the frozen North, it may be reasonable to do the majority of your cooking with wood, heating your home (and potentially your water) at the same time. Because different methods are appropriate for different seasons and weather conditions, weaning your cooking from fossil energy will take time. Whatever methods you choose, once you're no longer dependent on lengthy connections to pipelines filled with polluting fossil fuels, we guarantee you'll find your food more delicious and satisfying.

OUR STORY

At first, we were quite dismayed by our prospects of being able to achieve our cooking needs without any fossil fuels. We planned on putting in a woodstove, and knew we could do some of our winter cooking there, and we had been working on improving our solar oven for a while, but both of these technologies had their limitations. One by one, as we knocked out the other fossilized aspects of our lives—electricity, hot water, transportation, and so on—our propane camping stove that accomplished the bulk of our on-demand cooking needs seemed like it had started to sprout roots and dig into the countertop. Stephen had read about biogas production for some time and felt this was the missing link. But the information available was limited and lacked detail. We might have been able to rig something together based on what he had learned, but it wasn't necessarily clear that it would work or produce enough gas, or that it was something we could write about and recommend that others try. From the available information, much of it from India, it seemed like we needed to build a concrete tank in the basement. We had been planning on building a ferrocement tank (a built-in-place concrete tank reinforced with metal) in the basement for rainwater catchment. Before this, however, we were going to build one to catch rainwater off a detached garage in the backyard as a practice run, the water to be used for the exterior landscaping. That way, if it leaked a bit, it wouldn't matter much and we would learn from the process.

Building a tank in the basement to catch our humanure as our first try that might potentially leak was not something we were eager to tackle. Ironically, after we purchased the house we realized that an old bathroom setup in the basement had been funneling much of the previous residents' waste onto the basement floor rather than out to the sewage line that ran under the street. Cleaning this inch-thick layer of stinky goo off the basement floor slab had not been pleasant, and we certainly weren't eager to repeat the process anytime in the future, even if this time it would be our own stinky goo!

In the interim, we had a few setbacks. We purchased a beautiful old cast-iron cookstove for $250 from an antiques store. It had a few chips and cracks, but we figured our welder friend Jeremy would be able to fix them right up. Little did we know at the time (although we do now!) that you cannot weld cast iron. This beauty sits in our front room as we write, making a tolerable plant stand. On another tangent, in search

of an oven for use when the sun wasn't shining, we purchased a stovetop baking oven from Lehman's, to sit on top of our conventional woodstove. The folks at Lehman's are great, but they missed the boat with this one. The oven was designed to sit atop a gas stovetop. Glossy black, with stainless-steel hardware, it was pretty to look at. Unfortunately, when we put it on top of our woodstove (an activity that Lehman's had condoned) with the thought of baking dinner, the black paint began to smoke and catch fire, releasing waves of toxic gases into our house and sending us scuttling outdoors into the cold with all the windows open. Lehman's gave us a refund, but we were still without an indoor oven, and remain so, as of this writing, although we have plans to build one before winter out of scrap metal, based on some of the many designs from Aprovecho's publications (see the resources).

After the oven-fire fiasco, we turned our attention to other things: solar hot water, photovoltaics, the green roof, writing the book in earnest, and those pesky day jobs. Our year for wrapping up our house project was drawing to a close. The manuscript for this book was due in just a few months, yet the propane stove sat there, still seeing regular use. Were we wrong? Was it not possible to quite cut all ties to fossil fuels in our daily lives? Although the amount we were using compared to the average American household was very small, less than 1 percent, still, we weren't carbon free! Salvation came from the Internet, that vast cornucopia of ideas (and trifles and vanities, too, of course). We read about the exciting development of the Protos Plant Cooker, which uses a variety of vegetable oils as an energy source. A renewable stovetop fuel! This was very exciting, even if it meant we would not be producing the fuel ourselves. We had long ago dropped our lone-wolf, produce-everything-ourselves mentality. We already had a used-veggie-oil setup for our Mercedes 300D. And since this would be just one of several cooking options, our dependence on an outside source for our cooking fuel did not bother us terribly, although the biogas dream is still there, waiting for a free weekend or two or three.

Alas, the Protos was unavailable to us. The ethic was to get this stove, devloped by Bosch and Siemens, where it was needed most, in developing countries like the Philippines, and produce it there as well to support the local economy. We couldn't find fault with these fine intentions, of course, but still, *we wanted one*!

After a lovely chat with the project manager, Mr. Schiroff, he explained that, as a cooking device, the Protos needed to be tested for such things as safety, emissions, and so on, for each country where it was sold. Since the demand in the United States had not yet manifested itself, the company had not pursued this yet. Our renewable stovetop cooker was not yet legal.

This created some despair, but we turned our minds to other things. Time was running short. As if to prompt us, the propane stove gave out when some part of the regulator clogged. Coleman makes some dozen or so versions of the two-burner propane cooker but neglects to put any model numbers on the actual stove itself. We literally couldn't figure out which was the correct replacement part among the multitude of models.

Sometime during that frustrating time spent simultaneously on hold with Coleman and on the Internet searching for parts, the words *camping* and *stove* yielded something about a homemade alcohol camping stove. Well, of course! Alcohol burns and it's made out of plants! Therein lay our salvation. There are dozens of designs for homemade alcohol stoves. We were looking for something a little more permanent, and that's when we found Origo, which has been making alcohol stoves for boats for 50 years. It even makes one with an oven, although at over $1,000 this was out of our price range, not to mention we didn't want to neglect our solar oven and future woodstove oven, so we stuck with the Origo 3000, a two-burner model at around $350. It burns denatured alcohol, which is 90 percent plant-based ethanol mixed with 10 percent wood-based methanol (the methanol will make you go blind if you consume it, and it thereby avoids drinking-alcohol taxes). This is a clean-burning unpressurized fuel, making it extremely safe (no pressurized propane fireball worries). The denatured alcohol costs between $13 and $15/gallon, which is a little steep. Generally, a gallon lasts us a month or two, and longer in the winter when we mostly use the woodstove. We suspect that this price is what E85 (the ethanol-gasoline mix touted as a replacement for straight gasoline) would be if that product were wholly unsubsidized, which is about five times its current selling price. If we can find a source for 100 percent ethanol (rather than E85), we will switch to using that with the Origo. The 15 percent gasoline in E85 makes for hazardous indoor air quality and creosote buildup if it is burned in the stove.

We've saved fuel on our alcohol stove by using a pressure cooker we received from Stephen's mother. It's one of the new generation of pressure cookers and has three distinct safety measures to ensure that it will not explode. By raising the cooking temperature to 250 degrees F from 212 degrees F, pressure cookers are able to cook many foods in a fraction of the usual time. Beans especially benefit from this, as most can be completely cooked in less than 30 minutes, even without presoaking (although they'll cook faster and use less energy if you presoak them). This means we can use dried beans whenever we need them, even if we didn't plan in advance. Once we discovered how well it makes a risotto with no stirring (and in just 8 minutes), our pressure cooker became worth its weight in gold!

Our variety of cooking options serve us well. Since we're already keenly aware of the weather (a result of obtaining most of our energy from the daily available sunshine and being solar nerds generally), taking advantage of the solar cooker has not been a problem. The top of the conventional woodstove gets used for cooking many winter nights, and the alcohol stove is available when the first two options aren't, mainly for on-demand needs like pan-frying and making coffee in the morning. And, of course, our nonfossilized locally grown food tastes great!

Another thought we've had that we're still ambivalent about but feel is worth mentioning is using a microwave. Now, we know microwaves have been castigated for irradiating food and making it tasteless. Nevertheless, they do an excellent job of heating up food in a hurry and doing it with much less energy than a traditional electric range. Especially for off-grid

FIG. 4.1. **Origo ethanol stove. First made for boats, ethanol (or denatured alcohol) stoves are clean burning and easily adapt to use in the home. Larger models with an oven are available.**

folks, using some of the surplus of solar electricity on sunny days to reheat leftovers for lunch can basically mean tapping into some free energy.

SOLAR COOKING

Perhaps nothing is better capable of demonstrating the power of solar energy than a well-built solar cooker. Even simple inexpensive designs are capable of temperatures approaching or exceeding 300 degrees F in full sun, hot enough to cook stews, roasts, and even breads and cookies. Many cost little to construct and are small and light enough to be easily portable. They do what solar energy does best: turn the sun's rays directly into heat for our benefit. And they are an almost universally applicable technology, working well from the tundra to the tropics.

Cooking with the sun is exceptionally rewarding. Although its utility varies depending on location, even in the rainier parts of our country solar cookers can still be used several times a week on average. On the downside, relative to a stovetop range and oven setup inside the home, solar cooking can seem burdensome and overly limiting. Primarily, things are baked or slow-cooked, meaning well-planned meals and a somewhat limited menu. Solar cookers will not meet your on-demand cooking needs.

Don't let solar cooking's limitations lead you to neglect this most rewarding of cooking methods, however. Using a solar cooker for what it does best will ensure a satisfying experience. For those readers who would like to learn more about renewable energy but are often intimidated by the costs and complexities of such things as photovoltaics or solar hot water, solar cooking provides an excellent, inexpensive, and empowering introduction. The wonder and possibility of living a life powered by the sun is revealed by constructing and using any of the designs listed below.

Solar ovens and cookers invite tinkering and creative design. There are almost as many solar-cooker designs are there are folks who have built one. For the three we've detailed here, we've stuck with tested models that have been refined and perfected over time.

The first two designs detailed here are courtesy of Solar Cookers International. The third solar oven detailed is the Barbara Kerr Solar Wall Oven. The wall-oven model incorporates a solar oven into the structure of the house and makes it accessible from the inside, possibly even the kitchen if yours has a south-facing wall. Eventually, we all need to figure out how to incorporate solar cooking into our lives and make it as easy as possible. Barbara Kerr has gone a long way toward realizing this achievement with her oven. Presented here is a thorough summary that we hope will be sufficient for most handy folks to build and install one of her models. Readers are encouraged to peruse a more thorough presentation, which can be found at the Web site www.solarcooking.org/bkerr/DoItYouself.htm.

Finally, we'll show you what we built. We pieced together leftover construction materials from various other projects we were working on to build a solid outdoor solar oven that we have found to be easy to use, effective, and weatherproof.

The first solar cooker below is a simple box cooker that can be made primarily from cardboard boxes, aluminum foil, and Plexiglas.

Simple Box Cooker

Renter friendly.

Project Time: Afternoon.

Cost: Inexpensive ($5–20).

Energy Saved: Low. Cooking's relatively low energy requirements (4 percent of average energy budget) and solar cooking's intermittent availability make dependence on at least one other cooking system all but certain.

Ease of Use: Moderate. Cooking can be done only on relatively sunny days and works better in summer than in winter.

Maintenance Level: Medium. How long this solar oven lasts depends on how well you take care of it. If it gets wet repeatedly, it will eventually turn to mush, so bring it inside when it's not in use.

Skill Levels: Carpentry: Basic.

Materials: Two large, shallow cardboard boxes—the inner box should be at least 18 × 22 inches, preferably just a little bit taller than your pots; the outer box should be a little larger in all dimensions so there is at least 1–2 inches of space between the two boxes when they are nested. You'll also need corrugated cardboard at least 6 inches longer and wider than the outer box to make the lid; window glass (or Plexiglas) at least 20 × 24 inches and longer and wider than the inner box by 2 to 3 inches; a thin, black metal sheet, sized equal to or slightly smaller than the inner box; 50 feet of aluminum foil; dry plant fibers such as leaves or straw or at least 50 sheets of newspaper, quartered and crumbled; glue silicone caulk; and rigid wire (hanger wire, for instance).

FIG. 4.2. **The completed solar box cooker.** Courtesy Solar Cookers International

Tools: Paintbrush, utility or other knife, pencil, straightedge.

Caution: Solar cookers, especially parabolic varieties like the CooKit (described next), have the potential to cause retinal damage from the concentrated solar rays. Be careful to avoid looking at the bright reflections from any of these solar cookers.

Construction Steps

Cut the window opening in the outer box. See figure 4.3. Turn the outer box upside down. On its bottom, center the inner box and draw a line around it. Cut out this piece to make a window opening the same size as the inner box. There should be a small rim on all four sides, 2–3 inches wide. On the lid piece—the extra piece of cardboard—center the outer box and trace around it (these are the fold lines). Extend these lines out to the edges of the lid piece. Center the inner box between the fold lines on the lid (that you just drew) and trace around this box as well. Cut only three sides of the inner line, two short sides and one long one. Fold up the resulting flap for the reflector, creating a window frame opening the same size as the inner box.

Adjust the height of boxes, if needed. See figure 4.4 Set a cooking pot next to both boxes. The inner box needs to be just a little taller than your pot. The outer box needs to be just a little taller than the inner box.

If the boxes are too tall:

On the inner box make a mark about 1 inch above the top of the pot and draw a fold line at this height straight around the four box walls. Score the fold lines with a blunt edge such as a spoon handle.

On the outer box make a mark about 2 inches above the top of the pot and draw a fold line at this height straight around the four box walls. Score the fold lines with a blunt edge such as a spoon handle.

Cut the corners of both boxes down to the fold lines. Fold the sides outward along the creases.

Trim the inner box flaps. When the walls of the inner box are folded down to the right height (or if you didn't need any adjustments), trim the flaps to make them as narrow as the small rim around the window opening on the outer box (refer to the first step if necessary).

Join the boxes. See figure 4.5. Turn the outer box right side up, so the window opening and rim are down. Spread glue on the inside of the rim. Turn the inner box upside down and lower it into the outer box, onto the glue. Press the small flaps against the inside of the rim around the window opening to join the two boxes into one double-walled box, now open at the bottom (which should be facing up at this point).

Insulate and seal. Without disturbing the drying glue, carefully spot-glue aluminum foil on all four walls and the underside of the inner box, covering all surfaces between the two boxes. This layer of foil helps insulate the cooker. Lightly fill the gaps between the two boxes with crumpled newspaper, plant fiber, or other insulation. Add a few strips of cardboard and more crumpled newspaper or other insulation on the underside of the inner box (which should be facing up at this point). Close and glue the flaps of the outer box to seal the bottom of the cooker.

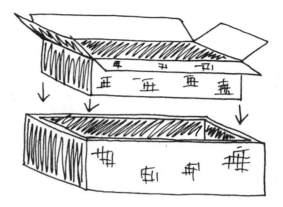

FIG. 4.3. Adapted with permission from Solar Cookers International

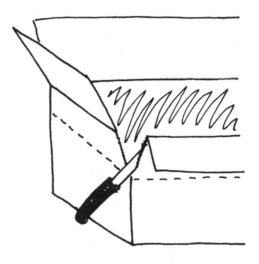

FIG. 4.4. Adapted with permission from Solar Cookers International

FIG. 4.5. Adapted with permission from Solar Cookers International

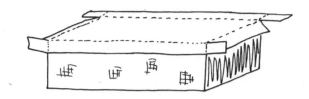

FIG. 4.6. Adapted with permission from Solar Cookers International

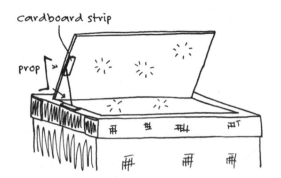

FIG. 4.7. Adapted with permission from Solar Cookers International

Glue foil inside the box and lid. Turn the box right side up. Dilute glue 1:1 with water and, using a paintbrush, spread it thinly on the dull side of sheets of aluminum foil. Press the glued sheets of aluminum foil tightly and smoothly like wallpaper to the inside and rim of the box. A few wrinkles won't hurt. Set the box aside to dry. Repeating the procedure, glue foil to the underside of the lid flap (the folded-up center part only).

Cut, fold, and glue the corners of the new lid. See figure 4.6. With the lid upside down (foil facing up), make one cut at each of the four lid corners, just to the first fold lines. (The cuts should be parallel to the long side of the lid.) Score all fold lines with a blunt edge and fold along the creases with a straightedge such as a board. Overlap and glue the corners, and secure them with clothespins or clamps until the glue is dry. To make quick clamps, cut cardboard-width slits in a small stack of cardboard pieces.

Insert the window. Spread silicone caulk along the underside edge of the window opening rim (outside the cut edge of the foiled reflector piece), then press

the glass in firmly but carefully to make a good seal with the caulk. Let the box and lid dry overnight.

Make an adjustable prop. See figure 4.7. Make small holes in a corner of the lid reflector and the side of lid. Loop string through the holes. Make several notches in a stick and tie the stick at both ends to hold up the reflector and allow angle adjustments.

OR

Bend a sturdy wire at both ends and glue corrugated cardboard strips to the lid and reflector as shown. The wire can be inserted into any of the corrugations for angle adjustment.

Add the black tray and "cook" the cooker. Put the black metal sheet inside the box. (The pots will sit on this light-absorbing sheet.) Put on the lid, with the lid reflector propped open, and aim the cooker toward the sun for several hours to drive out the last bit of moisture and any paint or glue fumes.

Cooking Directions

Put food in dark pots. Use with dark, tight-fitting lids.

Choose a cooking location. Set the cooker on a dry, level surface in direct sunshine away from potential shadows. For best results, solar cooking requires continuous, direct sunshine throughout the cooking period.

Put the pots in the cooker and replace the lid. Put the pots in cooker. If you're cooking multiple dishes, quicker-cooking items should be placed toward the front of the cooker (opposite the reflector) and slower-cooking items toward the back, where access to sunlight is best. Place the lid on cooker.

Orient the cooker. Orient the cooker according to the details below. Once oriented, the cooker doesn't need to be moved again during three to four hours of cooking. For longer cooking, or for large quantities of food, reorienting the cooker every couple of hours speeds cooking a little. Food cooks fastest when the shadow created by the cooker is directly behind it.

To cook a noontime meal orient the cooker so that the front side (opposite the reflector) faces easterly, or approximately where the sun will be midmorning. In general, it is good to get the food in early and not worry about it until mealtime. For most dishes you should start cooking by 9 or 10 AM.

To cook an evening meal orient the cooker so that the front side faces westerly, or approximately where the sun will be midafternoon. For most dishes, it's best to start cooking by 1 or 2 PM.

For all-day cooking orient the cooker toward where sun will be at noon or early afternoon. The food will be ready and waiting for the evening meal.

Adjust the reflector. With the adjustable prop, angle the reflector so that maximum sunlight shines on the pots.

Leave the food to cook for several hours or until done. There is no need to stir the food while it is cooking.

Remove the pots. Using pot holders, remove the pots from the cooker. (CAUTION: Pots get very hot.) If you won't be eating for a couple of hours, you may want to leave the pots in the cooker and close the lid. The insulative properties of the cooker will keep the food warm for a while.

Enjoy!

Care and Storage

Store your cooker away from rain and animals, preferably indoors. Keep the glass clean.

Panel Cooker

Renter friendly.
Project Time: Afternoon.
Cost: Inexpensive ($5–20).
Energy Saved: Low. Cooking's relatively low energy requirements (4 percent of average energy budget) and solar cooking's intermittent availability make dependence on at least one other cooking system all but certain.
Ease of Use: Moderate. Typically, solar cookers get used outside. Cooking is often an all-day affair, and the range of items that can be cooked is limited.
Maintenance Level: Medium. How long this solar oven lasts depends on how well you take care of it.

If it gets wet repeatedly, it will eventually turn to mush, so caution must be taken when leaving it for long periods outside when there might be rain.
Skill Levels: Carpentry: Basic.
Materials: 3 × 4-foot section of cardboard, 10 feet of aluminum foil, glue (nontoxic).
Tools: Cheap paintbrush, utility knife.

This panel cooker, known as the CooKit, is a simple, portable solar cooker. It can be made in one to two hours and can cook one large pot of food for about six people. For larger families, make a larger CooKit or several this size.

Construction Steps

Draw "cut" and "fold" lines on cardboard. See figure 4.9. Freehand drawing should suffice.

Cut out the CooKit shape and slots. Cut out the CooKit shape and the two 61-degree angled slots in the front panel. Be sure to make the slots narrow so the 73-degree angled corners from the back panel fit snugly to hold up the front panel. (Refer to the third-step in the cooking directions below.)

Score the fold lines. With a blunt edge such as a spoon handle, score the fold lines. Make straight folds by folding against a firm straightedge such as a board. Sscore the optional fold lines only if you intend to fold the CooKit for compact storage (see "Care and Storage" below).

Glue foil on the CooKit. Dilute the glue 1:1 with water. Using a paintbrush, spread the diluted glue on the dull side of the aluminum foil and press the glued sheets of aluminum foil tightly and smoothly like wallpaper onto one entire side of the CooKit. A few wrinkles won't hurt.

Leave flat until dry. Trim any excess foil.

Cooking Directions

Put food in a dark pot with a dark, tight-fitting lid.

Enclose pot in a transparent heat trap. Put the pot in a clear, heat-resistant plastic bag (a specialty product usually found in larger groceries) and bind the open end of the bag or simply fold it under the pot in such a

FIG. 4.8. **A panel cooker in action.** Courtesy Solar Cookers International

way as to prevent air from escaping. The bag should be loose enough that a small, insulating layer of air exists around the pot. Alternatively, clear salad bowls, plastic or glass, can be turned upside down over the pot.

Optional: Cooking efficiency may be marginally improved by placing the pot on a pot "stand," e.g., three or four stones, a couple of twigs, or a small wire rack, located inside the bag. This helps create a thin layer of air under the pot, reducing heat loss to the cooker itself. For optimal performance, Dr. Steven Jones of Brigham Young University recommends raising the pot just over 2 inches with a homemade open-mesh wire stand located inside the bag. This allows sunlight to be reflected underneath the pot as well as on the sides and top. For best pot stability, make the wire stand slightly wider than the pot and a little taller, resting the pot on two crossed bars just over 2 inches in height.

Assemble the CooKit. In a shaded area, lay the CooKit shiny side up so that the wide (back) panel is away from you. Tilt the back panel toward you and carefully slide the ends of its flaps into the slots on the shorter front panel that is nearest you. (As you do this, you will need to also tilt the front panel up.) Clamp the inserted flaps on the underside of the front panel using clothespins or a similar device.

Choose a cooking location. Set the cooker on a dry, level surface in direct sunshine away from potential shadows. For best results, solar cooking requires continuous, direct sunshine throughout the cooking period.

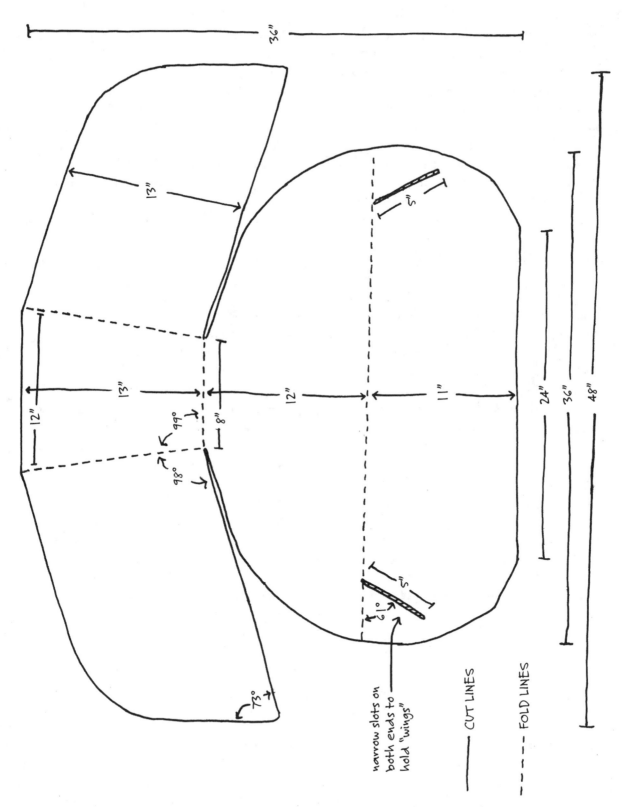

narrow slots on both ends to hold "wings"

—— CUT LINES

- - - FOLD LINES

FIG. 4.9. Courtesy Solar Cookers International.

Orient the cooker according to the details below.
Once oriented, the cooker doesn't need to be moved
again during three to four hours of cooking. For longer
cooking, or for large quantities of food, reorienting the
cooker every couple of hours speeds cooking a little.
Food cooks fastest when the shadow created by the
cooker is directly behind it.

To cook a noontime meal orient the cooker so that
the front side (opposite the reflector) faces easterly, or
approximately where the sun will be mid-morning. In
general, it is good to get the food out early and not to
worry about it until mealtime. For most dishes you
should start cooking by 9 or 10 AM.

To cook an evening meal orient the cooker so that
the front side faces westerly, or approximately where
the sun will be midafternoon. For most dishes, it's best
to start cooking by 1 or 2 PM.

For all-day cooking orient the cooker toward where
sun will be at noon or early afternoon. Food will be
ready and waiting for the evening meal.

Adjust the front flap. Raise or lower the front flap
so there is a small shadow, no more than half its width,
under it. The flap should be angled higher when the
sun is high and lower when the sun is low. You want
the front flap to reflect the sun, not block it.

***Set the bag-enclosed pot on the flat part of the
CooKit.*** *Optional:* On windy days, to anchor the
cooker, large stones or bricks can be placed on each side
of the flat part of the CooKit that extends beyond the
side reflective panels, as well as under the front panel.

***Leave the food to cook for several hours or until
done.*** There is no need to stir the food while it is
cooking.

Remove the pot. Using pot holders, remove the pot
from the CooKit. CAUTION: Pots get very hot! To
prevent steam burns, open the bag away from you
when removing the pot, and slide the pot lid toward
you when opening the pot.

Enjoy a delicious meal!

Care and Storage

Store the CooKit in a safe place away from moisture and animals, preferably indoors. Periodically wipe
reflective surfaces gently with a dry cloth. If the cardboard accidentally gets wet, lay it flat, shiny side down,
until dry.

Allow plastic bags to air-dry or gently wipe them dry
with a towel. Heat-resistant bags, handled properly,
should last 10 or more uses. Bags gradually become
brittle from exposure to sunlight and heat and will
eventually develop small tears. Cellophane tape can
be applied to the outside of small tears to temporarily
extend bag usefulness.

The CooKit is designed to be compact and portable.
When not in use it can be simply folded lengthwise
into thirds or, if needed, folded flat to about 13 square
inches.

Solar Wall Oven

Project Time: Several weekends.

Cost: $50–100.

Energy Saved: Low. Cooking is typically only 4
  percent of a home's energy needs, and a solar wall
  oven cannot be used for every meal.

Ease of Use: Easy. Works when sun is shining.

Maintenance Level: Low.

Skill Levels: Carpentry: Advanced.

Materials: Plywood, 2 × 4s, glazing, silicone, insulation, screws.

Tools: Saw, drill, caulking gun, tape measure, pencil.

Note: The following description is a condensed
version of how to build a through-the-wall solar oven
written by Jim Scott of the Kerr-Cole Sustainable Living
Center in Taylor, Arizona. A solar wall oven will not be
for everyone depending on the orientation of the home
(discussed in more detail below). Where possible, incorporating an accessible oven into one's home can greatly
increase the solar oven's ease of use, an important factor
in bringing solar cooking into the mainstream.

This section describes the considerations for designing and building a slant-faced, reflectorless, through-
the-wall solar box cooker. The discussion assumes a
northern hemisphere location. Readers "Down Under"
will need to reverse north and south in the following
description.

The solar wall oven also works very well as a portable freestanding cooker. However it is used, the rear-opening door of this design is a major convenience compared to conventional top-opening cookers. For maximum convenience, you may want both a freestanding and attached cooker. This section will emphasize aspects of the through-the-wall oven.

Reflectors. The basic design concept of the solar wall oven is to eliminate the need for reflectors to as great an extent as practical. Despite that, one may be tempted to add reflectors to "soup up" the performance beyond the original design objectives. Although there are situations where adding reflectors would be necessary, it comes at a cost in design complexity, difficulty of operation, danger in overheating and damaging the oven, risk of overcooking unattended food, and wind vulnerability.

One way to approach the reflector issue is to construct the oven without reflectors, then add them later if the cooking situation seems to warrant it, such as when cooking in the winter at higher latitudes where the sun will be low to the horizon, or during partly cloudy days.

Site. Slant-faced, reflectorless cookers mounted in a wall are suitable for temperate latitudes only. In tropical regions, the sun will be on opposite sides of the home during summer and winter, progressively restricting the seasons of usefulness of a fixed mounted cooker the closer to the equator it is installed.

In northern temperate regions, the structure must have a south-facing wall available for installing the cooker. True due south (as opposed to magnetic south) orientation is preferred for the cooker. A wall-mounted cooker cannot be turned to follow the sun. A cooker aimed southeast or southwest will limit afternoon or forenoon cooking, respectively. A cooker facing true south will be effective from about 9 AM to 3 PM solar

FIG. 4.10. **The completed solar wall oven.** Photo by Laurie Stone

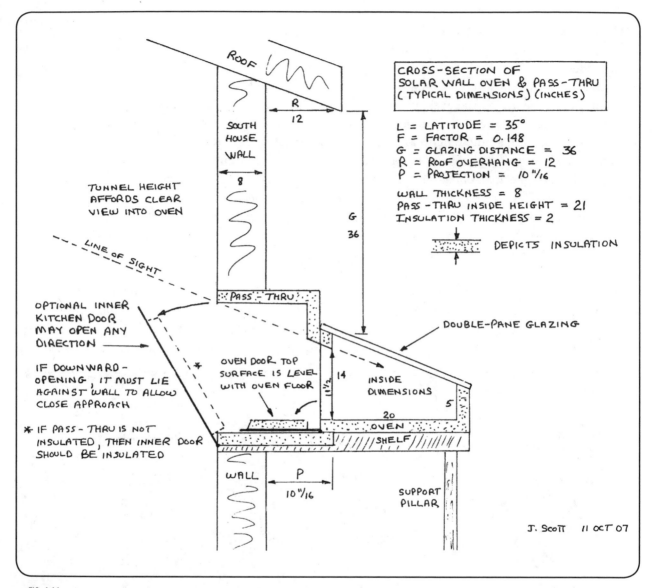

FIG. 4.11. Courtesy Jim Scott, Kerr-Cole Sustainable Living Center

time from mid February to the beginning of November (northern hemisphere). It will still work for more easily cooked foods for the balance of the year from about 10 AM to 2 PM.

The wall must be relatively free of shading by nearby structures, geological features, and trees for a large percentage of the day throughout the seasons. The roof overhang may partially shade the cooker in some seasons, hindering cooking, particularly in the latitudes nearer the tropics. Refer to the installation guidelines on page 64 for details.

Retrofitting an existing home for a solar cooker can be difficult. Smaller, south-facing windows are great candidates for filling in with a through-the-wall cooker. It would be relatively straightforward to remove the lower sash and then construct angled brackets out of 2 × 4s to hold a platform for a solar oven. (See the "Northern Window Conversion to Cold Box" section in chapter 5 for ideas.) Alternatively, a solar wall oven could be designed into the construction of a passive solar wall or greenhouse. If an oven is being inserted into a finished stud wall, the load of any studs that are removed must be deflected with a header. Another idea well worth considering is to place a solar wall oven on a shelf outside a window. This makes it easy to install, to move to another location, and to turn it to follow the sun to extend hours of cooking time. A post extending up from the shelf through the bottom of the cooker will prevent it from falling off when it is turned or subjected to high winds.

Cost and difficulty of construction. Building a durable, effective, slant-faced, through-the-wall box cooker to attach to a house is not as easy or as inexpensive as one might suppose. There are problems with angled construction, providing a door, proper sealing, and obtaining proper materials—particularly the glazing. The materials inside and outside the oven must withstand for the life of the cooker (potentially 50 years). The amount of potential abuse is substantial, including 350-degree F heat, high humidity, UV radiation, freezing, impact, sandstorms, moisture infiltration, abrasion by cooking vessels, and food spillage all while we expect to achieve good cooking capability, attractive appearance, food safety, and easy maintenance and cleanability.

Material considerations are paramount. Wood directly exposed to the extremes of a solar oven can warp, insulation can get wet, and plastic can turn brittle. Proper construction will ensure that the materials last as long as needed.

Dimensions. Size counts. Make the cooker big enough to cook a full meal for your family on a good solar day. A big solar oven also will successfully cook smaller amounts under less-than-ideal sun conditions. Furthermore, big pots, skillets, cookie sheets, and the like will fit in with room to spare for other cookware. A 20 × 30-inch interior floor space works well. It will require glazing about 24 × 32 inches overall. This much floor space will accommodate six "standard" 3-liter cooking pots (although cooking would be slow, even in strong sunlight, if this many pots were heavily loaded and all put in at the same time). Most of the cookers we have made over the years actually have been an inch or so larger than this.

When not in use on sunny winter days, the solar oven can also potentially be a source of meaningful solar

TABLE 4.1 Suggested Interior Dimensions for Solar Wall Oven	
Floor	20" x 30"
Back Wall Height	14"
Front Wall Height	5"
Door Width	26.5"
Door Height	11.5"
Glazing Angle	24 degrees (9" rise in 20")

Source: Kerr-Cole Sustainable Living Center

heat simply by having the door propped open. The larger the oven, the more heat it will make available.

The angle is not critical. Anything between 20 and 30 degrees is acceptable, but generally cookers have been built with angles between 20 and 25 degrees. Glazing in the 25- to 30-degree range might be a better idea farther north, say 45 degrees north latitude. The 14-inch height allows the upright placement of gallon-sized jugs across the back of the cooker for water pasteurization.

You may choose to increase the floor size some. The heights are well proven in practice, and you change them at your peril. Too low and your pots may not fit. Too high and the effectiveness of heat transfer into the food may suffer.

The door. The door generally will be the biggest problem in construction. Beware of metal door frames or a metal rim on the door itself. Even thin metal foil will rob a surprising amount of heat by conduction from inside to outside. Gaps around the door allow air infiltration and therefore can cause heat loss. If heat loss seems to be a problem, try adding some weatherstripping. Generally, even rather loosely fitting doors seem to work fine for solar wall ovens. The problem with freestanding cookers used outdoors likely comes from wind-infiltration losses.

The door (as well as the rest of the interior of the cooker) must be made of nontoxic materials that do not outgas when hot. Since the door does not receive direct UV rays, it can be made out of wood, although some shrinking and expanding can be expected. It's best for the cooker door to open downward and to stay open in a horizontal position, able to support the weight of dishes of food that will inevitably be placed on it. A chain on the side of the door that holds it open at the desired position is one effective way to accomplish this.

When an oven is tightly constructed all over, another problem often arises. Moisture from the food condenses on the undersurface of the glazing, blocking sunlight from entering the cooker and reducing the cooking capacity. A pot with a tighter-fitting lid will likely solve this problem except when baking. Two holes about ¾ inch in diameter drilled through the door will provide enough airflow to draw out the moisture, although some heat loss will occur. One may use ¾-inch plastic hot-water pipe to line the holes. One hole should be down low; the other should be up high. The upper hole should be closable to prevent unnecessary air circulation when the oven is dry. A plug of cloth or cotton will work, although it will be easily lost. A small sliding door over the hole is ideal. The lower hole may be left open unless there are rodent and/or insect concerns.

The wider the width of the door the better. We suggest 26.5 inches to clear a full-size 26 × 18-inch baker's tray slid in sideways. A tray this size allows cookware placed on it to be moved in and out en masse. With a door this wide, the upper doorjamb must be configured to carry a major portion of the structural load across the back of the cooker. A 26.5-inch door will open into the space between three studs on 16-inch centers if the center stud is cut out. This produces an opening 30.5 inches wide, providing enough room at either side (a couple of inches) for external door flanges and for the construction of insulated pass-through tunnel walls. This width is our preference, although narrower doors have been used and may be preferable on some houses, depending on construction details and the layout of the kitchen.

For a latch to hold your door closed, a small piece of wood screwed into the top of the doorjamb is very effective, assuming the door closes flush with the jamb. The screw is left just loose enough so that the piece of wood can pivot down and hold the door closed.

Insulation. Many materials have insulative properties, and you should consider insulating your solar oven with what you have on hand. However, some do better than others, and it's worth discussing the pros and cons in a little detail. Probably the best choice if you're purchasing new material is polyester batting purchased from a hobby or fabric store.

It's important not to allow any thermally conductive sheet metal or metal foil paths from interior metal surfaces to exterior metal surfaces anywhere, such as around the top where the glazing meets the rim. This will create a thermal bridge, and the heat loss via such a path can be substantial.

The walls, door, and floor should employ at least R-8 insulation, or close to it—the higher, the better. For most materials, 2-inch-thick insulation will be sufficient. Often 4 inches will give somewhat better performance, but heat loss through the walls is not of overriding concern in any case.

If you use foamboard insulation, you must check to make sure that it is rated for higher temperatures (300+ degrees F). Thermax is a commonly available brand that fits this purpose. Typical Styrofoam is not rated for high-enough temperatures for a solar oven.

A less appreciated consideration is the thermal mass of the interior walls that cover the insulation. Use very lightweight materials. It has been determined, for example, that in real-world cooking situations an ⅛-inch-thick Masonite hardboard oven liner soaked up 20 percent of the available heat, compared to the 10 percent passed by 4 inches of rice hull insulation. All of this heat loss becomes unavailable for cooking food. Use low-thermal-mass interior materials such as sheet metal or foil-faced or black-painted cardboard.

Fiberglass batt, an old down quilt, new quilt polyester fiber, feathers, rice hulls, sawdust, and crushed newspaper (each full-size sheet crumpled to the size of a lemon) are all effective. Be wary of fiberglass batting, as it compacts severely if it gets wet. Do not use wood ash. It settles over time. Beware of wool; weevils will eat it. Cotton has durability issues and is not recommended. Multiple layers of cardboard with aluminum foil adhered shiny side out to both sides (use diluted wood glue) gives excellent results. Slip straw (loose straw coated in clay, as described in chapter 7) probably has too high of a thermal mass to be effective.

Water vapor from cooking food will condense in the insulation if the oven cavity is not well sealed. Take special care to seal the inside of the oven and make sure it sheds water properly on the exterior. In Arizona we have never had a problem with this due to the low humidity and tightly sealed construction of our ovens. In Minnesota, which has humid summers, crushed newspaper insulation in an unsealed cooker settled into a pile of paper mush in a single season.

An excellent candidate for insulation that will take the heat is polyester fiber from a fabric store. This is sold in "fiber fill" form (bulk for stuffing pillows) and in batt form (sheets for making quilts). Polyester plastic typically is rated to withstand 425 degrees F. In a 350-degree F oven test that deformed test samples of high-heat foam insulation, polyester fiber showed no sign of degradation. This inexpensive and easily obtainable material does not sag, drains water when wetted, does not rot or deteriorate, is easily handled, produces no harmful fiber "dust," is easily cut with scissors, and is simple to install by stapling or stuffing. When saturated under a faucet, a sample compressed about 50 percent, then ceased to collapse, suggesting that when using bulk fiber to stuff a cavity it ought to be compressed 50 percent to forestall formation of voids. We have not tested the insulation R-value to date, so a thickness of 4 inches is suggested to be on the safe side.

Sealing. Silicone makes the best heat-resistant sealer, and food-grade varieties are available. Pure silicone is not paintable, however, and is a *real* mess to work with. Despite its messiness, silicone is our choice for all-purpose adhesive in solar-cooker construction. It is nontoxic during curing and inert when cured, producing no off-gassing, and does not conduct heat. Once cured, silicone remains flexible, which means it can accommodate the thermal expansion of the glazing.

For a wall-mounted oven, seal the oven and pass-through tunnel against rainwater entry. This is particularly important if the cooker is integrated with the structure of the building rather than simply mounted externally in the fashion of an air conditioner. If condensation from food or rain entry is not controlled, the water may leak out the bottom of the cooker and do damage to the building. To keep water from running along the underside of the oven back toward the house, add a line of silicone or a few indention lines (by making a few cuts with a saw a quarter-inch deep) along the underside of the oven parallel to the front edge.

Interior. Raise the floor plate a little so it does not directly contact the bottom of the oven box. Several thin wood strips will do the trick. Creating this air gap significantly reduces heat loss from the floor plate down through the insulation of the floor, as the floor plate is the primary solar energy absorber and gets *very* hot. The upper surface of the floor must be black (or another very dark color) to absorb sunlight and convert it into heat.

We suggest the use of a 0.062m (62-mil) black *aluminum* floor (best if "hard" anodized for durability and easy cleanup). The heavy aluminum readily conducts heat to cooking pots.

One can blacken oven surfaces and cookware with BBQ black paint. Black tempura paint, such as produced by mixing the dry powder with white glue, is used by some solar-cooking practitioners, but others point out that the paint develops a chalky white surface over time, lessening effectiveness in absorbing sunlight to produce heat.

Glazing. The glazing must be double-pane. Single-pane does not work for a reflectorless cooker except in very strong and direct sunlight, and then only if the cooker is free to be aimed at the sun. Triple-pane provides little advantage over double-pane.

Retail plastic sheets will not work satisfactorily as glazing. They will warp, cloud up, and disintegrate. Use Plexiglas only if it has a UV-rated surface.

For commercially purchased glazing, we use ⅝-inch overall, ⅜-inch spacing, double-pane, ⅛-inch thick, tempered, clear glass insulated windows with a black or dark bronze spacer bar separating the two sheets of glass. We specify butyl sealant for heat resistance. This substance does not outgas toxic vapor. Such glazing works very well, although it can be costly and heavy. Manufactured double-pane glass can often be special-ordered to a specific size from hardware or glass stores.

For a 24 × 32-inch window, we have paid as little as $50 and been quoted as much as $150, so it pays to shop around. Used double-paned windows can often be found at reuse centers, although it may be difficult to find the appropriate size. New double-pane glass often contains a low-E (low emissivity) coating. Avoid low-E coatings that block anything but infrared radiation.

Double-pane UV-resistant greenhouse plastic glazing is also a potential candidate. Using two separately purchased sheets of tempered glass with a homemade spacer won't save much money but does have the advantage of allowing disassembly of the glazing if crud builds up between the two sheets. If your homemade double glazing is experiencing condensation problems, a few 1/16-inch weepholes can be drilled very carefully into the top sheet, a few at the bottom and at the top. This will allow enough air to pass through to remove the moisture but not so much as to affect the insulative properties of the glazing.

Regular window glass is relatively inexpensive but is not recommended, as it is vulnerable to cracking from either heat stress or impact. However, cracks rarely allow airflow and hence heat loss and thus do not adversely affect the oven's performance. Cracks can be semipermanently fixed using clear 3M Magic Tape.

Tempered glass is very strong in some respects. It is quite likely to survive a hard blow from a baseball bat. However, be very careful not to nick tempered glass. If you do, you will end up with an expensive pile of glass pebbles. One touch with a metal screw, and the whole pane will magically crumble before your eyes. Take pains to carefully pad the glass during handling and storage, paying particular attention to the edges. If the glass is placed with its weight on a grain of sand on a hard surface, the effect will have you on the phone ordering replacement glass.

At some point in the life of your oven, you may very well need to replace the glazing no matter what you use. Keep this in mind as you build your oven, and don't make it too difficult to replace.

Solar Wall Ovens and Eaves

In order to clear the eaves and be in full sun the oven must be extended out from the house. This is accomplished via a pass-through tunnel. Note that some passive solar homes or retrofitted passive solar homes have very large eaves. This can mean that the oven projects very far out from the house. The higher up the oven is placed, the longer the pass-through tunnel will need to be, as the eave produces more shade the closer something is to it. A trade-off exists between the accessibility of the oven and the length of the pass-through tunnel. Very long pass-through tunnels could potentially be difficult to support structurally, as well as being inaccessible from the interior (and just plain looking weird). One potential solution to this is either to make the oven removable in summertime so that it can be placed away from the eave or to have a secondary solar oven for cooking in the summertime. In addition to making construction of the pass-through tunnel easier by making it much shorter or nonexistent, this would ensure the heat from the oven did not enter the house. If the southern wall does not contain much additional glazing (if solar heating in winter is obtained by solar air heaters on the roof, for instance), then additional overhangs (including trellising) are not as necessary and may be abandoned in favor of an accessible solar wall oven.

Installation guidelines. The floor of the pass-through tunnel should be set such that the oven floor is at elbow height. Assuming the door opens downward onto the pass-through floor, the upper surface of the door then will also be at the oven floor height, or close to it. This is about 42 inches high for a person 5 feet, 6 inches tall. The tunnel opening itself ought to be something like 18 inches in height to allow adequate access and visibility into the oven. The tunnel walls ought to be insulated to prevent heat loss from the home in winter or heat infiltration into the home in summer. Having the top surface of the opened door and the floor of the oven at exactly the same height makes it very convenient to slide vessels and trays in and out of the cooker (see figure 4.11).

One should consider installing a door at the kitchen (indoor) end of the tunnel. This would be a second door in addition to the oven door proper at the far end of the tunnel. The kitchen door may open downward 90 degrees to form a shelf or fold 180 degrees in any direction against the wall to allow closer approach to the oven. The kitchen door provides a barrier against loss of room heat via the pass-through tunnel walls—a potential problem in winter. Ditto for unwanted heat infiltration from outside in the summer. This consideration is significant if the tunnel walls are not insulated. Another benefit of having doors at both ends of the tunnel is that the space between them is often at a good temperature for raising bread dough or making yogurt. For security against intruders gaining entry via the cooker, say by removing the glazing, one might consider making this kitchen door stout and securely lockable.

On a southerly facing wall oriented somewhat to east or west, consider slanting the cooker relative to the wall so that it faces due south. For a house not oriented on a true north-south/east-west axis, location of the cooker on the most southerly facing wall as close as practical to the southernmost corner will give good results. In this position, the cooker will not usually suffer shading in the afternoon either from the roof overhang or from the house walls.

For a cooker mounted in a true south-facing wall, installing it close to the east or west corner will extend cooking time, particularly in summer when the sun rises and sets considerably north of the due east-west axis. For example, if mounted at the west corner, it will catch late-day sun for a longer time, particularly if fitted with a reflector that can be brought into play to scoop in the low-angle light until the sun hits the horizon. As is the case for all fixed-mount cookers, this optional reflector would have to be hinged or removable to keep it from getting in the way during portions of the day.

TABLE 4.2 Determining the Pass-Through Projection for the Solar Wall Oven

Latitude (L)	Factor (F)	Latitude (L)	Factor (F)	Latitude (L)	Factor (F)
26	.004	33	.116	40	.228
27	.020	34	.132	41	.244
28	.036	35	.148	42	.260
29	.052	36	.164	43	.276
30	.068	37	.180	44	.292
31	.084	38	.196	45	.308
32	.100	39	.212	46	.324

Source: Kerr-Cole Sustainable Living Center

The cooker may be installed flush against the house if there are no eaves. However, if the house does have eaves, one must space the cooker out from the exterior of the house far enough to clear the shadow of the roof overhang. This means that the pass-through tunnel must extend beyond the exterior wall of the house to reach the rear of the cooker. The length of this projection will be greater the closer to the equator the cooker is installed. The worst case will be at solar noon at the summer equinox.

Determining the pass-through projection. Assuming the cooker is installed in a vertical rectilinear wall oriented due south, the following formula applies to determine how far the top corner (northernmost edge) of the glazing must be positioned beyond the exterior wall of the house, given the latitude, the depth of the roof overhang, and the distance of the top corner of the glazing below the roof overhang.

Fill in the appropriate numbers to see how far your oven needs to project from your south-facing wall.

L = latitude

F = latitude factor from table 4.2

R = roof overhang (horizontal distance from eave edge to wall)

G = glazing distance below the roof overhang (vertical distance from horizontal plane of eave edge to horizontal plane of topmost edge of glazing)

P = projection of pass-through (distance from house exterior wall surface to edge of glazing).

$$P = R - (F \times G)$$

This equation is presented below as such calculations appear on tax forms.

1. Enter latitude degrees   1._____
2. Enter latitude (L) factor (F)
   from table 4.2   2._____
3. Enter glazing distance G   3._____
4. Enter roof overhang R   4._____
5. Multiply line 2 times line 3 and
   enter the result here   5._____
6. If line 5 is greater than line 4,
   enter zero on line 8
7. If line 5 is less than line 4,
   subtract line 5 from line 4
   and enter the result on line 8
8. Pass-through projection
   distance (P)   8. _____

OUR SOLAR OVEN

Since a solar oven is essentially just a small box with some glass, shiny metal, and insulation, it wasn't too hard for us to come up with scrap materials from other house projects to build a substantial and durable wooden one. We built our solar oven before reading much of the literature included in this chapter, and we've been satisfied with how this solar oven works, so we'd like to take a few moments to describe it.

Our solar oven sits outside on our green roof, keeping our plants, solar hot-water heater, and PV panels company. This is where we worship the sun, and where the sun returns our praise with delicious food, flowers, electricity, and hot showers.

To begin with, we built out of scraps of half-inch plywood a double-walled box that looked like figure 4.12.

This was done with wood glue and 1½-inch screws; we predrilled for each hole to lessen the odds of splitting the sides of the plywood. Three-quarter-inch plywood would be easier to work with if you have some. We made the gap between the two layers of plywood a bit larger than 2 inches to fit in some scraps of 2-inch

foam insulation we had lying around. Heat retention becomes increasingly difficult as the difference in temperature becomes greater; the problem is acute in solar ovens since the difference in temperature inside and outside the box can be over 200 degrees F. This means effective insulation is critical, so using a high-R-value insulation like foam seemed like a good idea.

Foam insulation has the potential to be compromised at temperatures greater than 300 degrees F. In the summer it may be wise to place a few dark rocks in the oven to regulate its temperature and keep it from going above 300 degrees F if overheating is a problem. This also helps even out the oven temperature so that a steadier cooking heat is maintained when clouds pass over.

Scraps of foam are easy to come by. Packing peanuts, crushed-up coffee cups, and takeout containers are potential sources. Pack these in your solar oven instead of throwing them in the garbage, since most places don't recycle them. Dipping these materials in a clay slip (see the "Insulation" section of chapter 7) can lessen the chances of these materials being degraded by the heat or potentially catching fire, although you want to keep the amount of extra thermal mass you add to your oven to a minimum so it doesn't steal heat away from your food. If you have any doubts about the insulation you are using, it might be worthwhile to make a removable panel that will allow you to periodically check on it to make sure the heat of the oven has not degraded it.

After the box was assembled as shown in figure 4.12, we built out a perimeter of wood to 2 inches thick on the underside of the bottom piece of plywood, filled in the gaps with the insulation, and then covered it with plywood. Elsewhere we filled in the plywood with the insulation and then capped it with strips of wood 1 inch thick that we ripped with a circular saw to the proper width.

On the bottom of the cooker we ran two strips of 1-inch-thick wood to elevate it and keep it dry.

To make the glass door we ripped 2 × 4s in half and built a simple rectangle with these, screwing through the sides (flat angle irons would also have done the

FIG. 4.12. **Inserting the insulation into the frame of oven.**

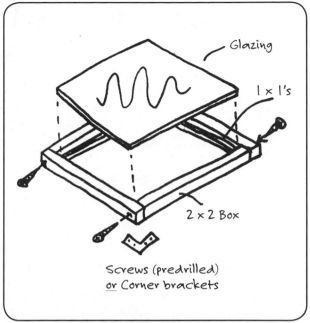

FIG. 4.13. **Assembling the door of the oven.**

trick), then tacked strips of 1 × 1s around the perimeter as shown in figure 4.13.

We made sure the door was square so that the glass would fit in there easily. We had a piece of glass cut to the dimensions of our opening minus ¼ inch on each side. The glass went in and then we glazed it. Double glazing, as suggested in the solar wall oven project above, might have made the need for our reflectors less necessary. We could also have decided on fixed glazing and an openable back door to avoid the glare when we put items in and out, and potentially save on heat loss when we open our oven from the top.

The box and door were primed, caulked, and painted as needed. On the interior we tacked up extra pieces of aluminum flashing we had lying around and then painted these black with flat paint. These pieces do an excellent job of absorbing the sun's rays and reradiating them back into the oven. If you don't have these, you could just paint the inside black and forget about the metal, although the air gap in between the sheet of metal and the wood helps prevent heat loss through the walls.

Next we ran two strips of 1 × 6 material up the back side of the oven, starting at the bottom. We needed

these to stick out high enough above the oven to hold the cover open, so we made them stick up a few inches more than the height of the glass door. We ran them up the sides of the oven, then put three or four screws in each one to hold it in place. Then we ran a board between them at the top for a crossbar.

The glass door hinges on the bottom and opens outward. We had to run an additional piece of 2-inch-thick material to support the door hinges. The metal cover over the glass hinges above the door on the two strips of 1 × 6 sticking up.

When the cover is closed, it protects the oven from rain and the glass from hailstones or other damaging objects. When it's open, it concentrates the solar gain when the sun is lower in the sky by having reflective flashing on its underside. We had extra material around from our roofing project for this. Scraps of roofing tin went on top for rain protection, and reflective aluminum flashing covered the bottom for reflection.

Weather-stripping runs around the perimeter of the glass door and there's a clasp to close it down tight. The cover is held up with a chain that loops into a screw set in the back side of the crossbar. By adjusting which loop of the chain we hook on the screw, we

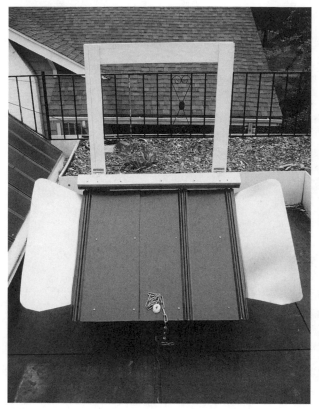

FIG. 4.14.

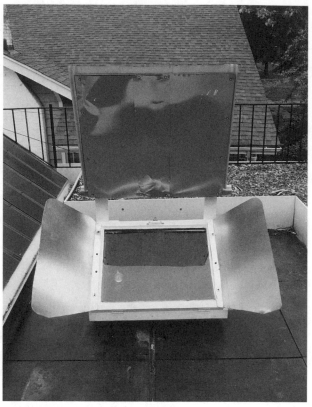

FIG. 4.15.

are able to adjust the angle of the cover according to the season to direct additional sunshine into the oven. Around the summer solstice, this provides little additional heat, but rarely is it needed then.

On the door we screwed in two "ears." These are two pieces of 24-gauge sheet metal we cut from a section left over from our woodstove installation. The 24-gauge metal is stout enough not to be bent in the wind but thin enough to cut with tin snips, and it helps direct additional sunlight into our oven. We rounded the edges so they wouldn't cut anyone. The bottom of these two ears stick out just enough so that when we open the glass door it's propped upright, resting on the lower edges of the two ears, which are stout enough to support the door.

Typically while we're cooking we don't turn the oven, leaving it facing due south. It will spin if necessary, and sometimes if we don't get started cooking until lunchtime we'll spin it a little to the west. If necessary,

we could always put it on a peg on a platform for easier rotation. Our finished oven weighs around 40 pounds and likes to stay put. It's definitely not portable, but it's not difficult to move with two people if necessary. Wind gusts, even with the cover up, have not bothered it, probably because it's so bottom-heavy, and it's held up very well exposed to the elements so far.

For cooler months we've added an aluminum reflector that props up on the bottom. Again, this has little additional benefit in summertime.

Typically on a sunny day with at least four good hours of sunlight we can cook most anything we want. We cook large batches of different varieties of beans, typically four dry cups at a time, which produces about double that amount cooked. We take these four pints, use one shortly thereafter, and freeze the other three in pint-size containers. Bread, stews, and chilis we make in quantity as well, freezing the extra if necessary.

FIG. 4.16.

On sunny days the oven stays between 250 and 300 degrees F from midmorning to midafternoon, usually around five hours. The hour on either side is usually between 200 and 250 degrees F and can still be a useful cooking temperature, although not for baking.

The solar oven does excellent double duty as a dehydrator. We have three wire racks that fit in the oven quite nicely. Extra fruit and/or mushrooms are stacked in the racks with the clasp propping the oven open rather than sealing it down tight. Propped open like this, the oven typically stays between 150 and 175 degrees F. Depending on the water content of the food you're dehydrating and the amount of sunlight available, it may take more than one day for proper dehydration, although this is rare. Obviously, nothing can be cooked in the oven when this is happening, and there are times when it would be nice to have a separate solar dehydrator. As the bounty of our fruit trees is increasing annually, we will probably need to build one in the future.

PREMANUFACTURED SOLAR OVENS

We have been happy to note the increase in the number of companies making premanufactured solar ovens over the last few years. Ideally, every home should have one. Those recently available include the Hot Pot Simple Solar Cooker ($120), Global Sun Oven ($240), and Tulsi-Hybrid Solar Oven with electric backup ($300). Tried and true is the Sport Solar Oven ($150) from the Solar Oven Society. We wish we could say we've tested them all, but we can't. If you want to go for reliability then the Sport is the only one that has been consistently recommended to us, and it's made by a nonprofit.

COOKING WITH BIOMASS

Wood is the most common and readily available biomass for cooking, at least in the eastern half of the country. The same clouds that limit the use of solar heating and cooking also bring rain, vital to the accumulation of stored carbon energy in plant materials. So on days when direct solar energy is inaccessible because of cloudy weather, we can still access it sustainably by judicious and responsible use of biomass, although we must bear in mind that the transfer of direct solar energy to stored biomass results in efficiency losses. For this section, we'll focus on cooking with wood. Cooking can also be achieved by using liquid fuels derived from biomass, such as plant oils and ethanol, and we'll discuss this in a minute.

Burning wood can produce a tremendous amount of heat. Unfortunately, only a fraction of it can be directed to the pots and pans holding our food. Great strides have been made in understanding how to improve the transfer of heat from fire to cooking vessels, thereby increasing the efficiency of biomass combustion. Unfortunately, these have not yet translated into improved manufactured products that a homeowner can purchase and install. Stoves more efficient than purchased products can be built at home, and existing stoves can be modified to improve the efficiency of their combustion and heat transfer. These principles are dealt with in greater detail in the "Rocket Stoves and Homemade Mass Heaters" sidebar in chapter 7.

Combustion produces radiant heat, which is dispersed in energy waves in many directions. For this reason, it's important to limit our use of cooking with wood to those times when our homes also need heating. Having alternative methods of cooking available ensures we can make the best use of our wood resources and keep our homes from being unbearably hot in the summer. Wood fires also have the potential to produce hot water when it's cloudy (see chapter 6).

New wood cookstoves can be quite expensive. Determine the exact model for your needs, making sure to match the heat output of your stove with your house heating requirements, and shop around. You'll want to check a local retailer, although our experience has been that individual dealers usually have a very selective display of what's available. To make sure you're aware of all the available models, an hour or two of Internet research will pay off handsomely, even if you decide to order the stove through a local retailer. See the resources section for nationwide dealers. Before you order from a national dealer, it's always worthwhile to call and see if a floor model is available for a discount, and remember that shipping costs can run into the hundreds of dollars. If you own or can borrow a pickup truck, you can save even more.

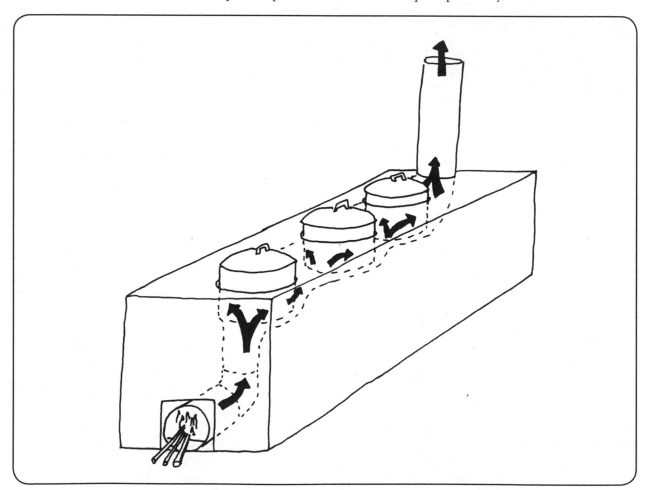

FIG. 4.17. **A tested rocket-stove design that greatly improves both combustion and heat-exchange efficiency. Running the heat of the fire around pots instead of under them greatly reduces the need for firewood.** Courtesy Aprovecho Research Center.

Picking up a stove at a nearby shipper's warehouse rather than having direct home delivery should save about half the shipping cost.

Used cookstoves are occasionally available. Keep in mind that these old stoves are unlikely to work properly and will almost certainly need some repair work. Broken cast iron is almost impossible to repair, so even small cracks or chips can mean a leaky stove. Since death by carbon monoxide poisoning is a possibility with a leaky stove, you'll need to proceed with extreme caution if you're considering purchasing a used stove. Basically, unless you already have one or can get one for free, they are likely to be too much of a hassle and potential danger. An outdoor firing will let you know how badly any woodstove leaks.

Cooking can be done on existing installed woodstoves, but much depends on the amount of flat space on top of your stove. We use clay tiles and copper trivets on top of our stove to give us a range of cooking temperatures.

For ovens, the only working option we know of for existing stoves is the Coleman camp oven. It's flimsy, small, and uninsulated, but it works if the fire is hot enough. We've heard tell of other options, including one that replaces a section of stovepipe, but we haven't been able to get our hands on any. Other options include Dutch ovens (cast-iron pots with tops) or clay ovens. Fireplaces are inherently inefficient and should not be used at all without some type of insert.

If cooking with wood during summer months is unavoidable, a cob oven outdoors is relatively straightforward to build and will keep the extra heat out of the home. Make sure to combine as many cooking tasks as possible for each firing.

Wood Cookstove

Project Time: Several weekends.

Cost: Expensive ($2,000–5,000 for new installations).

Energy Saved: Low if used only for cooking; high if also used for home and/or water heating.

Ease of Use: Medium. Takes time to get fire started and must be maintained. Temperature can be irreg-

ular and hot surfaces increase odds of accidental burning.

Maintenance Level: High. Maintaining a steady supply of cured wood is definitely a chore that requires lots of physical labor. Having wood delivered can lessen this but not eliminate it, and it comes at the cost of energy independence. The firebox requires periodic cleaning and the stovepipe must be occasionally checked.

Skill Levels: Carpentry: Advanced.

Materials: A purchased or assembled cast-iron cookstove, regular stovepipe to length, insulated stovepipe to length, a ceiling/roof chimney kit (available from hardware stores or woodstove dealers).

Tools: Tin snips, saw, drill, screws, hammer, roofing sealant, caulking gun.

Caution: Installing a heavy cookstove is an onerous task and will require three or four healthy adults with strong backs. Holes must be cut in the ceiling and roof, and great care taken to maintain the required clearances dictated by the particular model of stove you are installing. More so than in other projects, cutting corners is not acceptable, as the consequences could be a fatal house fire. If you have any doubts about your carpentry skills, hire a professional carpenter to assist you. In most locations woodstove installations require notification of both the fire marshall and your house insurer.

Classic wood cookstoves are beautiful and substantially better for cooking than a standard woodstove, especially since they include an oven. They can be quite expensive and difficult to install, so be sure you'll get your time and money's worth before proceeding.

Most wood cookstoves have a common basic layout. There is a firebox to one side under the stovetop, and it is filled with wood from a small door on the front. Once the fire is started, the smoke and heat are carried over the oven door and below the four to six burners located on the top. Often, there is a place on one side of the stove for an optional chamber to hold gallons of water that will be gradually heated as the fire burns. Newer stoves have combustion-control knobs to moderate the temperature of the burners and the oven. Older stoves might be lacking this feature and temperature must be controlled by adding wood or controlling the draft.

Temperature is regulated in the oven by how close the dish is to the fire. To ensure even baking, it is necessary to periodically turn the dish. In addition, most wood cookstoves have optional warmer boxes that can be placed above burners to keep already-cooked items warm.

The importance of using properly cured wood cannot be overemphasized, as cured wood has several times as much available heat as green, or unseasoned, wood. Read the section "Heating with Biomass" in chapter 7 for the basics on cutting, storing, and using wood.

Once you've determined where you want to locate your cookstove (presumably somewhere in your kitchen), then installation follows the same procedure as for a standard woodstove. Read the section "Woodstove Installation" in chapter 7.

Outdoor Cob Oven

Renter friendly.

Project Time: Several weekends.

Cost: Inexpensive ($50–100).

Energy Saved: Low.

Ease of Use: Medium. Takes an hour or so to really get up and going.

Maintenance Level: Medium. Requires a supply of seasoned wood.

Skill Levels: Carpentry: Moderate. Masonry: Basic.

Note: Some experience with cob is helpful but not required.

Materials: A cubic yard of sand, half a yard of clay, straw, strips of rot-resistant wood such as cedar or oak, scrap pieces roofing tin or equivalent wood shingles, 4-foot ridge cap, 4 feet of 5-inch or 6-inch black stovepipe with cap, two 80-pound bags of cement, unglazed tile (optional), foundation stones, gravel, landscaping cloth, four to eight 2½-foot pieces of rebar.

Tools: Shovel, masonry hoe, tarp or masonry basin, saw, drill, screws.

An outdoor cob oven makes much more efficient use of firewood than an open fire or grill and keeps heat out of the home on warmer evenings. It's a great alternative when the solar oven isn't getting any rays and makes a great neighborhood gathering spot.

This design allows multiple dishes to be cooked for each firing and has a roof to protect the unfired masonry (the cob) from water damage. This allows for multiple uses from each firing: baking of breads and pizzas, cooking of grains and legumes for stews and soups, and, as the oven cools, dehydration of fruits and vegetables for preservation.

This oven is a hybrid of a few different prototypes. The firebox is made of cement block filled with insulation. Cooking is done on a slab covered by a sloping A-frame cob oven. The fire heats the slab from underneath and the smoke exits through the stovepipe. The cob helps retain heat and allows the stove to be used for an extended period of time. The high thermal mass of this stove means that a great deal of wood will need to be burned to heat it up, although the retained heat will provide for a great deal of cooking and baking. The design of this stove could certainly be improved by incorporating elements of high-efficiency rocket-stove principles, although we are unable to offer detailed directions in this regard because of our lack of experience. We highly recommend reading Aprovecho's publication on building high-efficiency cookstoves before undertaking construction of an earth oven so that you can make sure the oven described here fits your needs. See the resources section at the end of the chapter.

Building with cob is time consuming, so we want the finished product to last. Fortunately, finished cob with adequate water protection has the potential to stick around for several centuries. To ensure this happens, we need a proper foundation.

Preparing the foundation. The footprint of the cob oven will be 3 × 3 feet. If the subsoil where you are building is clay, this is an excellent time to obtain the necessary clay for the cob oven you will soon be building. Dig out to below the frost line the entire footprint of the oven plus a few extra inches all around, making

FIG. 4.18.

sure to separate the topsoil from the clay. You don't want topsoil in a cob mixture, as it contains too much organic matter. Save it for your garden.

Lay down landscaping fabric. This is a petroleum product but will ensure that the foundation lasts a very long time. After you lay down the landscaping fabric, fill the hole with gravel, pouring it in a few inches at a time and tamping after each layer to make sure it is well compacted and settled. Rainwater that accumulates in this hole will drain through the gravel and seep away underground. Limiting the amount of water that gets in this hole will make sure the footing functions properly, so try to berm soil around the perimeter of your foundation to drain water away from your oven.

Once your gravel has filled the entire hole to ground level and is properly tamped down, it's time to lay the aboveground foundation. The easiest if not the most attractive aboveground foundation material is cement block. Although in general this book gives aesthetics short shrift compared to energy efficiency, your cob oven, soon to become a prominent feature of your

landscape, might deserve a little extra time and effort in this department. Depending on your masonry skills, you may want to lay some finer-looking fieldstone or brick. Note that if these materials are laid dry, it will be necessary to parget, or stucco, over the inside of the foundation to ensure a properly functioning firebox. If you do use cement block, you can hide it with a quick stucco job on the outside. Whatever you use, it should be about 16 inches high, and the top of the foundation wall needs to be solid (with caps if you're using block) and at least 8 inches wide.

Building the slab. To complete the "first floor," or firebox part of the cob oven, you first need to build your slab. This will be the portion of your oven that gets heated up and cooks any pizzas or breads that will be placed directly on it. If the idea of cooking directly on concrete does not appeal to you, you can finish off the top of the slab with clay cooking tiles or a cob floor.

To make the slab, build a simple square frame from scrap lumber, securing it with screws, such that it has a 2½ × 2½-foot interior. Put the frame on a flat surface, ideally a scrap piece of plywood or bare dirt (i.e., not something concrete will adhere to), and center a section of the stovepipe in the box 8 inches from one side, tapered end down.

Prop up the pieces of rebar with pieces of gravel or wire so they're about an inch up in a crisscross pattern (hardware stores sell what are called rebar "chairs" specifically for the purpose of elevating rebar off the ground). Don't skimp on the rebar, as the slab will be very difficult to replace later if it breaks. Mix the cement (which should be marked "S" for structural as opposed to "N" for nonstructural) and sand, in the ratio given on the label, in a wheelbarrow or masonry tub with some of the leftover gravel. Shovel this mix into the frame, making sure it doesn't knock over the rebar or stovepipe, and making it about 2 inches thick. If this will be your cooking surface, smooth the concrete with a trowel by jiggling it, which causes any of the larger pieces to sink, and use the unscored side of the trowel or float to make the face as smooth as possible, especially in the middle where most of the

Add sheathing and then roofing material of choice.

Fill gaps with slip straw to hold heat.

As cob layers are built, add "keys" to hold sheathing.

Add keys in face to hold door frame.

Build frame for cob out of scrap plywood.

Brace front to hold in place.

Build slab in place.

Leave stovepipe in place.

Stucco outside to seal cracks.

Fill in holes with insulation like wood ash.

Landscaping cloth folds over top of gravel.

Use clay and/or sand in cob.

Topsoil and subsoil in separate piles.

FIG. 4.19.

cooking will be done. Write your name and date along the edge and then go inside and make arrangements on the phone with a friend to come by the next day and help you lift the slab onto the top of the foundation.

After a day or so the slab will have set up. Remove the frame and then heave the slab onto the foundation, placing it all the way to the front with the stovepipe hole at the back. This should leave you with several inches of overlap onto the foundation wall and several inches of foundation wall still exposed. It's almost time to start cobbing.

The cob frame. To hold the cob build a frame out of scrap plywood in the shape of a triangle. See figure 4.19. The idea will be to build the cob layer by layer up the side of the forms and around back, with the stovepipe running up the inside. Once the cob has been built all the way up the plywood frame, you will then disassemble the frame and remove the plywood pieces out the front, so bear this in mind as you build your frame.

As you build up the layers, you will need to place "keys," or small blocks of wood with nails sticking out of them, into the face of the cob. You will be attaching your roof sheathing and door frame to these pieces of wood once you have completed the cob. Nails or screws that stick out of the keys allow it to embed in the cob and become locked in place after it dries.

Layering the cob. Mix the cob (see "Cob How-To" in chapter 7) and plop it onto the foundation wall around both sides of your plywood frame and around the back of the oven where your stovepipe is. At some height, the cob will begin to "ooge," or press out at the sides, probably at about 4–6 inches depending on the wetness of your mix. Once you've determined at what point your mix of cob will ooge, keep your fresh layer a little shorter than this. Once your first layer is done, add a few keys to hold your roof sheathing and door frame. It'll take a day or two of drying before this cob layer will firm up enough that you can add another layer, although you don't want the cob to dry out completely. Make sure to give it a good soaking before you add the next layer or if you can't get to it for another week or two. To keep the cob from getting

too wet from rain or drying too fast in the sun, it's best to cover the oven with a tarp. Direct sun can lead to too-quick drying and excessive cracking and structural weakness.

From here on out it's mostly repeat and wait until you get to the top. A strip of wood to catch the roofing material should be placed into the cob on the sloped sides horizontally every 12–16 inches. These strips also need to be well keyed, as they will support the roofing material.

As you near the top, the more of an arch you can create the better, as this will distribute loads better and contribute to the longevity of your oven. Remember to continue the stovepipe out the top before you finish your cobbing. Once you're done and the cob has set, remove the bracing you built to hold the cob in place.

Adding the door frame and door. You can safely build a wood door frame that won't burn as long as there is some cob separating it from the interior of the oven. Attach two strips of wood that come up to a point and make a triangle to the keys embedded in the cob. It's best to use rot-resistant wood such as cedar or oak (pressure-treated wood should not used near food preparation areas) or to protect the wood with linseed oil before application. If there are any gaps between the wood door frame and the cob, fill these gaps with some spare cob.

The door will need to be made of metal. Use some scrap thick metal (24-gauge or stouter). If you can double this metal up to make an air gap, that will help keep the heat in your oven. Leave the door separate from the oven so that it can be removed, holding it in place with eye locks, dead bolts, or a clasp.

Adding a rack. You can get extra mileage out of your oven with a rack halfway up. If you want to do this, get two pieces of rebar and an extra grill rack. Before placing the roofing material on, use a masonry bit to drill out two holes larger than the rebar into the side of your oven.

Slide the rebar through one hole and, using a level, mark the spot where the rebar hits the opposite wall. Remove the rebar and drill a hole about 2 inches deep

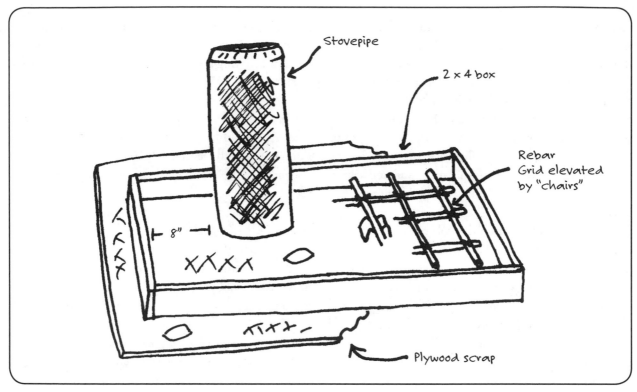

Stovepipe

2 x 4 box

Rebar Grid elevated by "chairs"

8"

Plywood scrap

FIG. 4.20.

at this spot, then put the rebar back. If the rebar is still sticking out, you'll either need to drill out the hole in the other wall more or cut the rebar with a metal blade. Repeat this in the other hole and fill the holes with cob. Place the grill rack on the two pieces of rebar. This makes an excellent place for baking and keeping foods warm.

The oven roof. If you've ever had a hankering to try out some new or forgotten roofing material, this may be the time to do it. Nothing beats roofing tin for ease of installation, and recycled rusty stuff has a classic look that complements the color of cob. Slapping some linseed oil on rusty tin yearly will get you a long-lasting roof even out of the roughest-looking pieces. Be sure to leave a few inches of roof overhang on the front and back to keep the cob out of the rain. Cut the ridge cap around the stovepipe and screw it on. Put on your stove cap if you have it.

You may find that the naturalness of cob calls for a more natural roof. In that case, you may want to consider wood shingles. These can often be purchased

from lumberyards, and you won't need many. Sometimes they're sold as framing shims, so ask for that also. Or you could make your own. Since we're not too particular about a leak or two for this project, you may want to try out making some.

Making wood shingles by hand is a dying art and uses specialized equipment like a froe and mallet. But for a small project, a chopping maul and a pair of wedges will do. Round up a dozen 2-foot sections of wood (preferably white oak) 8–10 inches in diameter. Draw parallel lines about a half inch apart across the top of the log section.

Then, working from one side to the other, use the wedges to separate the sections, alternating hits between the two wedges. This will produce a fair number of not very useful pieces in addition to the shingles, but these will make great kindling for your oven. If your wood is reasonably cured and dry, you can go ahead and affix the shingles after you make a few, leaving 6–12 inches of overhang for each layer. Be sure to leave a few inches of space between your wood shingles and the stovepipe, and cover the gap with some metal flashing. The pipe needs to extend at least a foot above the roofline.

Your cob oven is ready to go. Collect some firewood, invite some neighbors over, fire up the oven, and start making your pizza dough.

COOKING WITH BIOMASS-DERIVED LIQUID FUELS

Plants concentrate energy, and it's possible to take this concentrated energy, found in various plants' sugars and oils, and refine it into stored liquid energy. People run their cars on vegetable oil and ethanol, so it shouldn't be a surprise that you can cook with these liquid fuels, too.

What a much better use of these fuels it is to cook delicious and nourishing meals rather than expending it in the gluttonous automobile, with efficiencies typically less than 1 percent (see chapter 11). A typical taxi burns as much fuel in one day as a small family uses cooking in a year. However, the current problem is the lack of biofueled stoves on the market. We hope to see many more available in the future.

Two methods of cooking food with liquid biomass-derived fuels are possible, the first being ethanol, or drinking alcohol, which is derived from things like sugarcane, sugar beets, and, in the United States (because of massive subsidies), corn. It's also possible to run a cookstove using plant-derived oils, or what we commonly call vegetable oils, although the oils are actually derived from seeds and nuts, and not things like broccoli and spinach. Both of these stoves played an interesting role in our final departure from our formerly fossilized lives; we discuss them in more detail in the "Our Story" section earlier in this chapter.

Haybox Cooker
Renter friendly.
Project Time: One hour.
Cost: Free.
Energy Saved: Low.

FIG. 4.21. PROTOS PLANT OIL COOKER. **This stove, developed by BSH Bosch and Siemens, can use a variety of plant oils for cooking rather than firewood. This means much less pollution, fuel use, and unwanted heat in the kitchen.**
Courtesy BSH Bosch and Siemens

Ease of Use: Easy.
Maintenance Level: N/A.
Skill Levels: None.
Materials: Cooler, haybales, OR box and cushions
Tools: None.

Haybox cookers refers to any insulated boxes that finish the job of cooking begun on another stove by retaining the heat in the food. The first and easiest method of constructing one of these cookers is with bales of hay or straw, materials that are highly insulative. Things that need to be simmered for long periods of time can instead be brought to a boil and then covered with insulation. The haybox cooker then accomplishes the rest of the cooking, doing as good a job as the simmering would, but without using any additional fuel, although it does take longer. Effective cooking can continue as long at the food remains at about 180 degrees F or higher. The best thing about haybox cooking is that you don't have to worry about overcooking or burning resulting from forgotten simmering pots!

Since the principle of the haybox is so simple, there are a variety of ways to create an effective one. If you have a solar oven, then this can do double-duty as a haybox cooker on cloudy days or after nightfall. A simple insulated box with an insulated top will work just fine. For instance, a cooler could do double-duty as a haybox cooker. The less additional air space, the better. The pot could be placed in a cardboard box and covered with cushions on all sides (including the bottom). The pot could be put inside two bags with insulation sandwiched in between. And, of course, once brought to a boil and removed from the stove, the pot could be placed in a box made of four hay bales, with some scattered straw on the bottom and another bale thrown on top, again limiting the additional air space as much as possible.

The concept is simple and saves precious cooking fuel. Integrating a haybox cooker into your kitchen will help reduce your need for other forms of fuel, fossilized or not.

TABLE 4.3 Suggested Boiling and Hayboxing Times for Selected Foods		
Food	Boiling Time (minutes)	Hayboxing Time (hours)
Rice	5	1–1.5
Potatoes	5	1–2
Soup and Stock	10	2–3
Creamed Soups	2	1
Lentils	10	3–4
Pintos	10	3
Split Peas	10	2
Quinoa	5	1.5
Millet	5	1
Polenta	1	1
Winter Squash	5	1–2
Steamed Bread	30	3
Chicken	6	2–3
Beef	13	3–4

Source: Peter Scott et al., "Aprovecho's Guide to Hayboxes and Fireless Cooking," Aprovecho Research Center

COOKING WITH BIOGAS

Biogas is another name for methane (CH_4), a commonly occurring product of anaerobic decomposition. *Anaerobic* means "without oxygen," and anaerobic decomposition is what happens when organic material is broken down in a water-saturated environment, typically underwater. When this happens, an entirely different set of bacteria are involved than with typical aerobic decomposition, which is what generally happens in your compost bin and everywhere else outside not underwater. The primary bacteria involved in anaerobic decomposition are members of the family Methanobacteriaceae, the main by-products from their consumption of submerged animal waste and plant matter being methane gas, carbon dioxide, and an inert slurry of simple organic solids. As it happens, methane is flammable and is one of the finest cooking fuels known, and the inert organic solids make a fabulous garden fertilizer.

Today, biogas is produced from landfills and the waste from large animal farms and is often burned to produce electricity. But it is possible to produce a significant amount of biogas from human waste on a home-sized scale as a supplementary cooking fuel,

and where additional animal manure is available, the amount of biogas produced can be substantial. We will discuss biogas production in greater detail in chapter 9, along with directions on how to make some of your own. Although cooking does not have a large share of the fossil energy used in the home, biogas nevertheless is worth pursuing because it is such an excellent home-made cooking fuel and it accomplishes the additional energy-saving task of composting and recycling your home's humanure production.

RESOURCES

Books

Anderson, Lorraine, and Rick Palkovic. 2006. *Cooking with Sunshine: The Complete Guide to Solar Cuisine.* New York: Marlowe.

Bryden, Mark, et al. 2004. *Design Principles for Wood Burning Cook Stoves.* Eugene, OR: Aprovecho Research Center. Excellent booklet covering the basic principles in building a well-designed biomass cooker. A must-read. Downloadable from www.aprovecho.org.

Sass, Lorna. 2004. *Pressure Perfect: Two Hour Taste in Twenty Minutes Using Your Pressure Cooker*. New York: Morrow. Good recipes and information on cooking with a pressure cooker.

Internet

Aprovecho Research Center. Research papers on stove types and designs. Great site for those interested in building their own biomass cooker. www.aprovecho.org

Solar Cookers International. Great nonprofit and an excellent Web site. Also sells the CooKit premade panel cooker for around $25. www.solarcookers .org. Many how-to designs are archived at their plans page: www.solarcooking.org/plans

Solar Cooking Wiki. Collection of ideas and plans for solar cooking, including discussion and an excellent compendium of solar cookers so you don't reinvent the wheel. If you're looking to branch out and try your own solar-cooking design, this Web page is the place to start. http://solarcooking.wikia.com

Solar Oven Society. Nonprofit promoting solar ovens and makers of the highly regarded Sport Solar Oven, retailing for around $150. www.solarovens.org

Zen Stoves. Fabulous compilation of make-your-own alcohol stoves. Many can be made in just a few minutes. Great for camping and emergencies. http://zenstoves.net

Products

Lehman's Non-Electric Catalog. Lehman's sells new wood cookstoves. www.lehmans.com

Protos Plant Oil Cooker. www.plantoilcooker.com

CHAPTER 5

Refrigeration

Introduction • Our Story • Fixing Air Leaks • Efficient and Superefficient Fridges • More Fridge Thoughts • Resources

INTRODUCTION

As with all the topics covered in this book, the average household has lots of fat to trim from its refrigeration energy budget. Your family can easily adapt to less refrigerated space, most likely in positive ways. Small refrigerators mean knowing what's inside, and eating food instead of forgetting about it buried in the back. Replenishing your supply of fruits and vegetables more frequently will mean fresher and healthier food, and less going to waste. Though it started out as one the greatest inventions of all time, refrigeration has suffered woefully from the megalomania rampant in so much of American culture. We think you'll find taking a few steps back to be no trouble at all. As our refrigerator has gotten smaller over the years, we are eating more local fresh food and are less in need of refrigeration

Keeping foods cool is the easiest and most effective form of preserving their freshness and taste in the short term. Generally, the colder the better, and frozen foods can often be kept for up to a year or more, although freezing damages some foods, such as dairy products. Even providing moderate cooling can double or triple the lifetime of many staples. Mechanical refrigeration has existed for a very short time in the history of human civilization, however, and is just one of many methods for preserving food. While this chapter will focus only on methods of keeping food below ambient temperature for purposes of preservation, we think this should be only one tool out of many. Drying, canning, pickling, fermenting, jellying, salting, and smoking are time-honored methods and should also be explored.

Refrigeration takes a fairly large bite out of the average household energy budget (8 percent, according to the U.S. Department of Energy). Primarily, this is because refrigerators have inefficient compressors, are too large, are too poorly insulated, and use interior space inefficiently. That said, refrigerators have come a long way in just the past few years—inexpensive, more efficient models are now available and come close to energy parity with the most efficient and expensive models. Probably the fridge you have could use an energy upgrade, or you may already be shopping for a replacement, in which case you'll have to decide between a less expensive Energy Star model or a more

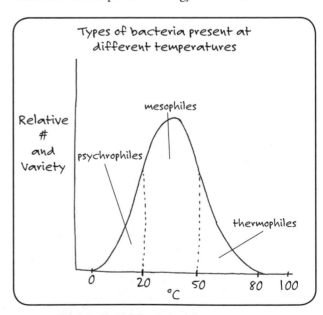

FIG. 5.1. **Food spoils quickest around room temperature, as mesophilic bacteria are the most common and reproduce rapidly.**

expensive superefficient fridge. Or it may be that once you research all the other food preservation processes, you'll decide can get by with an evaporative cooler or cold box.

Energy savings can be achieved on a much more limited financial budget if you work with what you've got rather than buying new. At a minimum, reinforcing the paltry insulation of a conventional fridge can reduce its energy use by up to half. However, we don't recommend refrigeration as a place to trim the budget. One thousand dollars spent on a new refrigerator can easily save $10,000 on photovoltaic panels later. Old refrigerators can use 6,000 watt-hours/day, as compared to new models at 1,000 watt-hours/day. Those extra 5,000 watt-hours would need on average 1,000 extra watts of PV array for power, which at the normal installed cost of $10/watt would equal $10,000.

When refrigeration is used, it's important to make the most of the available refrigerated space. Often refrigerated are items that need only to be stored in a cool location, these include bread, peanut butter, and many fruits and vegetables. Food at the back of the fridge, due to its inaccessibility, gets forgotten and can often turn into repositories of mold and fungus that can infect other stored items.

A simple remedy to this problem is the use of storage containers for a wider variety of items than the simple dairy and meat drawers. These come in a dizzying array of sizes and colors and can be easily stacked to take advantage of unused space near the top of shelves. Items that are used together often, such as salad ingredients, can be stored together to minimize the amount of time we spend rooting around in the fridge with the door hanging open.

In addition to refrigeration, other methods can be combined with cooling for extra effect. Dehydrated fruits and vegetables will last longer in a chilled environment. A solar, cob, or regular oven (see chapter 4) can be easily modified to facilitate dehydration by using it at lower temperatures, often simply by cracking the door. All kinds of milk, fresh or pasteurized, will keep longer in a cooler if first boiled and

cooled, and then stored in a sealed container. If you want the benefits of unpasteurized milk, you'll need to consume it quickly. Fresh meats keep better if rubbed with salt and wrapped in paper before being placed in the cooler. Cured meats can be rubbed with baking soda to prevent mold growth before being wrapped in paper and going in the cooler.

While refrigeration can improve the life of many fresh fruits and vegetables, they can suffer if the environment is too damp, especially if they are in direct contact with water. Many summer fruits suffer in taste and texture if refrigerated. Tomatoes are a great example. Often, the best method of storage is in hanging baskets in a sunless, cool part of the home. Softer fruits and vegetables store best when not in contact with one another, so arrange them on a cooking sheet or platter and cover with a cloth. Check all fruits and vegetables often, making sure to remove any that are beginning to show signs of decay, and consume these quickly or discard.

Hard cheeses, breads, and baked goods store best in metal containers. If items begin to mold, cut away the mold and disinfect the interior of the box with boiling water or vinegar, dry, then reseal.

Practicing these simple storage techniques can prolong the life of most fresh foods and minimize waste, even without access to any refrigeration. This ensures hard work in the garden or money spent at the grocery or farmers' market is not wasted.

OUR STORY

Our refrigeration choice ended up being fairly conventional. As we bought our home at the end of the hot Carolina summer, we needed some way to keep our food cool. Since our house is actually a duplex and we inhabit the southern side, we didn't even have the option of building a north-side icebox, although this idea has intrigued us for quite a while.

We ended up purchasing a new Frigidaire Energy Star model sized at 14.8 cubic feet. We wanted to have some freezer space for easy surplus food preservation, and, for us, there is ample room in this model for that purpose. Actually, we had wanted the 10–12 cubic-foot option, but our urban area is not large enough (or our fellow city-dwellers are not energy-conscious enough) for any local retailers to stock any of these models, so we have a bit more room in the fridge than we usually use.

We used plenty of double-sided carpet tape to attach sections of blueboard insulation on the sides, front, and top, covering the front with an additional layer of corkboard to hide the insulation and provide a message board space. We're not big fans of petroleum-based insulation, but space requirements and its ability to hold itself up made it the best choice for this application. Since our fridge and wood cookstove were going to share the same space, we cleaned out the pantry and installed the fridge there, installing a door to close up the pantry and keep the fridge from being over-worked by the woodstove (and hiding the blueboard insulation from sight). Next, we drilled holes through the floor of the pantry into the basement below just in front of the bottom of the fridge where it sucks in fresh air. Then we put a directional vent cover over the holes to direct this cooler air into the fridge air intake. (Our Frigidaire model actually takes in air on the left side and vents the warmer air out the right, so it was important to segregate these two airflows.) If we get around to insulating the bottom of the floor, we'll need to extend some pipes from the floor through the insulation to allow access to the fresh air coming from the basement.

This all worked reasonably well, and our 1.2-kilowatt solar array doesn't have a problem with keeping the fridge going, even in hot, cloudy weather. The fridge and insulation totaled less than $450, so compared with the superefficient fridges, many of which are $1,000 or more, it was considerably less expensive.

FIXING AIR LEAKS

An easy way to check for air leaks in your fridge is to use incense. Visible smoke is an excellent way to

FIG. 5.2. **A locking clasp can be installed on a refrigerator to keep it tightly closed and limit air leaks.**

detect drafts, so close all the doors and windows to the room and light up a stick and pass it along all the edges of both the freezer and the fridge door. Ideally, the smoke should be unaffected by its proximity to the refrigerator and will meander upward. But if there is a portion of the door where a draft shoots the smoke out into the room, then you are losing a significant amount of your fridge's coolness and running up your energy bills. Open the offending door and check to make sure the gasket is still in good repair, without any damage or becoming unstuck from the frame. Replace or reglue any sections that need it. Check the hinges to make sure they are not loose and in need of tightening.

If all these things appear in order and you still have a draft, then installing a locking clasp (also called a draw catch) on the errant door should solve your problem. The most common type looks like the one shown in figure 5.2.

This is the same type of clasp that is common on toolboxes and lunch pails. Installation is straightforward. Position the entire clasp on the side of the door, making sure all the screw holes sit where they can be attached, as near the problem area as possible. Take the larger section (the half with the loop) and place it on the side of the fridge next to the door in the chosen location. Mark the screw holes and predrill using a bit specified for metal that is slightly smaller than your metal screws, making sure not to push the drill too far into the fridge when your hole finally opens up. Screw the larger part of the clasp on. Now find where the smaller part of the clasp needs to go on the side of the door, making sure the door is closed tightly by leaning against it. Doing another smoke test with tell you if you're fixing the problem. Then mark your holes, predrill, and attach. Lock your fridge closed and check again for drafts. If it still leaks, you may be able to add some extra weather-stripping next to the gasket. The clasp will add an additional step to opening your fridge; while this may be a hassle some of the time, it will also help prevent unnecessary opening.

Insulation Of Existing Fridge

Renter friendly.

Project Time: Weekend.

Cost: Inexpensive ($50–100, depending on type of insulation used and size of frame to hold it).

Energy Saved: High. Average refrigeration uses 8 percent of the household energy budget. Insulating your refrigerator can reduce energy use by up to 50 percent.

Ease of Use: Easy. Does not affect day-to-day use.

Maintenance Level: Low. Lengthens life of fridge by reducing the compressor load.

Skill Levels: Carpentry: Moderate.

Materials: 2 × 4s, insulation, paneling, connector plates, screws, and nails.

Tools: Saw, drill, hammer.

Most household refrigerators needlessly use excess energy simply because they are poorly insulated or they do not close properly. Insulation can be added to the sides, top, and doors to greatly improve your existing refrigerator's performance. If you are considering putting a wood cookstove in your kitchen, then extra insulation is a must. Ideally, your fridge would be separated from any heat source by being enclosed in its own closet.

Because refrigerators work by radiating heat off the coils attached to the back (often covered with sheet metal in newer models), it is important to maximize airflow on this side, so insulation here is not a good idea. On every other side, the poorly insulated walls of the fridge allow precious cold air to leak out.

The easiest if not the most attractive way to insulate an existing fridge is to glue or tape insulation board to the sides and top. Cut the side panels so that they extend beyond the top of the fridge to the height of

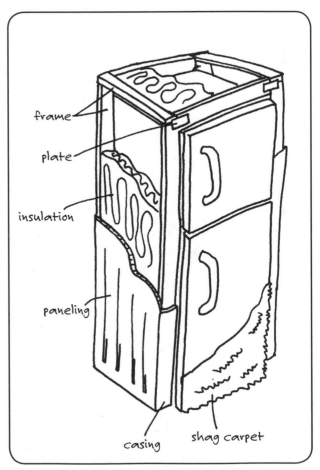

FIG. 5.3. **If your fridge is accessible, building an insulated frame around it is straightforward.**

the insulation you put on top. Carpet or corkboard or other panels can be used to hide the insulation and add a little more protection. Alternatively, corkboard or carpet can be applied on their own, although the insulating effect will be substantially reduced. Use only a few dabs of construction adhesive to hold the insulation and carpeting or panels in place, or use plenty of two-sided carpet tape, and make sure the surface is clean and dry.

For the fridge and freezer doors, it's probably best to skip the insulation, as the constant opening and closing could result in the bulky panels getting knocked off. Apply corkboard or carpeting directly to the doors, working around the handles. Clean the front of both doors with a nontoxic household cleaner such as vinegar or baking soda. Then simply cut out the right size of carpet or board and apply two-sided carpeting tape or a few daubs of construction adhesive around the perimeter and in a few strips in between. Get your edge lined up properly (rolling up the carpet will help), and then slowly apply the material. Shag carpet looks best and will impress your friends, who will secretly pet your fridge as they reach in for a beer.

For a top-notch insulating job that will look like fabulous cabinetry, build a 2 × 4 wall on each side, to a height of 3½ inches (one stud width) above the top of the fridge. Run a 2 × 4 along the front and back in between the two walls and connect with a plate. Fill in the two sides and top with the insulating material of your choice (see chapter 7). The sides of the box can be paneled and the front trimmed out for a sharp-looking fridge upgrade. Again, for the doors apply corkboard or carpeting directly.

Evaporative Cooling Box
Renter friendly.
Project Time: Afternoon.
Cost: Inexpensive ($5–50, depending on materials used).
Energy Saved: High. Can be high if used to replace an electric refrigerator. Can also quickly be made

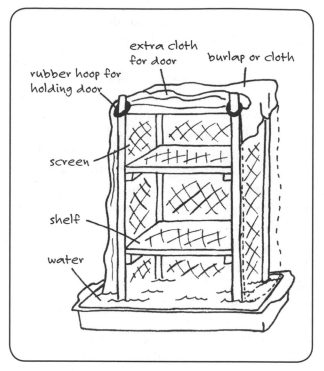

FIG. 5.4. **An evaporative cooler box.**

during camping trips or blackouts when no other refrigeration is available.
Ease of Use: Medium. Food temperature will be uneven, and in summertime the box will be considerably warmer than a mechanical refrigerator, resulting in quicker spoilage.
Maintenance Level: High. Pan must be kept filled with water. If kept outside, animal intrusion is a concern. The water will eventually degrade the wood and metal in the structure. If used for long periods of time, the covering cloth will need to be laundered regularly and will eventually degrade.
Skill Levels: Carpentry: Basic.
Materials: A large pan, wood or bamboo for shelving and basic framing, clean cloth or burlap, screen, nails or screws, old bike tires, staples.
Tools: Hammer or drill, saw, scissors, stapler.

Easily the most adaptable of all food-cooling contraptions is an evaporative cooler. Taking advantage of the fact that as water evaporates it draws heat out of the air, this type of cooler can be constructed in a variety of ways from the slapdash to the sturdy. The

FIG. 5.5. **Popularized in Africa by Mohammed Bah Abba, the zeer pot is a simple evaporative cooler used for preserving fresh foods. The space between the two pots is kept filled with sand and water, and a cloth covers the inner pot. As the water evaporates, it brings down the temperature of the food in the inner pot, keeping it fresher longer. Mohammed Bah Abba won the Rolex Award for his efforts in 2000.** Courtesy Rolex Awards/Tomas Bertelsen

basic premise is to keep food in the shade and covered with, but not touching, a wet cloth. The cloth is kept wet through capillary action by having its edges hang in a pan of water. The pan of water also helps keep away ants and roaches. The breezier the location, the better, as this will increase the evaporation rate and keep the temperature down.

Traditional evaporative coolers. This is the basic principle of the zeer pot, commonly used in West Africa for keeping fruits and vegetables fresh. In the zeer pot, a smaller clay pot fits inside a larger one. The gap between the two pots is filled with sand and then with water on a regular basis (usually once or twice a day). Fruit, veggies, and leftovers are placed in the smaller pot, which is covered with a lid or cloth. The water in between the pots slowly evaporates, keeping the food cool. Another example is the

coolgardie safe, an evaporative cooler that was quite common in Australia at the beginning of the twentieth century. Both these systems work best in drier climates.

Impromptu coolers. The simplest method of creating an evaporative cooler is with found objects around the house. It would be easy to combine a couple of garden pots of different sizes and some sand to make an effective small cooler similar to the zeer pot. Be forewarned that some ceramic garden pots have lead in the glaze, which could potentially spread to any stored food.

Building the box. For longer-term use or for more space, building a screened box with scrap wood or bamboo with a functioning door could be a big help. The principles are similar. The food sits on shelves above a pan of water covered with cloth. This can be kept in the home, out of the sun in a breezy location. The basic structure should look like figure 5.4.

A basic box frame is built, of any size and with the desired shelf arrangement; shelves should be made of slats or other material to promote air circulation and maintain even temperature and humidity. The two sides, top, and back can be kept bug-free by stapling on screen, as the cloth alone is usually not completely effective in keeping out flies and other bugs. Note that ungalvanized screen will rust relatively rapidly, so use stainless steel or nylon.

The door. The door is made separately. Cross-bracing will help ensure durability. Staple the screen to the door. Hinge the door on the top of the cooler, or leave it disconnected and hold it in place with rotating pieces of wood or rubber hoops made from cut-up strips of spent bike tires. The door can be left free of cloth. A flap of additional cloth can be left on the top of the evaporative cooler to cover the door when it is closed.

Variations on the theme. There could be many impromptu variations on this theme, based on one's resources, needs, and time. It's important to remember to take the simple steps for food storage described in the beginning of this chapter, because generally speaking an evaporative cooler will reduce the interior temperature only by about 15 degrees F (8 degrees C) compared to the ambient air temperature. Often this is well above the desired constant 40 degrees F (4 degrees C) of conventional refrigerators. Nevertheless, as the graph in the introduction relates, even a 15-degree F reduction will help inhibit the populations of fast-growing mesophilic bacteria that can spoil food quickly.

Northern Window Conversion To Cold Box
Renter friendly.
Project Time: Weekend.
Cost: Inexpensive ($50–100, but can be built with scraps, except the thermometer).
Energy Saved: High. Average refrigeration uses 8 percent of the average American energy budget.

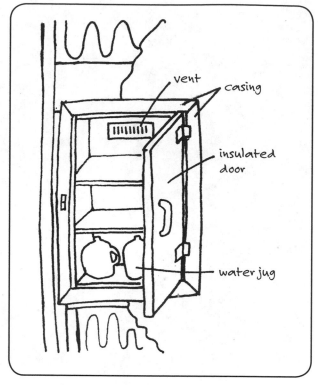

FIG. 5.6. **A window cold box.**

Ease of Use: Medium. Food temperature can be uneven, making it a little less effective than a conventional refrigerator. Requires some attention to ensure proper function.

Maintenance Level: Low. A well-built box, protected from the rain, should last longer than a conventional fridge.

Skill Levels: Carpentry: Moderate.

Materials: Plywood, insulation, wood glue, screws, paint, caulking, gallon jugs, closable heating vent, thermometer.

Tools: Hammer, flat bar, drill, saw caulking gun, paintbrush.

Many existing homes have an excess of windows on the north side. Ideally, no more than 5 percent of a home's windows will be on the north side, as windows inevitably lead to draftiness and heat loss in the wintertime, and northern windows are the biggest offenders. If you live in a cold climate and are in a home that has a north-facing window convenient to the kitchen, removing that window and converting it to an icebox

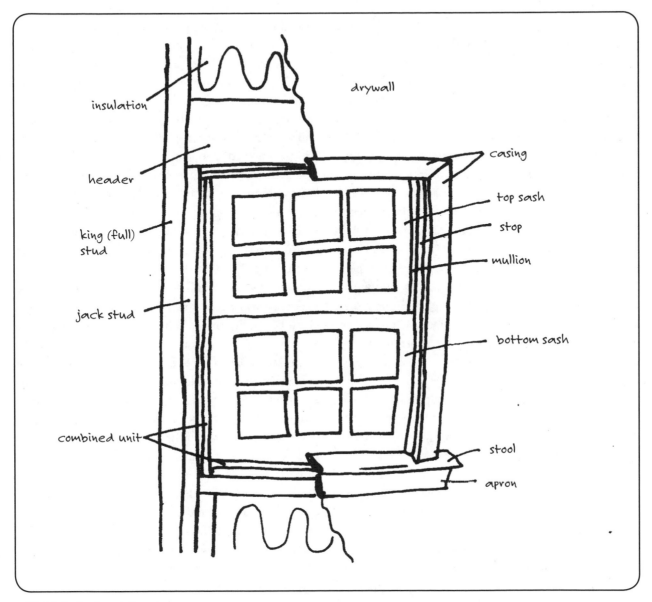

FIG. 5.7. **Parts of a window.**

could provide your refrigeration needs for over half the year. And this energy savings will come at a time when solar electric energy production is low due to short days, saving precious watts for other needs like lighting and movie watching.

Your goal in building a cold box is to take advantage of the coldest part of your home to do the work of preserving food, rather than using an energy-intensive appliance that cools down food in the heated part of your home. You will want to regulate this cold box to provide optimum unfrozen freshness while keeping the cold from entering your living space.

The basic cold box structure consists of a plywood box with an insulated door. A closable vent allows for temperature control. The vent is opened at night to allow in cold air and closed in the morning. In extremely cold places, it might be necessary to do the reverse and open the box for some part of the day in order to keep the box closer to 40 degrees F (4 degrees C) and above freezing. The shelf arrangement can vary to suit your needs but should allow for some movement of air within the box to maintain an even temperature. If you live in a climate where the average temperature is below freezing for a substantial part of the year, you can include a separate freezer compartment at the bottom of the box (remember, cold air sinks).

A great way to regulate temperature is with some kind of thermal mass that takes a while to heat up and cool down. The best readily available thermal mass is water. Plastic water jugs can be placed on the bottom shelf to maintain an even temperature, reducing overheating in warm spells and freezing in cold ones. Generally, the cold box will work whenever the nighttime temperature falls below 40 degrees F (4 degrees C), although it will still be somewhat effective at higher temperatures. Operation in colder environments may include replacing frozen water jugs with room-temperature water jugs, or increasing the insulation on the exterior of the cold box, or both. A thermometer (especially the min/max recording type) can be a big help to determining how well your cold box is working. During the shoulder seasons (spring and fall), adding ice in a bucket or tray to the top shelf can prolong the box's usefulness. Using a cold box into the summertime becomes difficult. In addition to the warm days, there's a good chance the outside of the box will get heated up by the morning and afternoon sun.

Measuring the window. If working during cold weather, before removing the window you'll want to build your cold box and have it ready to install. By removing the trim surrounding the interior of the window, you will expose the framing that locks the window unit into place without exposing the space to the outside, and you'll be able to get an accurate measurement of the rough framing in order to construct the cold box.

To remove the interior trim, first break the paint around the window by using a utility knife to cut around the window where it hits the wall. Then use a hammer to knock a flat bar between the trim and window unit (on the inside of the window so as not to damage the wall material) and pry it off. The framing

should now be exposed, making an accurate measurement possible.

To take accurate measurements for your box, you'll need to determine if your window is a **single unit** or if it is **double hung**. Newer windows are single units and are connected to the house framing with finish nails through the exterior trim. Since the entire unit will be removed, you can measure the rough opening (the 2 × 4s) to determine the size of your box. Double-hung windows are built in place and are typically found in older homes. Your cold box will fit into the space occupied by one or both sashes. By removing the bottom sash (after removing one of the stops), you can measure the opening and build the exterior dimensions of your box to this size (actually a little smaller to make sure you can fit it in). For both types of windows, you'll be sliding the cold box in from the outside, so keep this in mind as you measure and build.

Constructing the cold box. Building the box is straightforward, just like building a basic cabinet. The easiest material to use is plywood. Three-quarter inch is ideal, although ⅝-inch or ½-inch should also work. Cut the back of the cold box first. Next, cut out the perimeter sides, top, and bottom. You'll want these to be at least as deep as the water jugs that will rest on the bottom, with clearance for the insulated door. Glue the sides, top, and bottom to the back and screw together with 2-inch screws.

Building the shelves. The shelves need to leave room for air to circulate to maintain an even temperature, so if you're building them with wood, be sure to leave an inch of clearance between them and the insulation of the door. Alternatively, these could be built out of a simple frame stapled with hardware cloth. Old fridge shelves could potentially be modified to slide in. The unit needs to be primed, caulked, and painted on the inside and outside to ensure longevity. The interior environment will be moist, so protecting the wood is important. If the back will stick outside near to or beyond the eave of the roof, the exposed portion of the box will need some kind of roofing to shed water away from the house.

Removing windows. To remove a single-unit window, you'll need to pry the window free from the

Simplifying Coldbox Operation

The northern window box has the potential to be operated with much lower daily maintenance with the incorporation of a thermostatically controlled vent. While this would involve a source of electricity, the amount of power used would be minimal. Incorporated into the back of the icebox and set to open when temperatures are in a given range, from, say 32 degrees F to 45 degrees F, the automatic vent would regulate the interior temperature, keeping it from wild diversions outside of this range that would spoil or freeze food.

interior. When your cold box is built and ready to install, start the removal of the window unit from the inside of the house by sliding the curved end of your flat bar between the exterior casing and the outside of the rough framing and prying. Work your way around the window, making sure not to free the window completely, as it could drop to the ground. If you're at all worried about this, have someone else outside to steady and catch the window, in which case you can continue prying until the unit is free. If you're by yourself, loosen the window until you can see a gap between the casing and the adjacent siding on at least one side. Then go outside and, still using the flat bar, pry the window free from first one side and then the other. The moment when the window comes free can be tricky, especially if you're up on a ladder. Employ a helper to steady the window from the inside if you're at all uncomfortable.

If you have a double-hung window (composed of two separate sashes), the window will be easier to disassemble. The casing, stool, and apron can be left in place and the cold box can be fit inside the window casing from the outside once the sash or sashes are removed. If you remove the window stop on one side the bottom sash will come free into the inside of your home. The top sash could potentially be held in place

by an additional stop, or it may be possible to easily remove it once the bottom sash is removed.

If the bottom sash is weighted, the ropes will have to be cut to remove it. Potentially, you could build a small cold box that simply replaced the bottom sash. Or, alternatively, the bottom sash could simply be opened and screwed into the top sash to steady it, and a cold box could be built underneath it. If you're going to remove the bottom sash, you want to make sure not to lose the weights into the wall when you cut the sash free. Put a screw into the casing, hold on to the rope above where you cut it, and then tie the rope around the screw.

Installing the cold box. To install your box you'll need to enlist some help. Once your box is built, remove the sash and slide the cold box into the opening from the outside. Have your partner properly position the box and then screw it into place while you hold it steady.

Adding the cold box door. The cold box door can also be made of plywood, either a sandwich with plywood in between or just a single sheet of plywood with some insulation board glued to the inside. Attach with hinges. The door can be held closed using a sliver of wood that turns on a nail or screw or a locking clasp.

Place your jugs of water in the bottom and once the cold weather arrives, you're ready to go. Since installation in a traditional window is straightforward, you might consider seasonal use of the cold box, replacing it with the sashes during summertime.

EFFICIENT AND SUPEREFFICIENT FRIDGES

The most traditional approach to scaling down your food-storage energy requirements is to replace an older fridge with a newer model that is much more efficient. If your fridge is old, assume it is an energy hog until proven otherwise. To measure the actual electrical consumption for an individual appliance, a meter (such as the Kill-a-Watt) is an excellent item to have around. This may be the only way to determine how much juice your current fridge is drawing, since it's very difficult to determine the amount of time your fridge is on and hence its energy usage.

While there is a decent range of well-made, small, and efficient refrigerators, getting your hands on one can be a challenge. Many mainstream retailers are only starting to stock them, and direct shipping costs for such a bulky item can easily exceed $200. But efficient refrigerator technology is starting to spread and compared to even three years ago refrigerators have progressed by leaps and bounds. As an additional caveat, you might be tempted to think that the smaller the fridge, the less energy it uses, but this would be a mistake. It can be the case that smaller 2- to 4-cubic-foot dorm fridges use more energy than Energy Star–rated 15-cubic-foot home fridges. The difference is in the quality of the compressor that is doing the work and the level of insulation included.

Refrigeration has long been a thorn in the side of those wishing to power their homes with renewable energy. When photovoltaic enthusiasts started going completely off-grid in the mid-1970s, one of the biggest challenges was keeping food cold. The existing refrigerators were enormous, poorly insulated behemoths that would wrestle all but the largest PV systems into the ground. Renewable electricity pioneers were often forced to buy propane refrigerators, saving their precious watts for lighting and other necessities like water pumping.

Since then, the market has responded, although there's more room for improvement. Technical advances have improved the efficiency of the compressors, insulation has been beefed up, models have AC (common household alternating current) or DC (direct current from batteries or photovoltaics) power options, and many are top opening to ensure the best cold retention (although taking up more space).

In particular, three companies—SunDanzer, Sunfrost, and Vestfrost—have stepped in and started making high-quality fridges that are much lighter on the average energy budget, but hard on the wallet. As is common in many aspects of renewable energy, much of the cost must be borne up front.

In addition, smaller refrigerators made more for the low-voltage DC marine and RV market can be

Variations

Using electricity of any variety to keep food cold when it's already cold outside is just plain old bad engineering. Fridges have been designed to take advantage of the existing cold (rather than create new cold) by tinkerers ever since humans moved inside. The icebox is the simplest method of doing this, but there are lots of other ways to conceive of getting some of that cold into the insulated box where we store our perishable food. People become so accustomed to having things the way they are that they often overlook easy solutions. We'll never forget when a bad ice storm in December 2002 knocked out electricity for days in our area. Freezing rain brought down limbs and electric lines. On the third or fourth day of the blackout, the newspaper ran an article about how lots of folks were having to throw out their food because it was rotting inside their refrigerators! It hadn't been above freezing for a week and there were piles of ice just outside everyone's front door, which could have easily been moved into a low-tech cooler, or into the refrigerator itself (in plastic bags to contain the meltwater).

Sunfrost, a company discussed in the next section, made a few hybrid models using both electricity and outside cold that used 40 percent less energy than their already very efficient models, but these were discontinued due to lack of interest. It's time to get interested again!

purchased from outfitters and further insulated to improve their performance. Novakool is a brand that makes several smaller DC fridges that provide plenty of refrigerator space for families who use that space wisely, making them a worthwhile off-grid option.

One option to consider is a superefficient freezer combined with one of the nonelectric refrigeration

TABLE 5.1 Readily Available Medium-sized Energy Star Refrigerator Models		
Model	Size (Interior Cubic Feet)	kWh/year
Frigidaire	14.8	376
Kenmore	14.8	376
Maytag	14.64	376
Whirlpool	14.54	372

Source: www.energystar.gov

TABLE 5.2 Smaller Energy Star Refrigerators Often Available in Urban Areas		
Model	Size (Interior Cubic Feet)	kWh/year
Absocold	10.3	331
Avanti	11	277
Classic 50's	9.5	285
Danby	9.5	285
Summit	9.5	285
Vestfrost ConServ	10.5	~low 200's*

*This fridge was not rated by Energy Star. The watt numbers come from the company.
Source: www.energystar.gov

options detailed earlier in this chapter. Keeping food cool without machines is less of a challenge than keeping food frozen. And freezing food is an excellent, simple method of preservation for excess bounties of in-season fruits and vegetables. In addition, ice from the freezer can be used in a cold box or cooler in the summer.

To keep the fridge's energy use within the range of a renewable energy system, we'd like to keep its energy consumption at around 1,000 watt-hours (1 kWh) a day at 70 degrees F (or around 365 kWh/year, as the mandated energy label will describe it), with the most square footage per watt. The choices available break down into three general categories. For the commonly available models, we are looking only at combined refrigerator/freezers. If you're interested in only a freezer or fridge or just want more specifics, check out the Energy Star Web site (www.energystar.gov); go through the appliances link, then to the refrigerators section.

Readily available, Energy Star models. There are a few readily available models at 15 cubic feet that use only around 1 kWh/day and cost between $400 and $600. One or more of these models should be commonly sold by any major retailer (try to use a locally owned one) in your area. Although these fridges are better insulated than most, they can still greatly benefit from additional insulation (see "Insulation of Existing Fridge" earlier in this chapter). Table 5.1 lists the major brands of 2007 Energy Star–rated 15-cubic-foot fridge/freezer models, typically the smallest widely available size at large retailers.

Smaller models, available in urban areas. In more urban areas with lots of condos and apartments there tends to be more availability of several models in the

9- to 10-cubic-foot range that are Energy Star rated (plenty of room if you're not planning on storing lots of fresh garden produce). It may be worthwhile to call the retailers in your area and see if any of these models are available. Sometimes they have to be ordered a few weeks in advance. Generally, they retail again in the $400–$600 range (except the Vestfrost, which is about twice that but uses less energy). Many of these models can also be ordered directly through wholesalers, usually at around $200 direct shipping. If you have access to a vehicle that can cart a fridge around, ask about picking up the fridge at the shipper, as this can often cut the shipping cost by half. Table 5.2 lists the Energy Star model for each brand's 10- to-11-cubic-foot refrigerator/freezer.

Superefficient, designed for limited renewable energy budget. The last category is the superefficient plug-in models. Much of the impetus for their creation was to operate on the limited energy budget of an off-grid home. Expect to pay about $2,000 shipped for the equivalent of 12 cubic feet of fridge/freezer space. They generally use about 170 kWh/year.

Sundanzer is powered by DC (direct current) instead of AC (alternating current), reducing losses associated with converting the DC current created by off-grid systems into the AC current of the typical house and also reducing or eliminating starting surges. They are also top-openers, which do a much better job of retaining the coolness than front-openers. As such, they often take up more space. This is especially true since Sundanzer does not offer a combo fridge/freezer.

Absorption Refrigerators

An alternative method of refrigeration from the standard compressor fridge is what is known as a gas-absorption refrigerator. Typical fridges take heat out of the air in the fridge using a liquid with a very low boiling point, such as freon. By putting freon under pressure with the compressor, the fridge converts the gas into a liquid at a very cold temperature. As the liquid evaporates into a gas, it pulls heat out of the air in the fridge and freezer. This gas is then compressed again and the cycle starts over.

Absorption refrigerators also cool by evaporation, except they use ammonia trapped in a hydrogen environment. After the ammonia evaporates, drawing heat out of the air, it combines with the hydrogen to form water. Heat is then used to boil the ammonia off the water and return it to the hydrogen environment. Propane refrigerators, commonly found in recreational vehicles, boats, and some off-grid homes, operate on the same principles. The main difference in the ammonia versions is that the cycle is powered by a source of heat, such as solar power or waste heat, instead of an electric generator or battery.

Solar-powered gas-absorption refrigerators have been around for a quarter-century or so, most homemade by skilled tinkerers. A few have been mass-produced. Fridges of this type are often referred to as intermittent solar ammonia-water absorption cycle, or ISAAC, refrigerators. The idea is intriguing because the fridge has no moving parts and, theoretically, nothing to wear out, giving it a potential life span well beyond that of an electric compressor refrigerator. The main hurdle is the ammonia, which is poisonous if handled improperly and is therefore difficult to obtain and work with and is probably not suitable for residential use. It is possible to use other refrigerants. Energy Concepts is a company based in Maryland that makes solar-powered absorption refrigerators, although only for larger industrial customers.

Sunfrost offers more traditional front-opening models. They sell separate models for fridges and freezers but also have combos and also offer AC or DC models.

Both companies have good reputations. The drawback is the cost and, with the *Sundanzer*, fitting the models into an existing fridge space. With a grid-tied home, it may make more sense to use the additional money above the cost of a mainstream Energy Star fridge to purchase extra solar panels and go to the additional trouble of insulating the fridge. Superefficient fridges can make sense for off-grid homes, possibly saving more than their cost in the additional batteries and large PV array a less efficient fridge would require.

It's irksome that smaller, more efficient fridges are not readily available. Given how vital food preservation is to a comfortable life, there should be more energy-wise options out there to supplement the fairly pathetic Energy Star models or the expensive cost and delivery of the Sundanzer or Sunfrost models. The room for improvement is vast, and will hopefully include methods of accessing some of the outside coolness, potentially with radiators. Bugging your local retailer about the lack of options can only help hasten the arrival of better choices.

MORE FRIDGE THOUGHTS

People have, of course, been trying to keep food from going bad for thousands of years. Using the earth's own coolness is a common, time-tested way of preserving foods, especially root crops. For folks who are planning on growing lots of their own food or purchasing in bulk from a grower, an underground root cellar will save prodigious quantities of energy compared with a mechanically operated refrigerator. There is more up-front work, but just like accessing solar energy, the coolness of the earth will be there for as long as we are around. See the resources section for more information.

Similarly, if water storage will eventually be incorporated into your dwelling, it may be possible to access the constant temperatures and high thermal storage of water to store food, or even cool your house. Many homes, not being oriented for good solar exposure, could benefit from converting one of the northern-most rooms into water storage and expanding the south-facing portion of the home for passive solar gain with, for example, an attached greenhouse. Isolating this water storage room from the rest of the house with insulation would provide a buffer from winter chill, while maintaining a high-enough temperature to keep the water from freezing. The stored coolness of this room has the potential to act as a refrigerator in the winter and as a source of air conditioning in the summer. At this point this is just theory, as we've never seen or heard of any homes where this has been incorporated, but the reasoning seems sound to us.

Converting a chest freezer to a refrigerator results in a surprising amount of energy savings. This is because of the top-opening aspect of chest freezers (they have less cold loss when opened, as the cold doesn't roll out the bottom like with a conventional refrigerator door) and the fact that they are generally better insulated than standard residential refrigerators (even Energy Star models). The process is fairly straightforward, a matter of taking out the thermostat and replacing it with one that turns on and off at a higher temperature. This procedure is quite popular with homebrew-beer hobbyists who can fit kegs more easily in chest-style refrigerators. Those with a little electrical knowledge can simply remove the thermostat from an old refrigerator (these can be found at the local dump in the white goods section), remove the freezer thermostat, and replace it with the old refrigerator one. Alternatively, those without electrical skills can purchase a plug-in thermostat from homebrew shops that specialize in that kind of thing. They generally cost around $60.

RESOURCES

Books
Bubel, Mike, and Nancy Bubel. 1991. *Root Cellaring: Natural Cold Storage of Fruits and Vegetables.* Pownal, VT: Storey Publishing.

Delong, Deanna. 1992. *How to Dry Foods.* Los Angeles: HPBooks.

Farmers of Centre Terre Vivante. 2007. *Preserving Food without Freezing or Canning: Traditional Techniques Using Salt, Oil, Sugar, Alcohol, Vinegar, Drying, Cold Storage, and Lactic Fermentation.* White River Junction, VT: Chelsea Green Publishing.

Janssen, Jules, J. A. 1995. *Building with Bamboo: A Handbook.* Practical Action.

Katz, Sandor Ellix. 2003. *Wild Fermentation: The Flavor, Nutrition, and Craft of Live-Culture Foods.* White River Junction, VT: Chelsea Green Publishing.

Internet
Absorption refrigerator. Hildrand, et al. (2000). "A New Solar Powered Absorption Refrigerator with High Performance." Available at http://igt .heig-vd.ch/web/IMG/pdf/article_pour_site_ internet.pdf

Energy consumption comparisons of new-model fridges. www.energystar.gov/index.cfm?c=refrig .pr_refrigerators

Evaporative cooler. The *Coolgardie Safe* Web site includes a link to basic instructions on building a coolgardie safe. http://peacecorps.mtu .edu/resources/studentprojects/BryanJames /Coolgardie.htm

Freezer-to-fridge conversion. The Mt. Best site is worth a visit for lots of other low energy house ideas, too. http://mtbest.net/chest_fridge.html

Outside cold-assisted refrigerator by Sunfrost.
www.sunfrost.com/passive_refrig.html

Root cellars. Good site with lots of information
on building and using a root cellar. http://
waltonfeed.com/old/cellars.html

Zeer pot. Mohammed Bah Abba is credited with
repopularizing this traditional cooling technique
in Nigeria, and is the winner of 2006 Rolex
Award for Enterprise for his efforts. www
.rolexawards.com/laureates/laureate-6-bah_abba
.html

Products

ISAAC solar ice maker. From Energy Concepts,
manufacturers of industrial absorption coolers.
www.energy-concepts.com/isaac.html

Micromatic freezer-to-fridge temperature controller.
www.micromatic.com/draft-keg-beer/kegerator
-conversion-kits-cid-785.html

CHAPTER SIX

Domestic Hot Water

*Introduction • The Alternatives • Our Story •
Comparing Solar Water-Heating Systems • Resources*

INTRODUCTION

Let's face it: hot water is one of those modern luxuries that has definitely made the transition to necessity. Hot-water heaters, whether gas or electric, generally consume 20 to 30 percent of the household energy budget.

Electricity is one of the least efficient ways to heat water or air. Over three-quarters of the electricity in the United States is provided by natural gas and coal, which are burned to turn water into steam, the steam turning turbines to create electricity, with efficiency losses and pollution all along the way. So when you think about pulling that precious electricity into your home and turning it back into heat for your water, it starts to seem a little wasteful. That said, lots of us are stuck with electric water heaters. Maybe electricity was a little cheaper than gas when you went shopping for a new tank, or perhaps an electric water heater was sitting in your basement when you bought your house and you never gave it much thought. Fortunately, even without replacing your current water heater, there are lots of simple things you can do to reduce your dependence on fossil fuels: reset the thermostat on your water heater to a lower temperature, insulate your hot-water tank and hot-water lines, use low-flow shower heads and faucet aerators, and last, but definitely not least, *fix any leaking faucets*! (Don't put off fixing leaks just because you don't want to hire a plumber. Anyone with a wrench and a how-to book can change out a faucet fixture or fix a leak.)

THE ALTERNATIVES

The most common models of domestic electric water heaters draw in the vicinity of 4,500 watts when heating. This is a large load to expect a reasonably sized solar electric (photovoltaic) system to provide. Thus, when you convert your hot-water system away from fossil fuels, better ways exist to obtain hot water than using photovoltaics to produce electricity that would then be turned into heat. The best choice is using solar energy directly to heat water. If you don't have a sunny site that's appropriate for a solar hot-water heater, then you may have to settle for reducing your hot-water-related carbon emissions rather than eliminating them altogether.

The thing to ponder first when thinking about changing your current setup is this: how much hot water do you really use? Are there six people living in your house or two? How cold is your environment? People take longer, hotter showers in the depth of winter and shorter, colder showers in summer. If you live in the desert southwest, do you really need a constant supply of hot water? How much carbon will you eliminate from your life by installing a complex solar water-heating system if you don't use that much hot water to begin with? Read through the alternatives below with the answers to these questions in mind.

Solar water heaters (also called solar thermal). If you use hot water daily and have a south- or west-facing sunny roof that gets close to five hours of sun a day, you need to seriously consider installing a solar hot-water heater. Solar water heaters are the *best solar investment* we know of. Even if your sunniest spot encounters periods of shade throughout the day, a solar water heater can still work well (unlike photovoltaics, which falter in only partial shade). The payback time can easily be less than five years, the technology works amazingly well, and they're not as electronically complicated as photovoltaics. Solar water heaters can provide up to 100 percent of your hot-water needs. Average production from a household solar thermal system can provide around 80 percent of the hot water, but with a little care and patience, you can turn off your fossil-fuel backup and never turn it back on again. It's important to understand that if your current water heater runs on electricity, replacing it with a solar hot-water heater will eliminate much more fossil-fueled electricity from your life than purchasing an equivalent dollar amount of photovoltaics. This is because of the higher efficiency of solar water collector panels (around 70 percent) as compared to photovoltaic modules (less than 20 percent). The sidebar on page 16 crunches these numbers for two real systems side by side in California.

Solar water heaters are not simple to install, and they can be pricey. If you hire a professional installer, prices hover at or above $6,000 for a typical four-person-home-sized system. Generally speaking, 65 percent of that is materials cost, so there is some room to save money by installing your own. But you have to be comfortable soldering pipes, following complicated plumbing diagrams, and working on your roof. On the bright side, current federal tax credits of up to $2,000 (set to expire at the end of 2008) can pay back 30 percent of a system's cost. Check the www.dsire.org Web site for state credit information.

Solar showers. One great way to reduce your hot-water-related carbon emissions is to build a solar shower. Outdoor solar showers can be wonderful, exhilarating places to bathe, and in many places they are practical up to half the year. In most of the country, there are at least three months of the year when an outdoor shower with only minimally heated water is a perfectly delightful experience. If you are bathing in the sunshine, water feels acceptable at 90 degrees, and perfect at 100 degrees, instead of the usual minimum

120 degrees you expect in the bathroom. An outdoor solar shower is, in fact, a simple type of solar batch collector. Perhaps you already have a private location that would be perfect for an outdoor shower, or you might need to build a small enclosed wooden bathing platform. Many premanufactured solar showers are sold, but we've encountered a lot of bad apples and suggest that building your own shower is a better long-term solution (see the solar shower project later in this chapter).

Instantaneous hot-water heaters (also called on-demand or tankless). If you have a small household or don't use enough hot water to make a solar water heater a practical investment, your best bet for long-term carbon reduction will be an on-demand

FIG. 6.1. **Instantaneous, or on-demand, water heaters eliminate the need to constantly reheat stored water and can cut energy use by up to 30 percent. Gas models need to be vented.**

hot-water heater. These come in electric, propane, and natural gas models and can reduce your energy consumption by 10 to 40 percent (depending on what system you started with and how much hot water you use). Instantaneous heaters do just what the name implies: they heat water only as you draw it at the faucet, with a system of small-diameter copper tubing loops inside a heater box. Since the water is heated only when demanded, you don't have a huge tank of water constantly releasing and needing heat. An added benefit of these heaters is that you never have to worry about running out of hot water. Gas models need to be vented, and electric models need heavy-gauge, high-ampacity wire, sometimes on multiple circuits. But they are smaller than conventional water heaters and can hang on a bathroom wall, and they are not that much more expensive (and can pay for the initial cost difference in energy savings). There are federal tax credits for up to $300 for their installation, and some states offer green energy tax credits as well, so be sure to check the www.dsireusa.org Web site for listings for your state.

Last but not least—propane or natural gas tank heaters. Although the electric utility might tell you that heating water with electricity is cheaper than with gas, don't believe them (they might be right as concerns short-term dollar costs, but not environmental costs). As mentioned above, the inefficiencies involved in creating electricity and then turning it back into heat means that unless your electricity comes from renewable resources, gas will always be a more effective way to heat water.

OUR STORY

Over the years we've tried a lot of methods for heating our water—solar showers, instantaneous heaters, even woodstove pots! But we've now happily settled down with our closed-loop (pressurized) solar water heater and loudly proclaim its virtues to anyone who will listen. We live in a climate that freezes regularly and didn't want a batch-type collector that we might have

to drain out or use only sporadically in the winter (the different types of solar heaters are detailed below). We chose a heat-exchanging solar water system in which pressurized antifreeze solution circulates through collectors on our roof and then through copper tubes surrounding the specialized 80-gallon water solar tank in our basement (see figures 6.5 and 6.6). The solar-heated antifreeze exchanges heat via the tubing with the household water in the tank, and the two fluids stay separate. When we moved into our house, we replaced the nonfunctional rusty old water heater with the special solar tank, although the solar collectors on the roof didn't go into place for many months. The solar tank has a backup electric element, so we relied on that until the collectors went up on the roof. We chose evacuated tubes for the solar collectors more for the sake of experimentation than for any real cost-analysis reasons (Rebekah always installs flat-plate collectors at work and wanted to try something different). Tubes supposedly work better than flat-plate collectors in very cold environments, since they are a vacuum and slow conductive and convective heat loss, but North Carolina doesn't really qualify as a super-cold environment! We have 16 tubes, and four people use the hot water at our house. Having lived with our system through a few seasons now, Rebekah thinks we might have undersized the number of tubes slightly; 24 would have been a safer bet for a more continuous supply of hot water in our climate.

Rebekah hemmed and hawed about what type of pump to use to pump the heat-exchange fluid (antifreeze) through the system, but finally we installed a DC pump that runs directly off a small 20-watt PV module (its only purpose it to power the pump; it is distinct and separate from our solar electric system). The pump is extremely low power and pumps around 2 gallons a minute. We like the fact that it is a simple system and we don't have to rely on a separate AC power source or a controller.

The hardest part of installing the system was finding a route for the copper ¾-inch tubing that would carry the heat-exchange fluid from the roof to the basement, where our water tank is. We used flexible

Wood-Heated Water

There are three relatively common ways to heat water using wood. The first is the direct route: simply place a large pot or two of water on the top of a woodstove. The second, a jacketed woodstove, entails a water loop running through or around a woodstove. The third is the outdoor wood-fired furnace.

When our instantaneous propane water heater went on the fritz a few winters ago, we resorted to the direct woodstove method. Placing two 5-gallon pots of water on the woodstove for a few hours meant we could take a bucket bath, dump water in the tub, or wash dishes. We lived that way for two winters when our first cob house was under construction, and it wasn't (too) bad. However, traipsing around the house with heavy pots of heated (many times boiling) water can be treacherous, and safety is a concern! Many wood cookstoves come with an optional water-holding tank that hangs off the side to keep a reservoir of water warm for washing dishes.

A second way to heat water with wood, the jacketed woodstove, utilizes the stove as the functional equivalent to solar collectors on the roof. Coils of metal pipe either run straight through the wood box with gasketed entry and exit holes or wrap around and hug the outside of the box. Jacketed woodstoves can be plumbed in various ways, analogous to the solar thermal applications detailed in this chapter. If the water tank can be located above the stove, then the water-heating loop can function via thermosiphoning, with heated water moving up into the tank and cold water sinking down to be heated by the stove. Alternately, pumps, thermistors, controllers, and internal or external heat exchangers could be used. Retailers such as Lehman's sell prefabricated woodstove jackets for many different models of woodstoves. They can

also be constructed at home. The best resource we know of for those interested in a DIY water jacket project is *Hot Water from Your Wood Stove* (listed in the resources section).

Be forewarned: jacketed woodstoves can be dangerous. Woodstoves function at much higher temperatures than solar collectors (around 650°F for the average woodstove). You absolutely must take precautions and install pressure/temperature relief valves and fire-rated fittings, or you risk lethal explosions. Another downside is that woodstove-heated water isn't going to do much for you in the warmer months of the year when fires aren't necessary for household heat. The possibility for a hybrid system with a solar hot-water system for the warm months exists. When plumbing the systems you can install a diversion loop to reroute water to a solar batch collector for the summer, and you can drain the batch collector in the winter. For low-tech types, an outdoor solar shower could provide shower water in the warm months.

The third type of wood-heated water comes from an outdoor wood-fired furnace, which we do not recommend in any locale. This is basically a large furnace that resides outside the house, allowing use all year long. It can provide household hot water and heat via buried lines connecting the stove loops (water and/or forced air) to the house. These are popular because the mess and smoke of the woodstove never enters the house. However, many states are banning the use of outdoor wood-fired furnaces because they enable users to burn unseasoned wood and softwoods. Unseasoned wood has as little as a fifth of the energy content of seasoned wood, and because it burns at a lower temperature it produces many times as much polluting smoke. Nearby residents often rue the day someone in the neighborhood buys one of these behemoths.

copper tubing through the attic, as there were many twists and turns that would have required much extra soldering if we used rigid tubing.

We have yet to go through a whole winter with the system functioning, but we didn't use the backup electric element in our heat-exchanging tank from March through November. The water has gotten extremely hot over the summer, and we are looking for ways to use the excess summertime heat in the antifreeze loop, perhaps as part of a methane biodigester or for brewing all-grain beer. Overall we've been very pleased with the system. We truly believe that every house should have a solar water-heating system if at all possible. While it takes skill to install and at first seems confusing because of the array of options, it still ranks as the best possible solar investment we know of. It is definitely worth spending a few hours investigating the possibilities for your home.

The projects below move from simple to complex, but don't be fooled into thinking the simple projects aren't worthwhile. For example, even if you already have a solar water heater, you should still check the thermostat setting on any backup heat source! You might still be wasting energy if your backup thermostat is set too high.

FIG. 6.2. **Many water-heater thermostats come preset unnecessarily high. Resetting at a lower temperature can save 10 percent of the energy you use heating water.**

Resetting a Water-Heater Thermostat
Renter friendly.
Project Time: 1 hour.
Cost: Free.
Energy Saved: Medium.
Ease of Use: N/A.
Maintenance Level: N/A.
Skill Levels: Electrical: Basic.
Materials: None.
Tools: Flat or Phillips-head screwdriver.

Many water heaters come preset at 140 degrees F, which can be unnecessarily hot, meaning when you turn on the faucets you temper that hot water you already paid for with cold water. Most people never bother to check the temperature that their water-heater thermostat is set at, unless the water coming out

is either scalding or freezing. However, you can save energy by resetting your thermostat a little lower, and you will probably never notice the difference in water temperature. In addition, it is useful to know how to change the thermostat setting on a gas heater, because most models have low-heat "vacation" settings that keep the pilot light on but don't waste energy heating your water while you are gone. When you leave town for more than a few days, it pays to use this vacation setting. (With an electric heater, you can just flip the breakers off when you leave town and flip them back on when you come home; it takes a surprisingly short time for the water to heat up again.)

Shutting off electricity. If you have an electric water heater, please find and flip off its circuit breaker before you attempt to change the thermostat setting, because the thermostat is located in the midst of the water heater's electrical wires and poking around in there with a screwdriver can be dangerous. The water-heater circuit should be labeled in your electrical panel. If it's not labeled, look for a 30-amp breaker that takes up two slots (240 volts), called a double-pole breaker, and that's probably your guy. If there's more than one breaker fitting that description, it won't hurt anything to turn off all the double-pole breakers for a moment, unless your significant other is preparing for a dinner party at the same time (your electric range, dryer, air conditioner, and so on, could also be on a double-pole breaker). Occasionally electric water heaters, especially in mobile homes, are on single-pole breakers, so just be patient and take the time to relabel your panel if you have to do some hunting. To be absolutely positive you turned the tank off, you can buy an inexpensive device called a voltage detector, which looks like a plastic pen and lights up or beeps when you hold it near electric wires or extension cords that are live (hot).

Resetting the thermostat. Electric and gas water heaters have similar thermostat mechanisms. On a gas heater, look near the bottom for a dial with temperatures or "hot, hotter" ratings. For an electric heater, look for one or two covers somewhere on the front of the heater held on with screws, usually one at the top and one at the bottom for a dual-element heater. It is possible that a gas heater thermostat may be under a cover, too. Unscrew the cover, and you might see some insulation. Pull that out of the way (note how it is installed, as you'll have to squeeze it back in there to get the cover on again). You should see some type of thermostat, a dial or a movable plastic lever, labeled with temperatures. Roll it back if it is set to over 120 degrees. Perhaps try 115 degrees for a few days and see if that temperature agrees with you. If not, you can go back and set it a little higher. Don't forget to flip the breaker back on when you're done!

Insulating a Hot-Water Tank and Hot-Water Pipes

Renter friendly.

Project Time: 3 hours.

Cost: Inexpensive ($50–100).

Energy Saved: Medium.

Ease of Use: N/A.

Maintenance Level: Low.

Skill Levels: Carpentry: Basic.

Materials: Water-heater insulative blanket or roll of R-13 insulation, ⅝-inch or ⅞-inch-internal-diameter pipe sleeve insulation (Rubatex or Thermwell are two common name brands).

Tools: Measuring tape, scissors, razor knife, duct tape, pipe tape or glue or cable ties.

Insulating your water heater and pipes is simple, can save you 10 percent on your water-heating energy costs, and can be accomplished in a morning. The less heat you lose due to poor insulation, the less heat you must provide by burning fossil fuels. So what are you waiting for?

Insulating the tank. You can buy a special water-heater insulation jacket at any home improvement store (they run around $25), for the easiest installation. But a cheaper option is cutting up some R-13 or higher fiberglass insulation to fit and strapping it on with tape, especially if you have any pieces lying around left over from another job. If you have a gas heater, be cautious! Steer very clear of the space around the pilot-light access area, air intake, and thermostat, and don't insulate the top of the tank! If the tank is electric, leave a gap that will allow you to access the thermostat cover.

If you happen to have a stash of bubble wrap, the kind that comes with boxes in the mail, you might not even have to go out and buy insulation. We make sure to save any bubble wrap or foam we receive, as it often comes in handy for small insulation jobs. We recommend using bubble wrap only around an electric (not gas) water heater, and only around the actual tank, which doesn't get as hot as the pipes. It is possible that water pipes, especially copper, could get hot enough to melt plastic bubble wrap. We wouldn't recommend old blankets or fabric for the same reason. It's best to stay away from fire hazards. Your bubbles might pop after a few years, but then you can just add another layer.

There isn't a right way to wrap a hot-water tank; just swaddle the thing as best you can with insulation. Make it pretty if you must, but who's really going to be looking at your water heater? Formaldehyde-free fiberglass insulation is often nearly half recycled glass, so we don't feel too guilty about using it for small jobs like this one. The embodied energy in properly installed insulation is quickly replaced by energy savings, often in just a few weeks. Be sure to wear a good-quality dust mask and gloves, and don't roll around in it or eat the insulation. Beyond that, fiberglass's convenience, fire resistance, and durability make it pretty hard to beat for small jobs.

Insulating the pipes. This is somewhat harder than insulating your tank, because hot-water lines often run through places that are either inaccessible or unpleasant, like walls and crawl spaces. But the more of the run you can insulate, the more energy saved. An added benefit is that your pipes are less likely to freeze in the event of a winter-storm power outage. You can buy pipe sleeve insulation in different sizes and thicknesses. The internal diameter of the sleeve must be slightly larger than the size of your pipe, which will be either ½ inch or ¾ inch and probably a combination of both. Look for either ⅝ inch- or ⅞ inch-internal-diameter insulation. The external diameter changes the insulative value. The thicker it is, the higher the R-value. But thicker insulation is also harder to put on, so don't go overboard. Your local hardware store should carry a selection. You might find two types of insulation, closed cell and open cell. Closed cell looks smoother and more like rubber, is more expensive, and doesn't absorb water. Either one will work for this application.

Take a look at your hot-water lines. The ones coming out of your tank are most likely ¾ inch and at some point transition to ½ inch sections. Some houses have only ½ inch pipe. If your pipes aren't too old, try to read what's printed on them. It will generally tell you the size. Otherwise get out a tape measure and take your best guess.

Keep that measuring tape out, because it will come in handy to measure exposed pipe to get the lengths of pipe insulation you'll need to cut. Some insulation is presplit down the middle and has adhesive already applied, so you just cut it to the right length, split it open, hold it open, and slide it onto the pipes and stick it back together. Some insulation isn't presplit, so you have to cut down the middle yourself, cut to length, and then apply glue, tape, or cable ties to make it stick back together around the pipe.

Where the pipe takes a 90-degree turn or branches off, you can get fancy and cut a 45-degree angle at the end of your insulation so the two halves meet up perfectly, or you can just cut it straight and leave a little gap. Try to cover as much of the hot-water-pipe runs as you can. Obviously once they enter wall space you will not be able to insulate them, but if these cavities are empty you can blow insulation into your walls (see chapter 7). You might also want to insulate exposed cold-water lines if you ever have problems with freezing. It won't save you significant energy in the short run, but it might save you repair work in the future.

Outdoor Solar Shower

Renter friendly.
Project Time: One day.
Cost: $25–100.
Energy Saved: Medium to high.
Ease of Use: Medium; must be refilled to heat.
Maintenance Level: Medium.
Skill Levels: Carpentry: Basic. Plumbing: Basic.
Materials: Water tank, plumbing fittings, wood, nails, hose bibb.
Tools: Flat or Phillips-head screwdriver, adjustable wrench, hammer, nails.

For many years, prior to moving to Durham, our only summertime shower was a solar shower, and after running through a few leaky off-the-shelf models that either didn't heat up or dripped all the hot water out before we could use it, we found that the temporary solution of leaving a hose in the sun

FIG. 6.3. **Outdoor solar showers are fun and invigorating and, best of all, can provide carbon-free hot water.**

was just as effective, although sometimes the water would get too hot and the supply was very limited!

The best possible solar shower is one you make yourself: a small black container or water tank that sits in the sun, above your head on a wood or metal stand, and has a high-quality hose bibb or boiler drain valve that turns on and off securely, to which you can attach either a showerhead or a handheld sprayer.

There are also a lot of basic prefab models on the market; the most common is a 5-gallon thick-gauge plastic bag (either black or with a clear front and black back) that you hang in the sun, with a dangling small-diameter hose with a rudimentary closing clip or valve.

Siting the shower. There are three things you need to think about when siting a solar shower: first, privacy; second, water access; and third, sunshine. The most annoying thing about premanufactured solar showers is that you often have to take them down from the spot where they are hanging to fill them up, and then you have to struggle with a large heavy bag of water in the rehanging. If you can designate a spot for the shower and make it easy to get water into the container (usually

with a hose, or even better via rainwater catchment), your solar shower will see a lot more use. It is hard to generalize about the amount of sunshine solar shower tanks need. If you live in Arizona, you might prefer that your water stays in the shade to provide relief on 100-degree days. If you live in Vermont, you'll need at least four hours of direct sun on the tank to get it up to an enjoyable temperature. We found that in North Carolina, the water from the ground averages about 55 degrees, and it takes three hours in the sun for the water to reach a decent shower temperature. We can happily use a solar outdoor shower from May to September.

The tank and stand. We built a basic wooden stand for our previous cob house's solar shower (we don't currently have a solar shower, as our water is already heated by the sun and our current house is on a corner lot with an alley in back, making privacy harder to come by). Our first solar shower consisted of four posts (4 × 4s) and a flat plywood top. The diagram in figure 6.3 shows another possibility, with brackets tied into house wall studs holding up the platform. Make sure that shower water drains away from the house foundation rather than toward it. Water is heavy, about 8 pounds per gallon, so depending on the size tank you want to use, the stand has to be of sufficient sturdiness to support the weight (see "Building a Horizontal Trellis for Shading" in chapter 10 for information on attaching brackets).

If you oversize the tank, it will take much longer to heat up. Each outdoor showerer should use under 10 gallons of water, with 5 gallons often sufficient. The common 55-gallon rain-barrel-size tank is too large and would not heat up sufficiently. A 30-gallon or smaller tank is about right, depending on household size, showering frequency, and available sunlight. A black 5-gallon bucket can be a cheap solution for individual use. The more surface area the tank has relative to water, the faster it will heat up. The tank should either be black or be painted black, and it will need both a hose bibb (boiler drain) for the shower and a cap or cover that can be removed so you can fill the tank (see "Rain Barrel" in chapter 8 for advice on inserting a hose bibb into a tank). If you rescue an old tank, make sure it didn't contain something caustic or toxic in a previous life.

Building a solar outdoor shower is a good place to put your creativity to use. You might be able to fill the tank with rainwater overflow from your gutters. You could build an elaborate showering platform with built-in hooks and shelves and tiled walls. If you plumb the tank into the existing house water lines, refilling it will be a breeze. Just because you live in a city doesn't mean you can't have an outdoor shower. Nearly every home at the beach has an outdoor shower, and we've seen plenty of inner-city outdoor showers tucked away in the backyard behind simple board-and-batten walls. Just invest in a good bathrobe and you'll have no trouble.

COMPARING SOLAR WATER-HEATING SYSTEMS

A household (domestic) solar water-heating system falls under one of two categories: **direct heat** or **heat exchange**. *Direct heat* (often referred to as a batch collector since the water sits in a big batch of many gallons) means the water you use in the house is being directly heated by the sun, perhaps in a black tank sitting in the yard, perhaps in tubing on the roof, perhaps in a special device designed expressly for the purpose. There are hundreds of possible designs for direct-heating systems, from the simplicity of a hose lying in the yard to the complexity of an insulated glass-covered box filled with copper tubing and mounted on a roof (like the version shown in figure 6.5). The basic premise remains the same, however:

FIG. 6.4. **We get a lot of comments on our evacuated tubes, which we think look a cross between a crazy art project and an alien spacecraft.**

the sun directly heats the water you use in your house, meaning that your water needs a spot to make contact with the sun's rays.

Heat exchange, on the other hand, means that the fluid heated by the sun isn't your household water but a transfer fluid that exchanges heat with the household water, in a system of copper fins or tubing. The transfer fluid isn't heated in a batch of many gallons but flows constantly from the water tank up to the collectors and back again. One example of a heat exchanger is a water tank (of any size) that has copper tubes wrapped around or through it. The heat-exchange fluid runs through the copper pipes and the household water sits inside the tank. The two fluids are completely separate but can exchange heat via copper's conductive properties. Another type of heat exchanger, called an "external" heat exchanger, looks a bit like a small radiator and can sit next to your tank and be plumbed to work together with the tank. Both direct-heat and heat-exchange systems rely on some type of solar collector—most often a variety of flat-plate collector (solar panel) or evacuated tube—see the sidebar at right for a rundown of the possibilities.

Pros and cons of direct-heating systems. Direct-heating systems (batch collectors) are a big pain in areas that often experience below-freezing temperatures. Because it is your actual household water being heated, and not a freeze-proof glycol mixture, every part of the system (pipes, fittings, panels) that is outside is susceptible to damage by freezing. However, direct heaters are simpler and cheaper than heat-exchanging systems. Basically, unless you live in climate Zone 8 or warmer, we wouldn't advise you to install a batch collector unless you are prepared to constantly monitor the winter weather or are willing to bypass the system completely in the winter. A corollary to the susceptibility of batch heaters to freezing is that as your household water sits outside during cold nights, it will be chilled rather than heated! This means that if you use most of your hot water in the morning, a direct-heating system isn't for you. We've seen systems that have an insulated cover to close every night that eliminates a percentage of this problem, although obviously it requires regular attention and adds complexity to the system.

Solar Thermal System Types

- Direct heating: Household water is heated directly in the sun. One example is a 40-gallon solar batch collector affixed to the roof or in the yard and plumbed into household water lines.
- Heat exchange: Heat-exchange fluid (distilled water or antifreeze/water mixture) is circulated by a pump or via thermosiphon through the solar collector and warms household water via heat exchange. Collector loop contains minimal fluid (approximately 3 to 10 gallons) at any one time.
  a) Closed-loop: Antifreeze fluid under low pressure circulates through panels and heat-exchange loop when the sun is shining.
  b) Drainback: Unpressurized system with the heat-exchange fluid draining back into a holding tank when the sun isn't shining.

Solar Thermal Collector Types

- Batch collector: Runs the gamut from an old water tank placed on a roof to black hose in the yard to higher-end glass-box insulated collectors with large-diameter copper tubing.
- Evacuated tube: Sealed glass tube with internal heat absorber is evacuated to create a vacuum to limit heat loss to the environment (much like a thermos). Individual tubes are linked up in series; the heat is transferred to an insulated copper header (manifold) running on top of the tubes, connecting tube to tube and holding heat-exchange fluid.
- Flat plate: Large, approximately 4 × 8-foot panel containing thin copper tubes attached to heat-absorbing plates in an insulated, glazed box.

Pros and cons of heat-exchange systems. If you live in a colder climate than Zone 8, then you will most likely be installing some variety of heat exchanger—either closed-loop pressurized or drainback—in order to avoid freezing. The differences between closed-loop and drainback systems are related to the anti-freeze loop. In drainback systems the fluid runs back to a holding tank when not circulating (to avoid any chance of freezing). For the drainback system to work, the piping route from the solar panels to the fluid holding tank must have a constant slight downhill slope. Conversely, closed-loop systems are constantly under pressure, with the panels and supply and return lines always full of fluid and never draining back. There are pros and cons to both types of heat-exchange system, and we'll list a few here. You'll find that some solar-hot-water installers are religiously attached to one system versus another.

Closed-loop systems have a history of occasionally getting too hot, with the pressure rising, and blowing a bit of glycol out the pressure-relief valve. This can happen in summer when homeowners are on vacation and perhaps not using the system, thus accumulating hotter and hotter water. A drainback system can avoid overheating (and any potential freezing), because by being drained back the fluid is never stuck in the panels or lines.

In practice, because drainback systems start every morning with empty supply and return lines, to pump drainback system fluid to the panels means the pump must have enough power to overcome the head (pressure) in the supply lines. Alternately, in a closed-loop system, the fluid pressure (down) from the panels equals the pressure (up) to the panels, and except for friction losses in the lines, the head is negligible, and the pump doesn't have to exert as much force to get started. So with closed-loop systems, it is possible to run a low-power DC pump off a small (5- to 20-watt) photovoltaic module. The module is placed near the collectors, and when the sun is shining, the pump runs PV direct and fluid circulates—a beautiful solution. However, small modules and DC pumps aren't sized to have enough power to function in high-head (drain-back) systems. Also, if early morning sun hits the PV module, the pump can start running before the collectors warm up, cooling the water rather than heating it. There is one differential controller made specifically for use with 12-volt DC PV modules that could solve this problem, but it is a rarity—almost all controllers are made to work with 120- or 240-volt AC.

Many heat-exchange systems instead use an AC pump that works via controller. With a controller, you place thermistors (sensors whose resistance is affected by temperature) at the collectors and at the tank, and then the controller turns the pump on and off depending on whether the temperature at the collectors is hotter than at the tank, as indicated by the thermistors. But the controller and AC pump won't work during power outages!

Not to add to the myriad choices, but if it is possible to place the tank *above* the collectors, then you could rely on thermosiphoning—the fact that hot water rises due to convection—to circulate the fluid from collectors to tank, instead of a pump. There are premanufactured solar collector systems that rely on thermosiphoning.

One last thing to mention is that the piping in closed-loop systems from the tank to the collectors must be copper. We've tried experimenting with PEX (cross-linked polyethylene—plastic flexible piping) because it is cheaper and easier to run than copper, but the pressure and heat are too high for PEX.

Closed-loop Pressurized Solar Water Heater

Project Time: 3 to 4 days.

Cost: About $7,000 installed professionally, or $3,500 DIY (before tax credits).

Energy Saved: High.

Ease of Use: Easy.

Maintenance Level: Low.

Skill Levels: Carpentry: Intermediate. Plumbing: Advanced. Electrical: Intermediate.

Materials: Solar hot-water panels (flat or evacuated tube), heat-exchanging solar hot-water tank or external heat exchanger, 12-volt DC or 120-volt AC glycol loop pump, controller for AC pumps or solar PV module for DC pumps, ball valves, check valves, boiler valves, 75 psi pressure-relief valve, tempering valve, roofer's caulk, glycol, stainless-steel lag screws and washers, roof collars, panel mounting hardware, flexible and rigid ¾-inch copper piping, pipe hangers, pipe insulation, various copper fittings, expansion tank, pressure gauge.

Tools: Soldering kit (including flux, torch, solder, and so on), pipe cutter, measuring tape, drill and drill bits, holesaw kit, razor knife, pencil, screwdriver, hammer, fire extinguisher, rope, ladders.

Caution: This project is one of the most complicated and dangerous in the book—it involves extensive work on the roof, lifting heavy objects onto the roof, and soldering in tight spaces. You'll need to be certain of your soldering skills before you tackle this project. Use common sense, don't work on a roof without a safety harness, work slowly and safely, and don't do anything you aren't comfortable with!

There are four main parts to this system:

1. Collector panels (flat or evacuated tubes)
2. Heat-exchanging solar hot-water tank or external heat exchanger
3. Glycol loop pump, copper supply/return lines, expansion tank
4. Controller and thermistors OR photovoltaic panel connected to pump

A closed-loop system is perfect for cold environments that have many nights below freezing in the winter. With this system, you never have to worry about the solar panels or supply/return pipes freezing, because what flows through them isn't water but a glycol mixture that heats water through an exchanger. The food-grade (propylene) glycol mixture has a much lower freezing temperature (–55 degrees F or below depending on the mix) than water.

The heat exchanger. There are different ways to accomplish the heat exchange, but our preference is to install a special (80-gallon) tank made just for solar use. It looks just like a normal electric water

heater, but it contains only one electric heating element in the top of the tank. The element is only at the top of the tank and not the bottom because the heat exchanger loops around the bottom of the tank, heating the incoming cold water that sinks to the bottom of the tank. Underneath the external tank insulation, copper tubing wraps around the water tank and transfers solar heat to the water. The glycol loop and your household water never come into contact. A small, quiet pump works to send the glycol mixture through the piping and solar panels. An alternative is an external heat exchanger that sits outside the main tank or a supplementary solar feed tank, but the plumbing gets more complicated, as supply and return valves for the heat-exchanging loop have to be created.

Getting started. The first step in installing a closed-loop system is to tear out your old heater and replace it with a heat-exchanging tank (unless you're going to use an external heat exchanger). This can actually be done well in advance of installing any other part of the system, because the new tank has a backup electric element and will perform perfectly well without the aid of the solar panels. Because heat-exchanging solar tanks come only in electric models, if you currently have a gas tank it will be slightly harder to install the new tank. You must have a way to securely disconnect and cut off the gas supply to the old tank, and you also must run a new dedicated circuit from the electric panel to the tank.

Replacing an old electric tank. First, turn off the water-heater breaker in your electric panel and check to make sure the power is off (using a voltage indicator), then disconnect the electric wires at the old tank. Turn off the cold-water supply line (most tanks have one; if not you have to turn off all water to house). Disconnect the hot- and cold-water hookups that run into the tank, either by cutting through the copper or plastic pipes or by unscrewing unions.

Next, completely drain the water out of the tank, via the drain valve at the bottom of the tank; you might need to connect a hose to the drain valve and run it outside. Wrestle the old tank out of position and wres-

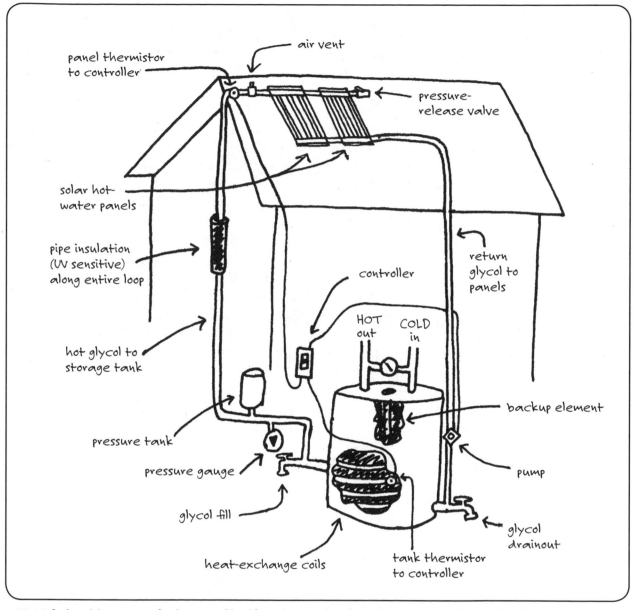

panel thermistor to controller

air vent

pressure-release valve

solar hot-water panels

pipe insulation (UV sensitive) along entire loop

return glycol to panels

controller

HOT out

COLD in

hot glycol to storage tank

backup element

pressure tank

pump

pressure gauge

glycol fill

glycol drainout

heat-exchange coils

tank thermistor to controller

FIG. 6.5. **A closed-loop pressurized system. Plumbing a heat-exchanging solar water heater is a challenging project.**

tle the new tank into place. Repair hot- and cold-water hookups (this will likely involve soldering new copper connections, gluing PVC, or crimping PEX connections). You will eventually need a tempering (mixing) valve that connects the hot- and cold-water lines to reduce the temperature of the solar-heated water when necessary. This is the most convenient time to place it in the system. It must be soldered in-line with the hot and cold supply lines. Fill the tank with water,

then replace the electrical connections. Finally, turn the breakers back on.

Guidelines for mounting flat-plate panels on a roof. Find your rafters and mark them. The best way to do this is to have one person in the attic with a measuring tape and another person on the roof with a drill. Drill a pilot hole through the roof and have the person in the attic measure from the hole to the nearest rafters, and from rafter to rafter, while calling out the measurements. The person on the roof can then mark the rafters. Don't forget to mark the hole you drilled so you can fill it with caulk later. Another, slightly less accurate way to find rafters is to use a hammer to sound along the roof and listen for the changes in pitch that occur when you are above a rafter. Common "stud finders" don't work through roof shingles.

Your panels should come with mounting brackets, usually four per panel, two on the top, two on the bottom. There usually isn't a specific place on the panel the bracket must go; just try to distribute the weight evenly. Measure the panel height and width. Figure out the most convenient place to attach the brackets to the rafters you have located (the brackets must be screwed to a rafter, and not just to the roof decking).

Install the bottom brackets first. Predrill holes at least one size smaller than the stainless-steel lag screws you will be using to attach the brackets. Fill the holes with polyurethane caulk such as Sikaflex-1a caulk, and also apply a good amount to the bottom of the mounting brackets. Screw down the brackets securely, but not so tightly that they spin in the rafter (this will mean a roof leak; if you get a spinner, take it out, fill the hole with caulk, and move the screw to a new location).

The next step is getting the panel on the roof. The safest way we've found to get a heavy panel on the roof is to secure it with ratcheting straps to a strong rope and pull it up along an extremely stable ladder, with at least two people on the roof pulling and one person following the panel up the ladder. This is a dangerous activity and should be approached very cautiously. You must make sure the ladder, ropes, and roof workers are all safe and secure.

After getting the panel up on the roof, place it on the bottom brackets. Now you can determine precisely the right position for the top brackets. Follow the same installation procedure for the top brackets. Tighten your hardware, apply a bit of roofer's caulk to the top of the screw, and you're done with the panel! If you are installing more than one panel, you will have to prepare the copper couplings that plumb the panels together and install them as you place the panels on the roof.

If you're installing evacuated tubes, the rafter locating and lag process is similar, but the racking is different and will come with clear instructions.

Plumbing the panels. The supply and return plumbing route will be different for every house. Perhaps it will be easiest to drop off the side of your roof and straight down to the basement, although you might lose a little heat in the winter. Alternatively, you might need to enter the attic through the roof and find a path to the water heater through the house. If the copper pipes go through the roof, you'll need a copper roof collar that fits under the shingles and keeps leaks out of the hole. Although the shortest path will be cheapest (less copper pipe), it may not be easiest. Give some thought to where you will have to solder connections, and don't solder near flammable materials like roof rafters. Be aware of your torch flame at all times. Have a friend man a fire extinguisher where you are soldering. Flexible copper tubing may allow you to avoid soldering at all in tight attic spots.

Follow the instructions that come with your panels when soldering the supply and return lines to the panels. Don't forget that you will need to plumb in a pressure-relief valve, to relieve excess pressure that could lead to explosions, at one of the four corners of the collectors, and an air-intake valve (also called a coin key vent) as well. The air-intake valve can be opened to allow all the fluid to drain from the collectors.

Once you get your copper lines to the tank, make sure you know which pipe is your supply line (enters at the bottom of the panels), and which is the return (exits at the top of the panels) because they will look exactly the same and have probably gone around some corners and perhaps switched places by this point. A heat-exchanging tank will have instructions about which line goes to which port.

Plumbing the tank. At the tank, you must plumb in the glycol pump (an AC pump if powered by a controller, a DC pump if powered by PV panel; see the section on pumps below for more info), a check valve (spring or gravity) to keep hot water from thermosiphoning at night, boiler drains on both the supply and the return line for charging and draining

FIG. 6.6. **A closed-loop hot-water tank. An 80-gallon solar hot-water tank with backup electric element. The heat exchange takes place at the bottom, where copper coils wrap around the base of the interior water tank.** Courtesy Honey Electric Solar

the system, an expansion tank to alleviate the effects of high temperature increasing system pressure, and a pressure gauge to monitor the system's pressure. See the plumbing diagram in figure 6.5.

Don't forget to insulate all the supply-and-return line piping with high-quality insulation such as Rubatex or Armaflex (see the section on insulating pipes earlier

in this chapter). Any insulation exposed to sunlight should be covered either with flashing or UV-resistant plastic to avoid deterioration and pollution of surrounding environment.

Charging the system. A 50/50 water/propylene glycol solution works well. This solution is freeze-proof down to negative 55 degrees Fahrenheit. This is not the same antifreeze you use in your car. It is nontoxic and food grade. Normal systems take somewhere between 5 and 10 gallons of fluid.

You can charge the system using either an electric pump or a manual pump. Electric pumps work better because they get more air out of the system, and the less air the better. You will need three hoses, one from a bucket of 50/50 water/glycol to the suction side of the pump, one from the pump to a boiler drain on the supply glycol line, and one on the other boiler drain on the return glycol line. As you pump glycol into the system, it pushes air out of the return hose.

Hold the return-line hose in the bucket, because eventually you will start to get glycol back from the return line after the copper pipes and the panels fill.

Once the glycol starts returning, let it continue to circulate for a few minutes. You should be getting less and less air in the line. Check the pressure gauge soldered into the glycol-loop line to make sure the pressure isn't too high. Close the boiler drains. Stop the circulation pump, and let the system settle for a few minutes. This is the pressure test, so a good pressure setting at this point is 30 to 40 psi. Check to make sure you don't have any visible leaks and, after waiting 10 to 20 minutes, that you haven't lost pressure. Pressure might rise if the sun is on the panels.

Turn on the pump again once you are sure you don't have leaks, open the boiler drains, and recirculate the glycol, to get any residual air out of the copper lines. You should repeat this process a few times. If the lines and pump are noisy, there is too much air left in them. Shoot for around 15 psi pressure in the glycol loop when you are done with the charging process, remembering that pressure changes as temperature fluctuates. If the pressure is too high, you'll have problems losing glycol through the pressure-relief valve on the roof.

The pump controller. Either you will need to install a differential temperature controller (such as shown in figure 6.7) and thermistors (temperature-sensitive resistors that allow the controller to tell relative temperature differences) to turn a 12-volt AC glycol-loop pump on and off, or you will need to purchase a PV module (5 to 20 watts depending on head and insolation) that will power a 12-volt DC glycol-loop pump whenever the sun is shining.

If you're using a differential controller and thermistors, be aware that the controller needs a 120-volt power source nearby, and that the pump power will come from the controller. One thermistor is in or on the tank, and one thermistor is clamped to the outgoing line of the panels. The thermistors have two 16-gauge wires running to the controller. Thermistors come in different resistance values, so you must make sure your thermistors match your controller's specs.

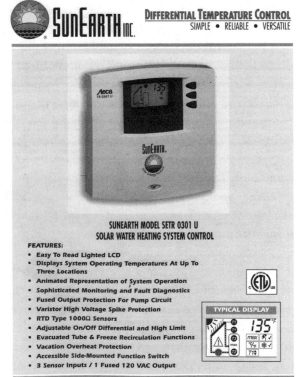

FIG. 6.7. **A differential controller can turn the solar loop pump on and off depending on whether there is heat to be gained at the solar collectors.** Courtesy of SunEarth, Inc.

If you're using a PV module and a DC pump, make sure the PV module provides enough watts to power the pump, but not too much current or voltage or it could burn out the pump. Check the pump manufacturer's specs. Also note that some DC pumps don't have enough force to open spring check valves and might work only with a gravity check valve installed in the horizontal position. If you're using a PV module, you must run wires to the pump from the panel on the roof for the DC power line.

Batch Solar Water Heater

Project Time: 3 to 4 days.
Cost: $500–3,000.
Energy Saved: High.
Ease of Use: Variable; depends on climate.
Maintenance Level: Low.
Skill Levels: Carpentry: Intermediate. Plumbing: Advanced. Electrical: Basic.
Materials: Variable, depending on complexity of system; include ball valves, check valves, boiler valves, 75 psi pressure-relief valve, tempering valve, roofer's caulk, glycol, stainless-steel lag screws and washers, roof collars, panel mounting hardware, flexible and rigid ¾-inch copper piping, pipe hangers, pipe insulation, various copper fittings, hose.
Tools: Soldering kit (including flux, torch, solder, and so on), pipe cutter, measuring tape, drill and drill bits, holesaw kit, razor knife, pencil, screwdriver, hammer, fire extinguisher, rope, ladders.

Sophisticated batch-collection systems are plumbed into household water lines, so the usual household pressure moves the water through the collector, as opposed to a pump moving antifreeze or distilled water through a heat-exchanging system.

Quite a variety of ways exist to plumb batch collectors. The batch collector can be the only source of hot water, or it can feed a backup tank adjacent to the normal tank, or it can feed straight into the regular household electric or gas heater. It is possible to plumb batch collectors with backup gas or electric tanks. This ensures the collector can be bypassed in cold weather

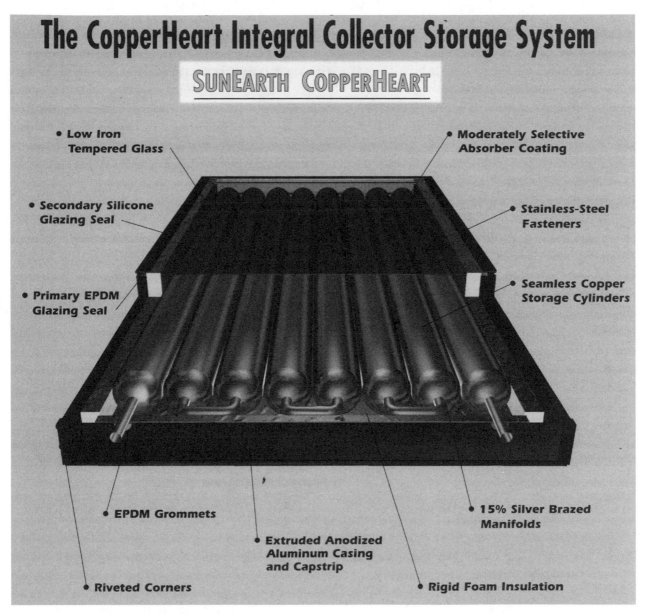

The CopperHeart Integral Collector Storage System

SUNEARTH COPPERHEART

- Low Iron Tempered Glass
- Moderately Selective Absorber Coating
- Secondary Silicone Glazing Seal
- Stainless-Steel Fasteners
- Primary EPDM Glazing Seal
- Seamless Copper Storage Cylinders
- EPDM Grommets
- 15% Silver Brazed Manifolds
- Extruded Anodized Aluminum Casing and Capstrip
- Riveted Corners
- Rigid Foam Insulation

FIG. 6.8. **A SunEarth Batch collector. A sophisticated batch collector made specifically for the purpose of heating household water in warmer regions.** Photo courtesy of SunEarth, Inc.

or, vice versa, the backup tanks(s) can be bypassed and turned off when it is sunny enough to rely solely on the batch collector. It is also possible to place a batch collector (or any other solar thermal system) in-line with an instantaneous hot-water heater, but it must be a model with incoming water temperature sensing.

Off the shelf, high-end batch collectors are installed in a very similar fashion to the closed-loop pressur-

ized system detailed above. The main differences lie in plumbing—adding the extra backup tank if there is one—and in the fact that batch collectors don't need a pump or controller because household water pressure pushes water through the collector. High-end batch collectors should come with a plumbing diagram to follow. Three-way (bypass) valves on the supply and return lines allow various configurations, including bypassing a backup tank or bypassing the batch collector. Many plans can be found at the DIY Web site www.builditsolar.com.

RESOURCES

Books

Lane, Tom. 2002. *Solar Hot Water Systems: Lessons Learned 1977 to Today*. Gainesville, FL: Solar Energy Systems, Inc. Available at www.ecs-solar .com/lessons_learned.htm.

Lehman's Non-Electric Catalog. *Hot Water from Your Wood Stove*. Adding a pressurized hot-water system to your woodstove is potentially dangerous. Read this booklet first and proceed with caution. Available at www.lehmans.com.

Ramlow, Bob, and Benjamin Nusz. 2006. *Solar Water Heating: A Comprehensive Guide to Solar Water and Space Heating Systems*. Gabriola Island, BC: New Society Publishers.

Trimby, Paul. 2006. *Solar Water Heating: A DIY Guide*. Snowdonia, U.K: Centre for Alternative Technology Publications.

Internet

Build It Solar. Great compendium of DIY solar hot water and other solar projects. www.builditsolar .com

Consumer's Guide to Solar Water Heaters. www.eere .energy.gov/consumer/your_home/water_heating /index.cfm/mytopic=12850

Interstate Renewable Energy Council. A nonprofit organization that supports market-oriented services targeted at education, coordination, procurement, the adoption and implementation of uniform guidelines and standards, workforce development, and consumer protection. www.irecusa.org

North American Board of Certified Energy Practitioners (NAPCEP). Develops and implements credentialing and certification programs for solar thermal installers. www.nabcep.org

Solar Energy International. A nonprofit offering renewable energy education including on solar thermal. http://solarenergy.org/workshops/index .html

CHAPTER 7

Heating and Cooling

Introduction • Our Story • Thermal Mass and Insulation • Sealing and Insulating • Windows • Insulated Curtains and Shutters • Insulation • Waste Materials • Cooling the Attic and Walls • Other Insulating Ideas • Thermal Mass and Passive Cooling • Cob • Earth Plasters • Solar-Heating Fundamentals • Active Solar Air Heaters • Heating with Biomass • Masonry Stoves • Conclusion • Resources

INTRODUCTION

For many folks, space heating and cooling consumes about half their annual energy budget (47 percent on average), so you should expect that eliminating fossil fuels from this aspect of your home will take some serious work. The renovations will likely take several years and will unfold on three fronts: sealing and insulating, increasing thermal mass, and increasing solar heat gain. Only the first two are needed for effective passive cooling.

Solar energy collected for heating purposes in a properly constructed building has the potential to supply all of a home's heating requirements, even in places of extreme cold. This is by far the most efficient way of collecting solar energy. Solar air heaters, passive or active, have the potential to allow in up to 70 percent of the heating energy from the sun, amounting to 300 Btus per square foot per hour. Once your solar-heating system of choice is installed, this energy is available free of charge until the end of time.

Homes as far north as Sweden or Minnesota are capable of providing all of their heating needs with solar energy. The Passivhaus movement, growing in popularity in Germany and Sweden since 1990, builds very well-insulated houses with plenty of thermal mass and triple-paned windows that need no external sources of heat beyond the sun and the heat radiating off occupants. Many such homes never drop below 50 degrees F even when unoccupied in the dead of winter. They do not require complicated forced-air heating systems that leave a home frigid during power outages. While it is easier to create a solar-heated house when such design considerations are implemented from the initial groundbreaking, applying the basic principles to retrofits of existing homes can achieve similar results. Our own example can attest to this. Since we're only in year two of our retrofit, we still have lots to do to make our home more comfortable.

OUR STORY

Our 1932 home had a good amount of thermal mass in the plaster on the walls but little effective insulation. So immediately after purchasing our home and before we moved in, we had fiberglass insulation blown in all the exterior walls. It was fortunate that we had this done before moving in, because drilling holes in the plaster wall made a huge mess, with the dust getting all over everything (drilling into drywall makes a much smaller mess). Cleaning up the dust was annoying, but the insulation instantly resulted in a warmer, quieter, more livable space. We also added fiberglass insulation to various areas of the ceiling and roof that had no insulation whatsoever, and we plan on an additional layer sometime soon. We are fortunate in that the existing thermal mass of the plaster is well distributed and has been effective in helping us store coolness in the summer and heat in the winter.

We put on storm windows and finished sealing by caulking where we found drafts in the interior walls. We added a metal roof, which brought our attic temperature down by 40–50 degrees F.

We enclosed our south-facing side porch. We made screened panels for it that are removed in the fall and replaced with corrugated greenhouse polycarbonate sheets for passive solar-heating collection. The heat is transferred to the house via the front door and front window that open onto the porch. We intend to add an active solar air heater to the remaining open section of our south-facing roof when we get a chance. For now, we use a woodstove for heat in addition to the moderate amount of passive solar gain we get from the south-facing windows and sun porch. We have fire-wood coming out of our ears from the willow oak that we harvested in the front yard, so we're making up our solar deficit by burning more wood than we would like. After the solar air heater is installed, we hope to burn wood only during times of cloudy weather, and since we often have chilly but clear and sunny winter days here, wood should be relegated to supporting cast member all but a few weeks of the year.

We planted grapes, kiwis, and passionflower vines to trellis over the windows to block summer sun but allow solar gain when their leaves fall off in winter. Instead of air conditioning, we open the windows and curtains at night and run fans to bring in the cool air and take away any heat built up during the day. The plaster does a decent job of retaining this coolness until the following evening, but we could certainly benefit from some additional mass. Since thermal mass and insulation are so vital to creating a comfortable home, it's worth delving into the subject in more detail.

THERMAL MASS AND INSULATION

Two main characteristics dictate how quickly a given body will equalize with the ambient temperature, whether it's your home or a rock sitting out in the yard. The first is that body's ability to hold heat. Different materials have differing densities, and the quantity of heat (or molecular movement) they can store is directly related to this density. Larger amounts of the same material have a greater capacity to store more heat. Dense materials like masonry and metals hold a lot of heat, while light materials like air hold very little. How much heat something holds is called its *thermal mass.*

The second characteristic affecting heat loss is how well that body is protected from the three forms of heat transfer: conduction, convection, and radiation. Recall from chapter 1 that conduction causes heat transfer through direct contact, convection causes heat transfer through the passage of fluids such as air or water around the object, and radiation causes heat transfer via electromagnetic waves produced by differences in temperature between two objects. Materials that inhibit this heat transfer are generally called *insulation.*

As discussed in chapter 1 different methods of heat transfer require different types of insulation. All three must be properly addressed in order for your home to hold heat and coolness with a sustainable quantity of energy. Generally speaking, the cardinal rule is:

> A body is able to maintain a given temperature when it has lots of thermal mass protected by lots of insulation.

When the outside temperature happens to suit you, that's great; you just open windows and run a fan if necessary. But much of the time you don't want your home to be the outside temperature. What poses a challenge is maintaining a comfortable temperature when it's too hot or too cold outside, and to do this using as little fossil fuel as possible (hopefully none). Almost all homes were designed to maintain their interior temperature by complicated fossil-fuel-burning systems that simply heat up the interior air when needed, and not by attempting to capture and hold solar and fluctuating ambient energy. In order to take full advantage of renewable energy, your home will almost certainly require a dual strategy of increasing both its thermal mass and its insulation to retain and store any additional warmth or coolness needed.

A great leap forward in the insulation of new homes occurred after the energy crises of the 1970s. Many older homes also received some additional insulation during this period. Unfortunately, this trend roughly coincided with a move away from high-thermal-mass plaster walls to much-lower-thermal-mass drywall interiors, which are easier to install. The reasoning for this was not entirely unsound. If the thinking was that all heat would be provided by the burning of fossil fuels, then heating up lots of interior thermal mass along with the inside air could be wasteful. Unfortunately, as we move toward homes that are heated naturally with only periodically available heating resources, either from the sun, an evening wood fire, or the warm air of an early spring day, we need the heat-storing ability of lots of thermal mass to tide us over during the cool periods of night or cloudy days.

SEALING AND INSULATING

Such a large undertaking deserves some forethought and planning. Read through this chapter thoroughly to get a good handle on some options for each of these three strategies. Then try to read through some of the recommended books and Web sites at the end of this chapter.

While reading and planning, try to accomplish some of the easier sealing and insulating such as sealing drafts (page 121) and putting in storm windows (page 119) If you expect to be using your furnace for the next three or more years, you should seriously consider installing a programmable thermostat in the interim. Effective models are available for as little as $30 and will make this up in energy savings in a few winter months. These are very simple to install by following the directions for the particular model you buy (and don't forget to turn off the power to the furnace before rewiring the thermostat!).

WINDOWS

Three things need to be achieved for an effective window treatment when and where it is very cold or hot. First, you need to have three layers of materials, minimum, to produce a double air gap. Second, your window needs to have a movable opaque barrier to stop the glass from radiating heat in and out but to let sunshine and light in. Finally, the airflow around the window needs to be reduced to a minimum to reduce heat loss.

For many houses, even newer ones, windows can be the primary source of heat loss and gain. As part of a comprehensive program to reduce heat transfer on the path to fossil-fuel freedom, it is almost certain that you will need to beef up the insulation around your home's "eyes on the world."

There has been much ballyhoo over replacing existing single-paned windows with double-paned windows in order to reduce heat transfer. While double-paned windows are more insulative than existing single-paned windows, the difference is quite small, raising R- values (the rate of resistance to heat transfer) from R-1 to R-2 generally. Oftentimes, they are very expensive and degrade the historic integrity of the homes where they are installed. Many are made of vinyl, a product that lasts only about 20 years before severely cracking when exposed to ultraviolet light, compared to wood or metal windows that can last 200 years or more when properly cared for. In addition, the seal around the double-pane is made of synthetic rubber that also typically lasts only about 20 years before it cracks and all the argon between the panes dissipates, resulting in condensation between the panes and loss of visibility. In our opinion, replacing a functioning window that could potentially last many decades if not several centuries with a window that will be defunct in 20 years is planned obsolescence designed to sell as much product as possible. It is inherently energy inefficient and not viable in the long run.

While many older windows are leaky and produce actual drafts, all windows, even sealed double-paned, produce substantial drafts when it's cold outside. This is because the glass in the window is such a great radiator that it is constantly absorbing heat from the room and reradiating it to where it is colder, i.e., outside. This heat flow is so great that it actually produces a breeze, or draft. The air gap in double-paned windows does almost nothing to stop this radiation. That's why its R- value is only a marginal improvement (at great cost) to that of single-paned windows.

Because windows are made of a variety of materials and because they can lose heat in several different ways (radiation, airflow, conduction through frame, and so on), an alternative measurement, the U-value, is used to describe their overall efficiency. While R- values measure the resistance to conduction of a given material, the U-value is an empirical measurement of how effectively an overall window *system* actually transmits heat from one side to the next. Because it is measuring heat transfer rather than heat-transfer resistance, the U-value is something of an inverse of R-value, although what it is measuring is more comprehensive. For this reason, a lower U-value is better, because this means heat is being transferred *less* effectively.

I'm not sure if they made it backward to be funny or just to be confusing, but it's important to know that installing a quality storm window over an existing single-paned window can produce a *lower* U-value (and is hence more effective at controlling heat transfer overall) than the fancy-pants vinyl double-pane argon gas windows that can often cost ten times as much as storm windows.

If you're putting in a new window and want it to open, you'll have little choice but to buy a double-paned window, unless you build one from scratch or salvage one from a deconstruction. We recommend the extra cost for a new wood window rather than vinyl because of longevity issues.

If you are putting in new double-pane windows and hope to be getting some solar heating out of them (which you should if they face east, west, or south), then there's another thing to pay attention to. Most new windows contain what is called a low-E, or low-emissivity, coating. Some low-E coating blocks out much of the solar radiation from these windows, in summer and in winter. Some folks have had the misfortune of installing this type of glass in their passive solar walls and been flummoxed when they received almost no heat gain during the day in winter. There are low-E coatings that allow for high solar gain, but you need to check and make sure. Heat gain in summertime can be solved with intelligent landscaping, using either a deciduous trellised vine or a shrub that blocks the sun from entering in the warmer months. See chapter 10 for more details.

Storm windows are a must. Even if you already have double-paned windows, you should install storm windows on the exterior. In almost every climate, except perhaps southern California and Hawaii, the extremes of climate are great enough that an effective R-2 for your window is simply not enough. The more extreme your climate, the more you'll need to beef up your windows.

Option for reducing heat loss from windows. Since you're retrofitting your home and not building it from scratch, your home's window placement is probably not ideal and more than likely there are windows that you almost never open. Instead of storm windows on the exterior, consider a permanent transparent cover.

While the light from rarely opened windows is likely welcome, the fact that they are designed to open means they probably leak a great deal of air. Taking stock of which windows are openers and which can be sealed will go a long way toward cutting down on air infiltration. Generally, smaller or hard-to-access windows, windows in rarely used rooms, and windows on the north side of the home are great candidates for potential sealing. This can be a cheaper and more effective option than purchasing storm windows (see "Sealing Unused Windows," below).

A word of caution is warranted, however. Keep in mind that windows serve as a means of egress in case of emergencies, especially fire. Don't permanently seal all the windows in one room, and make sure that all rooms have at least two functioning exits (doors and windows) at all times.

Windows open for a purpose: to let in cool (and sometimes warm) air to make the interior temperature more comfortable. Much more air will enter your home if there is cross-ventilation, so be sure not to seal any windows that facilitate this. Passive (nonsolar) heating strategies that warm the thermal mass of your home by opening windows on warm days are much more effective when windows that face south can be opened. This strategy is generally employed after a warm front has blown through in the shoulder seasons (spring and fall), and the wind is predominantly blowing from the south. This still works well even if northern windows are sealed as long as eastern and western windows still function and can be opened.

Once you decide which windows to keep operable, the next step should be to measure the openings of these windows, *each individually*, and order storm windows to fit. You may not want to permanently seal any windows, in which case you'll need to order storms for all of them. See "Storm Windows," below, for details.

For the windows that you are planning on sealing shut, instead of a storm window the best method of creating the first air pocket is by cutting and installing some kind of UV-resistant Plexiglas.

Sheets of Plexiglas are relatively inexpensive, allow in daylight, and are easy to install. Like storm windows, they do triple duty, keeping your home warm, deterring break-ins, and providing an additional sound barrier. The last two benefits are particularly welcome to urban dwellers like ourselves. It would not be too much trouble for the motivated homeowner to cut Plexiglas for every window, installing it in the fall and removing it in the spring.

There are many types of Plexiglas (also referred to as acrylic sheet plastic) out there. For the purpose of covering the exterior of your windows, there are two types of single sheet, and these two types come in a variety of thicknesses. They are rated on their impact-resistance strength. The less expensive type is rated as 25 times stronger than glass, the second 250 times. If you live in a place where there are frequent storms or you are concerned about break-ins, you may want to invest in the superstrong stuff. Costs range from $2–5/square foot. The cheapest type of Plexiglas has

no UV protection and will yellow in a few short years, so don't buy it.

Corrugated polycarbonate sheets are often used in greenhouses. These are similar to Plexiglas except they contain channels like corrugated cardboard. The sheets vary in thickness from 6 mm to 25 mm, the thicker having two layers of air instead of just one. The corrugated aspect of polycarbonate sheets means they produce a distorted, lined view, although they let in almost all available sunlight. By themselves, they achieve an R-value of between 1.5 and 3.5, based on thickness and number of air channels. They are not always readily available and cost between $1–5/square foot plus shipping, which can be substantial. Because of their limited availability, thickness, and somewhat strange look, they're not for every application, but if you have enough rarely used windows whose view you don't mind slightly distorting, they may make sense. They can be cut with a utility knife to fit any window. Ask friends and neighbors to be part of a large joint order, and you'll save substantially on shipping costs. In colder climates, the additional insulation is substantial and will quickly repay their cost by conserving heat inside the home. In our home we are using them as wintertime screen replacements on the south-facing front screened porch, to add a passively heated space without cutting in new windows.

Sealing Unused Windows

Renter friendly.

Project Time: One hour per window.

Cost: $10–100, depending on size and treatment.

Energy Saved: Medium. Windows account for up to 20 percent of heat loss from a home. Creating an additional air pocket to trap air enhances the insulative value of your windows.

Ease of Use: Easy.

Maintenance Level: Low.

Skill Levels: Carpentry: Basic.

Materials: Appropriate size sheet of Plexiglas, short screws, clear silicone.

Tools: Utility knife, permanent pen, drill, caulking gun, framing square, bevel square.

Caution: Windows serve as a means of egress during emergencies. Never seal all the windows in one room, and make sure there are always at least two operable exits (doors and windows) for each room.

Taking measurements. The most difficult aspect of sealing unused windows is to ensure an accurate fit. First, determine that the exterior of the window, where you'll be adding your Plexiglas, is free and clear of any obstructions such as old nails, chunks of caulk, or old paint. You need to be able to slip your piece of Plexiglas into the opening and press it against the exterior wood stops that are holding your window in place. If these are not properly aligned or are missing (there most likely won't be one on the sill, but don't worry about it), you'll need to address this before installing your exterior window cover. You'll also need to check that the stops have sufficient caulk to stop airflow around the Plexiglas's edges. If the paint and caulk are in bad shape, you'll need to recaulk this to have an effective window treatment. Scrape the glass clean and wash with vinegar and water before recaulking.

Once you're convinced the window is as it should be, you need to check it for square before you cut out your piece of Plexiglas. Take very accurate measurements. Don't assume the top and the bottom or the two sides are equivalent, but measure each separately. Double-check for square by measuring the two diagonals; they should be equal. Then take the framing square and check each of the corners. If they are reasonably square, then you have no worries and can cut your Plexiglas square and get a good fit. If the frame is far out of square, you'll need to use a bevel square (sometimes called an angle-finder) to determine each angle and transcribe it to the sheet you are cutting.

Cutting the Plexiglas. You'll want to cut a piece of Plexiglas that is a ¼ inch smaller on both sides and the top than the frame of your window. The sheet will rest on the sill.

After you make your cut, dry-fit the piece to make sure it goes in smoothly. Check for gaps. If you're using corrugated polycarbonate sheets, they specify taping the bottom and top for a seal (the insulative tubes will be open at the cuts).

Before you affix your window cover, you'll probably need to cut two small (¼-inch) weepholes, or notches, on the bottom edge. This allows any possible condensation buildup to drain freely out, allowing your sill to stay dry. More than likely, there will be a gap somewhere along the bottom where the Plexiglas doesn't touch the sill. Leaving the bottom unsealed will provide plenty of weep room without any notches if this is the case. However, too much of a gap will decrease the effectiveness of your window-cover application, so there's a trade-off between keeping the inside space dry and reducing heat transfer. It's likely the case that, in combination with interior shutters or curtains, there will not be large amounts of condensation buildup because heat transfer has been reduced enough by the double air gap to inhibit it. It might be worthwhile to seal the sides and top and wait to see how the window performs before sealing the bottom edge.

Placing the Plexiglas. To seal the edges, run a bead of silicone around the top and sides. Press the Plexiglas into place. Generally, the silicone is quite sticky and may very well hold it in place. This isn't a sure thing, though. Putting in a few small screws around the perimeter will keep the Plexiglas in place until the silicone dries in a few hours. The screws can then be removed and the holes daubed with a little caulk.

Storm Windows

Project Time: One hour per window (plus a few weeks for delivery).

Cost: $70 per window.

Energy Saved: High. Every home should have storm windows.

Ease of Use: N/A.

Maintenance Level: None.

Skill Levels: Carpentry: Basic.

Materials: Caulk, screws.

Tools: Measuring tape, caulking gun, screwdriver.

Before you skip this section because you already have storm windows, let us remind you to check the caulk and seal around your storms. Reapply if necessary.

Ordering custom-made storm windows is not terribly expensive, but it frequently takes a few weeks for them to arrive. You have two options for their placement, and this decision will affect the size of your storm windows. They can go inside the jamb against the window stop, or they can go on the outside of the casing (for a review of window terminology see figure 5.7, page 87). Both options function perfectly well, although the face-of-the-jamb option has the *potential* to let in water, although with a decently made window this should not be the case. Any potential water infiltration will quickly drain out the weepholes regardless.

Taking measurements. Take detailed measurements from the outside of the window to within an eighth of an inch for *each* window. Measure from one side of the casing to the other, at the top and the bottom, as well as from the sill to the bottom side of the top (horizontal) piece of casing. Even though some of your windows may appear to be the same size, they might vary substantially, so be sure to measure them all, even if it means dragging out the extension ladder. If your intention is to place the storms inside the casing against the window stop, accurate measurement is a must. Create a list with the measurements and window location. Hang on to the list with each window's detailed measurements so you don't get the storms mixed up when they arrive.

For interior jamb placement, you'll also need to check the window for square with a large (18 inches on a side or more) framing square. If several of your windows are substantially out of square, which could easily be the case for older homes, you may want to consider placing the storm windows on the face of the casing rather than inside it. While it is possible to shift the windows slightly out of square to get them into place, racking them too much will make them difficult to operate.

For inside-the-casing placement, take a ¼ inch off your measurements from both dimensions if they are reasonably square (not more than a ¼ inch off from

Rope Caulk

Rope caulk refers to inexpensive caulk that is put in place with your hands instead of a caulking gun. It does not harden and is easily removable. Ninety-foot rolls cost about $5 and can do up to six windows. In late fall, when the odds of needing to open the windows for any passive heating is past, rope caulk can be applied to the perimeter of any of the opening sashes, practically eliminating potential drafts. In spring, the rope caulk can be removed and saved in an old shoe box or something similar for reuse the following fall. The combination of storm windows with existing windows that have been sealed with rope caulk creates an effective insulative air gap for almost any window.

top to bottom). For placement on the face of the casing, add 2 inches to the width dimension (1 inch for each side) and 1 inch to the height dimension (the window will rest on the sill, so you don't need to add anything for this). When ordering, check to make sure that the dimensions stated are the outside edges of the storm window, which they should be.

Repair windows while waiting for storms. While waiting for the storm windows to arrive, you'll need to check the windows for any needed repairs. Cracked and broken panes will need to be replaced. Loose glazing should be pulled free and repaired. Caulk should be applied to any gaps in the casing and to any sections of the windows that will not be operable. Stray paint should be scraped off the panes. It may be necessary to do some touch-up painting.

Applying the storm windows. Applying the storm windows is fairly straightforward and simply requires following the manufacturer's directions. Once they are screwed in place, caulk the perimeter of the windows. The bottom of the storm window where it hits the sill should have two notches to allow for any water that happens to get in to drain out. Most of

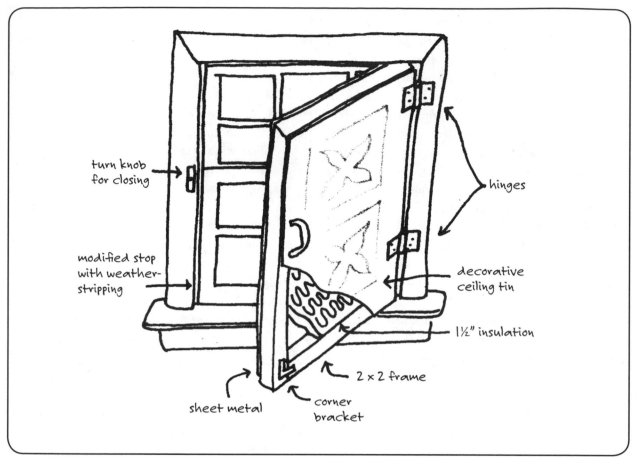

turn knob
for closing

hinges

modified stop
with weather-
stripping

decorative
ceiling tin

1½" insulation

2 x 2 frame

sheet metal

corner
bracket

FIG. 7.1. **The basic components of a DIY insulated shutter.**

the time, the manufacturer will specify not to caulk the bottom of the window, but we've found that air infiltration can still be significant from the gaps where the storm window hits the sill. Caulking the bottom, making sure to leave an open pathway at the two notches, can help reduce this airflow if you find it to be an issue.

INSULATED CURTAINS AND SHUTTERS

A variety of systems have been devised over the years to stop heat transfer through windows. The most obvious is the curtain. While curtains do address heat transfer via radiation, when improperly installed they can increase the convection over the window and potentially lead to a net heat loss. This happens primarily

from top to bottom when a large gap allows warm air to be pulled downward from the ceiling between the curtain and the glass. This cools the air, causing it to drop down below the curtain level and escape back out into the room. The cool air entering the room is replaced by additional warm air near the ceiling, and a thermosiphon effect can become established, quickly sucking the heat out of the room.

This can also occur to a lesser degree when curtains have large gaps between the sides and the wall. To make the application of curtains worthwhile from an energy conservation standpoint, it's necessary to go to some trouble to reduce as much as possible all gaps around the edges of the curtains. Historically, the thermosiphon effect has been reduced by the application of a valance (also called a pelmet) at the top of the window. Often these are applied with aesthetics as the main concern (covering the curtain hardware) instead of energy conservation. To be effective, the valance needs to hug tight to the wall above the window to prevent thermosiphoning. Cloth valances rarely achieve this end. Constructed wood valances, sometimes found in older homes, are more effective.

For windows without curtains or with poorly functioning curtains, there are two options: insulated curtains or shutters. Typically, insulated curtains are held tight to the wall by embedded magnets (or Velcro) in the curtain and window trim. Insulated shutters are typically hinged on one side, although they can be hinged on the top and opened via a pulley and held against the ceiling. They typically consist of a simple 2 × 2 frame with metal on both sides and insulation sandwiched in between, typically high-R-value foamboard. See figure 7.1.

Insulated curtains are either homemade or purchased affairs. Beware—many big-box retailers sell what they call insulated curtains, but these are thin and don't seal around the edges. Solar Components (www .solar-components.com/quilts) sells insulated material for making your own sealing insulated curtains. Cozy Curtains (www.cozycurtains.com) will custom-make sealing insulated curtains for around $10–12/ square foot. Generally, windows with sealing insulated curtains achieve an R-value of around 7 or 8. The curtains also have excellent sound-deadening and light-blocking qualities.

Sealing Drafts

Renter friendly.

Project Time: One weekend.

Cost: $5–50.

Energy Saved: High. Drafts can suck much of the heat out a home very quickly.

Ease of Use: N/A.

Maintenance Level: None.

Skill Levels: Carpentry: Basic.

Materials: Caulk, silicone.

Tools: Caulking gun, pry bar, screwdriver, incense or smoke stick.

Blow-in insulation. For older homes, the best way to seal up a drafty house is often by blowing insulation, either cellulose or fiberglass, into the walls and attic. Loose-fill insulation can reduce airflow to the point where air infiltration is essentially eliminated. If your home is poorly insulated, blowing in insulation in the attic and walls should be your top priority. It's probably best to hire someone for at least the wall insulation. The reason to hire out is because blowing in sufficient insulation to get up to R-13 or so requires pressure created by a high-powered compressor that is not easy to rent. Walls and attic can be done in an afternoon by a professional. However, the attic doesn't require high pressure and can be a DIY job if you're so inclined. Many rental places or big-box stores have the equipment needed to blow in attic insulation.

Checking for air leaks. If your walls are already insulated, you'll want to check all protrusions into the interior wall space for potential air leaks. This is easy to do with a stick of incense, when the interior temperature is substantially different than the exterior temperature. Hold a smoking stick close to things such as outlets, tops and bottoms of baseboards, chair rails, picture rails, window trim, plumbing intrusions, and vents, and watch the smoke. If it's not floating straight up, you found one.

Outlets and switch seals are made of rubber and match the profile of the outlet (receptacle or switch). These can be purchased at most hardware stores. Remove the outlet cover with a screwdriver and stick the seal in between the cover and the wall. Be cautious of live wires; to play it safe turn off the breaker for the circuits you will be working on whenever removing outlet covers.

Drafts from gaps in trim or plumbing and HVAC intrusions can be sealed with either pure silicone (which is preferred as it stays flexible, but it is not paintable) or painter's caulk with some silicone added. Expandable foam is an option for large cracks (more than a ¼ inch), although it often contains potential toxins like benzene and often uses HCFCs for blowing agents, known to be potent greenhouse gases.

Stopping vertical airflow. If your home is old and your interior walls are extremely drafty, you have two options. The first is to seal either the basement or the attic. This will close either the entrance (basement) or the exit (attic) for the cold air. Again, blowing in insulation in the attic does a great job of essentially eliminating potential basement-to-attic airflow through interior walls. The cheapest (but most difficult) choice is to go into the basement or crawl space and clog any holes made in the floor and walls for systems such as electrical and plumbing. There are often a surprising number of these. This can be done with expanded foam or by stuffing bits of fiberglass insulation into the holes. While fiberglass insulation does let through some air, it reduces airflow by over 90 percent.

If your house is on piers and not enclosed, you'll need to insulate your floor. This is an unpleasant and difficult task but will go a long way in sealing up your home. Flexible rods are sold to hold floor insulation in place, but we've seen these fail on a number of occasions. The best method for holding floor insulation in place is to start with a few of these flexible rods and then staple chicken wire to keep it in place.

Recessed lights and electrical boxes in the ceiling are a common escape route for air. Again, blowing some insulation in the attic will do wonders. Fiberglass batts in the attic also benefit from this treatment, as the gaps between the edges and the joists can let out a fair amount of heat.

Check all ductwork. If you have a conventional furnace or heat pump with forced-air heating, you'll need to check your ductwork annually. This is because some piece or other has quite likely become detached over the course of time and is lying on the crawl space floor, keeping the crickets warm. To detect a detached duct, check each heating vent in your house, while the heating system is running, by placing your hand over the vent to feel for airflow. What you can't check from above are slightly detached or leaky connections, which occur with great regularity. Grab the incense stick and check all the lines for leaks, using real duct tape (black, not gray, and quite expensive) to seal any problem areas. Also check for crimped ductwork or holes from squirrels or rodents. Repair any problem areas.

In a really well-sealed home, there's the potential to have an inadequate amount of fresh air coming in from the outside. If you've done a great job sealing your home, and especially if you heat with wood (which uses up a lot of oxygen), you'll want to install an *air exchanger*. This brings in fresh air and exhausts interior air through a highly conductive metal passageway that exchanges much of the heat of the outgoing air with the incoming air.

INSULATION

The first thing you need to insulate is yourself. Most of the objects in your room couldn't care less if they're 50 degrees F or 80 degrees F. Wool socks, thermal underwear, a warm sweater, and cozy slippers are perfectly comfortable additions that will greatly reduce your home heating needs.

Insulate, insulate, insulate. It's hard to insulate too much. In many instances, installing additional insulation in your home will save as much energy as it took to produce and install it, often in only a month or two's time, yet the insulation will remain effective for decades or centuries. And this easily translates into direct financial savings. It's not uncommon for the rate of return on installing insulation, especially in older homes, to approach 50 percent per year (check out an online rate-of-return calculator at www.chuck-wright.com/calculators/insulpb.html). If your financial adviser promised you returns in that neighborhood, you'd probably call the police wondering what nefarious activity he was trying to get you involved in. If our editors had asked us to limit the topic of this book to just one subject, we would have chosen insulation, because it's far and away the most important thing average homeowners can spend their time and money on to get them on their way to fossil-energy independence. Fortunately, that didn't happen or this would be one boring book! Still, there's a lot that can be said in a much smaller amount of space.

Types of Insulation

It's not worth fretting too much over which types of insulation are "green" or "sustainable." Pretty much all insulation is "green" when properly applied, even if it's very energy intensive in its manufacture, such as fiberglass or foamboard. The whole purpose of insulation is to be light and airy, so it often takes only a few dozen pounds of insulation for a good-sized attic. And instead of getting used only once, like the glass or plastic bottles we see overflowing from recycling bins, insulation gets used again and again, day in and day out, decade after decade. There are of course human health variables, in that some insulation off-gasses volatile organic compounds or formaldehyde, especially when first installed. If you are chemically sensitive, pay particular attention to your insulation choices. And foams are made of fossil fuels, which we hate, but properly installed they offset so much additional fossil-fuel use that they can be very useful on the path to carbon freedom.

Comparisons between different types of insulation are not often fruitful. Oftentimes, different types are used because different applications are required. For instance, spray foam or foamboard is used when a high R-value is required for a tight space or open application, fiberglass batts are used for insulating open cavities before drywall or plaster goes on, and loose-fill cellulose is used for blow-ins of attics and closed wall cavities. Use the type of insulation that is easiest for you to apply and fits within your budget and ethics. If it's the right one for the job at hand, don't let some aspect of a particular insulation's manufacturing process keep you from insulating, because the energy-saving benefits are so enormous. Variations exist between different products of the same type, so make inquiries from specific manufacturers before ordering (for example, the amount of recycled glass content in fiberglass insulation, formaldehyde-free versions, differing fire retardants, soy component in foam insulations, and so on).

With all that in mind, table 7.1 offers a quick rundown of the pros and cons of various insulation types.

Slip Straw and Clay Slip

The cheapest and most available of all insulation is an ancient concoction variously referred to as slip straw or clay slip. The basic principle is straightforward: straw is dipped in a clay slurry and, depending on the application, allowed to dry and then installed or packed in still somewhat wet.

The coating of clay residue that covers the straw serves a variety of purposes. First, it protects this organic material from molds that could potentially grow on it if left in a moist environment. The straw is in effect mummified. This also makes it much less appealing to bugs and rodents that might be interested in using it as bedding. Second, it provides fire protection. Uncoated straw will burn rapidly when removed from its bale and thus exposed to plenty of oxygen. The heavier the coating of clay on the straw, the more mummified and fire resistant it is.

Straw must be differentiated from hay. Hay is grass that is cut and then dried, to be fed to cows or other ruminants during winter when there is no fresh grass. It is rich in nutrients and weed seeds and is thus very attractive to molds, fungi, bugs, and rodents in addition to the four-legged creatures it was intended for. It should never be used for building or insulating anything. Straw is the dried stalk of harvested grains, such as wheat or rice. Although not actually woody, it is surprisingly strong and also has a very low nutritional value, making it much less appealing to critters of all stripes. The stems of almost all straw are also hollow, which provides an additional air pocket, increasing its insulative value. Straw can usually be purchased at any garden or farm supply shop.

Slip straw can be used in a variety of applications. When allowed to dry, it can be placed by hand in open attic spaces, on top of existing insulation if there is any, to the desired depth. Its R-value is not great, somewhere between R-1 and R-1.5/inch depending on the mix, especially compared to manufactured materials like fiberglass. However, it's easy to make in bulk, natural, and extremely cheap. Another application is in open wall cavities in between framing members

TABLE 7.1 Summary of Insulation Choices

Insulation	Type	R-value/Inch	Pros	Cons	Ease of Installation
Fiberglass	Loose fill or batts	2.5–3.5	Readily available, some recycled content, long-lasting, holds shape well, resists fire, batts are easy to install in many applications.	Can contain off-gassing formaldehyde, improper batt installation can reduce effectiveness, energy-intense manufacture, skin irritant.	Batts are easy to install before interior wall material is applied and in open attics. Additional insulation should be added perpendicular to existing batts if possible. Loose fill can be blown into empty wall cavities.
Cellulose	Loose fill	3	High recycled content (80% postconsumer cardboard and newsprint), no formaldehyde, less irritating during installation.	Contains fire retardants and mold inhibitors that could affect health, prone to settling esp. in walls, leading to substantial heat loss.	Relatively easy, but requires renting sprayer. Can't be applied to open wall.
Rock Wool	Loose fill	2.5	Made from mining waste, excellent noise reduction, naturally fire-resistant.	More expensive, possible lung irritant during installation, energy-intense manufacture.	Similar to loose-fill cellulose.
Sheep's Wool	Batts	3.5	Naturally occurring and benign, excellent R-value, fire-resistant.	Expensive, limited availability.	Same as fiberglass batts but less irritating.
Cotton	Batts	3.3	Naturally occurring and benign, excellent R-value, fire-resistant.	Expensive, limited availability.	Same as fiberglass batts but less irritating.
Foamboard	4' x 8' sheets	4–7	High R-value per inch, resistant to compaction, self-containing qualities good for open application such as basement or exterior walls.	Made of extruded plastic, manufacture emits ozone-depleting gases, application can be messy and inexact, leaving gaps for air leakage or thermal bridging.	Indispensable for certain applications. Large sheets can be difficult to handle individually. Precision cutting is difficult.
Liquid Foam	Spray	4–6	Fills entire cavity, eliminating air gaps; high R-value; some soy-based foam available.	Requires open wall cavities, usually made from petrochemicals, somewhat expensive, installation can be messy.	Requires contractor.
Slip Straw	Loose fill	1–1.5	Inexpensive, natural, readily available.	Labor-intensive, limited application for retrofits.	Easy to make and install.
Waste Materials	Loose fill	variable	Inexpensive and readily available; could potentially be good way to recycle waste materials instead of dumping them.	Labor-intensive, limited application, potential fire hazard.	Easy to make and install.

to create a filled-in wall space ready for an earth or lime plaster. For this book, we will refer to the former as *slip straw* and the latter as *clay slip,* since it has a substantially higher clay content and the application is different. For those interested in incorporating locally sourced low-impact natural materials into their home, or for those with more time than money, these two methods are great additions to the toolbox. See the resources for more information on natural building.

Making and Applying Slip Straw and Clay Slip

Project Time: Weekend or more depending on size of project.

Cost: $5–50.

Energy Saved: High. Adding insulation to your home is one of the best things you can do to save energy.

Ease of Use: N/A.

Maintenance Level: None.

Skill Levels: Carpentry: Basic.

Materials: At least one straw bale and two 5-gallon buckets of screened clay per bale.

Tools: Hardware cloth with half-inch holes, pitchfork, shovel, masonry tub or garbage can, 5-gallon buckets, hose with spray nozzle, tarp.

Gathering materials. You'll need to find some clay subsoil that is relatively free of organic matter. Set aside any topsoil and save it for your plants. The clay will need to be screened and soaked. To screen the clay, bend some hardware cloth (basically 2-foot-tall fencing with square holes) over the top of a bucket, and place a shovelful of clay on top. If you're going to make large quantities, it will be easier if you build a 2 × 4 box that fits over the top of the bucket with hardware cloth attached using staples or strips of wood. Scrape and push the chunks of clay through the hardware cloth with your

FIG. 7.2. **Making slip straw is straightforward. After your clay mix has achieved the appropriate goopiness, throw in loose straw and mix with a pitchfork, making sure the straw gets completely coated.**

FIG. 7.3. **The straw is completely coated when you can no longer see any brown left. Let it dry on a tarp.**

hands (wear gloves), a hoe, or a block of wood. Remove any debris that doesn't make it through, the exception being chunks of pure clay that won't make it through but that will soften with soaking. If you don't have any hardware cloth or don't want to buy any, simply pick the larger rocks out of your clay pile, again making sure not to discard the chunks of clay.

When the bucket is three-quarters full, fill it to the top with water. As the clay soaks up the water, you may need to refill the bucket once so that there is a consistent inch of water above the level of the clay. Let it sit overnight.

The next day or later (the bucket can sit there indefinitely, although it may develop a slight off-odor depending on the level of organic matter), mix the contents thoroughly with a stick. If you have an electric drill with a paddle bit (often used for mixing paint or drywall mud), this works great. If not, the stick will do.

Mixing the materials. Shovel some of the wet clay into your mixing tub or garbage can. For slip straw

you're going to want a thinner mix, and for clay slip a thicker mix. This is because the clay slip needs to have enough clay to hold itself up in the wall, so it requires more structural clay material.

Because it ends up having more thermal mass (clay) and less insulation (straw), clay slip is a hybrid that performs an intermediate role between these two different functions. Because of this, it tends to perform somewhat poorly during periods of extreme heat or cold.

For slip straw, add water until the mix is the thickness of a creamy soup. For clay slip, shoot more for a thick sauce. If you have some available, a shovelful of sand makes a great addition to clay slip.

Take several handfuls of straw and throw these handfuls into the tub, scattering the individual pieces. Push them in with a pitchfork, making sure each piece gets thoroughly coated. If the clay washes off your straw and you see patches of brown, your mix is too watery and you'll need to add another shovelful of thick, wet clay. For the clay slip, there should still be substantial

FIG. 7.4. **A clay-slip wall after the forms have been removed. Making clay-slip is much faster than making cob for applications that require lots of thermal mass. The clay slip applied here will help regulate temperatures for food storage on a farm, behaving similarly to a root cellar.**

clumps of clay mixed in with the straw. Pull the clayey straw out, allow it to drip for a few seconds, and then place it on a tarp.

For slip straw, allow the clay and straw mixture to dry thoroughly on a tarp in the sun. Then haul it to where it needs to go and pack it in.

Clay slip requires forms to hold it in place while it dries. Scrap pieces of plywood or other strips of lumber work great. Screw these scraps of wood into the studs where you're filling in with the clay slip. The wood pieces will hold the clay slip in place until it's dry enough to support itself, at which point they can be moved up higher and more clay slip can be added.

Attaching clay slip to studs. It's important to have "keys" attached to the studs to hold the clay slip in

place once it dries. All this means is you need to nail in a block of wood into the cavity that will be filled every 18 inches or so, or at a minimum have a few nails sticking out of the stud. It's wise to protect any wood it will be touching with linseed oil or primer to avoid condensation and rot issues. Clay slip can be put in place immediately after being mixed, but it will still be wet enough to leak a substantial amount of water. If puddling water is a concern where you are working, let the clay slip rest on a tarp for a few minutes before application. Watch out for any materials that have the potential to be damaged by exposure to dampness, such as wood floors or drywall, and make sure these are protected during application. Once you've reached the desired height, the

Insulative Paint

Flipping through a magazine, you might come across an ad for some form of insulative paint. A bevy of companies have sprung up over the years offering dramatic energy savings if you use their product. The idea is you buy their paint (or paint additive), slap it on the outside of your home, and instantly receive dramatic energy savings of "up to 40 percent!" Now, a coat of paint is only a millimeter or two in thickness, so you may be wondering how manufacturers manage to pack such tremendous amounts of insulation into such a thin coating. Various rationales are proposed: ceramic fibers block the heat; small microscopic bubbles provide millions of air pockets, et cetera. With anything that sounds too good to be true, the proof is in the pudding. And with insulating paints, there just ain't no pudding to be had.

Unfortunately, we share in some of the guilt of recommending one of these coatings. When our cob house was heading toward final inspection, our inspector rightly questioned the insulating value of our earth home. At first we couldn't understand why he was concerned. Our walls were at least a foot thick in most places, up to 18 inches toward the base. How could our walls not be insulated enough? Well, after a little research, we realized that earth, especially packed earth, is a very poor insulator, somewhere in the neighborhood of R-0.25/inch. Our foot-thick walls had an R-value of only around 3. By code, they needed to be around 13! What were we going to do?

It was under this duress that we discovered Industrial Nanotech and their paint, Nansulate. Using the latest in nanotechnology, they claimed to achieve an R-value close to 11 with three applications of their paint. The small nanotubes provided enough air pockets to achieve this. Since the other alternative was basically to frame a wall around the outside of our existing home, insulate it, and then add some kind of exterior siding, we leapt at this opportunity. Our inspector, gracious

---

clay slip wall can be left as is or finished off with an earth or lime plaster for additional sealing and thermal mass.

WASTE MATERIALS

Since most insulation is just a bunch of bubbles, it's not hard to imagine lots of suitable materials that get tossed every day that instead might find a second life helping you stay warm. Packing peanuts, old carpets, shredded newspaper or cardboard, and many other items seem like they would do a decent job of this. Instead of burying these things in the ground, why not recycle them as some attic insulation? So far as waste materials go, we've also had good luck finding perfectly good fiberglass insulation in construction and renovation Dumpsters.

The main reason lot of waste materials won't work on their own is because of their potential flammability. For instance, the polystyrene in most packing peanuts is highly flammable, as is Styrofoam to a lesser degree. These materials are, however, highly insulative. Newspaper and cardboard are recycled into cellulose insulation after they are treated with a fire retardant and fungicide, for instance.

The possibility exists to use the same mummifying and fire-retarding clay coating used in slip straw and clay slip with many of these materials as well. You should proceed with caution in this area, however. Safety should be foremost in your mind when considering such an undertaking. Making test batches and then subjecting them to flammability tests would go a long way in determining which materials could be recycled safely as insulation. Many household materials such as carpet, draperies, and clothing already have to meet relatively strict flammability tests (which usually means they are coated with chemicals, so do

Southern gentleman that he was, didn't ask too many questions. And neither did we.

Until we started working on this book. With the certificate of occupancy of our initial cob home hanging on the wall long enough to collect a little dust, it was time to ask ourselves if this stuff was really doing anything worthwhile. Was it really possible to get such a high R-value in such a thin layer of material? If so, why weren't they making inch-thick sheets of the stuff that had some crazy insulative value like R-4000? When we checked back with the company, we saw that they had used an article that Stephen had written for *Home Power* magazine in their promotions department. Why were they basing their sales on what a couple of hippies were doing in the woods of North Carolina? Where were the numbers? Where was the third-party testing?

Nowhere that we've found yet. One insulating-paint company we found did offer third-party verification for their product, so we followed that lead. It turned out that the third party was a private detective down in Tampa, Florida. When we contacted him to inquire what kinds of tests he had conducted, he told us he'd never heard of the stuff.

We wanted to tell this story to illustrate the dangers lurking out there. As energy consciousness increases, more scam artists are likely to move in looking for a quick buck. But the laws of thermodynamics are not so easily defied. Capturing and retaining heat is extremely difficult and requires plenty of forethought, time, effort, and space. Always check for third-party verification of any claims made, and for newer products, always check with the third party to make sure they're not an inadvertent part of the scam.

What paint is certainly capable of achieving is a change of color, and color plays a major role in whether a given material reflects or absorbs heat. Of course, this has nothing to do with whether some ceramic dusts or nanobubbles have been added to it.

any testing outdoors). If these materials could easily be shredded and then coated in clay the same way that slip straw is, they should make an extremely safe and durable insulation material. A type of construction material called "papercrete" is made of shredded paper encased in concrete. Tests have shown this to be highly resistant to fire.

A simple test could be done by coating the material with clay and allowing it to dry thoroughly. Then place it up on a screen with a candle burning below it and see how long it takes to ignite. Some materials will give off toxic smoke when they burn and this should be kept in mind. All tests should be conducted outdoors, the test material should never be left unattended, and there should always be a hose nearby. While we've never experimented with this ourselves, the idea seems intellectually sound, since highly flammable straw is rendered fire safe by the clay coating. In tests, wood chips have been shown to be highly insu-

lative on their own. We suspect that coated with clay and perhaps mixed with straw, a wood-chip concoction could potentially produce a higher R-value natural insulation. Just a few ideas for the experimenters out there. Be sure to let us know about any results!

COOLING THE ATTIC AND WALLS

Keeping your attic and exterior walls from overheating is of fundamental importance for keeping your home cool in the summertime. Heat hates to be bottled up and always wants to equalize with its surroundings, and the more heat there is, the more it wants to move. Higher temperatures in the attic and on your exterior walls mean greater heat flows through the ceilings and walls into your home. Insulation helps slow this, but remember, it can never stop it.

There are many landscaping options for keeping your walls cool, and we discuss many of these in detail in chapter 10. One of the most fundamental choices that affects heat buildup on exterior walls, as well as in the attic, is color. Some colors are much more reflective than others. White, for instance, reflects 80 percent of the light that strikes it, while black reflects only around 5 percent and absorbs the rest. Obviously, if you have darker-colored roofing material and exterior walls with lots of solar exposure, heat is going to build up and some of this heat is going to make it into your home.

The more poorly insulated your home, the bigger a problem color will be. While exterior walls can usually be shaded with intelligent landscaping options, this is more difficult to achieve for the roof. Large shade trees sometimes exist in the proper location, being ideally tall deciduous trees on the east and west sides of the home. Planting deciduous hardwoods and waiting for them to grow tall enough for this purpose is not practical, especially since as a general rule the faster a tree grows the weaker it will be, potentially putting your home in danger. We also believe that the benefits of sunshine on a home (for passive and active solar) far outweigh the drawbacks, and large shade trees are to be avoided for the most part.

Slope is also a factor in heat absorption for roofs. Flatter roofs are closer to perpendicular to the hot summer sun and absorb more of its rays, while steeper roofs reflect more of it away.

Options for the Attic

Besides color, the choice of roofing material can make a big difference in how much heat enters your attic. Asphalt shingles, besides wearing out quickly and leaching toxins into your yard, generally heat up the fastest and are the worst offender in this regard. White shingles, for instance, have a reflectance of only about 26 percent, while a white metal roof can reflect 66 percent or more. Everything about asphalt shingles bespeaks a short-term outlook that shows little regard for energy or the environment. Besides the above issues, they have a short life and are made of unre-

TABLE 7.2 Metal Roofing Reflectance	
Color	Solar Reflectance %
Bone White	66.1
Sandstone	50.1
Classic Green	11.2
Patina Green	24.3
Hartford Green	8.5
Pacific Blue	17.7
Slate Blue	19.5
Matte Black	5.6
Burgundy	12.4
Cardinal Red	36.9
Coral	34.4
Musket Gray	13.1

Source: Parker et al., "Laboratory Testing of the Reflectance Properties of Roofing Materials," *Florida Solar Energy Center*

cyclable energy-intense materials that take up landfill space and befoul the earth.

We are fans of metal roofs and provide installation details in chapter 8. The properties of metal make it a natural radiant barrier regardless of color (although lighter colors always help), and for that reason federal energy-efficiency tax credits (currently 10 percent) are available for metal-roof installation.

For shallowly sloped roofs (less than 30 degrees), extensive green roofs are a possibility, although at a steeper price. Green roofs are discussed in chapter 10 and can dramatically lower roof temperatures by up to 80 degrees F.

There are many other roofing options, including wood shingle, clay or concrete tile, and slate, to name a few. For these, the primary consideration for warmer climates is color. Although these are often an improvement over shingles as regards longevity, beauty, environmental impact, and water catchment, they provide only a marginal improvement, if any, for reducing heat buildup in the attic.

The traditional method of keeping the attic from overheating is providing proper ventilation. Typically, vents in the soffit (the underside of the eave) pull in fresh air from outside and allow the hot air in the attic to vent out a ridge vent at the top of your home.

Another common option is to have two gable-end vents on either side of a home, which allows cross-ventilation. Gable-end vents are usually not as effective as soffit/ridge-cap vents because the latter take advantage of the natural stack effect discussed previously. Because soffit vents are lower than ridge-cap vents, the hot air flows out the top and pulls fresh, cooler air into the attic.

Check to make sure your attic has some kind of venting system. If it has none at all, then almost without a doubt your attic is a blast furnace and this is making you forever dependent on mechanical air conditioning. If you have attic access, put a thermometer with a max/min function up there on a sunny summer day and check out how hot it gets. If it's getting more than 15–20 degrees hotter than the outside high temperature for the day, chances are that a good amount of the heat finds its way through your ceiling and into your home.

Radiant barriers can work in conjunction with an existing soffit-ridge venting system to help keep attics cool. Sheets of reinforced aluminum foil are tacked on the underside of exposed rafters. As heat infiltrates the roofing material and enters the attic, some of it gets trapped in the space created between the underside of the sheathing and the foil. As heat builds and begins to exit the ridge vent, cooler air is drawn in through the eave vents, and a thermosiphon develops, shepherding much of the unwanted heat out through the roof before it can enter the attic proper. Metal roofs applied in the manner, described later in chapter 8, will create a similar effect. Radiant barriers can also work on top of attic insulation, although they may be prone to getting dusty and losing effectiveness.

OTHER INSULATING IDEAS

Folks have taken the step of framing in an additional interior stud wall against their existing northern wall, then insulating, adding drywall, and painting. This is harder to do if the wall has existing windows and you want to keep them, but it is relatively straightforward

for the experienced carpenter. Electrical outlets and switches also need to be moved.

Some folks have developed hybrid conventional/natural homes by wrapping existing buildings with straw bales, then plastering over the bales with an earth or natural plaster. Since straw bales often approach an R-value of 40, this can be an extremely effective way of insulating an existing house. Because the bales are isolated from the rest of the home by the preexisting walls, there is little worry about potential mold problems from the bales in wetter climes. Although this type of retrofit would require extending the eaves well beyond the straw bales to ensure they stay dry, this could be done with a wraparound covered porch. This idea makes great sense for existing cinderblock homes, with the possibility of transforming these banal structures into beautiful natural homes. If the cinderblock walls could be filled, potentially with loose sand, then the ideal of a high-thermal-mass home wrapped in lots of insulation would be achieved. Don't forget that insulation functions for coolness retention as well as heat retention. An example of a straw bale wrap for coolness retention is the Myhrman/Knox family compound in the desert Southwest, detailed in *Natural Remodeling for the Not-So-Green House* by Venolia and Lerner (see resources).

THERMAL MASS AND PASSIVE COOLING

In our climate in the piedmont of North Carolina, we want our thermal mass to perform opposite functions at different times of year. In winter, we want our thermal mass to store the excess energy from our active and passive solar heating and woodstove to keep our home warm. In summer, we want our thermal mass to store the extra coolness that we get by opening up our windows at night, through the long, hot summer days after we close the windows in the morning. Different climates have different needs. Farther north, retaining cool may not be difficult. Farther south, retaining cool may be the main priority.

We mention these things because where you wind up putting your thermal mass will affect how well it works regarding these separate functions. Typically, passive-solar design manuals have emphasized things such as Trombe walls (large, high-thermal-mass walls with direct exposure to lots of south-facing glazing) that get direct sunlight in winter, heat up, and release this heat at night. Unfortunately, this takes only one aspect of the utility of thermal mass into account, and even this it does poorly.

Trombe walls are of limited utility mainly because they are so difficult to insulate at night and thus radiate most of their heat back out through the windows instead of into the home. While it is possible to insulate them, this usually involves complicated exterior insulated shutters or hard-to-access interior curtains. Furthermore, they block almost all of the incoming light. One of the great things about retrofitting for passive solar design is the fabulous amount of daylight that pours in, and the option of sitting directly in this sunlight for personal heating and general refreshment. Trombe walls are good theory but generally function poorly in reality.

For maintaining constant temperatures, thermal mass is much more effective when diffused throughout the home. This is because there are a variety of heat sources even in a fossil-fuel-free home. Besides passive solar heating, homes can be passively heated by opening the windows on warm spring and fall days. Greater surface area of the thermal mass means much more heat can be absorbed and, later, released. The same applies for cooling off the thermal mass with open windows and fans in the summertime. It is very difficult for one large chunk of thermal mass to be cooled down enough in the 8 to 10 hours of nighttime cool.

Solar-heating systems can result in zones of different temperatures throughout the day. The accumulated heat being held by the distributed mass will gradually disperse in the late afternoon and evening. Rather than a negative, having rooms of different temperature allows for adjusting one's comfort level by moving from room to room. Generally, it's not very important if places like bedrooms are cold during the course of the day. Excess fossil energy has led to the expectation

that every room in every home will be at a comfortable temperature regardless of when or if the home's occupants intend to use it. This facile assumption has made our homes fossil-energy hogs, to little end. When thinking about how to redesign your home for solar heating and passive cooling, always keep in mind that as long the temperature remains above 50 degrees F, very little in your home cares how cold it is (except tropical plants, which can be placed in the sun). It's only the living, breathing inhabitants, all of which are mobile, that do care.

The concept of increasing thermal mass is fairly straightforward. Basically, we want to have a bunch of heavy, dense stuff distributed throughout our home. Of course, the more heavy stuff we have sitting on floors and hanging on walls, the more concerns we have with our home being able to hold that stuff up. Distributing the thermal mass throughout the home will help.

The great thing about retrofitting your home over time is that you can evaluate how various projects affect your home's comfort level and then stake out your next course of action based on this. For heating, the three general strategies will be, in no particular order, adding windows or other solar collectors to the south side of your home to collect additional heat, increasing the insulation around your home, and adding more thermal mass to the interior to capture and release any additional heat. The last two are also needed for passive cooling.

Say, for example, that you have recently added a large passive-solar window wall to a south-facing room. The windows amount to roughly 10 percent of your home's square footage. The room is heating up very nicely, and, when at home, you use a small fan to help distribute the generated heat throughout the house. You still need your gas furnace, but you're using it much less often. The next winter, you finally have the time and funds to massively upgrade your home's insulation. You blow in more insulation in the attic and fill the wall cavities. You locate drafts and seal these as best as possible. You hang insulated curtains over all your windows and close them up at night. It's

TABLE 7.3 Heat Storage Capacity of Various Common Materials at 70°F

Material	Density (pounds/ft³)	Specific Heat	Heat Storage Capacity (Btu/ft³/Delta-F)	Thermal Conductivity (relative)
Adobe or Cob	80	0.15	12	4
Concrete	100	0.16	16	2*
Granite	160	0.2	32	4.5
Water	62	1	62	1.6
Cast Iron	450	0.11	50	109
Plaster	53	0.20	11	1.3
Drywall	42	0.26	11	3.1
Wood (Pine)	34	0.45	15	0.3
Brick	130	0.22	28	1.5
Steel	495	0.12	59	115

* The conductivity of concrete is heavily dependent on the materials in its composition (e.g., gravel, sand, stone, etc.).

late winter, and as you wrap up these projects, you find your home becoming uncomfortably warm during the course of the day, so much so that you must occasionally open the windows. Then at night, your home cools off uncomfortably, and when it's cloudy for several days, there's no option but to run the furnace.

In this example, you are losing perfectly good solar energy because you don't have enough thermal mass to store the additional heat produced by your south-facing windows. The next summer you spend a few weekends replacing the carpeting with a thick earthen floor in the room that receives the winter sunshine. The next winter, instead of overheating during sunny days, the solar room is comfortably warm and holds its heat overnight and even into the next day. There is no need to ever open windows because of excess heat, and instead of turning the furnace on, you have only the occasional fire in your efficient woodstove.

The point of this example is that, unlike building a home from scratch and calculating complex charts with ratios of passive solar area to the different densities of thermal mass, when retrofitting a home over the course of a few years, empirical data can be used to bring your levels of solar heating and thermal mass into balance. The additional thermal mass can take many forms and be a variety of thicknesses and materials. The greater the surface area of the thermal mass, the quicker it will take up and release extra heat or cool. Thinner thermal mass will obviously hold less heat or coolness than thicker thermal mass. Lastly, airflow over thermal mass can greatly increase the rate of exchange. This is especially important for storing coolness in the summertime. Opening windows will cool down the house, but to really cool down the thermal mass in the house and keep it nice and cool through the next day requires at least a fan or two (if not a whole-house fan) to move the air over the walls and take out as much heat as possible. Likewise, masonry stoves (see below) require the movement of air and lots of surface area for heat exchange from the fire to take place efficiently and keep the house warm long after the fire has gone out.

A few examples of some things you can add to build thermal mass to your house are concrete countertops, masonry stoves (homemade or professional), slab floors, thermal-mass walls made of brick, stone, cob, or other masonry, earth or lime plaster walls, indoor plants, et cetera. When we initially moved into our home it was heated by a gas-fired boiler/radiator system. Although we immediately disabled the boiler, we left the immensely heavy (and sort of cool-looking) radiators as thermal-mass plant stands in our rooms. Perhaps one day we will be able to use them with solar hot water.

Having a variety of different types of thermal mass of varying thicknesses ensures heat retention and release for short (hours) and long (days) periods. In addition to surface area, the relative thermal conductivity of the material affects its ability to retain and hold heat.

COB

Cob is a mixture of clay, sand, and straw that is similar in its final form to earthen materials used in construction throughout the world, such as adobe. It is a structural material with good thermal storage.

Cob has many advantages that make it worth considering adding to your home. It is one of the most beginner-friendly masonry materials there is. Using readily available materials, large amounts of cob can be made for very little money. It dries slowly and even after it has set up it can be rewet and then reworked, allowing for sculpting and a variety of shapes. The final product is earth-toned and does not clash with other colors; many people find it relaxing to be surrounded by earth structures. Being unfired masonry, it can help regulate interior humidity as well as temperature. Cob can be made into benches, interior walls, masonry stoves, and floors, for example. Its thermal storage qualities can be improved by the addition of denser materials such as gravel or scrap concrete (often called *urbanite*). Finally, cob is an excellent acoustic barrier, making it a great choice for separating bedrooms and offices from other living spaces.

Making Cob

Project Time: Depends on project; likely several weekends.

Cost: Low; $0–500, depending on local availability of clay and sand.

Energy Saved: Medium. Having a method of storing additional heat and coolness is vital to a carbon-free home.

Ease of Use: N/A.

Maintenance Level: Low. Occasional patching may be required if damaged.

Skill Levels: Carpentry: Moderate. Masonry: Basic.

Materials: Large amounts of clay (free of organic matter) and sand, at least one straw bale (not hay!).

Tools: Shovel, tarp, hose, machete or old handsaw, level.

Caution: Cob, like all earthen materials, has the potential to liquefy and collapse during earthquakes. Folks in earthquake-prone areas need to proceed with great caution and will almost certainly need to reinforce their cob with Portland cement (called stabilization).

Cob is built in place, layer after layer, rather than being made into bricks like adobe. The two methods combine wonderfully, however, and adobe bricks or patties can be worked into a cob wall, which can speed the construction process and keep much of the mess outdoors. Cob is often referred to as monolithic adobe. Obviously, depending on what you are building, the steps will be different, but we will touch on the basic method here and hopefully you will be able to adapt it to your particular situation (floor, masonry rocket stove, interior wall, et cetera). The more you read and the more practice you have before you begin an indoor project, the better off you'll be. See "Outdoor Cob Oven" in chapter 4 and the resources section for more information.

Mixing the materials. The basic procedure is to mix about two parts dry sand with one part dry clay on a tarp for a total of about 8 to 10 shovels full. Mix thoroughly by pressing with your feet (bare or shoed, depending on personal preference) and spraying with a hose. Then turn the mixture over by lifting one side of the tarp, and spray and mash some more. Eventually the sand and clay will mix and obtain an even moisture, the mixture becoming a coherent loaf. You want the mixture to have a certain stiffness and not turn into a mud pie. Adding too much water is the most common beginner's mistake. When your feet press into the mud, it should maintain some resistance, forming peaks on either sides of your feet like beaten egg whites. Once your cob has reached the desired texture, take two or three large handfuls of straw and work these thoroughly into the mix.

Generally speaking, a 2- or 3-to-1 ratio of sand to clay usually works, but if you're making a lot, you'll need to do some initial legwork to come up with a more accurate ratio for your specific materials. Unscreened clay or sand is often an impure mixture of the two, which can throw off your ratio. By placing samples in a clear jar with water, shaking vigorously, and then allowing them to settle, the ratio of clay to sand (and any organic matter) can be determined as the different materials will separate themselves out. You can then adjust your mixture accordingly. Nothing will better tell you what the best mixture is, however, than making a few sample batches with various ratios of clay to sand, letting them dry, and then seeing how difficult they are to break open. Mix a portion of cob the size of a bread loaf, making your samples wide and long rather than round. Once the cob loaf is broken in half, it is also possible to see how well the materials are mixed together and whether there is any cracking. Cracking is the result of too much clay or allowing the sample to dry too quickly (as it does in the sunshine).

Preparing the site. The site where you plan to put your cob must be properly prepared. Cob is a heavy material. If you are adding a great deal in one place, the floor must be beefed up, at a minimum by building one or more piers to take the weight of the load directly to the ground. Tying floorboards together by spacers between the floor joists is also a great way to help distribute the weight over more area. Ideally, large amounts of masonry (a bench or larger, for instance) would direct their loads to a foundation directly in the ground. Cob, being masonry, must be separated from wood and other organic material by a vapor barrier. Because masonry changes temperature at a different rate than the surrounding wood, condensation occurs and can lead to rot. A sheet of 6-mil plastic, or layers of thinner plastic, are easy barriers if you are putting cob directly onto a wood floor. Scrap pieces are easy to come by. Alternatively, a latex primer and paint or several coats of linseed oil will also work. Wherever cob and wood meet, the wood should be keyed to give a good grip to the masonry (floors excepted). *Keys* simply refer to projections out of the wood such as blocks or nails that are then surrounded by cob. The vapor barrier then goes between these two different materials.

A minimum 10:1 height-to-width ratio should be maintained to ensure adequate strength of the wall (so a 10-foot wall would be at least 1 foot thick). This ratio is enough even for load-bearing walls. The weight of a load-bearing wall always needs to be directed to its own foundation.

Building the layers. Cob structures are built by adding one layer at a time. Each layer will generally be about 4–6 inches tall, or basically as high as you can make it before it starts to lose shape. Layers could be substantially higher if you have premade any cob

patties or bricks and then work these into your structure. In a day or two, the cob will have set up enough that you can add another layer but still moist enough to bond well with the new layer. Several things can be done to help this bond. First, keep the top of the cob textured and not smooth; you could also flatten out the top and make a series of holes by pressing your thumb or a stick into it once you are done for the day. Avoid forming your cob into a rounded hump. Rather, the top of your cob wall should be flat, with a slight indentation in the middle ideal. Before adding the next layer, remoisten the top of the cob by adding water and letting it sit for 5 to 10 minutes. Work in the new cob layer by pressing it firmly into the existing layer.

Repeat this process until your work is finished. Finish with a plaster, if desired (see below).

If you are making a great deal of cob, a several-foot-high wall 10 or more feet long, for instance, then a cement mixer can greatly speed up the process. The only prerequisites are that the mixer must be lined with metal and be of sufficient volume (at least 3-cubic-foot mixing capacity). Proceed as above, mixing the appropriate amounts of clay and sand, spraying with water, and then adding straw. Dump the mix out onto a tarp. We've had great luck making cob in a cement mixer, although anecdotal evidence from other cobmakers is sometimes to the contrary.

EARTH PLASTERS

Another method for increasing the thermal mass of your house is to add an earth plaster to an existing interior or exterior wall. A facade of any masonry will increase your home's thermal mass, but again earth is easy to work with and quite forgiving. Besides adding thermal mass, interior drywall walls covered with earthen plasters look lovely! Natural dyes or oxides can be added to the plaster to create almost any color of the rainbow. Exterior walls without sufficient (about 2 feet) overhangs will experience degradation of the earth plaster over time due to rain splashback.

Earth Plaster an Existing Wall

Project Time: Depends on project; likely at least a weekend.

Cost: Inexpensive.

Energy Saved: Low.

Ease of Use: N/A.

Maintenance Level: N/A.

Skill Levels: Masonry: Basic.

Materials: Metal lath, screws, washers, plastic sheet or latext paint, clay free of organic matter, masonry sand.

Tools: Masonry tub, trowel, drill, hoe, ¼" hardware cloth for screening clay.

Before adding an earth plaster, install a vapor barrier such as plastic or latex paint over the wall. The next step is to add lathing. Traditionally, lathing was strips of moisture-resistant wood, often oak, that were nailed to the studs. The earth or lime plaster would then be troweled all over and into the lathing in several coats. Premade metal lathing can be purchased from hardware stores (it may need to be ordered). The lathing is then tied into the studs of the wall with screws and washers. Earth plaster is applied with a trowel to the lathing in layers, each layer as thick as it can be without falling off from its own weight (typically 1–1½ inches). As an alternative to metal, bamboo can be split with a bamboo splitter and these lengths used as lathing. Holes must be predrilled in the bamboo before screwing or nailing it into the wall to avoid splitting.

Earth plaster recipes are similar to cob recipes except plaster must be screened of rocks through half-inch or smaller hardware cloth, as rocks in the plaster will not allow for smooth troweling. Earth plaster also contains a higher proportion of sand to clay than cob, sometimes 10:1, in order to avoid cracking as it dries. When each new layer is ready to be applied, the existing wall is wetted with a spray bottle. The plaster can be finished smoothly or left rough for texture, depending on preference. Make a few test batches with different ratios of sand to clay to see which ones don't crack and hold tight to the lathing.

SOLAR-HEATING FUNDAMENTALS

Having a sound understanding of how much solar heat you'll be receiving and how much heat storage various materials can hold will go a long way toward helping you bring these two things into balance. These two factors need to be balanced, in turn, with the rate of heat loss of your home (how well insulated it is).

The use of solar energy to heat your home is broken down into two categories: *passive* and *active*. Passive solar heating (often referred to as just "passive solar") is the act of allowing solar energy to come through windows and heat your home. To maximize effectiveness, windows should be facing as close to true south as possible (or true north for the southern hemisphere). Significant solar gain also comes through eastern and western windows, half as much as south-facing windows. At night, the accumulated heat is kept inside by sealing the windows with insulated shutters or curtains.

Active solar-heating systems usually comprise prefabricated or homemade panels with an air space. These are positioned facing as close to south as possible, either on roofs or on the side of the house. Sunlight passes through the glazing, then strikes the back of the panel. Air is forced from the interior of the house, heated when it comes in contact with the panel, and then returned to the living space. The air can be moved by means of a fan, which is switched on when the exterior of the panel reaches a set temperature, around 90–100 degrees F, by an automatic switch.

It is possible to build a solar-heating panel that operates as a thermosiphon. The panel heats up and the hot air rises. This draws in cooler air from inside via a vent, and the warm air is forced into the room by means of another vent near the top of the panel. Using a fan is generally worth the electricity it consumes because it greatly increases the effectiveness of the panel. Efficient fans have very low electricity draws and can run direct from small photovoltaic modules.

Another option for active solar heating is to use a closed-loop solar hot-water heater (see chapter 6 for installation). The loop is routed into a high-thermal-mass storage device inside the home, which could be water or masonry such as a cob bench or concrete slab floor. The pros and cons of these approaches are summarized in table 7.4.

Which system is right for you depends on a number of variables: your heating needs, solar access, time, money, house construction, skills, et cetera. Some solar heating is certainly worthwhile for any home with sunshine available and heating needs. An equivalent area of solar-heating panels can displace up to six times as much fossil-fuel use compared to photovoltaic panels. This is because while the efficiency rating for photovoltaics is generally around 12 percent, solar heaters can be up to 70 percent efficient. And it's usually the case that solar air heaters, especially homemade ones, are much cheaper for an equivalent area than photovoltaics.

Determining heating requirements. There are two general rules of thumb you can apply to a decently insulated house in a moderate climate (Zones 5–7). The area of your solar heating, without significant thermal storage for night or cloudy days, should be roughly equal to about 7 percent of your home's total area. Colder areas should shoot for 10 percent. Exceeding these averages can be beneficial, but only if coupled with substantial thermal mass. Otherwise, overheating will likely be a problem.

There are two approaches to designing your solar heating. The first is the try-and-see approach. Add some solar heating based on the above numbers and then see how it does over the course of the winter. If it's not enough, you can work in another panel or mix in one of the other solar-heating methods. If your home is heating up too much and then cooling down quickly at night or during cloudy weather, then you need to store some of that extra heat by increasing the amount of thermal mass in your house. Since you're retrofitting, you can take a piecemeal approach as time and finances allow. If you're not fond of numbers, this is probably the way to go.

Calculating heating load. The second method involves more complicated math: determining your heating requirements and sizing your system(s) to

match. To get an idea of how much solar-heating square footage you'll need, start by finding out how much heat your home needs. To do this, determine your primary method of heating (natural gas, oil, or electricity). Look at the bill for this fuel type for a few heating months and a few nonheating months (stick with early fall and late spring to avoid summer-month electricity use if you use air conditioning). The difference will mostly be going to heat. Determine the amount you used—therms of natural gas, gallons of heating oil, or kWh of electricity. Convert this number to Btus using the following information:

Gallon of Heating Oil: 130,500 Btus

Therm of Natural Gas: 100,000 Btus

kWh of Electricity: 3,412 Btus

Heating degree days. For the given months, you can then go the National Climatic Data Center Web site and figure out how cold it was for the period you're looking at (local newspapers also often have this information in the weather section). This is recorded in heating degree days (HDD), which is a measurement of how many degrees below 65 degrees F the average temperature was for that day. These are then tallied to get monthly totals. Go to http://lwf.ncdc.noaa.gov/oa/documentlibrary/hcs/hcs.html to get historical information as well as averages.

Now you know how cold it was for those specific months and how many Btus you used. Determine your average Btus/HDD requirement from this. For example: if you burned 1 therm of natural gas a day, and your average HDD are 33 for the coldest month (for an average temperature of 32 degrees F for that particular month), this would be 100,000/33 = 3,000 Btu/HDD.

Also note the average HDD, as you will use this number to size your system.

Determining insolation. Next you would need to determine your average solar insolation per day in winter. This can be found through a couple of different Web sites. Our favorite is an NREL site called the PVWatts Calculator (http://rredc.nrel.gov/solar/codes_algs/PVWATTS). Go to Version 1, click on your state, then the nearest station, and press "Calculate."

TABLE 7.4 Comparison of the Three Solar-Heating Strategies

	Passive Solar	Active Solar Air	Active Solar Liquid
Daylighting	Yes, but can also mean loss of privacy.	No.	No.
Ease of Construction	Difficult. Opening up a south-facing wall and installing glazing requires expert carpentry skills. If each window is installed individually, however, the process is straightforward and supporting the wall during construction is much easier.	Medium. Building the panel is relatively straightforward, but opening up the walls and dealing with the vent pipes can be tricky. Large vent pipes are difficult to route, often requiring the building of chases to conceal them. Prefabricated panels are relatively straightforward to install.	Difficult. Expert plumbing skills are required. Some masonry skills may also be required for thermal storage. This method has some distinct potential advantages that may make it worth considering. Three-quarter-inch pipes can usually be run through existing walls, or at least concealed much more easily than 10- to 12-inch air ducts. Radiant heat is more pleasant than the feel of moving warm air. Thermal storage offers the potential for nighttime and cloudy-day heating.
Ease of Daily Use	Moderate. The system loses effectiveness if not properly managed. Insulated shutters or curtains must be opened in the morning and closed properly at night, or the windows will lose more heat than is gained. Creating an effective seal is difficult.	Easy. Operates via a thermostatically controlled switch or PV panel direct to fan. As long as there is access to electricity, it works great. Will heat home even during prolonged absence. Can potentially produce heat when it is not wanted if not turned off.	Easy. Operates via a thermostatically controlled switch or PV panel direct to pump. As long as there is access to electricity, it works great. Will heat home even during prolonged absence. Can potentially produce heat when it is not wanted if not turned off.
Maintenance Level	Low. Curtains can photodegrade and potentially need replacement.	Low. Fan motor will eventually burn out, requiring replacement.	Low. Pump could burn out eventually. Overheating in summer could lead to pressure buildup and fluid loss if heat is not dumped.
Efficiency	High, around 70%.	Good, around 50%; higher possible.	Good, around 50%; higher possible.
Cost	High. $20–50/square foot self-installed.	Low if homemade, around $10/square foot. High for premanufactured models, around $50–60/square foot.	Very high. Upward of $100/square foot.

There's lot of information here, but what's important for now is the monthly average insolation (it's in square meters; 1 square meter = 10.8 square feet) for the winter months.

For our example, let's say the winter months give us about 4 hours/day. Standard solar insolation is about 300 Btu/square foot/hour.

Calculating square feet. On average, then, 1 square foot of solar heating would provide 4 × 300 = 1,200 Btu/day *gross*. The *net* amount would depend on which solar-heating system we choose and its efficiency. At 50 percent efficiency, we would get about 600 Btu/day/square foot. To get all of our heat from solar on average, we would need

(Average number of HDD × Btu/HDD) / (Btu/day/ft^2)

If, for example, the average HDD for the coldest month was 25, then this would equal

(25 × 3,000)/(600) = 125 ft^2 of heating space.

Since this amount of solar-heating space would provide for the coldest month, it would likely result in overheating during other winter months. So for this example, 125 square feet would be the maximum amount of solar heating needed.

ACTIVE SOLAR AIR HEATERS

The good news about building a solar air heater is that it's hard to build one that doesn't work. The simple basic layout allows an almost infinite amount of variations. When the sun shines, air from the home is sent to the panel on the roof or south-facing wall via a fan turned on by a thermostatically controlled switch or PV panel. Sunlight heats the black metal in the panel and the glazing holds the heat in. As the air flows over the metal, it warms up and returns to the home. This cycle continues as long as the panel remains warm enough.

Unlike passive solar heating, solar air heaters require no active participation (such as opening and closing curtains) and heat your house even when no one is home. They are the easiest way to add solar heating to an existing home.

FIG. 7.5. **Several brands of premanufactured solar air heaters are available. They generally cost around $1,500 for a 4 x 8-foot panel and are relatively simple to install on south-facing walls or roofs. The model pictured is the SolarsHeat 1500.**
Courtesy SolarsHeat

Roof heaters can be large enough for adding serious amounts of solar heat to your home. The closer to perpendicular the heating panel is to the winter sun, the greater the efficiency. Take some time to plan out the best spot for your solar air heater where it will be easy to do the ductwork and where it will not interfere

Basic rules for an Active Solar Air Heater:

1. The more surface area the metal has, the easier it will be to heat up the air. Metal lathing painted black in addition to the sheet metal works great for this, as it breaks up the path of the air and forces heat exchange to occur.

2. The air gap in the panel should be between 1 and 1½ inches, with 1¼ inches ideal.

3. Avoid turns in the path of the air inside the panel, as the air in the corners gets trapped and heat exchange does not occur. Rounded corners can reduce this effect.

4. The air should flow horizontally through channels in the panel if this is possible. Horizontal channels should not be taller than 24 inches.

with potential solar hot water and PV. It is fine for the air to come from the ceiling and return to the ceiling if this is easiest, although some of the heat will get stuck up by the ceiling. It's best if the heated air can enter the house as low to the floor as possible.

There are some basic rules of thumb that must be followed, but beyond that there is great flexibility in the design of the solar heater. Many plans are available for perusal on the Internet. Check the resources section. If you are not using a PV-powered DC fan, the hardest component to find is the thermostatically controlled switch, which is available at www.mobile homerepair.com/solarheatswitch.html. Once the PV panel is getting enough sunlight, it is very likely that the air heater is producing warm air. It would be necessary to have a switch to turn off the fan in the warmer months, or you could disconnect it from the air heater and use the fan to blow hot air out of the house! (For you crazy experimenters out there, it might be possible

to create a solar-heated closed-loop ammonia fridge with the additional heat for warm-weather refrigeration. Read more about these chapter 5.)

Building an Active Solar Air Heater
Project Time: Several weekends.
Cost: $10–20/square foot of heater.
Energy Saved: High.
Ease of Use: Easy.
Maintenance Level: Low.
Skill Levels: Carpentry: Advanced. Electrical: Moderate.
Materials: Double-walled greenhouse polycarbonate sheets, 2 × 4 framing material, ¾-inch plywood, 2-inch insulated foamboard, insulated ductwork, temperature-controlled switch or PV panel, fan, vents, sheet metal (prepainted black is best), metal lathing (optional), roofing material, silicone, screws, nails, duct tape (black, not gray), duct clamps, lag screws, washers, primer and paint.
Tools: Saws, hammer, drill, adjustable wrench or socket set, paintbrush.

Building the box. Build a 2 × 4 box with a ¾-inch plywood back to match the size heater you want. Break the plywood panel up into two or three 16- or 24-inch channels by running 2 × 4s horizontally across it (you're attaching the thin side to the plywood). Apply silicone everywhere two pieces of wood meet, including the plywood and 2 × 4s. For solar heaters longer than 8 feet (i.e., one sheet of plywood), you'll need to leave one end of the box open. Build your additional sections of plywood box, but keep them separate. You'll need to assemble these separate sections in place on the roof, as any piece larger than a single sheet of plywood will be too awkward to handle. Once connected on the rooftop, the separate pieces can then be firmly attached to one another by using flat connector plates.

Prime and paint the exterior of the box (or separate components of the box).

Outline and cut a hole for the vents in the panel with a jigsaw for the duct entry and exit for each channel.

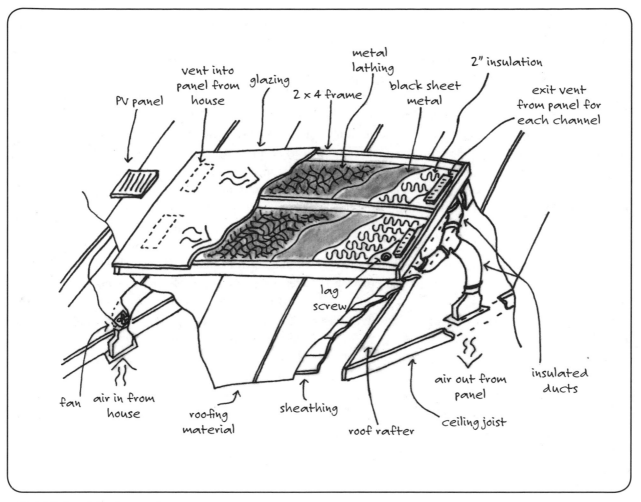

FIG. 7.6. **Solar air heater panel.**

The entry should be on the left or right side, with the exit opposite. Each channel needs an entry and exit. Bear in mind that the vent holes will have to be properly spaced so that they are located over gaps between rafters in your roof.

Placement on the roof. Determine the position of the panel on your roof. Locate the rafters by drilling a pilot hole. Outline the panel in chalk where it will go on the roof. The pilot hole can be caulked if necessary.

Measure, mark, and cut out the holes in the roof for the vent openings.

You'll need to space your panel up off the roof an inch or so, so that water and air can flow under it and keep it dry. The amount you can elevate your panel depends on the type of vent you purchased. The rectangular part of the vent extends for only a few inches before it starts to change shape to a circle to connect with the insulated ductwork. You're going to need to get through the roof (sheathing and roofing material) as well as the ¾-inch plywood and 2-inch foam insulation (total 2¾ inches) with this square section of the vent. You'll want to space the panel off the roof as much as possible given these constraints. This can be done by passing the lag screws through washers or short lengths of pipe between the panel and the roof. The panel needs to be lagged into the roof rafters at least 3 inches, so be sure to buy lags of sufficient length.

Install the vents through the roof so that they stick out the appropriate amount. Lock in place by screwing the vents into the roof sheathing. Caulk these holes. Flash around the vent openings or install a roof jack made for plumbing vents. Whenever making holes in your roof, make an inverted V of caulk on the roofing material over the roof opening to direct water away from the opening and minimize the chances of a leak.

Predrill the holes in the panel and the roof. You'll need to lag the panels every 32–48 inches or so, at the top and bottom.

Installing the panels. Here comes the hard part. You'll need at least one additional set of hands to accomplish this. Position the panel on the vents and then lag into place. Do this for each section, if applicable.

Connect any panels with flat metal connector plates. Silicone the seams. Screw the vents into the plywood of the panel and silicone.

Add the 2-inch foam insulation against the plywood. You'll need to press it into place, making an indentation in the insulation where the lags stick out. Cut out these indentations so the insulation sits flat. Don't attempt to install the insulation on a windy day.

Apply the black sheet metal (painted with high-heat metal paint or prepainted roofing tin) on top of the foam insulation and silicone all seams, including the vents.

Apply black metal lathing to the channels. This is optional but will improve performance. It's best if the lathing is spaced a ½ to ¾ inch off the black sheet metal. This can be accomplished by using 3½-inch screws through the lathing, through washers or short lengths of pipe, and then through the sheet metal and insulation into the plywood.

Cover the entire panel with greenhouse polycarbonate sheets (corrugated) or impact-resistant glazing, putting down silicone beforehand. Be sure to put the UV-resistant side of the polycarbonate facing outward and to tape the tops and bottoms.

Connecting to the house. Run the ductwork in the house to the entrance and exit vents, installing the fan in the entrance vent near where it enters the house. Connect a 12-volt DC fan to a switch and then to a 12-volt PV panel. Or install the thermostatically controlled switch in the panel, add an additional on/off switch, and tie these into the nearest 120-volt circuit.

HEATING WITH BIOMASS

Humans have burned wood to stay warm since we learned to control fire. It's certainly possible to burn wood in an unsustainable manner. A large swath of the Mediterranean and Middle East, for example, was forested with cedars and oaks just a few thousand years ago, but now much of this area is an empty desert. All from overconsumption by us humans.

Wood is not a fossil fuel, but it helps to think of it as a renewable fossil fuel. There is a tremendous amount of energy contained in the world's forests, and they *can* regenerate in a humanly significant time frame. But this fuel could also be burned up very quickly, and the soils on which regrowth depends can wash away if the forests are overharvested. Wood's convenience as an on-demand energy source, especially for home heating, makes it an inviting addition to the carbon-free home. But in order to be a carbon-free home, we need to not burn more wood in any given year than is being added by additional tree growth.

This number is quite variable and dependent on the local climate. Obviously, if trees don't grow naturally where you live, then the prospect for sustainably harvesting trees for firewood is quite low. But even if they do, using this resource as frugally as possible will ensure it lasts as long as possible, hopefully forever if we're conscious of its limitations and not gluttonous in its use.

Depending on your lot size, it may be possible to grow all of your own firewood. If this is the case, then chances are you live in a suburban or rural setting. Keep in mind that if this more remote setting is causing you to drive a lot, then your prospects of becoming fossil-fuel-free are quite low (see chapter 11). But even some urban lots have the potential to grow some of their own firewood. The best method for doing this is planting trees that have the ability to coppice, or to resprout from the same rootstock once they are cut down, again and again, 500 years or longer. Coppiced trees grow much more quickly than those started from seed, and the living rootstock ensures the soil maintains its structure and does not erode. Birch, beech, ash, oak, locust, maple, hornbeam, alder, willows, and others have the potential for coppicing, depending on their age (trees tend to resprout if they are not too young or too old). Of these tree types, black locust stands out as an excellent choice for coppicing. It is fast growing (especially when resprouting after being coppiced), is nitrogen-fixing, has excellent soil-binding characteristics, is easy to split, and has edible flower buds. It grows quickly from seed or from suckers obtained from a mother tree, and firewood can be harvested within a decade after planting. Some reports indicate black locust exhibits allelopathy, producing compounds that can suppress the growth of surrounding plants. To the extent that this is a concern, it may be worthwhile to isolate any black locusts you plant for coppicing. At any rate, keep potential coppicing trees in mind as you plan out your landscape (see chapter 10).

Because of the differences in climate, it is difficult to generalize about a sustainable level of tree harvesting. In areas that are naturally wooded, it is generally recommended not to harvest more than 2 percent of the given biomass each year. For a typical woodland, this is about one medium-sized tree (12-inch diameter at chest height; roughly one-third of a cord) per acre per year maximum.[1]

Woodstoves. Newer woodstoves (post-1988) are much more efficient than older ones, often approaching 70 percent combustion efficiency, which means burning less wood and emitting fewer particulates into the atmosphere. When installing a woodstove, it's worth the extra money for a newer model, as it will pay itself back in less firewood in a few years. If finances allow only a used model (which, granted, can often be found for very cheap on Web sites like Craigslist), make sure to sock away a few hundred dollars each year for a replacement when you get a chance. Keep in mind that new woodstoves almost always have 6-inch stovepipe, and that stovepipe is often half the price of

a new woodstove installation, so don't install any other diameter pipe.

Fireplaces are horribly inefficient and often result in a net loss of heat out of the house. Inserts can solve this problem.

You could, instead, build your own superefficient rocket stove. Well-built rocket stoves can approach 100 percent combustion efficiency. Unfortunately, there are no models for sale as of this writing. See the sidebar on page 146 for more information.

Even at 70 percent efficiency, new-model woodstoves add a fair amount of pollution to the air. The most important way to keep down smoke and particulate emissions is to burn very well-dried wood as hot as possible. Folks often refer to "seasoned" wood, meaning it's sat around at least one season (summer) before it goes into the woodstove. But there is much misunderstanding of this concept. New, or "green," wood must be split and dried at least six months, out of the rain but exposed to as much wind and sun as possible. Uncovered wood will not dry out sufficiently, resulting in an unsustainable amount of wood use, difficult-to-start fires, and excess smoke and pollution as a result of low fire temperatures. Green or wet wood typically has only about a quarter the heat value of dried wood (1 pound green wood = approximately 1,600 Btus; 1 pound properly seasoned wood = approximately 6,500 Btus). An ideal spot for a woodpile is roofed and facing west so that it gets blasted by the afternoon sun. Well-dried wood takes much of the chore out of starting fires, flaming right up with just a few twigs and pieces of newspaper.

Because of pollution concerns, burning wood in more urban areas is not ideal given today's conventional wood-burning technology. Of course, burning fossil fuels creates pollution, too. We haven't seen any studies, but we'd be surprised if a home that got the majority of its heat from solar with wood as backup put out more pollution than a conventional oil or natural-gas furnace or heat pump. Much cleaner wood-burning technology is on the horizon, however. Read the masonry stove and rocket stove sections later in this chapter for more information.

Other biomass heating options include corn and other grain stoves and pellet stoves. On the plus side, these stoves burn very efficiently. But the idea of burning food seems wrong to us, especially corn, the conventional cultivation of which depends heavily on fossil fuels. Pellet stoves likewise are dependent on large-scale agroforestry and logging operations. You need to decide how comfortable you are with these things before purchasing one. One other thing to note about these stoves is that they are dependent on an electric fan. While this fan improves the combustion efficiency of these stoves and means less fuel use and pollution, they don't work without power, so they cannot provide heat during blackouts unless via batteries and DC-to-AC inverter.

There is one other option for using biomass, and that's to use biodiesel in a conventional oil furnace. The main problem with this is that biodiesel gels (and hence won't flow) at around 32 degrees F, so if your furnace is outside this would be a serious problem. It is also possible to mix biodiesel with conventional heating oil (which is pretty much the same as fossil diesel). If the biodiesel is kept to less than 50 percent (or B50), gelling will be much less of an issue. A passive solar shed could also be built to help keep the tank warm. Biodiesel is discussed in greater detail in chapter 11.

Woodstove Installation

Project Time: Several weekends.

Cost: $1,000–5,000, depending on stove.

Energy Saved: Medium. Home heating can be up to 50 percent of a home's fossil-fuel use. A woodstove could potentially displace a significant chunk of this.

Ease of Use: Moderate. Hauling wood and starting fires takes some extra time and effort.

Maintenance Level: High. Growing, harvesting, cutting, and chopping wood are major chores. Stovepipe should be cleaned annually with a brush.

Skill Levels: Carpentry: Advanced. Masonry: Moderate.

Materials: Woodstove of choice, adjustable stovepipe to ceiling (single- or double-wall uninsulated,

depending on clearances), double-wall insulated pipe from ceiling to 2 feet above the roof or ridge (depending on clearances), pipe connectors, ceiling support, attic insulation shield, single-wall adapter, firestop assembly, stovepipe roof flashing, guy wire, stovepipe cap, stovepipe collar, roof caulk, extra roofing material.

Hearth materials: 24-gauge sheet metal, wood frame, masonry of choice (brick, tile, cob, et cetera).

Tools: Tin snips, circular saw, handsaw, plumb bob, drywall knife.

Caution: Most homes are made of wood. You burn wood in a woodstove. Obviously, there is the potential for your home to burn down. Determining the local codes (or using the Universal Building Code setbacks) and having your woodstove installation inspected are required for most municipalities. You will also need to alert your home insurance company (if you don't and your house burns down, you could be out of luck) and the local fire marshal. Please be very scrupulous in your attention to detail when following all setback requirements.

Usually, you can buy most of the things you will need in a woodstove installation kit. These come with recommended setbacks and installation instructions and are very helpful.

Securing the floor. The first step is to support the floor underneath where your woodstove will go because of the extra weight you will be adding. Ideally, the floor joists directly underneath the hearth will all be tied together and supported with a pier that takes the load directly to the ground. Use joist hangers and equivalent framing material (like a 2 × 8) to connect the joists if they're not already. At a minimum support the joist that will be in the middle of the hearth with enough cement block to get you down to the ground. Ideally, you would dig out a hole and pour a footing. This may be next to impossible, however, given space constraints under the floor. Don't forget to add a vapor barrier between the blocks and the wooden floor joists to avoid condensation issues.

Building the hearth and placing the stove. The next step is building the hearth. Again, there are requirements for how far the masonry must extend beyond the edge of the stove depending on local codes. Twenty-four-gauge sheet metal should go between the existing floor and any masonry. A simple hearth design is to frame a box and pour in cob. Tile can be embedded in the cob for a more sophisticated look. Your favorite choice of masonry will do just fine—bricks, heavy tiles, poured concrete, marble, and so on.

Once your stove is in place, you know where to put your stovepipe. It's wise to check where your ceiling rafters are before positioning your stove so that you can go between two of them. Sometimes you can see where the joists are by looking for seams or screws in the drywall or plasterboard. Or you can try measuring from the wall in 16-inch increments. Stud finders work if your walls are drywall.

Running the stovepipe through the ceiling and roof. Once you've located your joists, use a plumb bob to center your stove and pipe. Cut a square hole the size of your ceiling support kit in the ceiling. Box off your ceiling joists, using joist hangers if necessary. Use the plumb bob to determine the location of the roof opening. Hopefully this will also line up between two rafters. If not, you'll have to jog the stovepipe using two 30-degree turns. Open up the hole in your roof and box off the roof rafters.

Install the ceiling support, single-wall adapter, firestop shield, and attic insulation shield. Note that if you have another floor to go through, you'll have to cut another hole in the second-story ceiling and apply an additional insulation shield and firestop. You may want to enclose the pipe in a chase, although it shouldn't ever be hot enough to burn you, as the stovepipe will be double walled or insulated at this point.

Put in the roof flashing. Add enough additional roofing material to shed water properly (see figure 8.5, page 169). Caulk where necessary, making an inverted V to direct water away from the opening.

Run the course of double-walled insulated pipe from the ceiling support through the roof flashing to the proper height above the roof. Put on the storm collar. Put on the cap. Caulk. Lock the sections of pipe together using connectors. Attach two guy wires from the roof to the top piece of stovepipe. The easiest way to do this is to wrap a strip of stainless or galvanized steel around the top piece, bend the two edges, drill a hole through the two bends, run a bolt through the two holes, and then tie the wires to the bolt. Make sure the guy wires are taut. This one paragraph could take you several days. Another option is to use half-inch electrical conduit (EMT), bent on either end to attach to the stovepipe and roof and screwed into both with weatherproofing.

Be safe and take your time! This is very dangerous work, especially if you are on a slippery roof. A harness is very highly recommended. If you don't have a harness, tie a strong rope to a tree or vehicle and throw it over the ridge of the roof so you can hold on to it.

Attach the woodstove to the single-wall adapter with the length of adjustable stovepipe. Use a few self-tapping metal screws to lock these two pieces together. Cross your fingers and hope the roof doesn't leak the next time it rains!

MASONRY STOVES

Masonry stoves have been around for centuries, originating in Scandinavia. The essential principle is to create an extremely hot fire and send the exhaust through a winding flue surrounded by some type of masonry. The winding flue captures the heat of the fire in the thermal mass of the stove, slowly radiating the heat into the living space over the course of 12–24 hours.

Masonry stoves are beautiful to look at and hold heat overnight. The drawbacks are their large size and weight and their expense in construction, which usually requires a skilled mason specifically trained in building masonry stoves.

Masonry stoves behave differently than metal box stoves. Box stoves quickly heat a room by radiating high temperatures from the metal (steel or cast iron) to objects in the room, yourself included. Box stoves quickly heat up a room, but when the fire's out, objects in the room quickly transfer that heat to the air and this air then gets sucked outside via air leaks and radiation.

Rocket Stoves and Homemade Mass Heaters

Burning wood in urban settings has the potential to pollute the air and strip the surrounding countryside of its forests, damaging both ours and our ecosystem's long-term health. Since wood makes such an excellent potential renewable fuel, it is imperative that we get as much heat as possible out of the wood we burn and to produce as few pollutants as possible when we burn it. While conventional woodstoves are a great improvement in these regards over their forebears, the potential exists for even greater improvements. Unfortunately, for now store-bought woodstoves that reach hot enough temperatures (1,100°+F) to burn up the residual smoke are not available, although they can be fairly straightforward to build.

It is possible to approach combustion efficiency rates of nearly 100 percent with a well-designed woodstove, far above the 65–70 percent common with newer-model woodstoves. What's more, when these hotter-burning fires are combined with more efficient heat-exchange mechanisms, the same space can be heated using a fraction of the amount of wood used previously. And hotter-burning fires

produce only carbon dioxide and water from their chimneys, making their widespread use in urban settings possible without detrimental effects on air quality. Essentially, smoke is wasted fuel, but with hotter fires, the smoke itself combusts and instead of polluting helps heat your home.

Improvements in stove design and the invention of the rocket stove, so named because the air being pulled into these superhot fires sounds like a rocket, was pioneered by Larry Winiarski, a doctor of mechanical engineering, around 1980. Over the years, he has refined what makes a superefficient stove into eight basic principles. Improvements and variations have been achieved by a number of dedicated tinkerers besides Winiarski, primarily at the Aprovecho Research Center, which also maintains a testing facility and school, and also by folks with the Cob Cottage Company. Check the resources at the end of this chapter for more information.

These principles assume dry, well-seasoned wood, which is the most important ingredient for hot fire.

The eight basic principles of a rocket stove are:

1) Metering the Fuel. Smaller pieces of wood are applied more frequently. Smaller firewood means more surface area exposed to air and fire.
2) Making a Hot Fire. Fuel, fire, and air must be mixed by turbulence, at a high enough temperature, for a long enough time to completely combust.
3) Insulating the Combustion Chamber. Uninsulated chambers will not get hot enough to burn completely.
4) Igniting Escaping Smoke. Smoke must be redirected over the flame at high enough temperatures to burn.
5) Providing Plenty of Oxygen. Fires starved for air slow down and burn incompletely, producing smoke.

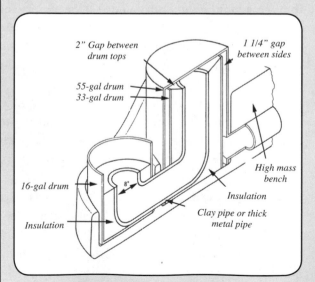

FIG. 7.7. **Rocket Stove.** Courtesy Aprovecho

6) Warming and Increasing the Velocity of the Air Entering the Fire. The area of air intake should match the area of the exhaust (the area of the stovepipe), although this can be reduced if a fan is used. The entering air should be preheated as much as possible by being pulled in next to the combustion chamber.

7) Forming a Grate Out of the Firewood. Firewood should be spaced evenly apart.

8) Creating Sufficient Draft. Use a tall enough chimney or even a small fan. Insulated chimneys (after a heat exchanger, if there is one) create a better draft than uninsulated ones. Low-volume, high-velocity jets pulled into the fire near the bottom of the coals create more turbulence and more complete combustion.

Rocket-stove fires burn hot and quick. Complete combustion of all the wood gases that make up smoke requires temperatures in excess of 1,125 degrees F. Obviously, fires cannot start out this hot, so there is some smoke at the beginning, but over the course of the fire almost all of the smoke is burned. This is fundamentally different than the way almost all woodstoves today work. Today's woodstoves have dampers that control the amount of air that can get to the fire. The problem with dampers of any kind is that limiting the amount of air that gets to the fire causes the temperature to drop and fewer, if any, of the wood gases get combusted. By allowing unresistricted airflow, the fire burns much hotter. To compensate for this and to keep the room from heating up too quickly, it is usually necessary to direct the heat into a large amount of thermal mass. The simplest method of creating this thermal mass is out of cob, although any type of masonry can be used. Cob offers the opportunity for less-skilled masons to make their own thermal-mass rocket stoves. See the resources for more on this topic.

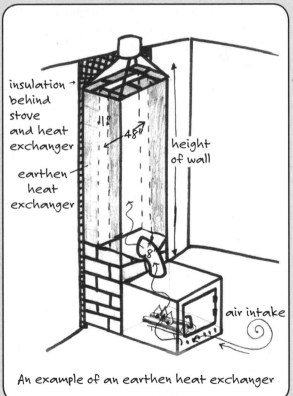

An example of an earthen heat exchanger

FIG. 7.9. **A conventional wood stove can be modified to maximize heat exchange efficiency by increasing the surface area of the exit flue before it enters the ceiling. Cob or other masonry surrounding the flue will help store heat and prevent the room from overheating.** Courtesy of Aprovecho Research Center.

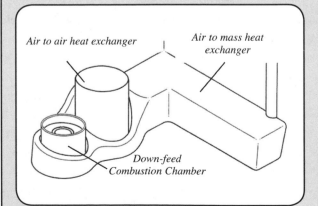

FIG. 7.8. **Rocket Stove with masonry thermal storage.**
Courtesy of Aprovecho Research Center.

The rapid dissipation of heat causes the room to cool down quickly once the fire is out.

The thermal mass in a masonry stove instead conducts most of the fire's heat into the masonry surrounding it. This heat is then slowly radiated into the room or can be directly conducted to other objects, including yourself. Some masonry stoves include benches that absorb the heat of the fire. Sitting on this bench can keep you warm even as the room temperature remains relatively cool because of the direct conduction of the heat into your buns. When your buns are warm, you're warm.

Having a masonry stove installed in your home is no small deal. Skilled masons are rare, and usually in high demand. The weight of the stove must be accounted for, usually by directing its load straight to the ground via a poured foundation. The cost is substantial, $10,000 in many cases, and can easily run much higher. If you can afford this and can find a skilled mason to build one for you, you will certainly end up with a gorgeous addition to your home and a great way to provide carbon-free heat to your home (assuming your firewood is harvested in a sustainable manner). The thermal mass will also be very effective for many passive cooling strategies.

Having a professional install a masonry stove is the more-money-than-time option. If your situation is the reverse, you can potentially build your own masonry stove using cob and the principles of the rocket stove. Even if you are just using a traditional woodstove, improvements can be made to increase the amount of heat exchange into your house by reading further.

CONCLUSION

No doubt about it, converting your conventional home to carbon-free heating and cooling will take a lot of up front work. Even brand-new homes built to conventional standards are not well sealed or insulated enough to stay comfortable on a more limited renewable energy budget. The good news is that it's

rewarding work. Time and effort spent sealing, insulating, putting up storm windows, building insulated shutters, and accessing solar and biomass heating will save you loads of money and make your home more comfortable in the bargain. All the while you continue to reduce your carbon footprint on your way to a sustainable life without fossil fuels.

RESOURCES

Books

Bee, Becky. 1998. *The Cob Builders Handbook: You Can Hand-Sculpt Your Own Home*. Murphy, OR: Groundworks. A great primer on building with cob.

Evans, Ianto, Michael G. Smith, and Linda Smith. 2002. *The Hand-Sculpted House: A Practical and Philosophical Guide to Building a Cob Cottage*. White River Junction, VT: Chelsea Green Publishing. Another great primer on cob.

Guelberth, Cedar Rose, and Dan Chiras. 2003. *The Natural Plaster Book: Earth, Lime, and Gypsum Plasters*. Gabriola Island, BC: New Society Publishers.

Lyle, David. 1984. *The Book of Masonry Stoves: Rediscovering an Old Way of Warming*. White River Junction, VT: Chelsea Green Publishing.

Venolia, Carol, and Kelly Lerner. 2006. *Natural Remodeling for the Not-So-Green House: Bringing Your Home Into Harmony with Nature*. New York: Lark Books.

Internet

Aprovecho Research Center. Articles and workshops on rocket stoves and other appropriate technology. www.aprovecho.org and www.aprovecho.net

Build It Solar. Solar heaters and everything else for the DIY crowd. www.builditsolar.com

Green Building Forums. www.greenbuildingforum .co.uk and www.informedbuilding.com

Hearth.com. Great articles on burning with wood.
www.hearth.com

Magazines

The Last Straw Magazine. Great natural building
magazine. www.strawhouse.com

Products

Cozy Curtains. Makes custom-made sealing insulated
curtains. www.cozycurtains.com

Endnote
1. Marcouiller, Dave and Steven Anderson. 2007.
   "Managing Your Woodlot for Firewood." Division
   of Agricultural Sciences and Natural Resources,
   Oklahoma State University: Oklahoma City, OK.

CHAPTER 8

Rainwater

Introduction • Our Story • Passive Rainwater Collection • Whole-House Rainwater Harvesting • Fundamental Components of a Rainwater Harvesting System • Sand Filters • Metal Roofs • Resources

INTRODUCTION

Letting water fall on your roof and run off your yard into the storm drain, and then pumping an equivalent amount of water from miles away for use inside your home doesn't make a lot of sense. Like other wasteful and inefficient modern city systems, the failure to harvest and use the water that rains down on our houses results in wasted energy, almost invariably fossil energy, with the concomitant carbon emissions.

Much urban and rural water arrives at taps after being pumped (using fossil energy) from underground aquifers. Some of these aquifers are now stranded, meaning they are not being recharged. Water from these aquifers is often referred to as fossil water, because it accumulated over thousands if not millions of years and will not be replenished in a humanly relevant time frame once depleted. Aquifers that are capable of being recharged do so faster when water is released slowly over a long period of time so that less is lost to runoff. In other areas, water is obtained from dams that cause massive ecological disruption and greenhouse gas emissions (due to the organic matter that settles and decomposes anaerobically on the bottom of the lake, methane is released as water flows over the dam)[1].

Water and fossil fuels are increasingly intertwined as they both become scarce, from overuse and ever rising human populations. Industrial agriculture depends heavily on both water and fossil fuels for the manufacture, packaging, distribution, and refrigeration of its "products." Depleting aquifers take geometrically increasing amounts of energy to keep the pumps running as the depth of the wells increase. With the biofuels boom, many of the grains grown are then being turned back into fuel to run our hundreds of millions of automobiles and transport trucks (more on this in chapter 11). Beyond realizing the energy required in the capture, treatment, and pumping of a typical municipality's water, an understanding of the precarious state of the world's water supply and how dependent it has become on fossil fuels is important to making informed decisions. (Read Lester Brown's *Plan B 3.0* for a detailed analysis of the world situation. See resources for more information.)

On a local level, nothing will make you think more about the status of your area's water supply, the fundamental requirement for all life, than becoming a personal steward of your water resources by capturing rainwater and using it in your home. As we write this chapter, much of the Southeast, including our hometown of Durham, North Carolina, is in extreme drought conditions. Durham currently has only 39 days of readily accessible water supply. We don't know when or if the rains will begin again in earnest, but we do think about every drop of water that we take from our taps and are thankful for even the minimal amount of water we've been able to catch in our rainwater barrels this year.

Please note that some jurisdictions, especially in the western United States, limit or prohibit rainwater catchment, as rainwater is counted in downstream water calculations when those water rights are sold. Despite how ridiculous we think this is, it is something to be wary of.

Rainwater can obviously be used to water gardens, but depending on the complexity of the system it can also be used for flushing toilets, washing clothes and dishes, and drinking water. Paradoxically, some folks consider the idea of drinking rainwater unpleasant. All the water we use has been rainwater many times, lots of it quite recently, and the process of evaporation (also called "distillation") that creates rainwater purifies it of salts, man-made contaminants, and bacteria. Understanding the main components of a rainwater-harvesting system and integrating a proper filtering system should alleviate any concerns you might have about the potability of your water.

While building your own rainwater-catchment system entails a fair amount of up-front costs, it nevertheless provides many benefits over the long term. Rainwater catchment:

- Provides water security.
- Makes us conscious of the amount of water our site would naturally receive.
- Will likely provide water that is much cleaner and purer than city water. Rainwater has been naturally purified of pollutants and microbes by distillation.
- Can be used for moderating temperature.
- Puts much less strain on municipal stormwater systems during heavy rains.
- Improves the ecology of our site by slowly releasing the water so that more of it can be used.
- Makes sure the "purifying" chemicals in your municipality's water don't kill off the vital bacteria in your compost, biogas digester, yogurt maker, or stomach.

While a whole-house rainwater-catchment system can be quite involved, it will operate synergistically with many other components of a carbon-free home, making its incorporation worthwhile over the long term. For example, installing a metal roof provides the best surface for water catchment, while helping keep your home cool with a roofing material that will last as long as your solar electric or hot-water systems.

OUR STORY

When we first moved into our new home, we were faced with an amazing array of leaking roofs of various substances and pitches. The main roof of the house was composite asphalt shingles at a fairly steep pitch—some of the sections of shingles were fairly new, around three years, and some were extremely old, perhaps 25 years. Whenever a big thunderstorm rolled through town the pots and pans appeared around the living room and on the staircase, creating that special music known only to owners of leaky roofs. The flat asphalt and gravel roof that eventually was to become a green roof actually sloped toward the house instead of away toward the gutter (not a good thing). There was no access to the flat roof, and it had leaked so badly and for so long that it had destroyed the eastern wall of a front room of the house, as well as the porch ceiling. In a classic example of addressing the symptom and not the root of the problem, the previous owner had replaced all the German siding and rebuilt the damaged wall but had not fixed the leaking roof! Tangentially, and ironically, we found out at closing that the previous owner was selling our house specifically to finance construction of a "green" house out in the country, while we were moving away from our "green" country house in order to lower our energy consumption. Well, we can only hope he eventually reads this book and takes a lesson or two to heart.

At any rate, we knew we were going to have to reroof, and we wanted to catch as much rainwater as possible off the roof. For the steeply pitched areas, we chose prepainted metal roofing, because of the purity of water runoff, energy-saving characteristics, and ease of homeowner installation. We redecked the green roof to slope away from the house, and any water that falls on the planter boxes or flat roof drains off and into the gutters. We already had metal gutters on the house, so we didn't need to add gutters.

We plan to build a large (about 3,000-gallon) ferrocement cistern in the basement to hold our rainwater, but unfortunately we haven't yet had time to start on that project. We will gather the rainwater via the gutters, purify it, and then gravity-feed the tank. The tank will be handbuilt with metal lathe, rebar, and stucco plaster and will need a booster pump and pressure bladder to supply the house, as it will be below the level of any plumbing fixtures.

For now, we make do with four 65-gallon plastic tanks sitting at the bottom of the gutters on the four corners of the house. It isn't nearly enough capacity to hold the quantity of water that comes off our roof in even a minor rain event, but it does give us a bit of reserve with which to water the garden.

To get started with rainwater catchment, you can begin harvesting your rainwater with a simple rain barrel, which will reward you and your garden with fresh and easily accessible water during short dry spells.

Rain Barrel

Renter friendly.

Project Time: Afternoon.

Cost: $20–100.

Energy Saved: Low. Catching rainwater preserves the mechanical energy of the falling water created by solar distillation and releases it later when plants need it.

Ease of Use: Easy.

Maintenance Level: Low to medium. An occasional cleaning may be required, and some spring and fall maintenance is likely in colder areas.

Skill Levels: Carpentry: Basic. Plumbing: Basic.

Materials: 55-gallon food-grade barrel or premanufactured rain barrel, 45-degree turn that matches existing gutter, self-tapping metal screws, extra length of downspout, two wood posts at least 4 × 4 × 8, scrap 1 × material, nails OR 6–8 cement blocks (8 × 16). If modifying regular barrel: ¾-inch PVC bulkhead

fitting or other ¾-inch fitting with gasket, ¾-inch hose bibb (sillcock), fiberglass or metal window screen.

Tools: Wood saw, hack saw, drill, drill bits, level, ladder.

The barrel. Rain barrels are often sold at garden shops and agricultural supply stores. Typically they are 55–80 gallons and made of solid black polypropylene plastic that will hold up well for 20–25 years. Some enlightened municipalities sell discounted barrels or hold rain-barrel-building workshops.

Modifying a regular barrel. All that distinguish a rain barrel from a food-grade barrel are a perforated, screened top to let in water but keep out mosquitoes, a hose bibb (also known as a sillcock or wall hydrant)

FIG. 8.1. **A standard 55-gallon rain barrel. While these are sold premade, making your own is easy and rewarding and can dramatically reduce the cost, especially if food-grade barrels can be found for free. See figure 9.1 for adding a hose bib into an existing tank.**

about a quarter of the way up from the bottom of the barrel that a hose can be attached to, and an overflow spout at the top.

Suitable food-grade barrels are not hard to find for free; just make sure the one you use didn't ever contain anything caustic. Large food producers are often willing to part with extras to whoever bothers to ask. Locally, we know of folks who have been given barrels by a Coca-Cola bottler, a pickle company, and a salad dressing maker. It's worth spending a little bit of time on the phone asking around if you're otherwise going to have to pay retail for a rain barrel, especially if you want more than one, because modifying a food barrel is relatively easy. There are also Web sites like www.freecycle.org where you can find useful materials for free in many parts of the country. Look for a waste or scrap exchange in your area!

For the faucet we like to avoid threading our own fittings, which takes a specialized tap tool. Instead, you can use what is sometimes referred to as a "bulkhead fitting" to make the watertight connection through the tank. These can be hard to find in home improvement stores but are readily available and inexpensive over the Internet. Browsing through the plumbing aisles you might find an even better fitting to use, for example, water heater pans include a nearly perfect fitting that can be unscrewed, with a gasket already attached.

Drill a pilot hole (with a spade-tip bit or small hole saw) into the barrel about 6–8 inches up from the bottom that matches the part of your fitting (whether threaded or straight) that will go through the tank wall. If you're using a bulkhead fitting, remove the locknut from the fitting, leaving the gasket on the body. Insert the body through the hole in the tank from the inside, trapping the washer between the *inside* tank wall and the fitting. Screw the locknut back onto the outside of the fitting for a leak-free installation. You may need to employ a friend to hold one side to get it tight. Next, screw the hose bibb onto the fitting. Depending on what type of fitting you ended up with, you will need either a male or female hose bibb.

Next you'll need to either drill holes in the top or cut a chunk out of the lid to let in water. If you're cutting many holes, use at least a ¾-inch bit and make at least a dozen holes, mostly in the middle. This will produce lots of obnoxious plastic filings, so do it someplace where you can sweep them up and throw them in the trash. If you decide to cut a square out of the lid, a jigsaw or hacksaw will do the trick. You should attach window screen (fiberglass or metal) to the top of the barrel to keep mosquitoes from entering. Drill pairs of small holes along the edge of the top and then weave scrap pieces of wire through the holes and the screen in about 10 different locations. Alternatively, you can place a large piece of screen over the top of the entire barrel and tie it down around the outside perimeter with wire or twine. The downspout will rest on top of this screen.

In case of downpours when your tank is full, make an overflow drain on the top of the tank. You can follow the instructions above for the faucet hole, but install the overflow drain not more than an inch below the top of the tank. It is also possible to attach barrels one to another via the overflow port.

The stand. Getting that rain barrel up off the ground at least a few feet will mean more water pressure and easier watering. Depending on the lay of the land and where your garden is, you may want it to be up as high as 4 feet, although making a steady stand that high is a little more difficult and rain barrels that high up look somewhat strange.

The easiest and most reliable stand is made from stacked pairs of cement blocks. Level the area underneath where your barrel will go, usually directly in front of your gutter, although you can use side turns for your gutter to move it a few feet to the left or right. Place a pair of blocks side by side, preferably with the holes facing up, as this is stronger. Alternate direction for the next set and build up the base to the desired height.

For a wood stand, cut four 4 × 4 posts to the desired height. Using scrap wood, make a square by nailing equal-length boards to the sides of the four posts about halfway up. The length of the sides should be slightly larger than the diameter of the barrel so the barrel can sit on top without overlapping the edge. Add another row of boards around the top, and then nail in scraps of wood on top to support the barrel. Do a thorough job of nailing and use boards at least ¾ inch thick, because a full rain barrel can weigh more than 400 pounds.

Level the stand and put up your barrel. If you don't have an overflow faucet on your barrel, be conscious of where the overflow will go. You don't want to cause erosion.

The downspout. Full rain barrels in cold climates can freeze solid and potentially burst, so in most of the country it's wise to remove the barrel during winter months. Black barrels that get plenty of sun can keep water above freezing in marginal climates, but you are taking a risk leaving the barrel full. Cold climates make dealing with the downspout a little more difficult, as the removed barrel will leave the curved downspout high above the level of the home, potentially spraying the home or causing erosion during drainage.

The best way to deal with this is to keep the existing length of downspout intact and purchase additional gutter (measure the width before you go to the store) for the rain barrel. Basically you'll be making a summertime section of gutter for when the barrel is in operation and then replacing it with the original gutter when it starts to get cold.

To install the new downspout, once your barrel is in place, remove the old downspout and with a hacksaw cut a new piece of downspout that will end about 6 inches above the tank. Attach the new shorter piece of downspout to the gutter. Next you will cut a second short piece of downspout that will run from the wall to the top of the tank. Measure from the new downspout to the tank at approximately a 45-degree angle and take into account the added length of the 45-degree piece that will connect these two pieces (probably adding about 2 inches). Cut a piece of downspout to this length, and attach it to the 45-degree turn using some self-tapping metal screws, and then screw this whole piece to the downspout along the house.

The other option is to use a length of flexible gutter to connect the gutter to the barrel. You may find it more difficult to keep this in place, however.

PASSIVE RAINWATER COLLECTION

Passive rainwater collection refers to sculpting the topography of your yard to slow runoff and increase infiltration. This is done using swales, spirals, site leveling, and mulching. Water that percolates through the ground is naturally filtered and purified before reaching streams, recharges underground aquifers, and ensures plenty of soil moisture. Keep in mind that this can produce boggy areas if rain is frequent and your soils don't drain relatively freely. Before you start sculpting your landscape, do a perc test to measure infiltration. See the "Graywater" section in chapter 9.

WHOLE-HOUSE RAINWATER HARVESTING

In many areas of the country, a water-conserving household can provide for all its water needs from what it can catch off its roof. If the graywater and potentially the blackwater/humanure is also recycled for landscaping, each home can become an independent and sustainable part of the local ecology. We often speak of living off our annual income of solar energy, so it makes sense that we should try to live off our annual income of rainwater as well.

FUNDAMENTAL COMPONENTS
OF A RAINWATER HARVESTING SYSTEM

Typically, the roof of your home will be the main rainwater-catchment *surface.* Supplemental water can be captured from other outbuildings if necessary. The *gutter system* captures the water that flows off the catchment surface. *Leaf screens, first-flush diverters, and roof washers* remove debris, such as bird droppings, dust, and leaves from the water before it is directed to the *cistern.* The water must be brought up to household water pressure through a *delivery system,* which is typically an electric booster *pump* and a *pressure bladder,* but in some places the water can be gravity-fed. Potable water systems will

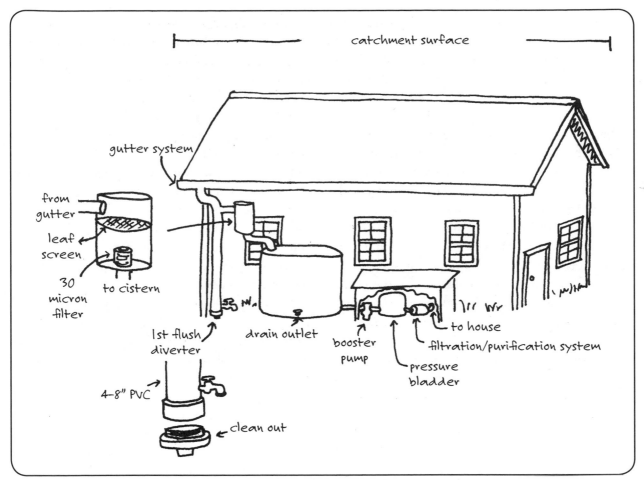

FIG. 8.2. **Typical components of a whole-house rainwater harvesting system.**

need to have some or all of the water filtered by some kind of *treatment system*.

Catchment surface. The first required element for your rainwater harvesting system is a proper roofing material for your catchment system. Acceptable roofing materials are slate, terra-cotta tile, copper, untreated wood shingles, concrete, and metal painted (or prepainted during manufacture) with an epoxy paint. All of these materials provide a reasonably stable, nontoxic surface for collecting rainwater. Unacceptable materials are asphalt shingles, metal without epoxy paint, older concrete tiles (which can contain asbestos), tar, or treated wood shingles.

Asphalt shingles are by far the most common roofing material. Unfortunately, they leach toxins into the water that runs off them. Since this water is going into the ground around your home anyway, if you're considering rainwater collection strictly for landscaping purposes the roofing material isn't so important. But for bathing and especially for drinking, you'll need one of the acceptable materials listed above. See page 163 for how to install a prepainted 5-V metal roof over an existing asphalt shingle roof.

Gutter system. Gutter installation is straightforward and can be accomplished by following the directions specific to the manufacturer. There are issues to consider before deciding whether to use your existing gutter system or whether to install a new system, especially if you will be drinking your rainwater.

PVC (polyvinyl chloride) gutter is probably the easiest to install, but there are serious issues with toxins produced in its manufacture and the potential for leaching. Where possible, avoid PVC that has been dyed other than white or that may contain other chemicals such as fungicides. Aluminum and painted steel gutters are slightly more difficult to install. Painted steel is the preferred choice in our opinion for highest water quality. Often companies that sell prepainted roofing metal also sell matching gutters.

The best way to ensure good water quality from your gutters is make sure that there is a continuous downslope for each run. Where water puddles, the potential for leaching of any chemical is much greater, and the opportunity exists for organic matter to collect and decay, potentially breeding microbes and imparting an off taste to your entire water supply.

Existing metal gutter systems could be suspect, since the solder at the joints could contain lead, which again could leach into your water and contaminate the entire supply. If you are unsure, effective lead test kits can be purchased for a few dollars each from hardware stores, from water quality departments, or over the Internet. Painting existing gutters with epoxy paint should eliminate this risk if lead is determined to be present.

Half-round gutters are much more complicated to install than standard ogee style (the more squarish variety) and are prone to spillage. Although the half-rounds have a great look, they should be avoided if you've never installed gutters before. Occasionally half-round gutters are available in greater widths (up to 10 inches), which may be worthwhile in areas of high flow.

One thing you'll need to keep in mind if you are adding a metal roof onto an existing shingle roof is that rainwater could now potentially spill past your current gutters. This is because of the increase in height of the roof as well as the velocity of the water as it comes off your new metal roof. These two changes can cause much of the water to be projected beyond the gutter. This problem could be rectified by adding metal flashing above the current rim of the gutter to increase the gutter's height and hence its water-catching capabilities. If you're adding new gutters, always buy the largest size possible to ensure that most of the water can be caught during large downpours.

Screens, first-flush diverters, and roof washers. Between rains, undesirable material such as dust, bird poop, and leaves collects on the surface of your roof. Keeping this material out of your cistern will help reduce bacterial buildup and make sure your water is clean before it even gets to your filter.

Screens along the length of the gutters have been touted as a way of keeping leaves out, but they do nothing for the smaller particles like soot or bird poop that you also want to keep out. Many gutter systems do not slope downward enough from the edge of the roof for these screens to be effective. The debris simply collects on top of them, gets wet, and eventually collapses the screen or at a minimum keeps the rainwater from being collected.

Our cultural obsession with "maintenance-free" has a downside. Vinyl siding, city water, coal-fired electricity—all these things supposedly remove the "hassle" of having to take care of our environment, on the micro (home) and macro (global) scale. The unintended consequences of prolonged maintenance deferral range from rotten sills to lead-poisoned drinking water to acid rain. Maintenance-free living is a myth. We recommend that you forget about adding screens and accept the fact that once or twice a year you're going to need to clean out your gutters.

Much more effective in keeping the undesirables out of your cistern is a first-flush diverter. The principle is simple: the first flush of rainwater, which contains most of the junk, flows into a large-diameter pipe, just like a downspout but with a screw cap plumbed in at ground level. Once the pipe is full, any additional water flows past this pipe and continues on to the downspout of the cistern. Sometime in between rainfalls, you must empty the diversion pipe by unscrewing the cap at ground level. The diverted water then flows out. Using 4-inch PVC or larger for the diverter allows whatever was flushed off the roof to funnel through. Rich in organic matter, this water is great for thirsty garden plants.

Recommended quantities of water to divert are around 10 gallons per 1,000 square feet of roof area. If you live in an area with less frequent rainfalls, you may

TABLE 8.1 Summary of Cistern Options

	Average Cost ($/gallon, based on 5000 gal. tank)	Expected Lifetime	Availability	Do It Yourself?	Notes
Fiberglass	1.00	30 yr+	Moderate	No	Generally, fiberglass is used for larger volumes (10K gal.+) and polypropylene for smaller
Polypropylene	0.40	25 yr+	High	No	
Metal		20 yr+	High	No	Can be assembled on-site; need food-grade liner
Concrete Precast	1.00	20 yr+	Low	No	Need food-grade liner; new septic tanks can be used but not above ground
Ferrocement	0.25	30 yr+	High	Yes	Swimming-pool installers can also make these, but the cost will approach that of concrete precast
Wood	2.00	15 yr+	Low	Possible	Most aesthetic; need food-grade liner
Plastered Tire	0.20	30 yr+	High	Yes	Installed underground or bermed

want to consider diverting more because additional debris will have accumulated on your roof between rainfalls. Ten gallons can be held in approximately 12 feet of 4-inch PVC. You'll likely need several shorter sections rather than one long section depending on the height of your gutter and cistern (6- or 8-inch PVC can be used for shorter sections with potential equivalent volume). Make sure to empty your diverter quickly in cold weather; otherwise the pipe can freeze solid and potentially burst.

Potable-water-catchment systems (to supply household drinking water) must filter water more thoroughly than with just a first-flush diverter. There are various methods for this secondary filtering, sometimes called roof washers. Essentially the incoming water is prefiltered through a 5- or 10-micron filter or its equivalent before it enters the cistern, greatly reducing the quantity of suspended particles and consequent water turbidity and cistern sludge buildup. This can be accomplished either with sand and gravel filters in 55-gallon drums or with commercially available filters. In addition to this prefiltering, water intended to be potable should be further purified (more information on purification options follows in this chapter).

Cisterns. By far the largest item in terms of both expense and size will be your cistern. Finding a location for the 5,000 or more gallons of water you'll potentially need can be a serious challenge. The top of the tank needs to be below the roofline, so that the water entering the tank is gravity-fed. While it may seem like a good idea to have an elevated tank to provide your home's water pressure, this is rarely practical. To achieve the typical household 30 psi requires a tank 70 feet up in the air. Making 50,000 pounds of liquid stay 70 feet up in the air is no mean engineering feat. Having a more down-to-earth tank and a pump and pressure bladder will almost always be easier.

The first things to determine are the type and size of the tank. All tanks need to meet some fundamental criteria for long-term use. They must

1. Be opaque to inhibit algae growth
2. Not leach toxic materials
3. Be covered to prevent drowning and accumulation of debris
4. Be accessible for cleaning

There are a range of choices depending on budget, aesthetics, and time. The basic options are fiberglass, polypropylene, metal, concrete, ferrocement, plastered tire, or wood. Aboveground swimming pools are sometimes used, but we believe they should be avoided due to their long-term structural weakness and potential for leaching toxins from their linings. Table 8.1 summarizes the options available.

Ferrocement tanks are a good option for the do-it-yourselfer. These can be freestanding or buried and built by those with a limited amount of masonry experience. They've been field-tested for decades and hold up well, with some limited repair possible.

Plastered-tire cisterns are another homemade option, although less tested. Essentially these are mimicking the cheapest way to store rainwater, the pond, but building up bermed tires allows the creation of an aboveground cistern without large earth-moving equipment. Check the resources section for leads on where to find more information on how to build your own.

Sizing your system. Now that you know your cistern options, you'll need to size your rainwater-harvesting system. How much water does your family use and how much is available? Bringing the supply and demand into balance is essential and often means using low-flow plumbing devices, recycling graywater, fixing all leaks, and other conservation measures. It might also mean increasing supply by harvesting additional water off outbuildings.

Keep in mind that some appliances are simply verboten with a rainwater-harvesting system. Older toilets that use more than 1.6 gallons per flush, top-loading washing machines, and high-flow showerheads must go. We encourage folks to consider a humanure toilet system (see chapter 9), as this can cut a household's water use by up to half in addition to cycling necessary nutrients back through the land.

For every horizontal square foot of roof space there's the potential to collect 0.625 gallons for every inch of rainfall. In practice, this number is rarely achieved. Overflow of gutters and piping in torrential downpours, leaks, and water absorption by rough roofing materials such as tile or slate are all factors that limit the amount harvested. Assuming 75 percent efficiency is conservative, but 90 percent efficiency is routinely achieved by well-functioning systems and should be your ultimate goal. Bad luck and erratic weather prevent the last 10 percent from making it into the tank.

To determine your building's potential, you'll need to figure out your roof's footprint. Measure the exterior dimensions of your home and figure out the area, then add in the horizontal overhang of the eaves. For example, a 25 × 40-foot home with 18-inch eaves over the long sides would be

$25 \times 40 = 1,000$ ft^2 + (2)$40 \times 1.5 = 120$ ft^2 for a total of 1,120 square feet.

When an inch of rain falls, this house could collect $1,120 \times 0.625 \times 90$ percent = 630 gallons of water.

To determine how many average inches of rainfall your location gets, check the weather section of your local newspaper. Or go to the National Climate Data Center Web site (www.ncdc.noaa.gov), click on the Free Data link, scroll down to section B, then choose Station Summaries. Put in your nearest locality when prompted. You'll be rewarded with a wealth of data that includes probabilities of weather extremes such as prolonged dry spells.

All this information will be vital in determining the size of your system. If your area has more intermittent or seasonal rainfall, you'll need a larger cistern. If you're depending solely on rainwater collection for your water supplies, then you'll need a rainwater-harvesting system that can persist through the longest possible dry spell. Hybrid systems that still have access to city water, a well, or, heaven forbid, trucked-in water can weather average dry spells.

The first thing to determine is the potential supply for your home and how this matches with the typical use of 50 gallons/day per household member of a water-conscious home (compared with 100 gallons a day for the average household). Checking the NOAA Web site, here in Durham, North Carolina, we receive an average 48 inches on our 1,500-square-foot roof, which gives us a potential supply of $48 \times (0.625)1,500$ = 45,000 gallons a year.

Assuming 90 percent capture, we get 40,500 gallons a year.

Since there are four people living in our house, this gets us about 10,000 gallons a year per person, or about 27 gallons a day. So we need to be extremely conservative to achieve water independence in our

TABLE 8.2 Conservative Water Use for a Family of Four.

Purpose	Gallons per Day
Cooking/Dishwashing	20
Laundry	35
Bathing	65
Flushing	80
Total	200

Source: Art Ludwig, *The New Create an Oasis with Greywater*. Oasis Design, 2006. Santa Barbara, CA

home. Currently we are close to achieving this goal, with the help of our humanure-composting system, recycled graywater, and the building of an additional cistern to catch the water off a detached garage for landscaping purposes.

With weather becoming more wacky all the time because of global climate disruption, it's not a bad idea to have in mind an area that could potentially provide additional storage space if experience reveals that you sized your cistern too small for the extended dry spells. Consider, also, your house members' willingness to do without most of their daily water use in extreme dry spells.

It's not hard to see from table 8.2 that as the water level in your cistern gets low, the majority of your family's water use could be curtailed. Composting human waste and taking bucket baths would cut the usage by well over half. If you intend to do these things fulltime regardless, then make sure to size your system appropriately. Tanks that are too large for the required system waste money and space.

Looking at your current water bills will let you know how much your household uses, although sometimes municipalities list water usage in meaningless numbers and you have to call them up to find out what they represent. Ideally, it's best to achieve wateruse reductions before you size your cistern so you will know more exactly how low you can go, rather than assuming you can live with goals that are unrealistic. Keep in mind your area's natural climate and try to live within its limitations. If you live in the deserts of Arizona as opposed to the mountains of Hawaii, then you have more of a responsibility to be frugal with your water.

The most conservative assumption, and the one used by many professional installers, is to plan on three months of reserve. This would be increased if your area receives only seasonal rainfall. This threemonth assumption would mean that there was always enough water for whatever you wanted to do and you would never need to think about conservation during dry spells.

This type of planning will produce a system that is extremely large and expensive, and it is a product of the convenience mentality that is pervasive throughout our society. Like an off-grid photovoltaic system that makes sure its owners never have to flip off a switch if they don't want to, such a large system dramatically increases its price, physical space, and maintenance only to ensure that no one has to consume less during periods when there is, in fact, less available.

Typically, this results in diminishing returns. Sizing a system, whether it's PV or water or whatever, to meet standard usage 100 percent of the time instead of 95 percent of the time can often be twice as expensive, because planning for that last 5 percent means having lots of additional capacity to meet standard demand in times of the greatest scarcity. This is a typical example of the perfect being the enemy of the good, because oftentimes trying to be perfect (100 percent) instead of just good (95 percent) means pricing the system out of the budget of the average homeowner. Plan on changing your behavior during the times of scarcity—consuming less when there is less around—and you will save yourself much trouble, effort, and expense in the long run.

To get a reasonably sized cistern, look at the climate charts and find the driest median three-month period. Using medians instead of averages will help cancel out outlier events that raise the general averages. It's quite likely that your rainwater-harvesting system would overflow during these high-rainfall events. For us here in North Carolina, hurricanes and tropical storms can seriously drive the averages out of whack.

Total these three months and assume that rainfall is two-thirds of normal for this quarterly period. For us, that's the last three months of the year for a total of 9.79

TABLE 8.3 Calculating Gallon Capacity of a Rectangular Cistern

1 ft³ = 7.48 gallons

Depth (ft)/Area (ft²)	3	4	5	6	7	8	9	10
16	360	480	600	720	840	960	1,080	1,200
25	563	750	938	1,125	1,313	1,500	1,688	1,875
36	810	1,080	1,350	1,620	1,890	2,160	2,430	2,700
49	1,103	1,470	1,838	2,205	2,573	2,940	3,308	3,675
64	1,440	1,920	2,400	2,880	3,360	3,840	4,320	4,800
81	1,823	2,430	3,038	3,645	4,253	4,860	5,468	6,075
100	2,250	3,000	3,750	4,500	5,250	6,000	6,750	7,500
144	3,240	4,320	5,400	6,480	7,560	8,640	9,720	10,800
169	3,803	5,070	6,338	7,605	8,873	10,140	11,408	12,675
196	4,410	5,880	7,350	8,820	10,290	11,760	13,230	14,700
225	5,063	6,750	8,438	10,125	11,813	13,500	15,188	16,875
256	5,760	7,680	9,600	11,520	13,440	15,360	17,280	19,200

Source: Patricia Macomber, Guidelines on Rainwater Catchment Systems for Hawaii. College of Tropical Agricultre and Human Resourcesm university of Hawaii-Manoa. 2001. Manoa, Hawaii

TABLE 8.4 Calculating Gallon Capacity of a Round Cistern

1 ft³ = 7.48 gallons

Depth (ft)/diameter (ft)	5	6	7	8	9	10
5	472	566	661	755	835	944
6	738	885	1,033	1,180	1,305	1,475
7	1,062	1,274	1,487	1,699	1,879	2,124
8	1,446	1,735	2,024	2,313	2,558	2,891
9	1,888	2,266	2,643	3,021	3,341	3,776
10	2,390	2,867	3,345	3,823	4,228	4,779
11	2,950	3,540	4,130	4,720	5,220	5,900
12	3,570	4,283	4,997	5,711	6,316	7,139
13	4,248	5,098	5,497	6,797	7,517	8,496
14	4,986	5,983	6,980	7,977	8,822	9,971
15	5,782	6,038	8,095	9,251	10,231	11,564

Source: Patricia Macomber, Guidelines on Rainwater Catchment Systems for Hawaii

average inches, and two-thirds of that gives us 6.52. The catchment area for our duplex's roof is 1,500 square feet, so during this projected dry spell we'll get 0.625 gallons for every square foot of roof, or 6.52 × (1,500)0.625 = 6,112 gallons. If we capture 90 percent, we get about 5,500 gallons in this dry spell.

If the four people living in our house used 200 gallons a day during this period, our demand would be 90 days × 200 gallons = 18,000 gallons. This is 12,500 gallons above our supply, and we would need a cistern that large to accommodate this dry spell.

However, we're shooting to each use a more conservative 25 gallons/day. This reduction cuts our consumption by half over this three-month period to 9,000 gallons total, leaving only a 3,500-gallon deficit for the period (5,500 gallons of supply – 9,000 gallons of demand = 3,500-gallon deficit). We'll need a tank that's at least this large (note this is only a quarter the size of the previous example of 18,000 gallons of demand). In fact, the area we have marked out for our planned ferrocement tank in our basement is about 100 square feet and 6 feet deep, so we have a 4,500-gallon potential.

If you want to use cistern water for irrigating landscape plants, you would have to dramatically increase the size of your tank. Instead, recycle graywater. If this is not sufficient, consider a small outdoor retainment pond, filled naturally by swales. If you have the space, ponds are far and away the cheapest method of storing large volumes of water. Your neighborhood wildlife will love you for it. Plants generally love "dirty" water, so using your carefully screened and filtered cistern water for them is not only counterproductive but also expensive.

Delivery system. Once you've collected your water in your cistern, you've got to get it to flow from the tap. Typical household pressure is at least 20 psi. Less pressure still works for most things (it just takes longer) but *not* for on-demand water heaters. Anyone who's ever lived in the country is familiar with the setup: a pump fills a bladder tank that provides pressure, from which water flows into the house. A pressure switch plumbed into the water lines turns the pump on and off. During heavy water use, typically the pump itself provides enough pressure to keep the water flowing.

But this depends on the pump. A slow (low-electricity-demanding) pump can fill a large bladder, just not very quickly. Thus if you install a slow pump you need to oversize the bladder or put two in parallel. The only prerequisite for the pump is that it can handle the head of the bladder (20 to 30 psi). The speed (gallons per minute) of the pump at the specific head is what you look at to see how fast your water will flow when the bladder is empty or being refilled.

The purpose of the pressure tank is to keep the pump from turning on and off repeatedly every time someone opens a tap for a second or two. Frequent starts increase surge electricity usage and greatly shorten the length of the pump's life. With this in mind, it's best to invest in as large a pressure tank as possible, even for smaller households. The additional up-front cost of a larger pressure tank will save money on pump repair and replacement in the long run.

Water treatment. Much of the energy involved in household water supply goes into purifying all of the water that enters your home up to drinking-water standards, even though only a small fraction actually goes into your body. In fact, a great deal of it will be unpurified very quickly as members of your household urinate and defecate in this perfectly good drinking water (which then has to be "cleaned" again before it can be released again; more on this in the next chapter).

The key to keeping the water coming out of your taps pure and tasty begins with your catchment system. The cleaner the water that goes into your cistern, the easier it is for your treatment system, whatever it is, to function properly. This means pruning back overhanging trees and shrubbery that not only deposit organic matter in your system but also allow access to the roof by squirrels and rodents whose feces and drowned carcasses are a prime source of contamination. Installing a metal roof will go a long way toward prohibiting access to your catchment surface for rodents as well as birds, most of whom cannot get a footing on the slippery tin, especially roofs with steeper slopes. You can more than make up for this prohibition by creating wildlife-friendly environments on other parts of your property (see chapter 10).

When it comes to treating your water, many options exist. Many municipalities treat water with some type of chlorine; however, chloramine, another chemical compound, has been increasing in popularity. These treatments are effective at killing pathogens and are also the simplest method of disinfection for household systems. Most municipalities are starting with much dirtier water than the rainwater in a cistern, and the number of illnesses (at least immediate ones) from municipal water is vanishingly small.

No system is perfect, however, which is the main reason why there are so many different options. Chlorine is a poison not only to protozoa and bacteria but in large enough doses to humans as well. Applied directly to skin it will cause a chemical burn, and in

TABLE 8.5 Summary of Purification Options

Type	Eliminates	Pros	Cons
Sediment Filter	Larger particles	Effective prefilter, inexpensive	Doesn't remove pathogens, chemicals, or metals; filter needs maintenance
Ceramic Candle Filter	Particulates and some bacteria	Simple and inexpensive	Filters only small quantities, filter needs maintenance, not effective against viruses
Fine Filter	Smaller particles	Better than sediment filter	Most made to work on pretreated water
Chlorination	Most pathogens	Proven, widely used, inexpensive	Ineffective for some protozoan cysts, needs maintenance, toxic by-products
Distillation	Pathogens, metals, and other inorganic contaminants	Effective; solar units available	Requires energy source, slow, done in batches
Boiling	Pathogens	Effective	Requires energy source, slow, done in batches
Ozonation	Pathogens	Effective and fast	Expensive, requires energy source, toxic by-products
Ultraviolet Light	Pathogens	Effective and fast	Expensive, requires energy source, needs prefilter
Activated Carbon	Pathogens and metals	Wide variety available	Filter needs replacing
Reverse Osmosis	Pathogens and metals	Wide variety available	Expensive, needs a lot of maintenance

household systems its storage and application must be done with care to make sure there are no accidents. Chlorine imparts an off taste to water that many people dislike. And the chloroform gas that is produced when chlorinated water comes in contact with the open air is suspected of increasing the strain on the lungs, possibly resulting in higher incidence of asthma and bronchitis. Much of the chlorine in your drinking water, however, can be filtered out with an inexpensive tabletop filter, or it can be allowed to evaporate off, keeping in mind the potential health hazards.

Not so the chloramine that more municipalities are using, which is more stable. Supposedly not as

carcinogenic as chlorine, it nevertheless has a spooky off-green tint and kills fish dead in aquariums. These chemicals are the simplest method of disinfection, but the water they produce is not necessarily "clean."

Table 8.5 lists the most readily available conventional options. It is not exhaustive, and the arena of water purification is undergoing intense development as the worldwide need for low-energy, low-chemical disinfection increases. Remember that if you maintain your rainwater-catchment system, you are starting with some of the purest water available. In many parts of the world, rainwater is not treated at all. In a study done in rural southern Australia where 42 percent of the residents drank primarily from rainwater stored in tanks, there was no discernible difference in childhood gastroenteritis from those drinking from tanks as opposed to treated city water.[2] This is despite the fact that the majority of homes did not use first-flush diverters (7 percent did) or screens (40 percent did), had not cleaned their gutters in over six months (50 percent had), and had not cleaned their tank in the last five years (25 percent had). While not employing any water treatment is foolhardy, too heavy a dose of paranoia can be paralyzing. Water testing regularly (quarterly is best) will help ensure a properly functioning system. These systems are capable of filtering all the water used in your home.

SAND FILTERS

Sand filters (also called biofilters) are a biological way of purifying drinking water. Low turbidity (suspended sediment in the water) is a requirement for sand filters to function effectively. Fortunately, a well-functioning rainwater-catchment system should meet this requirement. Sand filters can purify only small amounts of water at a time, as they are unpressurized and work using gravity, so purifying is limited to drinking water. Essentially a sand filter is a large drum filled with sand. Water enters the top and slowly percolates through. A thin, biologically active layer (called the hypogeal layer) quickly forms on top, feeding on the bits of organic residue and other impurities in the water. By the time the water has made it through the several feet of sand, it is potable and remarkably clean. Eventually, the hypogeal layer becomes too thick and needs to be either scraped off or destroyed by drying and backflushing (the water from the flush being disposed of into a nearby thirsty plant). A new one quickly forms and water filtration can continue.

METAL ROOFS

Metal roofs are long lasting and make a great surface for rainwater catchment. Although most are profes-

sionally installed, 5-V metal roofs can be installed by the handy homeowner, saving over half of the cost of installation. The work requires skill and can be dangerous, so the following information is for experienced carpenters. Those who are interested in a metal roof may want to skim the following section as part of their research or work alongside a hired roofer. In addition to facilitating rainwater catchment, metal roofs applied in the manner described in the following section (applied over existing roofs) also will keep the attic much cooler in summertime.

Install a 5-V Metal Roof
Project Time: Several weekends.
Cost: $1–2/square foot.
Energy Saved: High. Beyond catching potable rainwater, a metal roof, especially installed as described below, will greatly reduce summer heating from the sun.
Ease of Use: N/A.
Maintenance Level: None.
Skill Levels: Carpentry: Advanced.
Materials: Prepainted steel 5-V roofing (referred to as "tin") sized to roof, 1 × 6s (a little less than one linear foot per square foot of roof space), roofing screws, flashing for vent pipes, valley, ridge cap.
Tools: Drill, cordless drill, circular saw with metal blade for cutting lengths of tin, permanent marker to match color of tin.

Caution: This is a complicated project that involves some danger. If you don't have some experience as a carpenter or roofer, it might be best to skim through this project, thus ensuring you can ask enlightened questions, and then hire a professional. Roofing work is not for everyone. Some people can't stand the thought of it. But 5-V metal roof installation is straightforward enough for the handy homeowner to accomplish. A majority of the cost for a metal roof is the labor, and if you are willing to do this, you'll save a bundle of money for other projects.

There are many other quality metal roofs besides 5-V on the market, including standing-seam and shingle

Special Precautions

If your roof is very complicated, i.e., it has lots of dormers or other changes in pitch resulting in lots of valleys and ridges, installation of a metal roof can be quite complicated and result in a lot of wasted material. Also, metal roofs are much more slippery than asphalt shingle roofs, so if your roof has a lot of pitch to it, you'll need to invest in a harness. If your roof has less than a 3-in-12 pitch, then a 5-V roof may not shed water properly. Check with the manufacturer. Also, before ordering your tin, keep in mind that any overlapping pieces of tin (generally tin doesn't come in lengths greater than 16 feet) need to overlap at least 6 inches to ensure capillary action doesn't pull water upward and cause a leak.

As a caveat, the instructions we're going to include here for screwing down the tin match the old method of installing 5-V roofs and may not match the manufacturer's installation instructions. The reason we are sticking with the traditional method is based on our experience with these roofs on older homes. Specifically, we recommend putting the screw through the V of the tin, rather than through the flat of the tin. This ensures that the roof will shed water without depending on the neoprene washer, which we suspect will degrade over time as it is exposed to UV radiation and intense heating and cooling. Also, we recommend "skip" sheathing (strips of sheathing with approximately 12 vertical inches between strips) rather than continuous sheathing. This means that there are large gaps of unsupported metal that could bend if you stepped on them. When walking around on a skip-sheathing roof, be sure to step only in line with the visible screws and avoid the areas far from the screws. If you have any concerns with these alterations, then you should follow the manufacturer's instructions precisely to ensure your warranty.

varieties, but 5-V is by far the easiest for the homeowner to install. Prepainted 5-V roofs are warrantied for 45 years or more (5-V tin is so called because of the five ridges, or Vs, that give the metal its stiffness and help form an interlocking pattern that ensures water is shed properly). We've seen metal roofs that are still in good shape after 150 years. Installing one will ensure that your roof lasts as long as any solar panels (water or PV) that go on top of it.

Ordering the roof. Today these roofs are no longer made of tin, even though you'll often hear them referred to that way (including in this book). They're made of steel and have a very stable epoxy paint baked on. This is the original do-it-yourself roof, and you'll notice them on farms and outbuildings throughout the country. While the most common variety is galvanized and isn't as good for rainwater catchment because it leaches zinc, the newer prepainted variety is regularly offered from metal or hardware suppliers or can be ordered through suppliers over the Internet. Typically, this style of roofing material comes in 29- or 26-gauge (remember, with metals the lower the gauge number the thicker the metal). Spend the extra money on the 26-gauge if it's available. These stouter sheets will flop around a lot less while you're installing them and show fewer irregularities in your roof once installed.

Skipped sheathing. In our opinion, the best way to go with an existing asphalt shingle roof is to place new 1 × 6 skipped sheathing directly on top, and then put the 5-V roof on this new sheathing. This is much simpler than having to remove the old shingles and ensures that you'll have a backup roof underneath your new roof, never a bad thing, especially if this is your first installation. Even though this will use more material in terms of the wood needed for the sheathing, this method of application will provide a tremendous cooling effect for your home. The skips in the sheathing will allow plenty of cross-ventilation, keeping most of the day's heat out of your attic and thus your home, in effect acting like a giant parasol for your house. If cooling needs are not great in your area, consider eliminating the skip sheathing and applying the 5-V roof directly on top of the original decking. Again, check with the manufacturer if you are concerned about the warranty. Remember that lighter colors absorb less radiation (see table 7.2 in chapter 7).

Once you've chosen your color and ordered your 5-V roof tin, including all the ridge cap, valley, and screws, you'll need to locate a source of 1 × 6 wood. Consider a purchase directly from a local sawyer, as this will likely save you money and you'll know that your wood was harvested locally. To determine how much you'll need, assume one 1 × 6 for every 15–18 inches. Most shingles are 5 inches tall, so every third shingle is every 15 inches. Use the existing shingles both to determine the amount of wood needed and as a guide when you're installing. After determining the height of your shingles, count up the number of rows, divide by the proper amount (3 if your shingles are 5 inches and you're going to place sheathing every 15 inches), and then multiply by the width of your roof to get the total number of *linear* feet you'll need for that section. Tally up all the sections.

Starting with an easy section of roof. Once you have all your materials on hand, wait for a stretch of dry weather, and choose a roof section you can complete in its entirety before it rains again, preferably a straightforward one that is a little less visible to give you some practice. Although you'll be keeping the original roof, you'll still be putting lots of holes in it when you nail on the 1 × 6, so it's best to be completely finished before the next rainfall.

Nailing the sheathing into the rafters. It's best to nail the new sheathing into the rafters, but you'll need to have access to your attic to accomplish this. Measure from the edge of the existing shingle roof and put in two 3-inch or longer screws equidistant from the edge and 4 feet apart to form a line parallel to the edge of your roof, making sure to be over your attic and not still over the eaves. Go into the attic and find your two screws, measuring from each of them to the edge of a rafter. Hopefully these numbers are the same and the rafter is parallel to the edge of the roof. If not,

---

Linear Feet and Board Feet

A note on *linear* versus *board* feet: This will be very important if you're ordering your wood directly from a sawyer. *Linear feet* refers to the amount of lumber for a specific dimension, while *board feet* refers to a section of wood 1 foot by 1 foot by 1 inch but is used to describe lumber of any dimension. For example, if you needed 100 1 × 6 × 10s for your project, this would be 10 × 100 = 1,000 *linear feet* of 1 × 6. In *board feet,* this works out to be (100 × 1 × 6 × 10)/12 = 500 *board feet* of 1 × 6. To calculate the amount of *board feet* directly multiply all the dimensions, multiply times quantity, and then divide by twelve. Make sure to pay attention to which method your sawyer uses when pricing and ordering.

---

you'll have to do some figuring to make sure your nails hit the rafters.

Assuming a well-framed house and equal readings, this number tells you how far you need to shift from your two screws to get above your rafters. Check to see how far apart your rafters are spaced. They should be spaced equidistantly, probably 16, 20, or 24 inches apart, but check them all the way down to make sure they don't wander off, at the top and at the bottom.

You should now have the necessary spacing information to go back up on the roof and mark off your rafters. At this point you may want to tack in a row of 1 × 6s along the bottom to make sure you have proper footing, nailing into the sheathing. Plan to leave a half-inch gap between sheathing boards meeting in the same horizontal line to allow for upward airflow. Make sure your nails aren't poking through any woodwork in the eave. For installing the sheathing we highly recommend using a nail gun if possible. Not only is a nail gun faster, but it also allows holding a board in place with one hand and nailing it with the other, which can be a huge help.

FIG. 8.3. Adding new sheathing over an existing shingle roof before applying the metal roof allows for cross-ventilation. This will dramatically lower attic temperatures by as much as 50 degrees F. The existing shingles are also a great help in placing the new sheathing boards.

Using a board as a straightedge and resting it on the bottom piece of sheathing, mark off your rafters from top to bottom with a carpenter's pencil or permanent marker, measuring off the two screws for your first line. (You can accomplish this with a chalk line if you prefer.)

Now you know where to nail all your sheathing. Work up from the bottom, making sure to cut all the board ends square. Don't worry about breaking the boards over the rafters, as the sheathing underneath the shingles will provide ample support. Again, leave a gap between horizontal boards and keep back the boards about 1 inch from the edge of the roof. This will help hide them after completion. Make sure the middle of your top piece of sheathing lines up with the edge of where your ridge cap will go.

If you're unable to locate your rafters, nailing into the sheathing underneath the shingles will suffice, as long as your nails are long enough and the layers of old asphalt shingles aren't overly thick. Make sure to use

lots of nails (rows of three, every 16 inches or so), and get ringshank ones if available for better purchase.

Paint exposed sheathing and old shingles black. Use flat black outdoor paint to coat all areas of the sheathing that will be visible after you install the tin. This includes the edges of the sheathing along the roof edges, the bottom few inches of these same pieces of sheathing, and the bottom edge of the bottom piece of sheathing. Doing this will hide the entire sheathing system after completion.

Putting on the tin. Once you have your sheathing down you're ready to start with the tin. Getting the first piece lined up correctly is of paramount importance, as each new piece locks into the previous piece, so any misalignment becomes exacerbated the farther along you go. To make sure of proper placement, screw two short boards on the bottom corner of either end of the roof, essentially an extension of the fascia board, so that they overlap the edge by at least 5 inches. Do not allow these boards to stick out above the plane

Behavior of Water

The main purpose of installing a roof is to keep water away from your home. Water is incredibly lazy, and it helps to think like a drop of it while installing your roof. If the roof is flat, water wants to stay, and if it's steep water wants to roll. Water does two other things that are important to bear in mind: it mildly adheres to most other materials and it can move great distances, even vertically, by capillary action.

These two characteristics create two common problems with metal roofs. The first is the tendency, if the roof is at a slight pitch (6/12 or less), to roll back under the bottom of the tin toward the house. This can happen with any roofing material, but because metal is so smooth the distance water can travel in this way is greater. If you're concerned about this rollback, then install some sort of drip edge.

Capillary action can result in water getting sucked back up between two overlapping pieces of tin and making it to your roof framing. Again, lower-sloped roofs are more affected. Tin should always be overlapped at least 6 inches vertically. Freezing can exacerbate this problem, so if you live up north overlap your tin at least 1 foot.

of the roof. Then determine how much overhang you want at the bottom. If you have gutters or will in the future, then you'll want to only have an inch or so of overhang. If you're not installing gutters, shoot for an overhang of 2–3 inches. As rainwater rolls down your metal roof, it will do so with much more velocity than over a shingle roof, so keep this in mind.

Determining overhang. Measure out the desired overhang and put a screw on the outside of your board (away from the house) at this distance. Do this at both ends, then wrap a string tightly from one screw on one side of the house all the way to the other screw at the other side of the house. Make sure there is no sag in the string by winding it around the screws until it is taut. This string along the bottom of the roofline will be your guide.

Attaching the roof to the sheathing can be accomplished in one of two ways. If you're putting the screws in the flat of the tin, you can use a hammer to puncture the tin with a nail or the roof screw and then use a cordless drill to drive in the screw. If you're putting the screw in the top of the V, you can make a dent in the V, then put a hole in the dent with a nail or roof screw, driving the screw in until the rubber washer just pulls up snug but doesn't crimp the tin. Many cordless drills have settings that ratchet up to a certain pressure and then stop driving.

Consider predrilling the sheets. An alternative method is to predrill the sheets of tin for the entire section of roof you're working on. Predrilled sheets are easier to handle once you're up on the roof, because you can hold the sheet with one hand and screw it in with the other without worrying about making holes. You'll want screws every 20–30 inches (every other piece of sheathing), and more frequently along the top, bottom, and edges as these areas see considerably more wind shear. Measure out to the center of your sheathing from the guide string you have running along the bottom (but don't hook your tape on the string, as this will affect the measurement) for the desired screw spacing, making a list of your numbers. Check the list by measuring again in the middle and the opposite end to make sure these numbers work.

Stack up the appropriate number of sheets upside down on two long boards resting on a pair of saw benches, and clamp them down. Cut to length if necessary, making sure to cut the top so that the factory edge will be on the bottom, with the top edge running to the top piece of sheathing. This can be done with a circular saw fitted with a metal blade. Note that this will require gloves, safety glasses, dust mask, and earplugs, and that the cut edge will be VERY SHARP! Tin can also be cut individually with hand snips or electric snips.

The double V with the broad valley rests on top of the skinny valley. This ensures that any water that

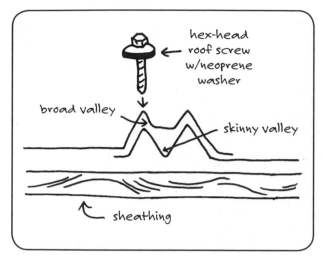

FIG. 8.4. **The proper method of placing 5-V sheets leaves a gap where the ridges overlap, allowing moisture to drain.**

might get in the channel has a pathway to escape. Keep in mind that if you live in an area that experiences high prevailing winds, ideally the sheets will lap away from the wind to diminish uplift.

If you're putting the screws through the V, you'll need to drill through the inside V of the broad valley and the outside of the skinny valley. You'll also need screws through the middle V.

Mark out your measurements with a permanent pen. It's worthwhile to have a permanent pen that somewhat matches the color of the roof. This allows drawing on the painted side of the tin when necessary without it being seen from below after the tin is installed.

Before you drill, keep in mind that you don't want holes on the outside rows of ridges at either side of your house, as these will be hanging over the edge of your roof and will not be getting any screws. Your first piece will have the broad valley double V overlapping the edge, and your last piece will have the skinny valley double V overlapping. Take off the second piece and drill out the holes in the skinny double V using a ⁵⁄₁₆-inch metal drill bit. Put the second piece back on and drill out the middle holes. Take off the top piece (this will be the first piece) and then drill out the holes in the broad valley double V. Take off the second piece and set it aside (this will be your last piece).

Putting up your first sheet. Placing your first piece is greatly helped by having a second person on a ladder at the bottom of where the first sheet will go (ideally you would have a helper through the entire project). Take the first sheet up onto the roof, keeping in mind that working with sheets of tin (basically sails) when it's windy can be very dangerous. Put on your harness. Remember that if a gust of wind catches the tin or you drop a tool or a screw, let it go! Chasing it down will do neither it nor you any good whatsoever!

Sheets can be held up on the roof temporarily by two methods: A single sheet can be screwed down into any piece of sheathing through one of the predrilled holes. Multiple sheets can be held in place by putting two roofing screws on the bottom piece of sheathing and resting the sheets against them (if the sheets will be there long, screw them down as well).

Lining up the sheets. Line up the sheet *exactly* with the string along the bottom. It's easiest to see this from the ladder. The line of the string and the bottom edge of the tin should be *perfectly parallel*. This is key, as any deviation will cause the tin to gradually edge off the roof and your predrilled screw holes will either not line up or migrate off your sheathing. You'll want to place the first sheet with about 1 inch of overhang over the existing side of the shingle roof, but this will vary depending on the total width of your roof. It's likely you'll have to rip the last sheet to width, but try to avoid this if possible by adjusting the proper amount of overhang. Generally, 3 inches of overhang is the limit. Remember the sheets are 24 inches wide when overlapping but there's an additional 2 inches from the final sheet.

When the sheet is in the right location generally, put a screw in the top hole of the single V. The person on the ladder can now line up the bottom of the sheet with the string as well as checking to see that the overhang of the sheet is reasonably consistent along the side. Get down and have a look. This is always a good idea whenever in doubt with roofs because what may look wacky up close is often not noticeable from the ground. Once the sheet is where you want it, again, *precisely* lined up with the string, put in the rest of the screws in the single V, making sure the sheet doesn't move when you lock it in place with the second screw.

It will now be necessary to put screws in the flat along the edge. Do this on every piece of sheathing. While it's not a problem to skip every other piece of sheathing in the middle of the roof to save screws (which are surprisingly expensive), it's not wise to do this along the edge. You can feel the edge of the sheathing through the tin with your hand. Make a hole with a hammer and 16d nail and drive in the screws, trying to keep them in line with the other rows when applicable for neatness's sake.

Now you're ready to roll. Bring up the next sheet and line up the screw holes. Again it's easier if you have someone working from a ladder down below. Get the sheet lined up on the bottom with your string. Again, the second piece needs to be *perfectly parallel* with the string. If it's already deviating, then you'll definitely get in trouble later on. It may be that you have to readjust the first sheet. While this is annoying, it's much better than having to take up a dozen sheets and start over. Get it right! This is the most important part of the entire installation.

Screw in ALL the double-V holes first, then the middle single-V holes. This will keep the sheets sitting flat on the sheathing.

Screw down all the sheets, making sure you stay relatively parallel with your string. If the sheets start to migrate off, you can cheat the next one up or down a little bit without it being noticeable from the ground. If you do this too much the holes will no longer line up. If the problem is serious, go back to the first sheet and readjust.

If the last sheet is going to overhang the side edge too much (more than 3 inches), you'll need to rip it to length. Check to make sure the piece needs to be equidistant at the top and the bottom by measuring the remaining exposed shingle roof. Cut the piece to width and screw it down, making sure to screw into the flat along the edge in every piece of sheathing, as you did with the first piece.

Working around plumbing vents, stovepipe, et cetera. To work around circular obtrusions in your

FIG. 8.5. **Flashing around a vent pipe. Notice the inverted V of caulk that deflects most of the water away from the opening.**

roof requires overlapping two pieces of tin on the top and bottom with flashing sandwiched in between (see figure 8.5). It may be possible to remove the existing vent or stove flashing and reuse it. If not, you'll have to purchase new material. You'll need about an extra foot for the overlap, so be sure to consider this before ordering your tin.

To make sure this sheds water properly there needs to be plenty of overlap between the sheets. Shallower-pitched roofs require more overlap, but 6 inches is the minimum for any roof. You won't be able to achieve this amount at the ridge cap, but there's much less water to be concerned about up there also.

Installing valleys. Valley installation is straightforward. Cut the edge of the tin to match the angle of the pitch of your roof for a consistent 2-inch space along the bottom.

Ridge cap. It's easiest to install the ridge cap once one side is completed and then tuck the pieces of the other side up under it. This will minimize the amount of butt-scooting you have to do along the top of the ridge, a potentially dangerous and definitely uncomfortable

FIG. 8.6. **Cut the sheets so that they end a few inches from the ridge of the valley to allow the water to flow freely off the roof.**

activity. As you install tin on the second side, screw down the ridge cap as you go, staying on the sheathing boards whenever possible. Put one screw in for every set of Vs, including the middle V. Ideally, this would be done through the ridge cap and then through the top of the Vs, but this can be extremely difficult. Go for the side instead. The minuscule amount of water that may potentially get through this hole will instantly dry up as soon as the sun shines, as large volumes of hot dry air vent up the Vs and out the top of the ridge cap. And remember, you have another roof underneath. Put an extra screw near the edge, as this part of the ridge cap will see the most wind shear, making sure not to go past the edge of your sheathing. Overlap your ridge cap 6 inches from piece to piece, and 3 inches or so over the 5-V sheets.

If at any time you find that you need to add a screw or have made a hole where there is not new sheath-ing underneath, remove the washer from one of the roofing screws and fit it on a 3½ inch or longer screw, going through the old roofing material and into the original sheathing. Make sure to not drive this screw in too far or you could crimp your tin.

Getting around on your new roof. When you get to those other projects, chances are you'll need to walk around on your new roof a good deal, to install a solar hot-water rack and evacuated tubes, for instance. When the need arises to clamber around on your roof, you can temporarily install a solid walk board by removing the screws from the section of roof where you'll need it. Line up your walk board with the roof holes and mark them on your board. Using a square, bring these marks down to the center of the board and then predrill them. Put in screws that will stick through the board at least an inch and a half. Line up the boards on the roofing so that the screws go into your metal roof holes and screw this board down into the sheathing.

RESOURCES

Books

Banks, Suzy, and Richard Heinichen. 2004. *Rainwater Collection for the Mechanically Challenged.* Dripping Spring, TX: Tank Town Publishing. Great detailed explanations of all aspects of rainwater harvesting, including whole-house systems.

Kinkade-Levario, Heather. 2007. *Design for Water: Rainwater Harvesting, Stormwater Catchment, and Alternate Water Reuse.* Gabriola Island, BC: New Society Publishers. Great detailed explanations of all aspects of rainwater harvesting, including whole-house systems.

Lancaster, Brad. 2006. *Rainwater Harvesting for Drylands.* White River Junction, VT: Chelsea Green Publishing. For landscaping catchment in arid areas.

Ludwig, Art. 2005. *Water Storage: Tanks, Cisterns, Aquifers, and Ponds for Domestic Supply, Fire, and Emergency Use—Includes How to Make*

Ferrocement Tanks. Santa Barbara, CA: Oasis Designs.

Internet

Guidelines on Rainwater Catchment Systems for Hawaii (www.ctahr.hawaii.edu/oc/freepubs/pdf /RM-12.pdf) and *The Texas Manual on Rainwater Harvesting* (www.twdb.state.tx.us/ publications/reports/RainwaterHarvesting Manual_3rdedition.pdf). Two excellent and free introductions to whole-house systems. We recommend reading both if you are considering one.

Instructions for Building a Rain Barrel. http://home.comcast.net/~leavesdance/ rainbarrels/construction.html and http://miami-dade.ifas.ufl.edu/pdfs /environment/How2Build.pdf

Plastered-Tire Cisterns. www.tnstaafl.net/Earthship /Cisterns/body_cisterns.html

RiverNet. Worldwide organization dedicated to decommissioning dams. www.rivernet.org

Endnotes

1. Fearnside, P. M. 2002. "Greenhouse gas emissions from a hydroelectric reservoir (Brazil's Tucurui dam) and the energy policy implications." *Water, Air and Soil Pollution* 133:1.

2. Heyworth, J. S., Garique F. V. Glonek, E. J. Maynard, P. A. Baghurst, and J. Finaly-Jones. 2006. "Consumption of untreated rainwater and gastro-enteritis among young children in South Australia." *International Journal of Epidemiology* 35 (4): 1051–1058.

CHAPTER 9

Waste

Introduction • Graywater • The Options • Our Story • Graywater
Safety • Graywater Use • Humanure (Aerobic Decomposition) •
Biogas (Anaerobic Decomposition) • Resources

INTRODUCTION

In nature, there is no such thing as waste. If any single statement summarizes the attitude adjustment needed to make our world a sustainable (and survivable) place, this is it. Waste is a construct of industrial society. Treating human feces and urine as "waste," not to mention the hundreds of gallons of nutrient-enhanced graywater most households dump down the drain daily, is to industrialize our very selves—to attempt to take ourselves out of nature and become machines.

Whenever we go against nature, the effort is enormously energy intensive. Whether it's failing to have southern windows to heat our homes in the winter, attempting to grow monocultures in the desert to feed the masses, or treating our feces and urine as so much industrial waste that needs to be disposed of, we rely on concentrations of energy that are very difficult to obtain except by exploiting the eons of accumulated solar energy found in fossil fuels.

This does not mean that we cannot live a wonderful life without these concentrations of old energy. In fact, the potential exists for a much healthier and rewarding life, one where we take responsibility for our actions and their effects on our surrounding environment and thus live in harmony with and even potentially enhance that environment. But this better life is not a given, and it requires forethought, wisdom, and some hard work along the way, as well as some attitude adjustments.

Perhaps no attitude adjustment is more difficult than looking at the crap that comes out of our bodies and seeing a resource rather than a repulsive brown lump that needs to be flushed away without even a glance. Obviously, no immediate need can be fulfilled via that brown lump. Our bodies went through a lot of trouble to get rid of it.

But this shortsightedness ignores our future needs, the needs of other species, and the remaining stored energy in that lump. While our complicated mammalian bodies have taken everything they needed and discarded the rest, many smaller critters still see great potential in that "waste." Great potential exists for us humans in that refuse after the smaller critters have had their fill of it. After it has been properly composted, the final product is a rich, pathogen-free organic fertilizer that will increase the health and vigor of all the plants growing around your home.

Instead of dropping your poop into a receptacle filled with drinking water and flushing it into the nearest stream, consider composting your own manure, either aerobically (with air) or anaerobically (underwater), and using the resulting rich fertilizer to help fix the broken nutrient cycle that we are now perpetuating. The remaining stored energy in your urine and feces is not waste, because you are a part of nature and not a machine. Instead, it is simply sunshine on the move, going from plants to animals to rich humus and then back to plants again. With a little extra trouble, you can turn your "waste" into black gold and eliminate your need for additional gardening inputs of purchased fertilizers. What was an energy-intensive one-way street leading to nothing but dead ends can become an energy-resourceful cycle of life.

GRAYWATER

Graywater refers to all water exiting your home from all fixtures except your toilet. In most cases, this water is perfectly acceptable for landscaping use, provided the water does not come in *direct* contact with any food being grown. The annual potential for a typical household is 30,000 to 50,000 gallons of nutrient-rich water for thirsty plants and fruit trees.

For those connected to a municipal sewer and water system, purification of both incoming household water and outgoing wastewater can be extremely energy intensive, requiring maintenance of dams, pumping stations, and chemical manufacture and application. Often, this treated water is then directed into nearby streams and rivers with the residual excess nitrogen, phosphorus, and treatment chemicals causing fish-killing algal blooms (eutrophication) and burning of fish gills.[1] Although the damage generally takes place far from the eyes of the homeowner, that does not negate one's personal responsibility, especially since many homes can be retrofitted to take easy advantage of at least some of this nutrient-rich resource.

As Art Ludwig describes in his book *Create an Oasis with Graywater,*

> Ideally, water should cascade through the house and yard by gravity, from the highest vertical level and degree of purity to biological land treatment at the lowest level. Every house could be surrounded with an oasis of biological productivity nourished by the flow of water and nutrients from the home.

There are two points of effective and natural water purification in the typical water cycle. The first, distillation, occurs when water on land and sea evaporates and leaves impurities such as salts and organic matter behind. The second phase of water purification happens when surface water passes through a biologically active area and microorganisms in the soil consume whatever nutrients it contains, including bacteria and other pathogens that may be present. This water then is taken up through plant roots to be transpired back into the air, flows underground to be discharged into nearby waterways, or sinks back into the earth to recharge aquifers.

Water that has passed through conventional municipal sewage treatment plants is neither clean nor pure. It has been poisoned with various chemicals so that it does not contain any active pathogens, but it still contains the residues of these treatments and much of the organic matter it started the voyage with. As we strive to eliminate fossil fuels from our lives, we have to ask ourselves how necessary this energy-intensive water treatment really is.

While Art Ludwig's ideal is difficult to achieve in most existing homes, a low-energy version of it can be readily applied in most places with the judicious use of a pump or two and some clever plumbing. Caught rainwater is necessarily stored near the level of the building, if not below it in a basement. Supplying water pressure to a home through gravity requires steep elevations of as much as 70 feet, so pumping is almost always needed (see chapter 8). And it's sometimes the case that existing landscapes, because of poor sloping conditions, require some pumping for effective graywater use.

Many homes have sufficient elevation and slope to tap into at least some of their vast graywater resources. The drier the climate you live in, the more imperative it is to act. Dumping good irrigation water down the drain to undergo energy-intensive chemical treatment while plants wilt outside your door just doesn't make any sense.

THE OPTIONS

Graywater systems can vary from as basic as schlepping a bucket of bathwater over to flush the toilet to expensive automated systems that are theoretically maintenance-free. As with most things in life, simple systems require daily attention but mean less complex and expensive initial equipment, resulting in fewer breakdowns and greater longevity overall. When starting out with any type of project, graywater included, it helps to adhere to the cardinal rule of engineering, the KISS principle: "Keep it simple, stupid." The same concept is expressed by the term "appropriate technology," which David Eisenberg, director for the Development Center for Appropriate Technology, defines as the "lowest level of technology that can be used to do well what needs to be done." Systems that adhere to these general principles are invariably easier to maintain, self-empowering, more egalitarian, more efficient in resource use, and longer lasting and preserve our personal connection to our environment through our continual involvement.

If you get the basics down and still think that a more complicated approach would be necessary (hopefully it won't be), then you can try to tackle graywater systems that include such things as replumbing, pumps, and float switches. As usual, it is best to pick the low-hanging fruit first, and we'll detail one such system that is straightforward and widely applicable. One reason it's difficult to collect graywater is that most home plumbing systems mix graywater with blackwater from toilets. Employing a humanure composting system (aerobic is by far the much easier retrofit) makes gaining access to your home's graywater simpler. For a comprehensive summary of your graywater options, including construction diagrams, we highly recommend Art Ludwig's book *The New Creating an Oasis with Graywater* (see resources).

While we detail only one graywater system in this chapter, washing machine catchment, the basic premise can be applied to sinks, showers, et cetera, as long as you completely isolate the graywater from the blackwater (toilet).

Once again keep in mind that many jurisdictions outlaw graywater and you may be risking hefty fines and perhaps even incarceration (heaven forbid) by using your graywater.

OUR STORY

The year 2007 was the worst drought in our part of North Carolina for decades, so accessing some graywater moved up the priority list as we watched lots of newly installed edible landscaping wilt in the blistering August heat. For the green roof on the second floor, this was simply a matter of stopping up the bathtub while showering and then schlepping buckets out to the thirsty (nonedible) plants.

Our kitchen sink completely clogged up, and that provided us with the necessary motivation to replumb it and tie it, along with the washing machine, into a 30-gallon graywater tank that sits just outside the kitchen wall. This provides us around 10–30 gallons of extra irrigation water on a daily basis.

We put in a humanure composting system as described by Joe Jenkins in an excerpt from his *Humanure Handbook* below. It is working great and has made crapping much more fun! We always felt guilty about using purified drinking water to flush the toilet and we're very happy we no longer have to do this. It is also fascinating to watch the hyperactive critter life in the hot humanure compost pile (which, by the way, doesn't smell at all and isn't in any way as repulsive as Rebekah initially assumed it would be). Sow bugs and silverfish have moved right in and made themselves at home.

GRAYWATER SAFETY

A few simple design considerations will ensure that your graywater system operates safely for many years. Most graywater is the water that you were just using, for bathing or for washing clothes that you were recently wearing, for instance. As such, there's no reason to be afraid of it. It does have the potential, however, to transmit infectious diseases if treated haphazardly, since it may contain trace amounts of pathogens that, given the right circumstances, can multiply rapidly. It is exactly this worst-case scenario that is the impetus for graywater's heavy regulation and municipalities treating it the same as blackwater.

The two principles that ensure the safety of your graywater system, as summarized by Ludwig, are:

1. Graywater must pass slowly through healthy topsoil for natural purification to occur; and
2. Design your graywater system so no human contact takes place before purification.

These two principles can be easily abided by if some simple precautions are taken:

- Do not apply graywater directly to plants or fruit that will be eaten raw.
- Do not put graywater through a sprinkler, since this can cause inhalation of airborne pathogens.
- Be certain your graywater is percolating through the soil and not running off into streams or gutters.
- Use biodegradable detergents and soaps for all sinks, washers, or tubs that produce graywater.
- Do not allow graywater to sit around for more than 24 hours, as this allows time for pathogens to multiply.
- Always keep in mind that buckets with even a small quantity of water are drowning hazards for toddlers.

GRAYWATER USE

The simplest systems use gravity or appliances with their own pumps, such as washing machines and dishwashers. Make an initial assessment of which plumbing fixtures and appliances in your own home could be easily replumbed so that, by gravity or internal pump,

TABLE 9.1 Determining Landscape Area Requirements for Graywater Percolation		
Soil infiltration rate (minutes/inch)	Loading rate (gal/day/ft²)	Area needed (ft²/gal/day)
0–30	2.5	0.4
30–45	1.5	0.7
45–60	1.0	1.0
60–120	0.5	2.0

Source: Art Ludwig, *The New Create an Oasis with Graywater*

you can water your orchard or landscape plants. How accessible are the pipes? If they're from a bathroom, can you access the tub and sink before the water that exits them combines with that from the toilet? This is often very difficult except on the ground floor of a house. Are members of your household willing to use biodegradable soap and shampoo if you will be recycling bathwater? Are you willing to use a biodegradable soap for your dishwasher? Do you really need a dishwasher? Some people are unsatisfied with the results of biodegradable dish detergents, so try some out first before you replumb your dishwasher for graywater use. Keep in mind that if you wash diapers in your washing machine, then that water should be treated as blackwater and should not be used in a graywater system.

Perc Test

To be a responsible graywater user, you need to make sure that the soil where your graywater is headed percolates well (i.e., drains neither too fast nor too slow). To check your perc rate:

1. Dig holes to the depth your graywater will discharge (typically 6–12 inches).
2. Place stakes into the holes with reference marks in inches.
3. Fill the hole with water, and time how long it takes for the water level to drop a given number of inches. Repeat this procedure two or three times for each hole.

Note: If it takes several hours or less than a minute to drop an inch, your soil is unsuitable for graywater use. In order to use your graywater, you'll need a more elaborate system such as a constructed wetlands, or you can use it only for manual chores like flushing the toilet or watering houseplants.

Use the number from your perc test to get a percolation rate in minutes per inch. Consult table 9.1 to determine the landscape area you will need for your graywater flow.

Here's some typical graywater production from various plumbing fixtures:

Washing Machine, Top-loading: 30 gallons/wash*
Washing Machine, Front-loading: 15 gallons/wash
Automatic Dishwasher: 5–10 gallons/load
Shower: 10 gallons/low-flow, 20 gallons/high-flow
Bathtub: 25–40 gallons
Bathroom Sink: 1–5 gallons/day/person

Laundry Graywater to Catchment Container

This system catches the graywater that comes out of your washing machine in a relatively small barrel or water-storage tank situated above the level of where the graywater is headed. The storage tank keeps a narrow outlet hose from being overwhelmed by the machine's pump surge (washing machines evacuate water at a high flow rate) and also gives the water a chance to cool down before being applied to any plants. Sometime within 24 hours of the wash cycle, the hose valve is opened and water flows via gravity to mulched plant beds. The system can be combined with kitchen sink graywater catchment, where applicable.
Renter friendly.

Project Time: Afternoon.

Cost: Low; $5–100, depending on cost of barrel.

Energy Saved: Low. Reuses water, eliminating additional water purification and sewage treatment.

Ease of Use: Moderate. This method requires attention. The tank should be emptied within 24 hours to keep the graywater from becoming pathogenic. It's easy to empty the tank after hanging up the laundry, allowing time for the water in the tank to cool.

Maintenance Level: Low. This is one of the most useful and maintenance-free graywater systems. You may want to rinse out the barrel every now and then.

Skill Levels: Carpentry: Moderate. Plumbing: Moderate.

Materials: Barrel set up like rainwater barrel (see page 152) and large enough to hold two loads of wash water (30 to 45 gallons), washing-machine drain hose or 2-inch PVC pipe of sufficient length to reach barrel, ¾-inch hose flagged for graywater use of sufficient length, bricks or blocks to raise up barrel for additional pressure, clamp for drainpipe.

Tools: Drill and hole saw, tape measure, pipe wrench.

Location of your washing machine. The basic idea is to divert the wash water that's going down the laundry drain and get it outside into a barrel. This is much easier if your washing machine is up against an exterior wall and may not be possible if your washing machine is in a basement below ground level. If your machine is in the interior of the house, you may be able to run a length of drainpipe under the floor and then outside and up to the top of the barrel. The pump on the washing machine is relatively powerful and is capable of moving the wash water reasonably long horizontal distances. Additional vertical distance will put strain on the washer pump and could potentially shorten its life, so aim to have the exit of the drain hose near the height of the top of the washer. *Note that the drain hose or pipe must at some point rise above the height of the washing drum or water will drain via gravity as the machine is trying to fill.*

Exiting to the outdoor tank. If your washing machine is against an exterior wall, the procedure is relatively simple. Often it's the case that the washing machine drainpipe is resting in a drainpipe in the stud wall. Sometimes washing machines drain via laundry sinks. You'll be bypassing the existing drainpipe by drilling a hole in the exterior wall large enough to pass the drain hose to the outside and to the top of your graywater barrel. Due to the accordion nature of the

---

* You should eventually replace with a front-loader. See chapter 3.

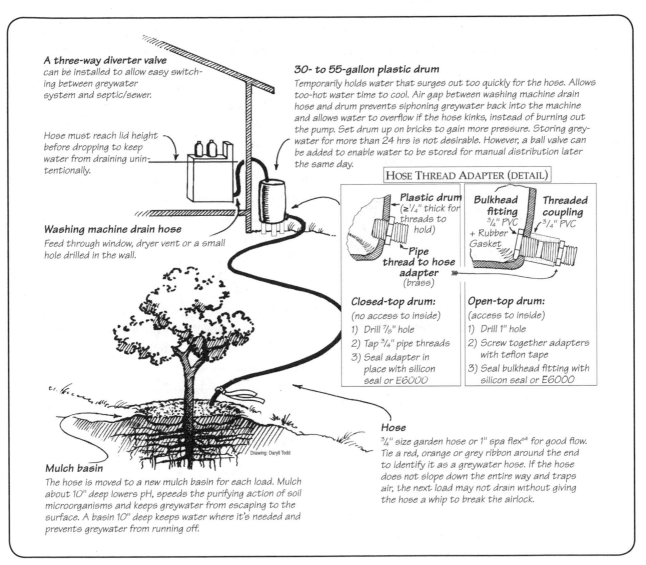

A three-way diverter valve can be installed to allow easy switching between greywater system and septic/sewer.

Hose must reach lid height before dropping to keep water from draining unintentionally.

Washing machine drain hose
Feed through window, dryer vent or a small hole drilled in the wall.

30- to 55-gallon plastic drum
Temporarily holds water that surges out too quickly for the hose. Allows too-hot water time to cool. Air gap between washing machine drain hose and drum prevents siphoning greywater back into the machine and allows water to overflow if the hose kinks, instead of burning out the pump. Set drum up on bricks to gain more pressure. Storing greywater for more than 24 hrs is not desirable. However, a ball valve can be added to enable water to be stored for manual distribution later the same day.

HOSE THREAD ADAPTER (DETAIL)

Plastic drum (≥1/4" thick for threads to hold)

Bulkhead fitting
3/4" PVC
+ Rubber Gasket

Threaded coupling
3/4" PVC

Pipe thread to hose adapter (brass)

Closed-top drum:
(no access to inside)
1) Drill 7/8" hole
2) Tap 3/4" pipe threads
3) Seal adapter in place with silicon seal or E6000

Open-top drum:
(access to inside)
1) Drill 1" hole
2) Screw together adapters with teflon tape
3) Seal bulkhead fitting with silicon seal or E6000

Drawing: Daryl Todd

Mulch basin
The hose is moved to a new mulch basin for each load. Mulch about 10" deep lowers pH, speeds the purifying action of soil microorganisms and keeps greywater from escaping to the surface. A basin 10" deep keeps water where it's needed and prevents greywater from running off.

Hose
3/4" size garden hose or 1" spa flex[34] for good flow. Tie a red, orange or grey ribbon around the end to identify it as a greywater hose. If the hose does not slope down the entire way and traps air, the next load may not drain without giving the hose a whip to break the airlock.

FIG. 9.1. **Laundry graywater to catchment container.**

drain hose it is difficult to accomplish this neatly. If your plumbing skills are up to snuff, you can fit the end of the drain hose into a new length of PVC drainpipe and glue together whatever fittings are necessary to get through the wall and to the top of the barrel. The existing drainpipe has a trap on it to prevent backdrafting of sewer gases (the trap constantly holds water in a P or S shape that doesn't drain). If you are running the new pipe out to a tank, it would be a good idea to place a new trap in the line in order to avoid drafts of outside air. The trap can be outside the house prior to the tank or inside the house if there is space. How you proceed,

either with the flexible drain hose or with rigid PVC connections, depends on your concerns for aesthetics, the route to the outside, and air and rain infiltration through the hole you're going to make in your wall.

Don't forget to screen the entrance to your tank to avoid mosquito and other bug issues. If instead you make a threaded, glued, or otherwise airtight connection to the top of the tank, you will encounter vacuum issues and will need to install a vent pipe teed into the line somewhere after the trap. Drain your tank at least once every 24 hours to avoid multiplying bacteria, and don't forget to use biodegradeable soap!

Concerns for colder climes. If you live in a very cold climate, you may want to abandon this graywater system during the winter, replacing the machine's drain hose in the original septic drain and covering the hole to the outside with a piece of sheet metal or wood until the thaw sets in (add a piece of insulation). Running wash water into a barrel only for it to become frozen stiff in an hour doesn't accomplish much. There are systems for dealing with graywater in cold climates during winter, including greenhouses for passive solar heat and winter veggies, but they are much more extensive than what is detailed here. Nevertheless, accessing graywater during the warm season can still be extremely useful and resourceful, but plan accordingly.

HUMANURE (AEROBIC DECOMPOSITION)

Author Joe Jenkins has been composting his family's feces and urine for three decades, using the final product to grow great organic veggies. He does not have some fancy $10,000 Scandinavian composter. He has four plastic 5-gallon buckets, an indoor hand-built collection toilet, and an outdoor compost bin. It does not smell indoors or out, and the energy saved by recycling his own waste in this way over the decades is enormous. No pumps are needed, no chemicals are manufactured or applied, and there are no trucks required to haul away the stuff. Additionally, he has no need to buy outside supplements for his garden.

Many such systems exist the world over, and creating and maintaining such a system at your own home is straightforward and requires little maintenance. We are detailing the system that Mr. Jenkins outlines in the third edition of his book, *The Humanure Handbook*.

What Is Compost?*

Composting is the breaking down of complex organic matter into simpler organic molecules. Leaves, straw, food scraps, feces and urine, weeds, old cotton shirts, grass, et cetera, all make great additions to the compost pile. In order for composting to happen, four conditions need to be met: 1) The compost material cannot be frozen; 2) The compost material cannot be too dry; 3) The microorganisms need oxygen; and 4) A balanced diet of carbon and nitrogen is required.

Fortunately for us, the pathogens that could potentially contaminate the compost (from the addition of fecal matter from a sick person) also are complex organic molecules that make good eating, at least if you're a microbe in a thermophilic (more than 105 degrees F) compost pile. These potential pathogens are unable to make it out of a functioning compost pile alive.

As Joe Jenkins writes in his book, "Organic material should be recycled by every person on the planet, and recycling should be as normal as brushing teeth or bathing." It's ironic that many home compost piles do not reach a thermophilic temperature level of decomposition because they lack the nitrogen-rich urine and feces of a living breathing mammal. Instead, they straggle along at lower temperatures, unable to make it back into the garden in a timely matter. It's almost as if we're *supposed* to throw our poop on the compost pile.

Fortunately, it's not hard to do. Here is how Joe describes it:

> Simple methods of collecting and composting humanure are sometimes called cartage systems, as the manure is carried to the compost bin in waterproof vessels. People who utilize such simple techniques for composting humanure simply take it for granted that humanure recycling is one of the regular and necessary responsibilities for sustainable human life on this planet.
>
> How it works is a model of simplicity. One begins by depositing one's organic refuse (feces and urine) into a waterproof toilet receptacle with about a 5-gallon (20L) capacity. Food scraps should be

---

* We are speaking in this section about aerobic decomposition. For the details on anaerobic decomposition, see the following section on biogas.

collected in a separate, covered receptacle to prevent a fruit fly infestation. A 5-gallon toilet capacity is recommended because a larger size would be too heavy to carry when full. If a full 5-gallon receptacle is still too heavy for someone to carry, it can be emptied when only half full.

The contents of the toilet are *always* kept covered with a clean, organic *cover material* such as rotted sawdust, peat moss, leaf mold, rice hulls, or grass clippings, in order to prevent odors, absorb urine, and eliminate any fly nuisance. Urine is deposited into the same receptacle, and as the liquid surface rises, more cover material is added so that a clean layer of organic material covers the toilet contents *at all times.*

A lid is kept on the toilet receptacle when not in use. The lid need not be airtight; a standard, hinged toilet seat is quite suitable. This lid does not necessarily prevent odor from escaping, and it does not necessarily prevent flies from gaining access to the toilet contents. Instead, *the cover material does.* The cover material acts as an organic lid or a *biofilter*; the physical lid or toilet seat is used primarily for convenience and aesthetics. Therefore, the choice of organic cover material is very important and a material that has some moisture content, such as rotted sawdust, works well. This is not kiln-dried sawdust from a carpenter shop. It is sawdust from a sawmill where trees are cut into boards. Such sawdust is both moist and biologically active and makes a very effective biofilter. Kiln-dried sawdust is too light and airy to be a 100 percent effective biofilter, unless partially rehydrated. Furthermore, kiln-dried sawdust from woodworking shops may contain hazardous chemical poisons if "pressure-treated" lumber is being used there.

During a cold winter, an outdoor pile of sawdust will freeze solid and should be covered or insulated in some manner. Otherwise, containers filled with sawdust stored in a basement will work as an alternative, as will peat moss and other cover materials stored indoors. A large, plastic refuse container with wheels is great for storing sawdust indoors during winter months.

The system of using an organic cover material in a toilet receptacle works well enough in preventing odors to allow the toilet to be indoors, year round. In fact, a full toilet receptacle with adequate and appropriate cover material, and no lid, can be set on the kitchen table without emitting unpleasant odors (take my word for it). An indoor sawdust toilet should be designed to be warm, cozy, pleasant, and as comfortable as possible. A well-lit, private room with a window, a standard toilet seat, a container of cover material and some reading material will suffice.

Full toilet receptacles are carried to the composting area and deposited into the pile (not on top of it). You'll know that a receptacle is full enough to empty when you have to stand up to take a shit. Since the material must be moved from the toilet room to an outdoor compost pile, the toilet room should be handy to an outside door. If you are designing a humanure toilet in a new home, situate the toilet room near a door that allows direct access to the outside.

It is best to dig a slight depression in the top center of the compost pile in the outdoor compost bin, then deposit the fresh toilet material there, in order to keep the incoming humanure in the hotter center of the pile. This is easily achieved by raking aside the cover material on top of the pile, depositing the toilet contents into the resulting depression, then raking the cover material back over the fresh deposit. The area is then immediately covered with additional clean, bulky, organic matter such as straw, leaves, or weeds, in order to eliminate odors and to trap air as the pile is built.

The toilet receptacle is then thoroughly scrubbed with a small quantity of water, which can be rainwater or graywater, and biodegradable soap, if available or desired. A long-handled toilet brush works well for this purpose. Often, a simple but thorough rinsing will be adequate. Rainwater or wastewater is ideal for this purpose, as its collection requires no electricity or technology. The soiled water is then poured on the compost pile.

It is imperative that the rinse water not be allowed to pollute the environment. The best way to avoid this is to put the rinse water on the compost pile, as stated. Under no circumstances should the rinse water be flung aside nonchalantly. This can be a weak link in this simple humanure recycling chain and it provides the most likely opportunity for environmental contamination. Such contamination is easy to avoid through considerate, responsible management of a closed system. Finally, never use chlorine to rinse a compost receptacle. Chlorine is a chemical poison that is detrimental to the environment and is totally unnecessary for use in any humanure recycling system. Simple soap and water is adequate.

After rinsing or washing, the bucket is then replaced in the toilet area. The inside of the bucket should then be dusted with sawdust, the bottom of the empty receptacle should be primed with a few inches of sawdust, and it's once again ready for use.

Finally, always wash your hands after feeding the compost pile, after using the toilet, and before feeding yourself.

When first establishing such a toilet system, it's a good idea to acquire at least *four* 5-gallon receptacles with lids, that are *exactly the same*, and more if you intend to compost for a large number of people. Use one under the toilet seat and the other three, with lids, set aside in the toilet room, empty and waiting. When the first becomes full, take it out of the toilet, put a lid on it, set it aside, and replace it with one of the empty ones. When the second one fills, take it out, put the other lid on it, set it aside, and replace it with the other empty one. Now you have two full toilet receptacles, which can be emptied at your leisure, while the third is in place and ready to be used. This way, the time you spend emptying compost is cut in half, because it's just as easy to carry two receptacles to the compost pile as one. Furthermore, you potentially have a 20-gallon toilet capacity at any one time instead of just 5 gallons. You may find that extra capacity to come in very handy when inundated with visitors.

Why should all the receptacles be exactly the same? If you build a permanent toilet cabinet, the top of the receptacle should protrude through the cabinet to contact the bottom of a standard toilet seat. This ensures that all organic material goes into the receptacle, not over its edge. Although this is not usually a problem, it *can* be with young children who may urinate over the top of a receptacle when sitting on a toilet. A good design will enable the receptacle to fit tightly through the toilet cabinet. If using plastic buckets for toilet receptacles, remember that many are slightly different in height and diameter, so you should build your toilet cabinet to fit one size bucket.

You should have extra identical buckets when backup capacity is needed to accommodate large numbers of people.

The advantages of a humanure toilet system include low financial start-up cost in the creation of the facilities and low, or no energy consumption in its operation. Also, such a simple system, when the refuse is thermophilically composted, has a low environmental cost as little or no technology is required for the system's operation and the finished compost is as nice and benign a material as humanure can ever hope to be. No composting facilities are necessary in or near one's living space, although the toilet can and should be inside one's home and can be quite comfortably designed and totally odor-free. Also, all urine and fecal material is collected in the toilet, as is all toilet paper. There is no need to segregate urine or paper when using a humanure toilet.

No electricity is needed and no water is required except a small amount for cleaning purposes. One gallon of water can clean two 5-gallon receptacles. It takes one adult two weeks to fill two 5-gallon toilet receptacles with humanure and urine, including cover material. This requires 1 gallon of cleaning water for every two weeks of humanure toilet use as opposed to the standard 10 gallons per person per day used for even a low-flow toilet.

The compost, if properly managed, will heat sufficiently for sanitation to occur, thereby making it useful for agricultural purposes. The composting process is fast, i.e., the humanure is converted quickly—within a few days if not frozen—into an inoffensive substance that will not attract flies. In cold winter months the compost may simply freeze until the spring thaw, then heat up. If the compost is unman-

aged and does not become thermophilic, the compost can simply be left to age for a couple of years before horticultural use. In either case, a complete nutrient cycle is maintained, unbroken.

A humanure toilet requires three components: 1) the toilet receptacle; 2) cover materials; and 3) a compost bin system. The toilet will *not* work without all three of these components. The toilet itself is only the collection stage of the process. Since the composting takes place away from the toilet, the compost bin system is important. Humanure toilets are technically not composting toilets as no composting takes place in the toilet, nor *can* composting occur inside the toilet due to the small mass of the material in the receptacle. Humanure toilets are simply collection devices for bin composting. In a kitchen, one may have a compost receptacle for food scraps. When recycling humanure, one uses a compost receptacle in the toilet room. All of the collected organic materials are fed to microorganisms in a compost bin system.

1) *Use at least a double-chambered, above-ground compost bin.* A three-chambered bin is recommended. Deposit in one chamber for a period of time (e.g., a year, or until it fills), then switch to another for an equal period of time.

2) *Deposit a good mix of organic material into the compost pile,* including kitchen scraps. It's a good idea to put all of your organic material into the same compost bin. Pay no attention to those people who say that humanure compost should be segregated from other compost. They are people who do not compost humanure and don't know what they're talking about.

3) *Always cover humanure deposits in the toilet with an organic cover material* such as

sawdust, leaf mold, peat moss, rice hulls, ground newsprint, finely shredded paper, or what have you. *Always cover fresh deposits on the compost pile with coarse cover materials* such as hay, weeds, straw, grass clippings, leaves, or whatever is available. Make sure that enough cover material is applied so there is neither excess liquid buildup in the toilet nor offensive odors escaping either the toilet or the compost pile. The trick to using cover material is quite simple: if it smells bad or looks bad, cover it until it does neither.

4) *Keep good access to the pile* in order to rake the top somewhat flat, to apply bulky cover material when needed, to allow air access to the pile, and to monitor the temperature of the pile. The advantage of aerobic composting, as is typical of an aboveground pile, over relatively anaerobic composting typical of enclosed composting toilets is that the aerobic compost will generate higher temperatures, thereby ensuring a more rapid and complete destruction of potential human pathogens.

The disadvantages of a collection system requiring the regular transporting of humanure to a compost pile are obvious. They include the inconvenience of: 1) carrying the material to the compost pile; 2) keeping a supply of organic cover material available and handy to the toilet; and 3) maintaining and managing the compost pile itself. If one can handle these simple tasks, then one need never worry about having a functioning, environmentally friendly toilet.

It's very important to understand that *two* factors are involved in destroying potential pathogens in humanure. Along with heat, the *time* factor is important. Once the organic material in a compost pile has been heated by either mesophilic or ther-

mophilic microorganisms, it should be left to age or "season." This part of the process allows for the final decomposition to take place, decomposition that may be dominated by fungi and macroorganisms such as earthworms and sow bugs. Therefore, a good compost system will utilize at least two composting bins, one to fill and leave to age, and another to fill while the first is aging. A three-binned composting system is even better, as the third bin provides a place to store cover materials and separates the two active bins so there is no possible accidental transfer of fresh material to an aging bin.

When composting humanure, fill one bin first. Make sure the bottom of the bin has been slightly dished out like a bowl and the excess dirt placed around the inside edges of the bin. Should there ever be an excess of liquid in the compost bin, this simple technique will make sure it remains inside the bin. Start the compost pile by establishing a thick layer of coarse and absorbent organic material on the bottom of the bin. This is called a "biological sponge." Its purpose is to act as a leachate absorption barrier. The sponge may be an 18-inch *or more* layer of hay, straw, grass clippings, leaves, and/or weeds. Place the first container of the humanure/cover material mix from the toilet directly on the top center of the sponge. Cover immediately with more straw, hay, weeds, or leaves—the cover acts as a "biofilter" for odor prevention, and it causes air to become trapped in the developing compost pile, making physical turning of the pile for aeration unnecessary. A standard bin size for a family of four with an active garden is about 5 feet square and 4 feet high ($1.6 \text{ m}^2 \times 1.3$ m tall). Smaller bins may be necessary for smaller families or for individuals. If the bin is too small, however, the compost will not develop enough mass to heat up.

Continue in this manner until the bin is full, which is quite likely to take a year when used by four adults, being sure to add to this bin as much of the other organic material you produce as is practical. There is no need to have any other compost piles—one is enough for everything produced by the humans in your household. If you have small animals such as chickens or rabbits, their manure can go into the same compost pile.

You need do nothing special to prepare material for adding to the compost pile. You do not need to chop up vegetables, for example. Just chuck it all in there. Most of the things compost educators tell you cannot be composted *can* be composted in a humanure compost pile (such as meats, fats, oils, citrus fruits, animal mortalities, et cetera). Add it all to the same compost pile. Anything smelly that may attract flies should be dug into the top center of the pile. Keep a shovel or pitchfork handy for this purpose and use the tool only for the compost. Keep a clean cover material over the compost at all times and don't let your compost pile become shaped like a Matterhorn—keep it somewhat flattened so nothing rolls off.

When you have a sudden large quantity of cover material available, such as an influx of grass clippings when the lawn is mowed, weeds from the garden, or leaves in the fall, place them in the center bin for storage and use them to cover humanure deposits as you need them. It is assumed that you do not use any poisonous chemicals on your lawn. If you do, bag the lawn clippings, take them to a toxic waste dump, and on the way, reflect upon the folly of such behavior. Do not put poisoned grass clippings in your compost pile.

Filling the first bin should take a year—that's how long it takes us [Joe Jenkins and family], usually four, with a lot of visitors. We have used this system continuously for 28 years (as of 2007), and every year at the summer solstice we start a new compost pile. During March, April, and May, the pile always *looks* like it is already full and can't take any more material, but it always does. This is due to the constant shrinkage of the compost pile that takes place as summer approaches. When the pile is finally completed, it is covered with a thick layer of straw, leaves, grass clippings, or other clean material (without weed seeds) to insulate it and to act as a biofilter; then it is left to age.

At this time, the second bin is started following the same procedure as the first—starting with an empty bin and a biological sponge. When the second chamber is nearly full (a year later), the first one can begin to be used for agricultural purposes. If you're not comfortable using your compost for gardening purposes for whatever reason, use it for flowers, trees, or berries.

An active compost pile can accept a huge amount of refuse, and even though the pile may seem to be full, as soon as you turn your back it will shrink down and leave room for more material. One common concern among neophyte humanure composters is the pile looking like it's filling up too fast. More than likely, the compost pile will keep taking the material as you add it because the pile is continually shrinking, especially if it's heating up. If, for some reason, your compost pile does suddenly fill up and you have nowhere to deposit the compost material, then you will simply have to start a new compost bin. Four wooden pallets on edge will make a quick compost bin in an emergency. When using pallets, however, be careful to stuff clean cover material around the outer edges of the pile to prevent anything falling through the slats.

The system outlined above should not yield any compost until about two years after the process has started (one year to build the first pile and an additional year for it to age). However, after the initial two-year start-up period, an ample amount of compost will be available on an annual basis.

Happy crappin'!

Humanure Toilet and Hacienda

Project Time: Weekend.
Cost: Inexpensive; ($50–200).
Energy Saved: High.
Ease of Use: Moderate.
Maintenance Level: Moderate.
Skill Levels: Carpentry: Moderate.
Materials: Rot-resistant posts, plywood, 1x material, nails, screws, roofing material, toilet seat, rain barrel (optional).
Tools: Saw, drill, hammer, post-hole digger.
For instructions, see figures 9.2 and 9.3.

BIOGAS (ANAEROBIC DECOMPOSITION)

The other on-site method of turning human waste into a resource is through anaerobic decomposition.

Anaerobic means "without oxygen," and anaerobic decomposition is what happens when organic material is broken down underwater. When done properly, anaerobic decomposition of animal wastes mixed with plant matter will be dominated by methanogenic bacteria. The main by-products from this decomposition are methane gas, carbon dioxide, and an inert slurry of simple organic solids. As it happens, methane is flammable and is one of the finest cooking fuels known, and the inert organic solids make fabulous garden fertilizer once the digestion process is complete.

Like burning wood, the process of creating and burning biogas is a closed carbon cycle. Only as much carbon dioxide is released as was initially captured during the photosynthesis of the original plant matter before it was eventually consumed and turned into waste.

Certainly, if we are attempting to achieve independence from fossil fuels, using our waste to produce the fuel to cook our food as well as the fertilizer for growing it is very appealing. Meaningful quantities of biogas can be made from humanure alone, but not in sufficient quantities to provide the majority of most households' cooking needs. For this reason, homes with some livestock are excellent candidates for pursuing biogas production. The manure of a dozen chickens or a few head of goat or sheep mixed with your home's humanure could potentially be sufficient to supply all your home's cooking fuel. Gas is a very high-quality cooking fuel, far superior for on-demand cooking needs compared with a solar oven or wood-fired stove. It also burns very cleanly, producing only water vapor and carbon dioxide ($CH_4 + 2O_2 \rightarrow CO_2 + 2H_2O$). The biodigestion process kills pathogens in all types of manure but retains all of the other nutrients, such as nitrogen, that make for a great, organic fertilizer. It is an amazing symbiosis.

If your home does have some livestock, consider building the following bench-scale biodigester to learn the fundamentals of biogas production and to get an estimate of the potential quantity of gas that could be produced. For all biodigesters

- The slurry (mix of water and organic matter) must be kept warm, typically around 95 degrees F.
- The slurry needs to be 6–8 percent organic matter.
- The carbon: nitrogen ratio needs to be between 25 and 35:1.
- Any carbon-rich matter needs to be shredded or macerated so as not to clog pipes and pumps.
- The effluent needs to be passed through a secondary biologically active filter such as a mulch bed.

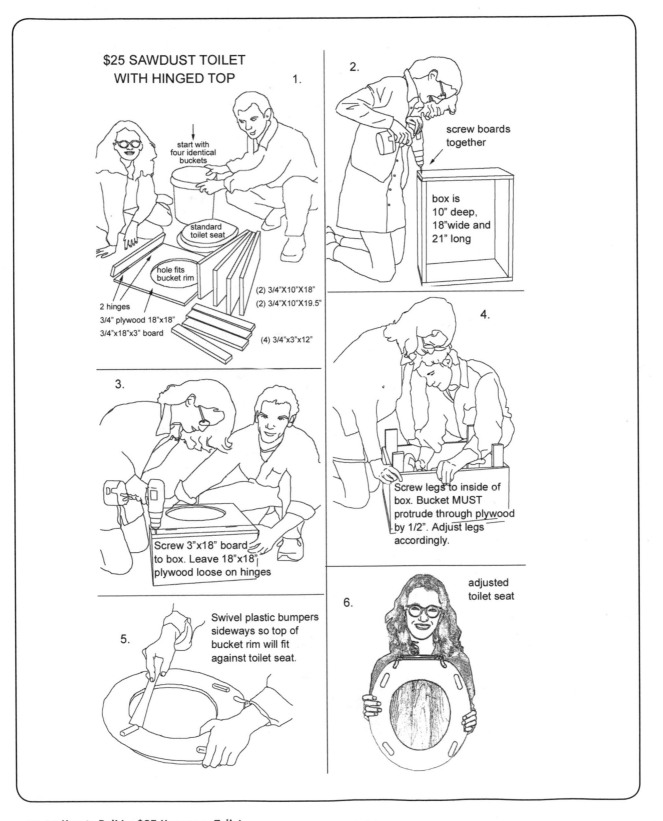

$25 SAWDUST TOILET WITH HINGED TOP

1.
start with four identical buckets

standard toilet seat

hole fits bucket rim

2 hinges
3/4" plywood 18"x18"
3/4"x18"x3" board

(2) 3/4"X10"X18"
(2) 3/4"X10"X19.5"

(4) 3/4"x3"x12"

2.
screw boards together

box is 10" deep, 18"wide and 21" long

3.
Screw 3"x18" board to box. Leave 18"x18" plywood loose on hinges

4.
Screw legs to inside of box. Bucket MUST protrude through plywood by 1/2". Adjust legs accordingly.

5.
Swivel plastic bumpers sideways so top of bucket rim will fit against toilet seat.

6.
adjusted toilet seat

FIG. 9.2. **How to Build a $25 Humanure Toilet.** From Joseph C. Jenkins, *The Humanure Handbook*

$25 SAWDUST TOILET WITH HINGED TOP (CONT.)

7.

8.

Drill holes.

Mark holes for toilet seat attachment.

A hinged sawdust toilet box will be 18" wide by 21" long. Get two boards 3/4"x10"x18" and two 3/4"x10"x19.5". Get two hinges, one piece of 3/4"x18"x18" plywood and one 3/4"x3"x18". Hinge the plywood to the 3"x18" piece.

Cut a hole in the larger piece of plywood to fit the top of the 5 gallon bucket. Set the hole only 1 & 1/2 inches back from the front edge of the plywood. Start with four identical buckets so you have extras. Buy a standard toilet seat somewhere.

When screwing the legs to the inside of the box, make sure the top edge of the box will sit about 1/2" below the top edge of the bucket (the top of the bucket rim should protrude through the box by 1/2"). This allows the bucket rim to sit tight against the underside of the toilet seat (which is why the toilet seat bumpers are pried loose and swiveled to one side, as shown in #5 and #6).

9. Attach your seat. Stain, varnish or paint the wood. You now have a compost toilet!

HOW TO CONSTRUCT
THE HUMANURE HACIENDA

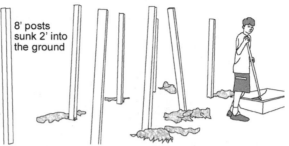

8' posts sunk 2' into the ground

1. Dig 24" deep holes, drop in (8) 4x4 locust (or other suitable) posts, back fill with soil mixed with concrete. Posts are about 5' (1.6 meters) apart. Leave four center posts high. Cut four outer posts to a height of about 4'.

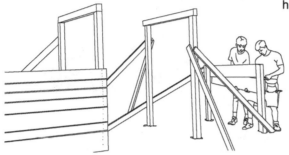

2. Plumb and brace posts. Nail 4x4 header across higher center posts.

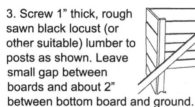

3. Screw 1" thick, rough sawn black locust (or other suitable) lumber to posts as shown. Leave small gap between boards and about 2" between bottom board and ground.

4. Cut rafters and install in a simple gable roof design. All the lumber for the roof can be recycled. The posts and side walls should be rot resistant lumber, but not lumber treated with toxic chemicals. It would be better to use scrap lumber for the sidewalls and replace it periodically than to use toxic lumber. The roofed center section will hold cover materials and will keep them dry, protected and unfrozen. The roof will also collect rain water, which should be used to clean compost buckets when not frozen.

FIG. 9.3. **How to Build a Humanure Hacienda.** From Joseph C. Jenkins, *The Humanure Handbook*

HUMANURE HACIENDA (cont.)

5. Nail sheathing boards to roof rafters. Make sure rafter tails have plumb cuts so a fascia board can be attached.

6. Install fascia boards, then the finished roofing. Recycled slate makes an excellent roofing material.

7. Install the rain spouting. Install a rain barrel adjacent to the Hacienda. A recycled oak wine barrel is an excellent rain water collecter. Remember that you will have to drain the barrel during freezing weather.

Joe Jenkins Humanure Hacienda, shown at right, is expected to last a lifetime. The rain water system makes cleaning compost buckets very convenient spring, summer and fall. The center roof also keeps bales of hay and straw dry and available for use throughout the winter.

Peak Phosphorus

Phosphorus is one of three macronutrients required by all plant life. Phosphorus is highly reactive and is typically found bound up in phosphates residing in inorganic rock. Since industrial agriculture is not a closed loop where nutrients can be recycled, it depends on continued inputs from outside sources. Phosphorus is one of the most important of these inputs, one for which there is no substitute. As such, limitations in its availability have the potential to severely limit worldwide food production. Worldwide phosphorus production appears to have peaked in 1989.

Unlike oil, phosphorus can be recycled. The easiest and least energy-intensive method of recycling phosphorus is by returning the composted waste of the animal that ate the crop along with any crop residue back to the soil where the plant came from. This cycle could potentially be continued indefinitely. Obviously, if that waste is instead flushed into the nearest stream and eventually dumped at the bottom of the ocean, that phosphorus is no longer available. Industrial agriculture has created the need for raw phosphorus, as well as the problem of its scarcity, neither of which previously existed. Fortunately, the solution is easy: return "waste" products to the nutrient cycle where they belong.

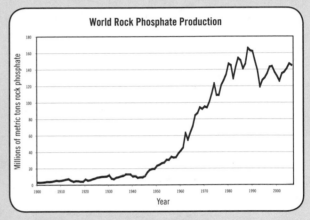

FIG. 9.4. Compiled from Patrick Déry's work. Read an excellent summary of his paper at www.energy bulletin.net/33164.html.

Bench-Scale Biogas Digester

Renter friendly.

Project Time: Afternoon.

Cost: Low; around $50.

Energy Saved: Low. Can potentially be scaled up to produce large quantities of biogas.

Ease of Use: Moderate. Requires attention while in operation.

Maintenance Level: N/A.

Skill Levels: Carpentry: Basic. Plumbing: Basic.

Materials: Styrofoam cooler, 1-gallon clear plastic bottle with gas-tight removable top, aquarium heater, quarter-inch clear vinyl flexible tubing, tube shutoffs, quarter-inch PVC sheet, 12-inch or so length of 4-inch PVC pipe, 8-inch or so length of 3-inch PVC, PVC glue, silicone, manure, biogas starter (see below), balloon, Bunsen burner or gas stove.

Tools: Hacksaw, drill, caulking gun, jigsaw, 12-inch straight ruler.

Caution: Biogas is potentially explosive as well as flammable. Please be extremely careful and read up as much as possible on this subject before proceeding. Generally, the pressures and volumes in a home-scale biodigester are low and the explosive potential is small, especially with the Bench-Scale Biodigester, but care should still be taken. Working outside during the summer months is recommended for this project.

Sanitation is also very important when dealing with any manures, but especially humanure. Maintaining a clean worksite and washing your hands frequently are general requirements to prevent the potential spread of disease.

Feedstock. Biogas production can vary greatly depending on the feedstock. If you have access to lots of potential feedstock material and are considering

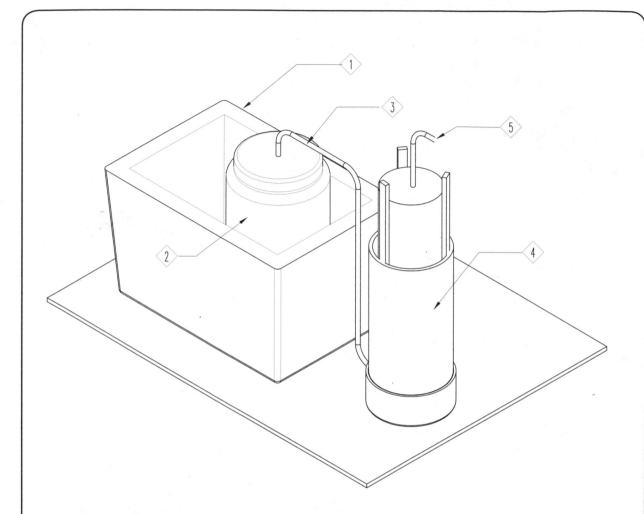

1   STYROFOAM COOLER: FILL WITH WATER TO JUST BELOW THE LIQUID LEVEL IN THE
    DIGESTER (TO KEEP JAR FROM FLOATING). MOUNT AN AQUARIUM HEATER IN THE
    WATER BATH TO KEEP IT AT SET TEMPERATURE (95 DegF FOR MESOPHILIC). AN
    ALTERNATIVE SOLUTION WOULD BE TO USE AN ELECTRIC CROCK POT FOR A WATER
    BATH.

2   DIGESTER: CLEAR PLASTIC JAR WITH GAS-TIGHT GASKETED LID. DRILL HOLE IN LID
    TO ACCEPT 1/4" PLASTIC GAS TUBE FITTING.

3   GAS TUBE: 1/4" VINYL HOSE. CONNECT FROM DIGESTER TO GAS COLLECTOR.
    ADDING A SHUTOFF VALVE(OR PAIR OF SHUTOFF VALVES AND A COUPLING) ON
    TUBING WILL FACILITATE MAINTENANCE.

4   GAS COLLECTOR: SEE CONSTRUCTION DETAIL.

5   GAS OUTLET. CONNECT TO BALLOON. ADDING A SHUTOFF VALVE(OR PAIR OF
    SHUTOFF VALVES AND A COUPLING) ON TUBING WILL FACILITATE MAINTENANCE.

FIG. 9.5. **Bench-scale digester.** Courtesy Robert Crosby/Biorealis, Inc.

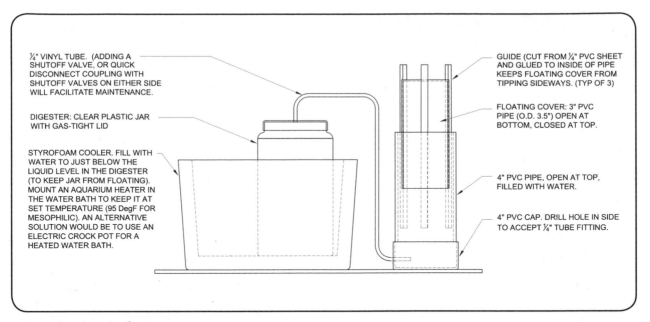

FIG. 9.6. **Bench-scale digester.** Courtesy Robert Crosby/Biorealis, Inc.

whether it's worthwhile to build a full-scale digester, then building a bench-scale digester to quantify biogas production will be worthwhile. Figures 9.5 and 9.6 are diagrams for building a test digester created by Bob Crosby of Biorealis Systems. You can get a rough idea of biogas production by using Bob's interactive Biogas Calculator at his Web site (http://biorealis. com/wwwroot/digester_revised.html).

The setup. Figures 9.5 and 9.6 show the basic setup for the pilot digester. The digestion takes place in a clear plastic bottle set in a water bath in a Styrofoam cooler. An aquarium heater keeps the water at 95 degrees F. Once gas production begins, the gas is piped over to the gas collector, an inverted 3-inch PVC pipe (OD = 3½ inches) in a 4-inch PVC pipe. Water creates a seal, and quarter-inch strips of sheet PVC are used to guide the inverted 3-inch PVC as it rises from gas collection. This gas can then be released by directing it to a larger storage mechanism (such as a balloon, inner tube, or larger inverted drum setup) or burned directly. The purpose of the initial gas collector is to measure the volume of the gas.

Assembling the digester. Drill a pilot hole for the vinyl tubing in the plastic bottle you'll be using for the digester. Insert the tube an inch or so and silicone around it.

Cut three half-inch strips of the quarter-inch PVC sheet and glue these with PVC glue, evenly spaced, to the interior of the 4-inch PVC pipe so that they stick out several inches above the top (so the strips will be about 16 inches long).

Trace an outline of the outer dimension of the 4-inch PVC onto the PVC sheet and cut out with the jigsaw (use a fine-toothed metal blade). Glue this cap onto the 4-inch PVC pipe using the PVC glue.

Once the glue is dry, drill a pilot hole for the vinyl tubing into the cap of the 4-inch PVC pipe. Use hose clamps to insert a shutoff in the tubing. Insert the free end of the vinyl tubing into the cap at least an inch or so and silicone.

Trace an outline of the outer dimension of the 3-inch PVC onto the PVC sheet and cut this out with the jigsaw. Glue this cap onto the 3-inch PVC pipe.

Once the glue is dry, drill a pilot hole for the vinyl tubing into the 3-inch PVC top. Use hose clamps to insert a shutoff into this tubing, then insert a new length of vinyl tubing and silicone.

All you need now is a starter and some feedstock. Remember that you're shooting for a combination of feedstock with a C:N ratio near 30:1.

Obtaining starter material. To make sure you have

TABLE 9.2 Nitrogen Content and C:N ratio of Various Organic Matter

Material	C:N Ratio
Human feces	10
Human urine	1:1
Chicken manure	12
Sheep manure	15
Goat manure	17
Pig manure	14
Horse manure	28
Cow manure	21
Animal blood	3.5
Grass clippings	20
Kitchen waste	20
Clover	25
Leaves	60
Sawdust	200
Cardboard, shredded	350
Newspaper, shredded	200

Both aerobic and anaerobic decomposition performs best with a carbon:nitrogen (C:N) ratio of the stock material in the range of 25–35:1. Fortunately the range is fairly broad, so exactness is not required. By knowing the general C:N ratio and applying materials in the approximately correct proportions based on the weight of the material, you can keep the decomposition process humming along.

plenty of methanogenic bacteria, you'll need some starter material. This can be obtained from a fresh cowpat or other animal manure. Take some manure from the middle of the pie and place it in a jar of warm water, filling as close to the top as possible to eliminate as much air as possible. The more starter you add, the quicker you'll start getting methane. A 50:50 feedstock-to-starter ratio will potentially produce gas in just a few days. Lesser amounts of starter might take upwards of a month to begin production, if at all. With less starter, care must be taken to buffer the sample with some baking soda to make it more basic so that the acidogenic bacteria do not overpopulate and kill off the methanogenic bacteria. Runaway acidogenic bacteria production will result in only CO_2 production and no methane. With less starter, mostly CO_2 production at the beginning of gas production is inevitable.

Measuring output. One way to measure gas output is to measure how high the 3-inch PVC pipe rises above the water level using a 12-inch ruler. Release the secondary storage (or flare it off), and then repeat. You'll probably have to do this more than once per day after the gas really gets going, but this depends on the lengths of your PVC pipes. At peak production, your digester can produce up to three times its volume in a single day. Multiply the height difference in inches and multiply times the cross-sectional area of the 3-inch PVC (pi × r² = 7.065 inches) to get volume. This method is labor-intensive, and Bob has been developing other automated systems that would be much simpler. For a fuller discussion of this bench-scale digester, you should definitely visit the Biorealis Web site and see what Bob has cooking these days.

To make sure you're getting flammable biogas, you should definitely try burning your gas (this is why you're going to all this trouble, right?). Use your biogas to heat up some water and make a glass of tea or coffee, and contemplate the wonder of it all. If you want to get an accurate measurement of the energy content of the biogas content you are producing (which would allow you to retroactively assess the proportions of biogas to CO_2), you can use the biogas to heat up 1 pound of water. Each degree Farenheit the water goes up roughly corresponds to 1 Btu. Some knowledge of the efficiency of your stove is required for this method. A typical gas burner might only be 50 percent efficient

Determining methane content can be tricky, involving passing the gas through a liquid that takes the CO_2 out of the mix, called a CO_2 scrubber. If your gas burns, it's at least 60 percent methane, although it could be higher, so you can make a conservative estimate based on this (1 ft³ methane = 1,000 Btus, so 1 cubic foot biogas = 600 Btus typically).

Diagnosing problems. If your biodigester isn't producing methane, it is most likely that the methanogenic bacteria never became established and instead acid-loving bacteria have proliferated. To check, you can remove the top of your digester and stick a piece of litmus paper or a pH meter in. You can also prevent or mitigate against this happening by adding a buffer to the initial mix. (Warning: don't try this with anything larger than this small bench-scale test digester. Opening a digester can be dangerous.) If you get a pH reading below 6, chances are your biogas experiment was a flop. Try again with more starter or with starter from a different source.

RESOURCES

Books

UN Food and Agriculture Organization. 2007. *Biogas, volumes 1 and 2*. Warren, MI: Knowledge Publications. Reprints of thorough FAO instructions on building a biodigester from the 1970s.

Jenkins, Joseph C. 2005. *Humanure Handbook, 3rd Edition*. Grove City, PA: Jenkins Publishing. Lift up the toilet seat and take a detailed look at a truly fascinating subject.

Ludwig, Art. 2007. *The New Create an Oasis with Graywater*. Santa Barbara, CA: Oasis Design. If you're considering recycling all of your water, this book is a must-read before you get started.

Woelfle-Erskine, Cleo, July Oskar Cole, and Laura Allen, eds. 2007. *Dam Nation: Dispatches from the Water Underground*. New York: Soft Skull.

Internet

The Internet is loaded with free graywater plumbing diagrams and information on how to get started. Of particular note are Arizona's and California's graywater guides. www.watercasa.org /publications/Graywater_Guidelines.pdf and www.owue.water.ca.gov/docs/graywater _guide_book.pdf

Appropedia. A collection of appropriate-technology information set up as a wiki that anyone can add to. Look for information on a variety of subjects and help this great site develop. www.appropedia .org/Graywater

Biorealis. Bob Crosby's Web site. Tons of information on Bob's biodigester setup, biodigester Web forum, experiments, et cetera. The place to start if you're thinking about building one. www.biorealis.com

Humanure Handbook. Joseph Jenkin's Web site. Tons of great crap here, including an online humanure forum with such interesting topics as large-scale event composting and neighborhood composting. www.josephjenkins.com/books _humanure.html

Oasis Design. Loads of information. www.graywater.net

Endnote

1. Cloern, J., E. Duffy, and T. Krantz. 2007. "Eutrophication." *Encyclopedia of Earth,* ed. Cutler J. Cleveland (Washington, D.C.: Environmental Information Coalition, National Council for Science and the Environment).

CHAPTER 10

Food and Landscaping

*Introduction • Our Story • What and How to Grow • Edible Perennials •
Fruit Bushes and Trees • Perennial Vegetables • Mushrooms • Green Roofs, Living
Walls, and Thoughtful Landscaping • The Potato and the Chicken • Resources*

INTRODUCTION

You might think it was the business of agriculture to capture the energy of the sun for our nourishment. If you are thinking about the "food" that comes to reside on most Americans' tables at mealtime, you would be very wrong. Sunshine has little to do with it.

Instead, what you would find would mostly be a product of fossil fuels. There's the oil and natural gas for the manufacture of fertilizer (31 percent), for the operation of the machinery (19 percent), for the product's transportation (16 percent), irrigation (13 percent), pesticides (5 percent), and other miscellaneous squanderings (16 percent).[1] And this doesn't even count the fossil fuels burned for the packaging, refrigeration, and transportation of that sunlight-deficient product from the retail outlet to the home. In sum, on average an American consumes 12 barrels of oil equivalents (504 gallons) for energy used in the home, 10 barrels (420 gallons) for food production and distribution, and another 9 barrels (378 gallons) for transportation.[2]

The 420 gallons of oil equivalents used to produce the average 2,175 pounds of food a year the average American eats (compared to the world average of 1,630 pounds) boils down to spending 10 fossil-fuel calories for each one food calorie. It doesn't sound like a good idea, nor does it sound efficient, but that's what most of us depend on to stay alive every day—fossil calories.

How did things get to such a sorry state? As with many things, our move toward convenience has come at the cost of our independence. Where at one time many families grew some of their own food and knew the grower of any other food they consumed, now the grower of our food is on average 1,500 miles away, and oftentimes much farther. We had the misfortune of buying some garlic grown in China recently. Growing this staple 8,000 miles away seems like a bad idea to us, but most Americans don't realize nor do they care where the garlic they buy comes from. In 2005, garlic imports rose to 100 million pounds, while being almost nonexistent five years earlier.[3] If this is what the wisdom of the marketplace dictates, then we suggest that the market is not very bright.

The very large distances we are making our food travel has another downside. This is the removal of nutrients from where they are needed: where the food is being grown. Exporting produce thousands of miles away ensures that the nutrients locked in that food cannot ever be returned to the soil from which they came to cycle through again. This deficiency ensures the missing nutrients must be replaced by fossil fuels or other fossil accumulations that are being rapidly depleted, such as phosphorus.

When we consider these facts in the context of peak fossil energy and global climate disruption, then it's not surprising if our first reaction is some good old-fashioned fear and loathing. Not only is our food system consuming unsustainable amounts of energy (a 10-to-1 ratio of calories in to calories out), it's also overconsuming our water and topsoil resources at a prodigious rate. Can there be any hope of rectifying a situation that has gone so awry?

FIG. 10.1. **The easiest way to reduce the amount of energy it takes to keep your belly full is to buy local, organic, unprocessed foods from your neighborhood farmers' market.**

The first thing to note is that, generally speaking, we in the United States could use a little *less* food, anyway, especially with obesity rates at all-time highs. So the fact that food prices might rise at first as we have less fossil energy available is, for most of us, not such a dire situation. Moving our diet from lots of higher-energy-input foods like meat and cheese to more vegetables, beans, and grains will not only be cheaper and use much less energy for the same amount of food calories, but the net result will be a healthier population. Heavily processed junk and fast food should also increase in price relative to healthier unprocessed items, since the processing requires large energy inputs. Unfortunately, the price of this type of food has never reflected its true cost in terms of pollution, animal welfare, fossil energy depletion, and adverse health effects, the latter afflict-

ing poorer folks disproportionately due to its subsidized cheapness and availability.

Fortunately, the same path that brought us down into this fossilized abyss is the same one we can take back out. By gradually relocalizing our food production we can return to an agricultural system that is much less energy intensive. If there's one good thing about a system being so grossly inefficient and out of whack (producing so little food calories for the energy calories that went in), it's that dramatic improvements can be made very quickly once we realize the need to turn around. The myriad problems that seem overwhelming all stem from a common disease: the fact that we've let our food production and distribution get out of our hands and into the paws of profit-grubbing corporations. If instead of buying nonorganic (and, hence, heavily pesticide-

and fertilizer-dependent) canned goods at some big-box grocer that we have to drive to, we grow some veggies in our own yard and get the balance from a local farmer, we've eliminated the vast majority of tomato-miles it takes to keep our tummies full. Spending a fall afternoon planting a few blueberry bushes will result in tens of pounds of blueberries in just a few years. Thinking about how many clear plastic half-pint blueberry containers this will save from being brought into existence almost blows the mind (not even to mention how many dollars will remain in your wallet!).

Aiming for total food self-sufficiency will quickly lead to burnout, as the labor demands of such an endeavor quickly become overwhelming. Instead of trying to leap to the finish line, consider your goal of fossil-fuel-free food to be a meander through a beautiful park. Each year, plant a few more edible perennials, grow some hardy low-maintenance veggies (see what's doing well in your neighbors' gardens), and maybe experiment with mushroom cultivation. Make sure to patronize local farmers' markets, food stands, and community-supported agriculture (CSAs).

Food is the foundation of community. A healthy garden naturally produces more than one person can consume. The surplus must be shared, stored, or wasted. Sharing the bounty of the garden will quickly lead to meals together with friends and neighbors, which in turn will lead to other socioeconomic connections: trading skills and lending tools, carpooling, taking care of a vacationing neighbor's cat or dog. Food weaves the community together like the vast interacting community of earthworms, mycelia, plant roots, and other microfauna and flora that exists in the soil just beneath our feet.

OUR STORY

Our home sits on one-fifth of an acre, or around 9,000 square feet. The house, which is a duplex, and a detached carriage house take up about 2,500 square feet, leaving us with 6,500 square feet of gardening space (not including 200 square feet on the green roof). While at first glance it looks like a small city lot, it really is an amazing amount of space to plant intensively, and we've just begun to make a dent in it.

Our preference now is to grow mostly lower-input perennials. After spending many an evening earlier in our lives in a vain attempt to grow a majority of our own food while simultaneously trying to build/retrofit our own house and hold down jobs, the vegetable garden came to seem more like prison labor than a pleasant diversion.

We've dropped the self-sufficient, lone-wolf posturing and taken a more community-minded approach to getting our food. Now our idea of a vegetable garden is to live three blocks away from the farmers' market. Keith and Kyra, our housemates, run an edible landscaping business and maintain a fabulous vegetable garden outside. We help out when we can and take some of the extra veggies. The bulk of our food comes from our farmer friend Obie, who has a gorgeous farm north of here, and with whom we trade our carpentry and electrical skills for a share from his CSA.

After we harvested the large oak in the front yard, we opened up a huge amount of orchard space to full sun. At first this was used primarily for launching various construction projects: the green roof, the tin roof, the passive solar porch, et cetera. But as these wind down, we're left with more and more available planting space. We have a large patch of land, about 1,200 square feet, in between the street and the sidewalk. It's technically the city's, but we're responsible for maintenance. It's open on all four sides with a sidewalk, two roads (we're on a corner lot), and our neighbor's driveway. That means we have more space here than the 1,200 square feet might imply. We've planted two Asian pears (Sueri and Chajuro), two Cornelian cherries, two native plums, two Jostaberry, and an Elberta peach.

Planting along heavily traveled roads may not be possible in northern areas where the practice of salting roads during wintry weather is common, leading to the proverbial infertile salted fields, but so far our plants have thrived despite the few saltings we get each year. We often get asked whether we're concerned about heavy metals and pollutants from the exhaust of automobiles passing by. Of course we are, and we wish everyone would stop driving and emitting all that pollution! Soil tests will let you know if any potential orchard area is unsuitable, but unfortunately after several centuries of the Industrial Revolution, we just have to accept the fact that almost everywhere in the world is contaminated to a certain extent. The good news is that soils rich in organic matter are excellent bioremediators, capable of breaking down many persistent pollutants and locking heavy metals in the ground and keeping them out of plants through a process called *chelation.*

On the other side of the sidewalk we planted strawberries, raspberries, and thornless blackberries. This is sort of a treat for our neighbors as they walk by, although hopefully they'll wonder as they pop an unbelievably fresh strawberry, perhaps the freshest, best-tasting strawberry they've ever had, why they don't having anything like that growing at their house.

Another 1,200 square feet of yard, which lies between the two doors of the duplex, is mostly the vegetable garden. Up against the house, however, we've planted a pair of figs, five heat-tolerant rabbit-eye blueberries, and five varieties of muscadines that will do double duty as a southern and western shade trellis. Similarly, on the eastern side we've planted a male and female hardy kiwi for a shade trellis.

Much of the back is still wildlands (unmowed grass), although a large dogwood, excellent for climbing and a good dynamic accumulator (meaning it's good at burrowing deep down in the earth and pulling nutrients up), takes up a large chunk of space and provides some much-needed shade. There's also a black locust at the top of the yard, a good nitrogen fixer that can also potentially be coppiced repeatedly for some firewood production. The flowers are edible (although very difficult to harvest), and folks around here sometimes make a kind of beer out of the pods, although we've never been lucky enough to try any.

So far in the back, we've fit in two hazelnuts, two Nanking cherries, four Juneberries (two Regents and two Princess Dianas), and a deerberry. From the oak we took down, we're experimenting with various types of mushroom cultivation: Shiitakes, shaggy mane, lions mane, garden giant, elm oyster, reishi, pearl oyster, and hen of the woods were all introduced.

We have about another 3,000 square feet of gardening space that is slowly opening up as the backyard is terraced. This is necessary because the ground slopes toward the north side of the house here, causing moisture problems. One section of this terrace, which runs about 30 feet along the back of the house, could potentially be used as an extended cold frame for growing veggies in wintertime. There are plans for a chicken coop/greenhouse attached to the garage, which is now more a tool and firewood shed.

We still have room for more fruit trees in this space, in addition to plans for a patio area, a small pond, and a large rainwater barrel to catch water off the garage (around 800-gallon capacity). We're going to plant a pair of pawpaws, a pair of Asian persimmons, a jujube, and a medlar. Toward the back edge we'll build our Humanure Hacienda (see chapter 9).

Our first winter in the house, 2006–2007, was one of the craziest winters we can remember here. Early in the fall it got unusually cold, then in January unbelievably warm. Then really cold in February, warm again in March, and in April we had a severe cold snap down into the lower '20s, very unusual for our area. The blueberries, one hazelnut, and the Cornelian cherries all flowered during the January warm spell. Everything else came out during the March warm spell, meaning everything was out when we had our April cold snap. Everything did amazingly well, except we had a Vern's Brown Turkey fig that got zapped, although it survived. Its neighbor, a Celeste fig, was unaffected. After the Easter freeze, we had a wrenching drought, with no rain to speak of for three months straight. It speaks volumes about the adaptability of the low-maintenance perennials we planted that, out of 30 or so that we planted, only two perished.

How much food can we produce from all this? Well, at first it won't be much, as it takes a few years for many of the perennials to start producing. We're all right with a little long-term investment, however, since we figure it was a colossal lack of foresight that got us into a lot of this mess. Hopefully, in the long run we'll be taking in *tons*, not pounds, of fresh fruits, veggies, and eggs. The Dervaes' fifth of an acre in Pasadena, California, produces 6,000 pounds of food annually (read all about it at www.pathtofreedom.com). Although we don't intend to work on our garden full-time, the potential of thousands of pounds of food annually from an urban lot exists if the right plants are invited in to share our home. And those are thousands of pounds of food that will never know what a fossil fuel is (or was).

FIG. 10.2. **A full-grown fruit tree will produce more fruit than the average family can consume. Share the bounty with your neighbors, but don't be surprised when they come knocking with presents of their own.**

WHAT AND HOW TO GROW

Many gardeners behave like they own a mini-industrial agricultural farm. Even those who don't use industrial pesticides and fertilizers often use tillers to turn the soil, perpetuating a holocaust on the soil communities living there. In the process, millions of weed seeds are brought to the surface, guaranteeing many hours in the hot summer sun yanking up weeds (unless the gardener gives in and just nukes them with Roundup). Why grow plants in monocultures just like on an industrial farm, even though the home gardener does not have the benefit of a harvesting machine? A monoculture ensures that if an unfriendly bug or virus does find that cabbage or eggplant, they'll multiply like crazy.

In nature, a monoculture often results from a compromised environment. Usually one species of plant succeeds at the expense of all the thousands of others only if something is terribly out of whack. Of course, it's industrial agriculture's goal to maintain an environment totally out of whack. Polluted streams, loss of topsoil, and unintended wildlife and fish deaths have no economic cost to industrial farmers, so they see no reason to be concerned with them. The price of industrial food does not reflect the real cost to society. They go on growing square mile after square mile of the same thing without a thought. Mimicking this sick mentality in our yards and neighborhoods is suicidal. If you want to live a long and healthy life, surround yourself with life, and this means as many different kinds of life as possible.

Once your bed of perennials is established, maintaining it will be no more of a chore than mowing your lawn used to be. Instead of spending your money and time with noisy and polluting mowers and leaf blowers, you'll be saving money, grazing on tasty fruits in the sunshine with butterflies and hummingbirds floating by. We shouldn't be surprised to find that mimicking nature will naturally be easier than fighting it. Nature generally creates diverse plant communities, and mimicking this strategy can mean low maintenance and high yields even in relatively small yards.

Sheetmulching and Polycultures
Project Time: Afternoon.
Cost: Inexpensive ($5-20).
Energy Saved: Low.
Ease of Use: N/A.
Maintenance Level: None.
Skill Levels: None
Materials: Large sheets of cardboard free from tape (appliance boxes work best) or sections of newspaper, mulch, other organic debris or waste.
Tools: Wheelbarrow, pitchfork or shovel.
Home gardeners often till with the idea that their

hard work will produce a blank slate that will allow them to grow whatever they want. When the weed seeds, some of which have been dormant for 50 or more years, burst forth, the gardener goes into a tizzy. Tilling should be used not yearly for weed control but only for initial soil preparation in a spot that has never seen a garden, and only then if truly necessary for soil amending. Raised beds and sheetmulching are both good options to avoid tilling.

Replacing tilling with sheetmulching goes much farther in creating the desired blank canvas. Keep in mind that gardening can be as complicated or as simple as you desire. While the following methods may not produce the largest bounties, at least initially, they are the simplest way we know of to turn a lawn into a garden. If you're inclined to take a more proactive approach to your vegetable bed, check out some of the books in the resources section at the end of the chapter.

Sheetmulching involves placing overlapping layers of cardboard over the cutback area where you want your bed. It's easiest to use large sheets of cardboard, because you want the edges to overlap at least 6 inches, with a foot being ideal. Stores that sell appliances accumulate large sheets, and we've also had good luck asking at recycling centers. Newsprint can be used, since almost all papers use soy-based ink for both black and white and color, but the sheets are comparatively small and harder to overlap effectively. If using newsprint, soak the paper first in a bucket of water to keep it from blowing away. Use whole sections together instead of individual pieces. Soaking the cardboard can also help, especially with stiff pieces, because the surface can be slippery once mulch is added.

Next comes the mulch. Be creative about where you get your mulch. Neighbors' lawn clippings or leaf bags (inquire first about herbicides); wood debris and chips from the city, tree timber, electric utility, or landscapers; coffee shops and restaurants; dairies and horse farms are some of the places that produce prodigious quantities of organic "waste." Some are even willing to deliver for free or for a nominal fee.

Layer these materials together, alternating between fresher green layers with deader brown layers when possible. Don't sweat this too hard, though. Pile it all together in the desired shape. Remember, you won't be using a mechanical harvester, so there's no need to plant in rows. Instead, consider shapes that give you much more planting area in a much smaller space. Spirals, branching Y patterns, and keyhole shapes offer many more planting options than a couple of rectangular rows. Be mindful of where people walk, however, and make sure you keep these paths open so folks don't walk through your garden beds.

If the area you are sheetmulching is infested with some of the more pernicious plants known to humanity, than you may want to consider double sheetmulching. Invasive vines such as honeysuckles, kudzu, wisteria, and English ivy are capable of wending themselves through the layers of sheetmulch and reappearing at the surface. Some types of grasses, such as wire and Bermuda grass, are also capable of such feats. The tiresome weeds are then that much more vigorous thanks to all the extra nutrient-rich mulch. If you're concerned about the aggressive nature of the plants you're trying to extirpate, then an additional layer of sheet mulch, sandwiched in between several of the layers of mulch, should help exhaust any plants before they reach the surface. Be sure that the cardboard or newsprint overlaps at least a foot, and you should also sheetmulch pathways through the garden. You may also want to consider biodegradable landscaping cloth to hold down these pernicious weeds, which is available from some gardening stores or over the Internet. This stuff gradually breaks down over 4–6 years. By this time your unwanted visitors should have perished due to lack of sunlight.

The layers of mostly undecomposed materials will not provide much plant nutrition during the first growing season. This isn't a big deal, because most perennials use their first year becoming established, sending out roots and generally recovering from the big move. A common garden saying is that, after planting, perennials "sleep, creep, then leap," meaning they don't do much their first year, show a few signs of life their second, but then burst into productivity in their third year. To get you started, we've included a sampler of these more carefree food crops later in this chapter to get you started.

When forming your bed you may want to consider adding an edible mushroom into the mix, especially if the spot you're planting will get plenty of water. This way you can get double duty out of your bed, picking great-tasting mushrooms while the mycelia provides additional soil structure and nutrient release.

If you started your beds in the spring, then by fall much of the nitrogen will be freed up after a summer of decomposition. Now you can plant whatever edible perennials strike your fancy—fruits, nuts, or veggies— and you can plant heavier feeders like broccoli or collards that love the cold if you so desire, or keep it low maintenance and stick to perennials.

Nature abhors a vacuum, as the saying goes, and your blank slate will not stay blank for long. Don't sheetmulch until you're nearly ready to plant, and cover-crop any areas that remain bare. Cover cropping simply means planting a short-lived annual that helps improve the soil until you figure out what you want to plant there, or to give the soil a respite from heavy feeders. After the cover crop flowers but before it goes to seed, cut it down and then plant whatever you fancy. This will help keep any aggressive weeds from occupying your blank canvas. A good fall-spring cover crop is red clover, and good spring-fall cover crops for us down south are clay and iron peas. Up north, oats and buckwheat work better for this time of year. Check the resources section for more information.

FIG. 10.3. **Recently a lawn, now an established polyculture bed including edible thornless blackberry, herbs like mint, hyssop, and calendula, lantana, and edible daylily flowers.** Courtesy Bountiful Backyards Collective

When ready to plant, add another layer of mulch in the spring to keep down any weeds and provide more sustenance for your plants and mushrooms. Some folks use a perennial living mulch like low-growing white clover, a variety of sedums, or herbs like chamomile after their plants are established to inhibit weed growth and/or fix additional nitrogen. Keep planting until your bed is full up with herbs, flowers, and veggies, all perennials if you want to minimize maintenance, making sure to eat and share your garden's bounty. If grass or other undesirables still lurk in your yard, it's time to start another bed.

EDIBLE PERENNIALS

For about the same amount of time, perennials can be planted instead of annuals. For all the hard work that garden preparation can entail, even with time-savers like sheetmulching, we much prefer putting plants in the ground that, instead of dying after one season, will come back year after year, producing more each time. Granted, most perennials are not the staples that we traditionally think of as the main ingredient for dinner each evening. Instead, perennials are often all the other good stuff like fruits and berries, exotic vegetables, and rare mushrooms that create the rest of the meal and make it worth eating. While it's unlikely that you could survive on the production of the edible forest garden waiting to be planted just outside your door, you can produce a significant quantity, tons even, of great-tasting, fresh-as-can-be organic food, even on smaller city lots. While preparing beds and planting fruit trees is definitely hard work, the work is generally less every year as plants become established and the amount of food production increases. Growing these perennials requires developing a longer-term mind-set, being willing to accept payoffs in the future for work done now. But the sooner you get started, the sooner you'll be hauling your bounty of fresh organic fruits and veggies into your kitchen.

FRUIT BUSHES AND TREES

Many berry- and fruit-producing trees can easily fit into even the smallest of yards, and some do quite well even as container plants (for low-maintenance container gardening, consider self-watering containers that hold a reservoir of water at the bottom of the pot). Once established they are low maintenance, usually requiring only some watering during dry spells and annual pruning. Even a half dozen can provide hundreds of pounds of food a year. Unfortunately, a great many varieties of fruit bushes and trees are unknown to most grocery-store shoppers, usually because the fruits or berries are not conducive to being shipped by truck and hence don't make an appearance at the big-box grocery. This is because they are so tender and succulent they would get squished if stacked in a box. Beyond the usual suspects of apples, pears, and bananas lie dozens of varieties of fruits and berries that are more delectable than anything your neighborhood grocery store has to offer, all there for the picking. Furthermore, home berry and fruit production offers a fabulous return on investment. Twenty to 40 dollars spent on a decent-sized specimen will produce many times more than that in the highest-quality organic food after only 3–5 years, year after year, which can translate into a return of hundreds of dollars annually on your initial investment.

The wide variety of berries and fruits means there's something for all climate zones. While those living in drier areas will need to provide some extra irrigation, either through rain barrels or graywater use, cold is generally not a limiting factor. Look for a nearby grower of fruit trees and berry bushes who specializes in your climate zone. Also possible is ordering young plants over the Internet, but be sure the plants have been tested in your zone. Regardless of your source, be sure to inform yourself of all the available cultivars for each particular species before obtaining your plants. Each region of the country is unique and different cultivars of the same species fare differently in different microclimates. Cultivars of each species can produce at different times, keep better in storage, and/or have showier flowers or foliage. Plants sourced locally usually have a better chance of success. Many species require cross-pollination, so two individuals of the same species (but not necessarily the same cultivar) must be planted to ensure proper pollination, but check that different cultivars flower at about the same time so the bees can do their work. When possible, stagger the ripening time to create a longer season for each fruit or berry type.

Planting Edible Perennials

Project Time: An hour.

Cost: $5–50, depending on size and variety of plant.

Energy Saved: Low to medium. Over the course of their lives large fruit trees will potentially produce tons of organic food that needs no nonorganic fertilizers or transportation.

Ease of Use: Easy.

Maintenance Level: Medium. Some weeding will almost certainly be required. Watering is also likely necessary during dry spells, hopefully from graywater or rainwater. Also needs annual pruning.

Skill Levels: None required.

Materials: Fruit tree or bush or perennial vegetable of your choice. Organic amendments of essential nutrients (N, P, and K) for depleted soil are helpful to ensure the plant thrives.

Tools: Shovel and pitchfork.

Evaluate the site. Evaluate the solar potential of your planting site. Using a Solar Pathfinder can be very helpful in this regard to ensure that solar access is not blocked during late summer, which could inhibit fruit production. Generally, plants that require full sun need five hours of sun over the course of the day for the entire growing season to grow well and set meaningful quantities of fruit. Planting in the fall is optimal, as this gives extra time for the roots to settle in. Winter plantings when the ground is not frozen are also good, but there's more potential for the plants to become confused by the change and bud out too early. Spring plantings before leaf bud are possible, but extra

watering is a wise precaution. Summer plantings are possible with heavy watering but should be avoided.

Preparations for transplanting. Remove your transplant from its container and soak the root-ball in a bucket of water. Outline an area roughly three times the size of the root-ball where you want your transplant to go. Loosen the soil with the pitchfork in this area. Dig up the soil, removing any grass or other plants that may be growing on top. Loosen the soil in all areas of the hole, especially the sides, with the pitchfork. This will help decompact the soil but not ruin its integrity like a tiller would and allow for lateral root growth. Add any amendments (such as compost) in with the soil you just removed, but be sparing. Adding too many amendments will confuse your plant into thinking it is growing in lush soil, causing it to grow too quickly at first and also discouraging it from spreading its roots into the surrounding subsoil due to the lack of nutrients. Essentially, the plant will respond to excess fertilization by thinking it's still in a pot, which will lead to a small root area and extra stress on the plant during dry spells. Mixing only a modest amount of amendments in with the native soil will condition the plant to the new soil and encourage the roots to spread out as they seek additional water and nutrients.

Water the hole. Then take the plant from the bucket after a good soaking (15–30 minutes). If the root-ball is tightly wound, spend a few moments unwinding it. Place the plant in the middle of the hole. The hole should be deep enough so that the top of the root-ball is slightly below grade. Fill the native soil minus the top layer of vegetation back in the hole and around the root-ball. Water again and let the soil settle. Mulch with hardwood mulch, unless the plant requires an acid soil like blueberries, in which case softwood mulch like pine would be better. Unless you know otherwise, use regular hardwood mulch, at least 4 inches. Pile the mulch up high in a ring around the perimeter of the hole you dug, sloping it toward the base of your plant. Leave a few inches of exposed soil around the trunk to ensure it dries out after rains and waterings. Take special care to leave any grafts (scars near the base) uncovered or the potential exists for the grafts to fail. Once the tree buds out, if you are not receiving an inch of water a week then you'll need to water. After the first year extra watering is usually appreciated but is generally not necessary (at least in the wooded areas of the country).

Our purpose below is to introduce just a few of the lesser-known varieties to whet your appetite, but don't forget about the standards when drawing up plans for transforming your lawn or annual flower garden into an edible forest garden, like blueberries and raspberries. For each species, further research into climate specifics and various cultivars will likely be well rewarded.

For each berry or fruit type we have provided acceptable climate zones (USDA), height at maturity, preferred climate, ripening time, annual production at maturity, and decorative qualities.

Blackberry (Thornless) (*Rubus canadensis*). Even with their delicious berries, blackberries are often considered weeds. This is because of their annoying thorns and ability to grow nearly anywhere. Fortunately, a vigorous thornless variety has been around for some time.
Zones: 5–8.
Height at Maturity: 3–4 feet.
Preferred Climate: Sunny; tolerates both heat and cold well.
Ripening: Generally for one month in the middle of summer (mid-July through mid-August).
Yield per Plant: 3–5 pounds.
Decorative Qualities: Medium, white blossoms in mid-spring; fruit turns from red to black as it ripens.
Other Notes: Makes a great hedgerow, but usually needs to be supported with some kind of trellis. Plan on sharing some with your neighborhood feathered friends. Spreads easily by burying tops of canes (year-old stems), which will root where buried.

Cherry, Nanking (Bush) (*Prunus tomotosa*). Cherries can be finicky and high maintenance, especially where summers get hot. The Nanking cherry, a sour bush cherry, grows easily, is beautiful, and shouldn't be ravaged by birds the way sweet cherries often are. The fruits are sweet enough to eat straight off the bush but are also good for cooking or juice, although pitting can be tedious.
Zones: 3–7.
Height at Maturity: 6–8 feet.
Preferred Climate: Sun to partial shade; does poorly in prolonged heat.
Ripening: Midsummer.
Yield per Plant: 8–10 pounds.
Decorative Qualities: Excellent. In early spring the bushes are covered in whitish pink flowers, and the dramatic red of the fruits set against the green foliage is striking.
Other Notes: Needs mate to set fruit. Several cultivars available.

Cornelian Cherry (*Cornus mas*). Get in touch with your Neolithic side with this member of the dogwood family. The cherrylike fruits have been consumed by humans for at least 7,000 years, were a staple during Greek and Roman times, and are still popular in Turkey and eastern Europe. They are long-lived and prolific, and their profusions of yellow late-winter blossoms are a gorgeous harbinger of spring. Very similar in appearance to a dogwood, except when in flower.
Zones: 5–8.
Height at Maturity: 20–25 feet.
Preferred Climate: Full sun to partial shade.
Ripening: Long period from summer to fall.
Yield per Plant: 30–70 pounds.
Decorative Qualities: Excellent.
Other Notes: Needs cross-pollination. A small tree, the Cornelian cherry can grow quite large, but pruning can keep it shorter and makes harvesting easier. The unripened fruits can be pickled and have a taste and texture similar to that of an olive.

Gooseberry (*Ribes grossularia* and *Ribes hirtellum*). A delicious berry popular in England, the gooseberry faded in popularity because of its poor shipping qualities and a disease called mildew that could suddenly appear and wipe out all of its fruit. Resistant cultivars have since been developed, especially crosses between the American and European species. A little finicky, but worth the effort.

Zones: 3–6.

Height at Maturity: 3–5 feet.

Preferred Climate: Cool and moist.

Ripening: Late spring/early summer.

Yield per Plant: 8–10 pounds.

Decorative Qualities: Good in summertime when heavy with fruit; attractive lobed leaves.

Other Notes: More than most berries, finding the particular cultivar that most suits your area is very important. Many cultivars are bred for their size, which often comes at the expense of their sweetness. Unripe gooseberries are excellent for cooking, especially sauces. Josta berry is a more heat-tolerant relative.

Hardy Kiwi (*Actinidia arguta*). These fruits tolerate cold winters, unlike the common tropical grocery-store variety. The flavor is similar to that of ripe pineapple, but the fruit is smaller and green when ripe, and the skin is eaten. Large, vigorous, deciduous vines grow quickly and bear prolifically, making this an excellent trellising plant rivaled only by the grape. Three years to maturity.

Zones: 4–9 (some cultivars tolerate Zone 3).

Height at Maturity: Depends on trellis; can be up to 40 feet.

Preferred Climate: Needs 150 frost-free days to set fruit; susceptible to late spring frosts.

Ripening: Late summer to early fall.

Yield per Pair: 50–100 pounds.

Decorative Qualities: An attractive vine. Cultivars can be found with variegated foliage.

Other Notes: Fruit keeps well, up to nine months if kept in the fridge. Very high in vitamin C, many times more than an equal weight of orange. Besides the fruit, this is a plant of many uses, from glue to paper to cat sedatives.

Fig (*Ficus carica*). Not having a few figs in the yard borders on madness. Tolerant of a wide variety of conditions, the fig's only faults are that it does not ship well and can tolerate only milder winters, although growing in pots is possible above Zone 6. This fruit was one of the first plants cultivated for good reason: it's delicious, nutritious, attractive, and easy to grow. Its broad, lobed leaves do excellent double-duty for shading walls.

Zones: 6–9.

Height at Maturity: Up to 15 feet if not managed.

Preferred Climate: Hotter climates; generally suffers if exposed to temperatures below 10 degrees F.

Ripening: In warmer climes, an early summer and fall crop can be expected; in cooler climes, a single late summer crop.

Yield per Plant: 10–20 pounds.

Decorative Qualities: Good; the deeply lobed large leaves are striking.

Other Notes: Figs are excellent dried and keep up to eight months. Some figs will produce without a mate, but cross-pollination is recommended. Many cultivars are available, so find one that does well locally and research your options. In Zone 6, plant in protected microclimates like the south side of buildings. Can be grown in pots in Zone 5.

Juneberry (*Amelanchier* spp.). Similar to the blueberry in appearance and taste, but ripens much earlier, hence the name. Prolific and delicious; fills in the berry gap between the strawberry and the raspberry.

Zones: 3–8.

Height at Maturity: 6–15 feet, depending on species.

Preferred Climate: Does well in colder and warmer climates; prefers plenty of sun.

Ripening: Early summer (June or early July).

Yield per Plant: 5–10 pounds.

Decorative Qualities: High; early blossoms are white or pink.

Other Notes: Very popular with birds, so harvest as soon as ripe. Needs a mate. Many cultivars available.

Asian Pear (*Pyrus pyrifolia, Pyrus ussuriensis,* and *Pyrus x bretschneideri*). Different in appearance and taste from the European pear, rounder like an apple with crispy rather than buttery flesh, excellent in taste. We've seen single organic specimens priced at three bucks a pop, where a mature tree is capable of producing hundreds of pears. Again, another fabulous fruit whose only fault is its poor shipping qualities.

Zones: 4–9.

Height at Maturity: Up to 25 feet.

Preferred Climate: Sunny; some shade acceptable.

Ripening: Late summer to fall.

Yield per Plant: 100 pounds per plant common; more than 1,000 pounds for a full-grown tree possible.

Decorative Qualities: Good, pretty spring flowers, brownish yellow fruits.

Other Notes: Many cultivars available. More than any other fruit, Asian pear's prolific production and generally limited storage make sharing with neighbors a necessity. Hundreds of pounds of fruit from a mature tree for what amounts to a few hours a year of work. Some cultivars store well. Needs a mate that flowers at about the same time.

Lingonberry (*Vaccinium vitis-idaea*). A relative of the cranberry, the lingonberry is loved throughout Scandinavia, where it is made into juice, sauces, jam, and wine and popped in the mouth straight off the bush. A dainty, low-growing plant with a marvelous flavor, a must-have for residents of cooler climes.

Zones: 2–7.

Height at Maturity: 8–12 inches.

Preferred Climate: Cool, boggy, acidic soils with ample sun; afternoon shade needed for warmer climes.

Ripening: Often double crops in midsummer and late fall.

Yield per Plant: 5–10 pounds per 100 square feet of the low-growing plants.

Decorative Qualities: High; makes an excellent edible groundcover planted in partial shade with delicate spring flowers and showy red berries.

Other Notes: Prefers a mate. If happy, will spread to cover a large area. The berries keep well, up to two months. Versatile and delicious.

Persimmon, Asian and American (*Diospyros kaki* and *Diospyros virginiana*). For centuries the most popular fruit in Asia until displaced by the apple. Persimmons are not widely known or cultivated because of their astringent taste when eaten unripe. When ripe, however, they rival an apricot in flavor and texture. But, you guessed it, they do not ship well ripe.

Zones: American Zones 4–8, Asian Zones 6–10.

Height at Maturity: Up to 25 feet; dwarf cultivars available.

Preferred Climate: Asian varieties prefer sun and heat; American varieties tolerate cool and shade.

Ripening: From August to late November.

Yield per Plant: 50–100 pounds, with older trees capable of 400 pounds or more.

Decorative Qualities: Excellent. Brilliant fall foliage, often with some of the large red fruits remaining on the tree after leaf fall.

Other Notes: Asian, or Kaki, persimmons have many different cultivars and are self-fertile. Some species are less astringent when unripe. American persimmons are very cold hardy but need a mate. Fruits need to be squishy soft before harvest, often in late fall.

Pawpaw (*Asimina* spp.). Often referred to as the banana of the north, this North American native produces large yellowish green fruits that have a texture and taste similar to the banana. George Washington, Daniel Boone, and Mark Twain were big fans of pawpaws, the largest edible fruit native to the United States.

Zones: 4–8.

Height at Maturity: 10–25 feet, depending on cultivar and pruning.

Preferred Climate: Tolerates cold, but needs about 160 frost-free days for fruit to ripen.

Ripening: Late fall.

Yield per Plant: 25–50 pounds.

Decorative Qualities: Good. Deep purple flowers in spring are somewhat hidden, but leaves turn a golden yellow in fall.

Other Notes: Doesn't transplant very well. Best to start either from seed or from specimens grown in pots. Needs shade its first two years, but then ample sun afterward to produce a good quantity of fruit. Very low maintenance once established.

Hazelnuts (*Corylus avellana* and *Corylus americana*). Often overlooked in the home orchard are nut trees. While many nut trees are too large for smaller yards, the hazelnut is a carefree smaller tree that will produce bounties of delicious smaller nuts if given plenty of sun.

Zones: 4–9.

Height at Maturity: 8–12 feet.

Preferred Climate: Well-drained, sunny spots.

Ripening: August through September.

Yield per Plant: 8–10 pounds.

Decorative Qualities: Medium; highly regarded by many types of wildlife, including turkeys and squirrels.

Other Notes: Needs a mate. Can be made into a delicious butter spread and is excellent for a variety of desserts. A great cooking companion to a wide variety of fruits, including many of those mentioned above.

Again, the above are just a sampling of some of the easier-to-grow orchard plants that have the potential of offering hundreds if not thousands of pounds of food year after year for a minimal outlay of up-front time and expense. There's plenty more out there. See the resources section for where to find out more.

PERENNIAL VEGETABLES

Forgotten or unknown to most residents of North America are a surprising number of perennial vegetables. You may ask yourself, "Could it really be that not only

do I not need to till every spring and fall, but I don't even have to plant?" It's true, if you're willing to expand your horizons a bit and open your mind, and your mouth of course, to a new range of flavors, textures, and sensations. Many of these crops have been cultivated and harvested for centuries if not millennia. While perennial veggies are primarily a tropical phenomenon, there are dozens of varieties that will thrive even in the northern hinterlands if given the proper conditions. After that, it's collecting your harvest, occasional weed control, and figuring out how to play chef with your new ingredients!

This section relies heavily on Eric Toensmeier's *Perennial Vegetables*, and we are very grateful for his thorough research and excellent book. We hope we are able to whet your appetite sufficiently to dig deeper into these amazing and underutilized crops.

Multiplier Onions (*Allium cepa aggregatum*). There are two types of multiplier onions, shallots and potato onions. These onions reproduce by forming clumps. To harvest, the bunch are dug up, and some bulbs are returned to the ground to grow again. Excellent taste and storage capabilities.

Zones: 5–10.

Preferred Climate: Rich, well-drained soil; full sun.

Harvest: When tops die down in the fall.

Yield per Plant: Several onions for each one planted.

Taste: Potato onion's taste is indistinguishable from that of traditional onions; shallots have a milder, more delicate taste.

Decorative Qualities: Low. The tops look like traditional onions.

Other Notes: Greens can also be used. Shallots are less cold hardy.

Lovage (*Levisticum officinale*). Lovage behaves like an enormous perennial celery. The young stalks are harvested in early spring and used for cooking. It is too strongly flavored to be eaten raw. The roots and seeds are also edible.

Zones: 4–8.

Preferred Climate: Moist, well-drained soil; sun to partial shade.

Taste: Once cooked, very similar to traditional celery.

Harvest: Early spring.

Yield per Plant: 1–2 pounds of stalks per plant.

Decorative Qualities: Medium; a tall plant (up to 6 feet) with branching stems.

Other notes: The stalks are excellent for Bloody Marys.

Sunchokes (*Helianthus tuberosus*). A native of eastern North America and once a staple of Native Americans, the sunchoke, often called a Jerusalem artichoke (don't ask) is an exceptionally tasty, productive, and easy-to-grow root crop. Masses of yellow sunflowers appear late in the summer, so it does double duty as a beautiful garden plant.

Zones: 2–9.

Preferred Climate: Moist, well-drained soil; full sun.

Taste: Nutty and potato-like; crisp when raw, a little grainy but delicious when cooked. Does not fry well.

Harvest: Fall and winter. The bulbs can be left in the ground and dug up when needed, provided the ground is not frozen.

Yield per Plant: 1–2 pounds per plant. Can spread to form dense colonies. Highly productive.

Decorative Qualities: High. A tall, spreading plant, up to 12 feet. Ours often fall over, so some kind of containment is advisable.

Other Notes: Cultivars are available that are shorter and clump together rather than spreading out. Starch is stored as inulin, which makes it good for diabetics. Inulin also helps the body absorb calcium, among other benefits, although it does cause gas in some folks.

Achira (*Canna edulis*). One of the great Andean root crops. Related to the ornamental canna lilies (not a true lily), also reputed to be edible and delicious. The horticultural canna also has large flowers, although not quite as large as ornamental varieties, making this an excellent edible landscaping plant.

Zones: 8–10 without trouble; 6–7 with additional winter mulching and microclimate selection. Still possible in Zone 5 if completely harvested and stored indoors, with some roots saved for replanting in the spring, although growth may be slow.

Preferred Climate: Moist to wet soils; sun to partial shade.

Taste: Sweet, with a slight mucilaginous texture. Sweetness improves with a few weeks of aging.

Harvest: Fall. Spreads as a rhizome. Eat the smaller ones, and the save the larger rhizomes, which have a tendency to become woody, for replanting. Keeps very well in a root cellar environment.

Yield per Plant: Depends on length of season. Long summers without frost could potentially yield many pounds for each bulb planted.

Decorative Qualities: Excellent. Hopefully, breeding work will be done to combine cannas that are both beautiful and delicious.

Other Notes: Young leaves and shoots are also edible. Grown throughout the tropics as a staple crop. The roots are also an excellent fodder crop for livestock such as pigs and cattle.

Good King Henry (*Chenopodium bonus-henricus*). A traditional European vegetable, good King Henry is grown primarily for its edible shoots. Often appears several weeks before asparagus, making it one of the first veggies available in the spring, with a long harvest season of several months.

Zones: 3–9 without special care.

Preferred Climate: Moist, well-drained soil; sun to partial shade.

Taste: Asparagus-like; needs to be cooked. Can be made sweeter by blanching.

Harvest: Late winter/early spring.

Yield per Plant: Established plants have the potential to yield several pounds of shoots over a long spring season.

Decorative Qualities: Low. Looks like a tall spinach plant.

Other Notes: Sometimes grown for its grain, so has potential as a perennial grain crop. It is related to the South American staple quinoa. Also, the leaves can be eaten (cooked) all summer long, even after flowering when many other greens have gone bitter.

Ostrich Fern (*Matteuccia struthiopteris*). A North American native that is a prized early spring vegetable in New England, often appearing in farmers' markets. The tightly wound frond resembles the spiraled head of a violin, from where the plant derives its common name.

Zones: 2–8

Preferred Climate: Moist to wet soil; partial to full shade; avoid afternoon sun in warmer climates.

Taste: Excellent. Nutty and crisp when young.

Harvest: In early spring, fiddleheads are cut and cooked like asparagus, at least 10 minutes. Harvest season is relatively short.

Yield per Plant: ¼–½ pound.

Decorative Qualities: Excellent. Ostrich ferns make up for their short harvest season by their early spring spore-bearing fronds and gorgeous summer foliage.

Other Notes: A great food crop for shady areas and a no-maintenance cover crop. Dislikes heat. Can grow up to 6 feet tall and slowly forms dense stands if given proper conditions.

Groundnut (*Apios americana*). Another Native American staple, the groundnut is one of the easiest vegetables to grow. As a vine, it makes an excellent candidate for trellising against walls for protection from the summer sun. Where summers are long, the harvest can be up to 8 pounds from each plant. Recent work done at Louisiana State University has yielded significant improvements in yield size and harvestability. As a member of the pea family, it also fixes nitrogen.

Zones: 3–9.

Preferred Climate: Moist to wet soil; sun to partial shade.

Taste: Like an earthy, nutty potato, although the texture is mealier like the flesh of a yam.

Harvest: Can be harvested whenever the ground is not frozen, so makes an excellent insurance crop.

Yield per Plant: Several pounds per plant.

Decorative Qualities: High. Makes a good trellising vine, with soft pink pea flowers.

Other Notes: Can be naturalized in well-suited areas and basically forgotten, allowing it to sprawl over existing vegetation. Come back and harvest whenever you desire after your groundnuts have become established.

Sorrel (*Rumex* and *Oxyria* spp.). Sorrels are another neglected European perennial vegetable group, including mountain sorrel (*O. digyna*), garden sorrel (*R. acetosa*), sheep sorrel (*R. acetosella*), and french sorrel (*R. scutatus*). These names are often interchangeable, but the plants behave similarly. The leaves of all varieties produce greens, many of which can be eaten raw or cooked, throughout the growing season except when in flower.

Zones: 3–9.

Preferred Climate: Sun to shade; prefers somewhat acidic soils.

Taste: Zesty. Excellent as an addition to salads and in creamy soups, especially combined with lovage.

Harvest: All season long, from early spring to late fall, although bitterness increases when flowering.

Yield per Plant: ½–1 pound per plant over the course of the growing season.

Decorative Qualities: Low. Similar in appearance to spinach.

Other Notes: Sheep sorrel (*R. acetosella*) can be quite aggressive and should be introduced with great caution. French sorrel (*R. scutatus*) is considered to have the best taste and texture, although it tends to be less hardy. Has potential as an understory edible groundcover.

MUSHROOMS

Ah, mushrooms, the forgotten kingdom!

When we were children, mushrooms meant the white button variety from the store or the multitudes of bizarre and certainly deadly varieties that sprang up after rainstorms. If it didn't come wrapped in cellophane in a container from the grocery store, it would surely kill you!

Fortunately, those days of ignorance are behind us. Now we know that there are dozens of varieties of edible mushrooms, some of which can be cultivated in the home garden. And the great thing is that once established, most can be perpetuated year after year with the addition of more organic matter. While the mycelium, the "root" of the mushroom, grows, it provides soil structure, breaks down dense organic matter (thereby freeing up nutrients for plants), and helps retain moisture. It achieves all this without needing sunlight (although it needs sun to fruit) and requiring little or no maintenance. With a little luck (and some extra watering most likely), you'll be rewarded with pounds of succulent morsels that can be cooked in a thousand different ways waiting to surprise you outside your door.

As mushrooms become more popular, the number of retailers selling inoculated dowels or plug spawn (described below) is increasing. Purchase your starting materials as locally as possible to increase your chances of success. You'll need to do extra research on what variety you want to cultivate, but from our (fairly limited) experience, pearl oyster and shiitake seem to be the two varieties that are easiest to propagate, so the beginner may want to start with these. Again, this section is more of an introduction. A little further research will go a long way.

Mushroom Cultivation

Mushrooms are the fruiting bodies of mycelial fungi that derive their nutrients from decaying organic matter. This organic matter *must* be moist in order for the threadlike mycelial roots to obtain their sustenance. A wide variety of moist organic matter will do the job, depending on the species. A pile of decaying organic matter—sounds a lot like compost, doesn't it? And the concept is the same as we can grow mycelium in piles of wood chips, grass clippings, straw, kitchen scraps, and other "waste" organic matter. This is stuff most of us have around the garden anyway. With mushroom cultivation, rather than having some random fungus, mold, or what-have-you break down our organic matter, we select species that will give us a bumper crop of mushrooms as they do so. For this reason, mushrooms have been aptly coined "Gourmet Decomposers."

The end result of rich, loamy humus is the same as with any compost, we just get tens of pounds of organic mushrooms in the interim, some varieties of which fetch $30/pound or more at fancy groceries or restaurants. Once a patch is established, it may be possible to keep it going by adding additional organic matter each year. Some varieties we can interplant in our vegetable patch, making our beds do double duty. The veggies up above soak up the sun and provide shade to the mycelia underneath, which help retain moisture and break down undecomposed organic matter for the plant roots. Come picking time, an entire meal may be awaiting us from a single bed: mushrooms, vegetables, herbs, and berries.

Inoculating Logs with Mycelium

Renter friendly.

Project Time: An afternoon.

Cost: $20–100.

Energy Saved: Low. The quantities won't likely be great, but considering how they direct some of the decomposition in your yard to producing mushrooms can be very worthwhile.

Ease of Use: Medium. Success is erratic.

Maintenance Level: Low. Once established, logs will produce for several years depending on log type. Propagation can take some time but is not labor intensive.

Skill Levels: Requires more luck than skill.

Materials: Inoculated quarter-inch spiral dowels or plug spawn, freshly cut hardwood logs (three weeks old and cut in late winter before budding out is optimal) and beeswax *or* hardwood mulch and burlap bags.

Tools: Drill, ⁵⁄₁₆-inch drill bit, hammer, pastry brush, small stove, old can to melt wax. No tools are required for the mulch and burlap bags.

Caution: Don't automatically assume the mushroom that appears is the one you propagated! To ensure an accurate identification, it is necessary to be able to identify all the common features of a mushroom and to take a spore print of the one you are considering consuming. A field guide will be extremely helpful in this regard, but having the mushrooms identified by a local expert is the safest method of identification.

Ordering mycelium. Starting a mushroom patch is usually done by ordering plug spawn or dowels. Depending on the type of mushroom, the plugs or dowels are either inserted into holes drilled into 2- to 4-foot-long log sections of the proper species of tree or mixed in layers with wood chips, lawn clippings, straw, et cetera. It generally takes about 6–12 months for the mycelium to become large enough to start fruiting, although it could take a shorter or longer period of time, depending mainly on the weather. Most mycelia are capable of adapting to even the coldest of climates, although growth and production are stronger with longer seasons. The maintenance level, especially where there is adequate rain, is essentially zilch. Watering during extended dry spells may be necessary. Or it may not, if you've chosen a shady enough spot and made your level of organic matter deep enough. You may want to simply forget about it and come back and check for mushrooms after heavy rains during fruiting season, but your chances of success will increase the more water you can provide, especially during hot, dry weather.

Putting the inoculated dowels in the logs. In sum, the process is as follows: Drill holes every few inches a little deeper than the length of the dowel. Knock them in with a hammer or mallet, and brush on wax to retain moisture. Water during dry spells or just come back later in the year and check on them.

Propagating your own mycelium. Starting your own mycelium patch from edible mushrooms you find, or even from those purchased at the grocery store, can be very simple, not to mention free. The easiest way to propagate the desired mycelium is to cut off the stem butts of several of the desired species of mushroom. This will require some care in the harvest or purchase of these mushrooms, as the stem butt could have been cut or broken off. The stem butt refers to the base of the mushroom where it was formerly attached to the mycelial network. It's where the stem starts to bulge out and lose its shape and texture. Often it has bits of dirt or other organic matter still attached. Cut off these stem butts, using the freshest mushrooms you can find. These will be your mycelial seeds.

It seems like almost all mushrooms love the corrugated interior of cardboard. The glues that hold cardboard together are wood-derived and seem easily digested by the mycelium for quick growth. Take several pieces about the size of your hand and peel the paper off one side to expose the corrugations. Soak for a few minutes, and then let the excess water drip off. Poke a few holes in the sheets with a fork. Spread your stem butts around on the exposed corrugations and top with another piece to make a sandwich. Pile on a few more sheets if you have them. Next, take this stem-butt sandwich and put it in a plastic container or a covered bowl or something else that will hold moisture. Put it away in a cabinet so it stays dark. Come back in two or three days and check. At this point, the mycelia, composed of tiny thin strands, usually white, should be snaking their way throughout the cardboard. If not, put it away for a few more days and check again. If there's still nothing, it's probably a bust.

To successfully grow mycelia, the strategy is "Move it or lose it," as veteran mushroom cultivator Paul Stamets says. If not given new organic matter to conquer, the mycelium will quickly lose its vigor. The easiest way to continue to propagate your mycelium is to place the inoculated cardboard in a plastic bag with some soaked hardwood spiral dowels. Birch dowels seem to work well and can be found from woodworking suppliers. Alternatively, soaked wood chips would make a decent secondary medium. Again, you want the organic matter to be saturated but not dripping, so soak overnight and then let it drain for fifteen minutes or so before using. Spiral dowels are the easiest, because once they are inoculated, holes can then be drilled in appropriate logs (using the same wood as where the mushrooms were found is always a good idea) and the dowels inserted without damaging the mycelia in the spiral crevices. The dowels should then be covered with beeswax to retain moisture. For inoculated wood chips, mix these in with more soaked wood chips in a burlap bag at a ratio of around 5- or 10-to-1 new

FIG. 10.4. **Mushrooms grown in a garden bed help plants by retaining moisture and making nutrients available, plus they are good to eat!**

chips to started chips (the lower the ratio, the greater the chance of success; you can always expand later if the mycelium is still "running"). Keep watered for the first week or two. Riding these mycelia waves has been likened to surfing. You won't catch every one, but when you do, it's great!

Companion planting with vegetables. Just as certain plants like one another or don't, this is also probably the case with various species of mushrooms and common garden veggies. Since companion planting of veggies and mushrooms is still a relatively new idea, it might behoove you to do a few controlled experiments to advance the cause of sustainability. If you're so inclined, try control patches of the same veggie in nearby beds with any mycelium, and see what happens. Try different kinds of mushrooms and different kinds of mulches. Be as scientific or not as you please, because even general information on what

does well together will be helpful to your surrounding gardening community.

Mycelium Running, a must-read on the lives of mushrooms and the state of our planet, tells how author Paul Stamets and colleagues experimented with growing brassicas and the elm oyster (*Hypsizygus ulmarus*) and the pearl oyster (*Pleurotus ostreatus*). In their limited trials, yields of broccoli and Brussels sprouts increased four- to sixfold when companion planted with elm oyster but actually decreased when planted with pearl oyster. Suffice it to say that little about the relationships between edible mushrooms and food crops is understood, but there appears to be great potential. A little experimentation could go a long way, so have fun with it.

It's worth noting that many of these mushrooms have been eaten and highly regarded by most other peoples of the globe. Eating mushrooms is not a new thing. Mushrooms are a low-maintenance, delicious food that is largely ignored in the United States because they cannot be shipped easily and hence commodified. Further reading beyond these pages should disabuse even the most skeptical of the importance of this neglected food crop as a welcome member of the garden. Check the resources at the end of the chapter for more information.

Using inoculated logs in the landscape. An easy way to incorporate mushrooms into your garden is by inoculating logs and using these as barriers between paths and garden beds. Since most mushrooms thrive in log cultivation and logs are frequently used to demarcate paths and beds, this is an area ripe for double duty for mushroom colonies. Another idea is to chainsaw sections of log using mycelium-inoculated bar chain oil and use these as stepping-stones in your garden or stack them to make fences.

GREEN ROOFS, LIVING WALLS, AND THOUGHTFUL LANDSCAPING

Plants can help us eliminate our use of fossil fuels in ways beyond providing us with local food. By incorporating vegetation into our landscape through the use of green roofs, trellising, and windbreaks, we can greatly diminish the supplemental energy our homes require by reducing the amount of excess heat and cold that enters in the first place. Just as monocultures that are isolated from other living things require fossil-fueled technofixes when problems arise, air conditioners, heat pumps and dehumidifiers, and air filters are needed when our homes remain segregated from the living world.

To the traditional home-owning American, the garden stops where the home begins. But by incorporating living things into and onto our home's walls and roofs, we can provide great benefit to ourselves and our surrounding community. The benefits break down as follows:

Aesthetic. Plants and flowers are beautiful to behold and attract beautiful creatures like butterflies and hummingbirds. By combining the random and organic growth of plants with the rectilinear and staid architecture of most existing homes, we can soften hard edges and incorporate our home into its surrounding environment. Doing so communicates the ecological concern of the home's inhabitants with the surrounding communities, both human and otherwise.

Environmental. Additional green space provides forage and housing to a wide variety of insects, birds, and smaller animals. Indoor and outdoor plants cleanse the air of pollutants created by furnaces and passing cars and trucks and take carbon dioxide out of the air. Storm water that can overflow sewage systems is instead retained and released back into the environment, reducing flood potential. If done on a large enough scale, green roofs and living walls can reduce the ambient temperature by several degrees in the summertime.

Economic. Greening of roofs can reduce roof temperatures by up to 70 to 80 degrees F. Substantial reductions in interior temperatures result, often by as much as 6 to 8 degrees F. Considering that a 1-degree F decrease in interior temperatures can reduce air conditioning use by 8 percent, this can lead to huge energy savings. Windbreaks can reduce heat loss in wintertime by up to 50 percent, while trellising of southern, eastern, and western walls can reduce heat gains in summer by a similar amount. By opening up additional areas for gardening and food production of high-value items such as fruits and herbs, families can save on their grocery bill in terms of both money and energy, especially in space-constrained urban areas.

Green Roofs

Green roof is a catchall term for any roof with vegetation on it and is also sometimes referred to as an ecoroof. The modern green-roof movement began in Germany in the mid-1970s. Its proponents were interested in creating green space in otherwise barren urban areas. As the number of green roofs increased and their environmental and energy benefits became better studied and understood, the movement spread to other parts of Europe and then to North America.

Green roofs on large civic buildings are now being built in cities such as Chicago, Illinois, and Asheville, North Carolina. Some new, architect-designed residences are also incorporating aspects of green roofs into their design.

For the owner of an existing home, the ability to create a green roof may be limited, due to concerns about weight, although not as much as might be initially supposed. Lightweight green roofs are possible on existing roofs with a pitch of up to 30 degrees. If the homeowner has access to the framing members of the roof via an attic, then reinforcement of load-bearing members is possible, and a heavier, more diverse green roof can be achieved. As a retrofit, the effect of going from a dead zone of tar or asphalt shingles to a thriving garden of flowers and birds can be very dramatic and is a joy to witness.

Green roofs are differentiated by the depth of the growing medium, as this directly relates to weight—the primary structural concern.

Intensive roofs are those greater than 4 inches in thickness, with some as deep as 2 feet or more, making a wide variety of plants, including bushes and even small trees, possible. Retrofitting a home for an intensive green roof requires structural analysis and almost certainly involves beefing up support members, not only of the horizontal span of the roof rafters but also the vertical support of the walls. Since access to wall members in an existing home is likely to be limited, creating an intensive green roof is more than likely cost- and time-prohibitive for most do-it-yourselfers. If, however, you are considering building some type of passive solar addition onto your home, then an intensive roof may be relatively simple to incorporate into your designs. This section will focus on the creation of an extensive green roof.

Extensive roofs are thin, from 1 to 4 inches thick, and can support less diverse plant communities. They are relatively easy to install and oftentimes require no additional structural support. Nevertheless, their environmental and energy benefits are still quite high.

Construction of your green roof will likely vary depending on your circumstances, making a general

FIG. 10.5. **The original tar and gravel roof. The tar was so thick and heavy there was basically a road on top of our house. The new green roof hardly weighed any more than this monstrosity.**

how-to difficult. For homes, we recommend only expert carpenters undertake such an endeavor, although less experienced carpenters may want to see what they can do with other outbuildings where the consequences of failure (i.e., collapse) won't be so catastrophic.

In general, all green roofs have five basic components, although sometimes one layer achieves two or more functions:

1. Weatherproof membrane
2. Root-protection barrier
3. Drainage layer
4. Growing medium
5. Plants

Weatherproof membrane. Generally, there are three options available to create a waterproof seal as the base of any green roof project: a *built-up roof*, which is composed of layers of asphalt roofing felt; a *single-ply rubber membrane*, also called a pond liner; or a *fluid-applied membrane*, which can be applied hot or cold and forms a continuous seal.

The first thing you may note is that a green roof is made from some not very "green" materials. While constructing our green roof, we took to referring to it as the "black roof," since this was its color for several months as the project was completed. While this is

FIG. 10.6. **The perimeter garden was created by using 4 x 4-foot planters. A drainage layer of brick rubble, from the old coal furnace chimney that we took down, is followed by landscaping cloth, soil, mulch, and plants.**

somewhat of a contradiction, it's important to keep in mind that most of these materials are no worse than the average asphalt shingle roof but will have much more positive environmental and energy effects during their lifetime. Also, a properly constructed green roof will substantially improve the roofing material's life by protecting it from direct sunlight as well as extremes of hot and cold.

Applying any of these roofing materials is fairly straightforward. Before they can be applied, a relatively flat continuous roofing deck free of all protrusions must exist, preferably with at least a few inches of fall for every 10 feet of deck. If the slope is greater than 15 degrees (about 2/12), then a latticework frame that creates 2 × 2-foot or smaller boxes will be necessary to ensure there is not slippage of the substrate mate-

rial. Roofs with slope greater than 30 degrees (or 4/12) should not be attempted unless a green roof professional is consulted.

Root-protection barrier. A root-protection barrier is necessary if the weather-protection barrier contains chemically organic materials such as bitumen or asphalt (which contains bitumen), which is the case with built-up roofs and some fluid-applied membranes. Single-ply membranes (EPDM or butyl rubber) are inorganic and do not need a root-protection barrier. Occasionally, single-ply membranes made of recycled material can be found. Hopefully this will be the case more often in the future.

Chemically organic materials in the weather-protection barrier are susceptible to rot and infiltration from plant roots. Ultimately, in order for a green roof to perform the two functions of water protection and plant container, some inorganic material is required. Rolls of PVC are the most common material used to create this impermeable layer (if needed), which should be at least 1 mm in thickness. Note that PVC as well as the single-ply membranes consisting of EPDM will degrade over time if exposed to UV sunlight. Plan to have all parts of these materials out of sunlight either via green roof cover or some kind of trim.

Drainage layer. For roofs with slope greater than 7 degrees (1/12) a drainage layer will most likely not be necessary. In fact, a drainage layer could lead to the growing medium drying out too quickly. For flatter roofs, a drainage layer prevents soggy, anaerobic conditions that could lead to plant death and roof leaks.

There are two methods for creating a drainage layer: channels or a bulky substrate. Channeled flat plastic material elevates the planting medium off the roof. Excess water can then percolate down into the channels and run off the edge of the roof. A wide variety of materials can be used for this, some specifically made for green roofs; others, such as wavy plastic roofing materials, can be modified with drain holes to achieve this purpose.

The second and much more common option is to have a granular substrate material that allows excess water to flow through. A wide variety of options

FIG. 10.7. **Previously a leaky, inaccessible, and barren tar roof that would heat up tremendously on a hot summer day, our flat one-story roof was converted into a green roof hangout spot by reinforcement, replacing a window with a door, and using specially designed planters. Now hardy flowers like zinnia and blanket flower share space with edibles like scarlet runner bean and herbs like parsley, sage, oregano, mint, thyme, lavender, and horseradish.**

are available for this layer, some much heavier than others. Gravel, brick rubble, lava stone, sand, pumice, pebbles, vermiculite, and light expanded clay granules are common. The cost as well as the weight varies greatly. Brick rubble can often be had for free (okay, and a few hours with a sledgehammer) and makes an excellent intermediate choice between weight, moisture retention, and drainage.

Thinner extensive green roofs can dispense with any additional growing medium and plant directly into the drainage layer. Keep in mind that in order to do this your drainage layer material needs to be heavy enough not to blow away and to hold enough moisture for the xerophytes (dry-climate plants) to survive. Brick rubble makes an excellent compromise between these two needed attributes. Free colonization of such simple extensive roofs by local mosses and grasses will ensure hardy species are planted and money is not wasted purchasing lots of expensive plants that could very well perish in the extreme conditions.

One exciting recent development are preseeded extensive mats that simply roll out on top of the membrane layer. The sedums then sprout and keep the roof cool and green with little maintenance. As usual, convenience comes with added cost.

Growing medium. Where deeper roofs of 4–6 inches, sometimes referred to as a semi-extensive green roofs, can be supported, a drainage layer is covered with a separate growth layer. Landscaping cloth that allows water and some root penetration but retains soil is spread over the drainage layer. A few inches of growing medium such as loamy soil is spread on top. The growth layer retains most of the moisture and nutrients for the garden, but the drainage layer also retains air and moisture for the plants. Semi-extensive roofs can support a broader range of herbs and prairie flowers.

Where access is possible, the roof becomes a potential gardening spot that would otherwise be barren. Soils that contain large quantities of organic matter should be avoided or diluted with more inert sand, as these soils can promote growth that is too vigorous and severely stress the plants during extended dry spells. If there's water access, although this is often rare or difficult, then a more dense organic soil is possible. Generally, green roofs behave similarly to any container planting, meaning they are more prone to drying out and experience wider fluctuations in temperature, increasing the stress level on plants with higher moisture requirements.

Beyond sedums, a wide variety of bulbs, grasses, and prairie flowers do especially well in extensive roofs and make dramatic mass plantings. Local wildflowers also have the potential to do quite well, especially those that thrive in full sun. Herbs like sage, thyme, rosemary, and lavender are usually quite drought hardy. You won't know what'll grow until you scatter a few seeds on your green roof and find out!

Structural considerations. Of course, a dramatic mass planting isn't very worthwhile if it falls down on your head, although it would still be very dramatic. Obviously, many green roofs involve placing a large amount of weight on your roof. Understanding structural issues is of paramount importance to creating a stable, functioning green roof.

To determine if your existing roof has the capacity to carry the weight of any type of green roof you must have a firm understanding of live and dead loads, lumber sizes and spans, and wood species and their related compression capabilities. All this is in addition to general framing and carpentry expertise. Failure in proper planning can have catastrophic consequences, including death. If you have any doubts about the potential loading of your green roof or your home's ability to support it, consultation with a structural engineer and/or building inspector is a must. This doesn't necessarily have to cost any money. Some counties' building inspectors are structural engineers by trade, and if you go in with some reasonably drawn-up plans and a thorough understanding of the concepts listed above, there's a good chance they will help you out. The American Wood Council (www.awc.org) has a wide variety of information on required spans and wood types available for free from its Web site. Much of this information is also available in local building code books or the Universal Building Code book.

Generally speaking, an extensive green roof (2–6 inches in depth) will increase the load on your roof rafters by between 14 and 35 pounds per square foot. The lower end of this is easily accommodated by any solidly built residence (please don't put a green roof on top of your trailer!). Obviously, the material used as a substrate has much to do with the final weight. A 1-inch layer of pebbles can increase the load on your roof by about 10 pounds/square foot when saturated, while saturated light expanded clay granules will increase the load by only 2 pounds/square foot.

Regardless, checking the spacing, span, and wood type of your rafters and checking to make sure they are free from rot and capable of accommodating this extra weight, in addition to the maximum potential snow load or other stresses of your particular area, is *required*. The information is available for free at the above Web site and there is no excuse for not checking to make sure your home can support your green roof.

Intensive green roofs, depending on the depths of the soil and the substrate used, can increase loads by as much as 200 pounds/square foot. Intensive green roofs require plans approved by a structural engineer.

Living Walls

Living wall refers to landscaping and trellising plants to provide a buffer between the inside of your home and the extremes of weather outside. There are three general strategies that can greatly reduce your home's energy needs through shading, windbreaks, and insulation. The first is the planting of deciduous shrubs or small trees that shade eastern, western, and sometimes southern walls from the summer sun. The second is the trellising of deciduous vines to create a shaded canopy over eastern, western, and southern walls and windows. The third is the trellising of evergreen vines on northern walls to act as both a windbreak and an additional pocket of air for increased insulation.

Like other greening strategies, living walls have many additional benefits beyond their energy savings. Habitat creation, air and noise pollution abatement, and aesthetics are all enhanced by living walls. It is much easier to plant something on the ground next to your home than on its roof! Much more so than green roofs, living walls can be created using food-producing plants, opening up additional, and often neglected, growing space.

Shading walls can reduce interior heat gain by more than 50 percent. By stopping the heat from entering the wall in the first place, living walls can be as effec-

tive in stopping heat transfer as a wall filled with fiberglass insulation. Particularly if exterior walls are darker in color (see "Cooling the Attic and Walls" in chapter 7), shading provides dramatic energy benefits.

For cooler climates, deciduous shrubs and trees work best, as they don't block heat gain in wintertime. This can be as fancy or as low maintenance as one desires. Espaliers are a traditional French method of training fruit trees, sometimes in intricate patterns, against the sides of houses. Done on the southern side of the home, this can allow the growth of trees that would otherwise not be possible in that zone. Judicious annual pruning can easily create the same shading effect for much less effort, if not necessarily with the

FIG. 10.8. **The horizontal trellis on the south side of this small passive-solar cabin creates a shaded hangout spot in the summer using deciduous, nitrogen-fixing native wisteria vines. Although a more complicated post-and-beam construction rather than the wire trellis we describe, the basic principle remains the same.**

same ornamental effect. Any deciduous fruit tree can be used, provided it grows high enough to shade the wall. Make sure to prune trees so that the vegetation does not contact the wall, especially any wood siding or trim. Allowing airflow for walls to dry after rains will inhibit any potential mold or termite problems.

Trellising. Idiotically, many existing homes were built with no regard for passive solar heating. To retrofit one's existing home for passive solar gain can often mean converting some or most of the southern wall to glazing (see chapter 7). However, the overhang of the eaves of the existing south-facing wall is rarely appropriate for shading the glass wall during the hot summer months. Since a substantial overhang is often required, sometimes 2 feet or more, it's usually the case that any existing overhang doesn't adequately shade the summer sun.

Trellising provides an ideal solution to this problem, better, in fact, than a permanent overhang that is part of the building. This is because there is a natural lag between the length of the day and the change of the season. For instance, the summer solstice is the longest day of the year, generally June 21st. Since this is the longest day of the year, it should follow that this is the middle of summer, as the days during the six weeks on either side of the summer solstice constitute the ones with the most hours of sunlight. All over the northern hemisphere, May 10th has the same number of sunlight hours as August 2nd, but, in fact, these twelve weeks are not the hottest of the year. Traditionally, June 21st is when summer is considered to have *started* not the middle of summer ("summer" here referring to the warmest three months of the year). Unfortunately, this, too, is inaccurate, as any plant can tell you.

Instead, generally speaking the warmest three months are from June 3rd to September 3rd, with the hottest week on average smack in the middle around the third week of July. The same is true in winter. December 21st is the shortest day and considered to be the start of winter, but actually in terms of average low temperatures, winter runs from December 3rd to March 3rd, with the coldest week usually the third one in January.

This three-and-a-half-week lag between daylight length and temperature makes permanent passive solar overhangs inaccurate. You're getting the same amount of sunlight on March 21st as on September 21st, even though September 21st is just outside of summer and March 21st is just outside of winter. In other words, it's almost always much colder on March 21st than September 21st, but a typical passive solar overhang won't be able to tell the difference.

A deciduous trellis, on the other hand, will be able to. On September 21st, it will still have leaves and be blocking most of the incoming sunlight. On March 21st, it won't have budded out yet and will be letting in all the sunlight. As it warms up through the months of April and May, the deciduous trellis will gradually block more and more sunlight until the southern, eastern, or western facade is completely shaded. In October, as things cool down, the deciduous trellis will lose its leaves, allowing more and more sunlight in.

Furthermore, fruit-producing trellises such as grapes can produce up to hundreds of pounds of food annually. They are simple to construct, especially on existing homes. And they provide all those other benefits (wildlife habitat, pollution reduction, CO_2 capture, et cetera) that a more conventional passive solar overhang does not, all for much less time and money invested, especially for retrofits.

Types of climbers. Trellising requires plants that climb. Different climbers have various ways of attaching themselves to whatever they're clinging to. Most ivies (especially English ivy, *Hedera helix*) should be avoided, as they have aerial roots that penetrate any spaces available as they climb. These roots can do extensive damage, especially to wood siding, opening up gaps that allow water in and generally breaking apart the siding. These roots can also damage the mortar between bricks or stone, causing structural damage. They are generally extremely aggressive exotic invasives. It's better to put one's energy into eliminating them rather than propagating them.

Virginia creeper (*Parthenocissus quinquefolia*) and Boston ivy (*Parthenocissus tricuspidata*) are two common types of climbers, both natives to North America, that use specialized tendrils with a gluelike substance on the tip to attach themselves to whatever they are ascending. They are both deciduous and easy to grow and have beautiful fall foliage. Their berries are useful to wildlife but are inedible by us humans. They make good candidates for covering masonry walls. (We can't recommend these climbers for earth plasters without any lime, although we have no specific knowledge that they would damage earth plasters. We've seen a cob wall with regular latex paint on it perform without any problem for several years, so the gluey tendrils may not be a problem.) On wood siding, they leave little footprints when detached that can be seen from up close, although this residue is harmless. More of a concern is the high moisture level these climbers maintain so close to wood siding. Unless the siding on your house is a rot-resistant wood such as cedar, avoid this type of living wall.

Twining climbers ascend by wrapping around stems, branches, or anything else they come across. These are some of the most aggressive of all climbers. Kudzu (*Pueraria lobata*), Chinese wisteria (*Wisteria sinensis*), and Japanese honeysuckle (*Lonicera japonica*) have escaped cultivation and compromised millions of acres of woodlands across North America. Fortunately, less aggressive native species of wisteria (*Wisteria frutescens*, nitrogen-fixing) and honeysuckle (*Lonicera sempervirens*) exist, because twining climbers make good trellising plants. Both plants thrive in Zones 4–9.

Native honeysuckle (*Lonicera sempervirens*) is evergreen, making it a great candidate for trellising on northern walls as a windbreak. Hummingbirds adore it. Native wisteria (*Wisteria frutescens*) is deciduous and makes a beautiful choice for trellising over windows. A wide variety of gorgeous clematis (*Clematis spp.*), some evergreen in warmer areas (Zone 7 and above), are possibilities. Hardy kiwi (*Actinidia arguta;* see description on page 205) is an excellent candidate for trellising for shade purposes. Both a male and a female vine are necessary for fruit production. Trumpet creeper (*Campsis radicans*) is a vigorous, deciduous vine, and its flowers are another favorite with hummingbirds. The seeds make excellent wildlife forage. Hops

(*Humulus lupulus*) die back to the ground each winter but grow so quickly from perennial roots that effective trellising is possible. They can be aggressive in cool, moist environments, so you may need to isolate their roots underground. Homebrewers will relish the fine floral bouquet fresh hops add to their beer. Scarlet runner bean (*Phaseolus coccinus,* nitrogen-fixing) is a fast-growing annual vine with beautiful racemes of purple flowers that mature into edible scarlet beans. They can be perennial in warmer zones and also often reseed themselves. Check your local garden shop for other potential twiners that will do well in your area. The main problem with twiners is their propensity for wrapping around themselves, sometimes forming a tangled mass of unsightly twigs. Occasional pruning is usually required.

Tendril climbers, sometimes called true vines, make perhaps the best candidates for trellising over windows. Most famous (and useful) by far is the grape. The two dominant species are the European grape (*Vitis vinifera*) and the North American grape (*Vitis labrusca*). Hundreds of cultivars and hybrids exist, many very location specific. Generally, the European grape is used for wine and the North American grape is used for juice, fresh fruit, and jam. Also of note are the muscadines (*Vitis rotundifolia*), which thrive into Zone 6. These are also excellent fresh or for juice or jam and are the most trouble-free grape if conditions are warm enough. Dozens of cultivars of muscadines are available.

It's hard to imagine why you wouldn't plant a few grapes. To many, the grape is the symbol of civilization. Even the leaves are edible. A single mature vine can produce 50 or more pounds of fruit. Choosing the correct species and cultivar is very important if you want your grapes to thrive. Generally, established grapevines are very drought hardy.

European grapes are the most finicky of the grapes and suffer from a large variety of bugs and other ailments. Growing them organically is nearly impossible in all but California. Hybrids between European and American grapes exist that make good wines and tend to be more vigorous and trouble-free. However, for use in trellising it's a much safer bet to stick with true American cultivars, especially the muscadines. Their vigor and growth are markedly better.

In recent years the Japanese beetle has invaded and does great damage to the leaves of grapes, as well as to other garden plants and some fruit trees. Again, muscadines are less affected. The beetle is easy to catch, falling to the ground as a defense mechanism when the vine is shaken. Poultry of all varieties absolutely love to eat this bug, so if you can have some residing underneath your grapes, you can debug your grapes and feed your hens simply by giving the trellis a shake. Taking some captured bugs and running them through a blender produces a slurry that when sprayed on grape leaves repels these voracious bugs.

A relatively bug-free tendril climber is the passion-flower (*Passiflora incarnata*), an herbaceous perennial with fascinating showy flowers that will rapidly cover any trellising each springtime (Zone 6 and above). The fruits are edible and have a citrusy taste. The interior of the fruit is heavily seeded like a pomegranate. Passionflowers can be somewhat aggressive in warm climates, so you may want to isolate the rootstock with a buried pot.

Maybe the best thing about trellising is the harder work doesn't happen for a year or two. Once you decide which climber suits your home, climate, and needs best, you stick it in the ground and let it grow for a year with only some easy staking. Once your climber is established, you'll need to construct your trellis. In the interim, a quick trellis can be put together using readily available bamboo and jute twine. Once you're ready for your permanent trellis, toss these on your compost pile.

Building a Horizontal Trellis for Shading
Renter friendly.
Project Time: An afternoon.
Cost: $50–200, depending on size.
Energy Saved: High. Shading, especially of windows, is extremely effective at reducing interior temperatures in summertime.

FIG. 10.9. **Horizontal trellis system.**

Ease of Use: Harvesting fruits can be somewhat more difficult when they are high up over windows.
Maintenance Level: Low. A well-constructed trellis could need some occasional tightening, and the climber will need some annual pruning.
Skill Levels: Carpentry: Basic.
Materials: 9-gauge galvanized or 12½-gauge high-tensile fence wire, trellis brackets (enough for every 10 feet or less), spring tighteners, washers.
Tools: Drill, wire cutters, needle-nose pliers, adjustable wrench or ratchet set, pilot drill bit for lags.

Building a well-functioning deciduous trellis for shading passive solar glazing is much simpler than building a permanent overhang. Even if you're just shading eastern or western walls, a wire trellis has the advantage of not only being long-lasting but also letting all available sunlight strike your home and enter any windows in morning or afternoon during winter. Concerning southern applications, since the deciduous vine will lose its leaves as the sun sinks in the sky in autumn and the solar gain becomes necessary, an accurate calculation of the horizontal overhang for shading purposes is not necessary. Generally, 2 feet of overhang for a one-story wall will provide plenty of shading during the hotter summer months as well as plenty of sun for your vine's happiness and well-being.

The basic components of a trellis system are shown in figure 10.9.

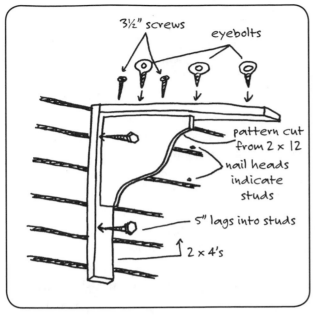

3½" screws

eyebolts

pattern cut from 2 × 12

nail heads indicate studs

5" lags into studs

2 × 4's

FIG. 10.10. **Horizontal bracket.**

Making brackets. Trellis brackets can be purchased from garden supply stores or made out of a few sections of 2 × 12 and 2 × 4, which, if not a moisture-resistant wood, should be protected from the weather with some linseed oil or primer and paint. Cut out something curvy (see figure 10.10) with a jigsaw, making a pattern with some cardboard first. Finish out the bracket with a 2-foot piece of 2 × 4 on the two straight sides, using several 3½-inch exterior screws. This bracket will require eyeholes to be placed in the top of the bracket for holding wire. Note that wire must be used and not lathing as is the case with many trellises, as the lathing will block too much sun in the wintertime. For more durable assembly, use stainless-steel components (including the wire) instead of galvanized.

Assembling the trellis. Assembly of the trellis system is relatively straightforward, although a few points are crucial. The trellis brackets must be secured by lag screws into the structural members of your home, not just into the siding. If your home is made of masonry, thread cement screws through predrilled holes in the mortar. For wood-frame houses, find vertical studs by looking for the line of nails in the siding, making sure to get purchase for all of the required lags in the trellis bracket. For the bracket described above, drill through

the vertical section of the 2 × 4 next to the attached 2 × 12, making sure to leave space for a washer. At least two 5-inch lags should be used to provide plenty of purchase through the 2 × 4 and weatherboard into the actual stud. For metal brackets shorter lags can be used.

Attaching the wire involves threading two sections starting at each end and meeting in the middle at a spring tightener, which will keep your trellis wire from sagging, when your grape or passionflower is laden with fruit, for example. The wire can be held in place at the ends by wrapping it numerous times around a washer that is larger than the hole in the bracket or simply being tied through the eyehole. Thread the two wires into the spring tightener and ratchet it tight.

There are other methods for tightening wire, including Daisy tighteners and Hayes-style Strainers. Tension springs are the most commonly available, at least where we live, but any style can be used.

Windbreaks and Other Landscaping Considerations

Much literature has been devoted to landscaping strategies that involve tall deciduous trees on the east and west side of homes for summertime shading. While this is certainly effective, it blocks many other solar options from being pursued. The roof can no longer be used for photovoltaic or solar hot-water or air systems, and large amounts of gardening and orchard space are lost as a result. Large trees are not a good match for tighter urban spaces, as they also undermine home foundations, underground sewer and plumbing lines, and sidewalks and streets and can foul rainwater-catchment systems, as well as shading any of your neighbor's attempts at PV or solar hot water. The same cooling effects can be achieved by other strategies while maintaining your access to the sun (see chapter 7).

For windbreaks on the northern and sometimes western sides of houses, evergreen trees can be used to greatly reduce heat loss by reducing the wind load. Again, keep your neighbor's solar gain in mind as these trees mature. Consider smaller trees or harvesting larger trees if they get too tall. For a windbreak to be effective, there needs to be foliage near the ground.

Tree windbreaks are most effective when what you are trying to protect is 8 to 10 times farther away than the trees are tall, although they are still effective much closer in. Medium density is preferred, meaning about half of the wind is allowed through (this corresponds to how much light is allowed to pass through when looking at a stand of trees, so it's not too hard to make a visual estimate by looking at the branches of a mature specimen of the type of tree you are considering planting). If you're using very dense trees like red cedars, you'll want to have some space in between your trees. Otherwise, turbulence can develop downwind of the break and reduce its effectiveness. Keep in mind that red cedar can cause apple and other blights. Check the compatibility of your evergreens with any fruit trees you're thinking about planting.

Generally, a great many trees are planted initially and then thinned as they grow. Alternately, a quick-growing species like Leland cyprus is planted for quick effect, and a row of slower-growing spruce, fir, holly, et cetera, is planted beside it. The Leland cyprus is then harvested once the slower, growing species grows tall enough.

There are at least a dozen species of pine nut that produce excellent edible seeds, can do double duty as a windbreak, and grow in almost every zone. The Korean pine (*Pinus koraiensis*) is the most widely cultivated in the United States. Pine nuts are harvested from the cones and contain up to 31 grams of protein per 100 grams, the most of any nut. Many of these species will eventually grow very tall, upwards of 100 feet, and lose their windbreaking characteristics although their food production will be going strong. The dwarf Siberian pine (*Pinus pumlia*) tops out at 9 feet, although it is much less frequently cultivated.

Trellising Walls as a Windbreak

Alternatively, you can create a windbreak right where it's needed, on the northern wall of your house. An effective way to do this is either by planting evergreen shrubs on the north side and keeping them pruned or by creating a trellis and growing evergreen vines. Keep in mind that the north side of your home is the most vulnerable to insect damage, especially termites. You never want to create a permanently damp area on any side of your home, but the northern side is the most vulnerable, the northeast corner especially so. The idea is to greatly reduce the airflow between your home and its coldest side, not eliminate that flow altogether. This is something that will require annual maintenance, usually an early spring pruning. For shrubs, prune off the lowest branches so the bottom part of your home can dry out.

If your northern wall is masonry, dampness is much less of a concern. What is a concern in this regard is the poor insulative value of masonry in general if your wall is, indeed, solid masonry and not just a veneer. If it is solid, you want to build up as many layers of vegetation as possible to actually create stagnant air gaps that provide insulation. Vining is an easy and effective method for accomplishing this. Greater care needs to be taken with facade masonry walls, by far the more common type in the United States, to ensure that the interior wood wall is not getting damp.

For masonry walls, English ivy (*Hedera helix*) is a common choice as an evergreen vine, although as previously mentioned it can be very aggressive. Variegated or duckfooted cultivars are showier and easier to contain. For the vertical trellis described below, native honeysuckle (*Lonicera sempervirens*) or evergreen clematis makes a good choice. Remember, in climate zones colder than 8, evergreen vines are for northern vertical trellises and deciduous vines are for all others in order to allow winter passive solar gain. Also, wire trellises are best for twining or tendril-type vines.

Building a Vertical Wall Trellis for a Windbreak

Renter friendly.

Project Time: An afternoon.

Cost: $50–100.

Energy Saved: High; can cut winter heat loss by up to 25 percent.

Ease of Use: N/A.

Maintenance Level: Low; requires some early spring pruning.

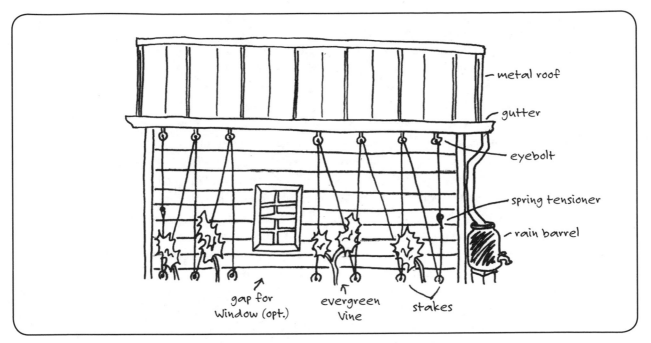

FIG. 10.11. **Vertical trellis system.**

Skill Levels: Carpentry: Basic.

Materials: 9-gauge galvanized or 12½-gauge high-tensile fence wire, spring tensioners, 12+-inch stakes, eyebolts.

Tools: Drill, wire cutters, pilot bit for eyebolts, heavy hammer, plumb bob.

First, be sure that the grade slopes away from the north side of your home before adding any permanent landscaping there. If the area is wet or boggy, it may be necessary to increase the drainage of your site before you begin.

Laying out your trellis. Once you are satisfied that the area below your wall drains well, building a trellis is relatively straightforward. There are many ways to build a trellis; this is the most simple we know of. The basic idea is to run wire from a stake in the ground to either an eave or an eyebolt in the wall with a spring tensioner set in to keep the wire taut.

If the north side of your home is eaved, then the eyebolts can be attached to the underside of the eave. If the north side of your home is gabled, then the eyebolts will need to be placed in the wall. Most vines will easily reach two stories, although the coverage is apt to be less dense as height increases.

Consider window placement and the relative value these northern windows have for summer cooling and lighting. Northside windows are some of the worst violators in terms of cold air infiltration. At a minimum, these windows should have both exterior storms and interior insulated curtains or shutters if they are not eliminated altogether. If the above are employed along with a northern-wall trellis, heat loss from these windows can be dramatically reduced. A fair amount of light will still enter even if the windows are permanently shaded by an evergreen trellis close to the wall. It may be worth skipping the windowed sections of wall with your trellis if the light gain is crucial to the comfort of the interior rooms.

Locating rafters. For eaves, locate the rafters by finding the nails holding up the underside sheathing. For gable ends, decide how far up you want your trellis to go and locate the studs in the wall by finding the nails holding up the weatherboard. You'll want your eyebolts to get at least 2 inches of purchase in your rafters or studs; 4-inch eyebolts should work fine. Predrill holes the length of your eyebolt. The drill bit should be equal in width to the shaft of the lag (excluding the threads).

You'll want your trellis to be at least a foot away from the bottom of your wall. You'll need to place your stakes at least as far out from the wall as your eave extends, or your vines won't get enough sun to grow. If your eave juts out less than this or if the end is gabled, your wires will end up inclining toward your wall. The foot of space at the bottom will ensure there is enough air circulation down there for the siding and foundation to dry out.

Most rafters are spaced either 16 or 24 inches on center. Sixteen-inch spacing is close enough for most evergreen twining vines (there are no tendril evergreens that we're aware of) to wrap around and form a continuous wall. If the spacing is greater than 16 inches, then some overlapping of the wire will be needed.

Placing the stakes. Once your eyebolts are in place, drop a plumb bob (one can be made with a string and a rock) to find your stake placement. Doing this will add a professional appearance to your trellis. Drive in your stakes, spaced at least a foot out from the wall (sandier soils require longer stakes). Using stout stakes that have an eye or hook will allow for the use of one continuous wire to run from the first stake to the eyebolt and then through the successive stakes and bolts. These can then be maintained taut by one spring tensioner in the middle. It may be easier, although requiring more materials and thus being more expensive, to run separate lines of wire from each eyebolt in the wall to the stake in the ground, with a spring tensioner in each line. Installation is straightforward, but be sure not to overtighten the tensioner and pull any of your stakes out of the ground. As the vine grows and adds weight to the trellis, it may be necessary to occasionally tighten the spring tensioner.

Once all your wire is up, if you haven't done so already, it's time to plant your vines!

THE POTATO AND THE CHICKEN

Permit us a few words on these two paragons of food creation. Often overlooked, they can be amazingly productive additions to even some of the smallest of urban lots.

The Potato

For creating food calories with minimal inputs of time, maintenance, and energy, the potato (*Solanum tuberosum*) simply cannot be beat. Spuds can be grown almost everywhere in the country, and many locales can harvest a spring and autumn crop.

Much to both our and the potato's misfortune, today's average spud is one of the worst fossil-fuel offenders that regularly makes an appearance on our plates. Often grown several thousand miles away (Idaho, where lots of potatoes come from, is about 2,400 miles from us, for instance), the common spud is also a prodigious consumer of fossil-fuel-derived fertilizers and pesticides.

There is, quite simply, no reason for this. Even folks with no gardening experience can organically grow tens or even hundreds of pounds of this extremely versatile vegetable with a minimal input of effort. Because the industrial potato is one of the worst offenders of sustainability and rectifying this problem by growing your own spuds is so straightforward, no garden should be diminished by their absence.

The potato requires heavy loads of pesticides only when grown in monoculture. Once the potato beetle or blight appears, it spreads like wildfire, easily hopping from plant to plant. Agribusinessmen (formerly known as farmers) prevent this from occurring on large potato farms by saturating every square inch of leaf and soil with herbicides and pesticides. There's a good chance, depending on where you live, that your homegrown spuds won't be troubled by any serious pests. Again, you won't know until you try!

Here's how to grow your own.

Potato Barrel

Renter friendly.

Project Time: An hour.

Cost: $5–10.

Energy Saved: High; conventional potatoes require large fossil-fuel inputs.

Ease of Use: N/A.

Maintenance Level: Low.

FIG. 10.12. **Baby potatoes emerging in spring from an old barrel filled with compost and mulch. An easy harvest of up to ten pounds of potatoes can be accomplished by turning the barrel over once the plants have flowered and yellowed off. The compost/mulch mix is then added to a nearby garden bed, and the potatoes are taken into the kitchen for cooking and storage. Potato barrels are a simple and easy method of increasing food production in tight spaces.**

Skill Levels: None required.

Materials: At least one old bucket with holes in the bottom or 6-foot sections of at least 2-foot-tall chicken wire or hardware cloth; a few seed potatoes; compost; leaves or straw.

Tools: Shovel, wire cutters.

Obtaining planting stock. Selecting a strain of potato that does well in your area is crucial for success. Buy a locally grown, preferably organic variety from a farmers' market or one of hundreds of heirloom varieties from a supplier that specifies your region. The potato thrives in cooler but not freezing weather. It requires around 100 days to mature, during the bulk

of which time you want the average temperature to be in the neighborhood of 60 degrees F, avoiding heavy freezes or long periods of days well about 80 degrees F. Where we live, for instance, we can usually get away with planting in mid-March, harvesting when the tops have flowered and the plants turned yellow in late June. If we want, we can plant again in early August and harvest again in mid-November.

Planting your bucket. What makes the potato so easy to grow is that it will thrive in a variety of organic matters, including compost, and that it loves to grow in buckets. Think of your potato barrel as the final stage of your compost as it moves from the compost bin to the garden. Take a bucket at least 12 inches tall with holes in the bottom or no bottom at all. Alternatively, or in conjunction, take 6-foot lengths of 18- to 24-inch-tall chicken wire and form tubes (they don't call 'em "tubers" for nothing). Shovel in some straw or leaves for drainage, then a layer of compost. Do this until you get about 10 inches from the top, or until you have at least 10 inches of organic matter, then throw in your spud eyes, about 6–8 inches apart from each other and a few inches from the sides of your bucket (further in from the sides if you're using wire tubes). Layer on more leaves or straw and then another layer of compost, totaling at least another 4–6 more inches.

Water heavily once, then sit back and watch your spuds grow. The buckets and mulch will keep your taters weed free and moist in all but the driest of climates. Spread your buckets or tubes out through your garden to make sure any potential diseases or pests don't find their way from barrel to barrel, making sure they get at least 5 to 6 hours of sun a day.

Harvesting. After the plants flower and the tops yellow and die back, your potatoes are ready for eating (you can dig new potatoes before this if you wish). Turn the bucket over and pick up your tubers. Eat fresh or air-dry for several days and then store in a cool, dark place.

The compost you dumped out is ready for dressing any of your other garden plants. Fill the bucket with new compost for your next potato barrel to ensure plenty of available nutrients and that no diseases or other potato pests stay in the soil.

The sweet potato can be grown in a similar manner and is almost as prodigious. Sweet potatoes, however, love heat, although varieties have been bred that can tolerate even cool northern summers. Sweet potatoes are propagated from slips (shoots sprouting off a mature sweet potato), which can be purchased locally or grown by placing a sweet potato in a cardboard box of damp wood mulch in early spring. As the potato sends up new shoots, they are picked off and planted after all danger of frost has passed. Sweet potatoes require at least 120 frost-free (preferably hot) days before harvest.

The Chicken

Having a productive omnivore as a garden companion can do wonders for recycling potential wastes into assets. By far the most useful in our opinion is the chicken. A few hens can eat a wide variety of things that otherwise might go straight to the compost pile, producing quantities of delicious eggs as they do so. And the egg is as versatile in the kitchen as the hen is in the garden. Taken together, the potato and the egg provide homegrown foundations for a variety of garden-only meals that otherwise would be much less fulfilling. Generally, within city limits hen-only flocks are mandated, although some municipalities ban even these (in which case, pester your councilperson and start a petition!).

Chickens can eat near about anything, including kitchen scraps, extra worms from the vermiculture bin, spent grain used first in brewing and then for mushroom cultivation, weeds, damaged fruit or the leftovers from juicing, et cetera. They also can provide for themselves quite well, digging up earthworms and snacking on other bugs, especially Japanese beetles, and eating a wide range of clover and grasses. Their nitrogen-rich waste can be collected and is a boon to methane production in the biodigestor or simply composted and added back to the garden.

Additional grain is usually required to keep your hens robust and laying. Beyond that and a place to dwell, it doesn't take too much to keep them happy. One hundred square feet can easily maintain a few birds, and this can also be used as orchard space once the trees or bushes are tall enough to stay out of their hungry beaks. Grapes are an excellent companion, providing shade for the chickens and plenty of protein when the Japanese beetles are shaken off.

Another idea is enclosing your hens in a perimeter garden fence, known as a "chicken moat," developed by Joe Jenkins (for more of Joe's ideas, see "Humanure (Aerobic Decomposition)" in chapter 9). The birds can be penned in an elongated fenced-in area around the perimeter of the garden. Grapes and other low-growing berry bushes can be trellised on top, and fruit not harvested will be eaten by the hens. Rhizomatous weeds and grasses will be kept from creeping into the garden, and the fence will keep out unwelcome garden guests like dogs, rabbits, and even deer if built tall enough. The birds will eat most any weed you toss at them from the garden and are great company.

Although raising animals does require some additional responsibility, they're great entertainment and good companions. Chickens take about as much maintenance as the family dog, but you don't have to take them on walks. Kids that might otherwise be inside wasting electricity being brainwashed by the TV will spend hours watching chickens grub in the dirt for worms. While obviously not a requirement of a fossil-fuel-free home, they're definitely a bonus for everything they provide.

RESOURCES

Books

Coleman, Eliot. 1999. *The Four-Season Harvest: Organic Vegetables from Your Home Garden All Year Around*. White River Junction, VT: Chelsea Green Publishing. A great resource on organic gardening and extending the season to all twelve months—even as far north as Maine—via unheated greenhouses and cold frames.

Dunnett, Nigel, and Noël Kingsbury. 2008. *Planting Green Roofs and Living Walls*. Portland: Timber Press. Great introduction to green roofs, with in-depth information on loads, construction, and appropriate species.

Flores, Heather. 2006. *Food Not Lawns: How to Turn Your Yard into a Garden and Your Neighborhood into a Community*. White River Junction, VT: Chelsea Green Publishing. Food is the foundation of all human relations, and our relationship with it needs some fixing.

Kourik, Robert. 1986. *Designing and Maintaining Your Edible Landscape Naturally*. Santa Rosa, CA: Metamorphic Press. A great introduction to the topic.

Reich, Lee. 2004. *Uncommon Fruits for Every Garden*. Portland: Timber Press.

Smith, Edward. 2006. *Incredible Vegetables from Self-Watering Containers*. North Adams, MA: Storey. Low-maintenance container gardening; great for folks with tight spaces.

Stamets, Paul. 2000. *Growing Gourmet and Medicinal Mushrooms*. Berkeley, CA: Ten Speed Press.

Stamets, Paul. 2005. *Mycelium Running: How Mushrooms Can Help Save the World*. Berkeley, CA: Ten Speed Press.

Toensmeier, Eric. 2007. *Perennial Vegetables: From Artichoke to Zuiki Taro: A Gardener's Guide to Over 100 Delicious and Easy to Grow Edibles*. White River Junction, VT: Chelsea Green Publishing.

Internet

American Community Gardening Association. www.communitygarden.org

Bountiful Backyards. Durham's edible-landscaping collective. www.bountifulbackyards.com

Fungi Perfecti. Paul Stamets's spore and spawn company. www.fungi.com

Food Not Lawns. Promotes edible landscaping in the Northwest. www.foodnotlawns.com

GardenWeb. Excellent forums on every aspect of gardening. www.gardenweb.com

Local Harvest. Information on nearby farms, community-supported agriculture (CSAs), farmers' markets, and food co-ops. www.localharvest.org

Mushroom Expert. Great information and pictures for identifying mushrooms. www.mushroomexpert.com

MykoWeb. Great compilations of photos, mushroom clubs, recipes, et cetera. www.mykoweb.com

North American Fruit Explorers. Listservs, library, consulting services, and supplier information for almost all fruits and nuts, even the fruitier and nuttier ones! Great site. www.nafex.org

Sources of rare edible plants and seeds: www
.usefulplants.org (NC), ww.southernexposure
.com (VA), www.fedco.com (ME), www
.jlhudson.com (CA), www.rareseeds.com (MO),
www.forestfarm.com (OR), www
.bountifulgardens.org (CA), www.horizonherbs
.com (OR), www.oikostreecrops.com (MI),
www.tripplebrookfarm.com (MA), www.eat
-it.com (VA)

Summer Cover Crops. From North Carolina State
University. Great breakdown of cover crops and
their planting and function. www.ces.ncsu
.edu/depts/hort/hil/hil-37.html

Magazines

Permaculture Activist. Great magazine with thought-
provoking articles and supply resources.
www.permacultureactivist.net

Products

Greentech, Inc. Green roof planters (4 × 4 foot).
www.greentechitm.com

Xero Flor. Sells roll-out preseeded green roof mats.
www.xeroflora.com

Endnotes

1. Pfeiffer, Dale Allen. *Eating Fossil Fuels.* 2006. New
   Society Publishers: Gabriola, BC, Canada.
2. Pfeiffer, Dale Allen. *Eating Fossil Fuels.* 2006. New
   Society Publishers: Gabriola, BC, Canada.
3. Barrionuevo, Alexei. "Imports Spurring Push to
   Subsidize Produce." *New York Times*, December 3,
   2006.

Transportation

INTRODUCTION

No other decision affects the sustainability of your transportation options as much as location. It's a cliché that the three most important factors affecting your real estate decisions are location, location, and location, but the same could be said for the three most important factors affecting the sustainability of your transportation options. Living near where you work, shop, eat, and play is vital to reducing the amount of energy dedicated to your mobility to a level that can be sustained without fossil fuels.

OUR STORY

Mobility is another area that produced almost endless debate in our currently two-person household. A big reason for our move from the country to the city was to become less dependent, if not totally independent, of the automobile. Moving downtown meant we were close enough to friends, groceries, and entertainment that the potential existed to not ever get in a car. The bus system here in Durham exists, but public transportation is definitely not a priority for most, but not all, of our ill-informed politicians. Even basic amenities like benches at bus stops, much less some kind of awning to protect from the heat and rain, are all but nonexistent. We do not use the bus as much as we should.

Part of resolving our transportation problem revolved around our careers. Rebekah installs photo-voltaic and solar hot-water panels for a living; Stephen is a carpenter who works on things like metal roofs and passive solar retrofits. For Rebekah, there's not currently enough business in the core of downtown to keep her employed locally. Plus, her tools and the materials have to be brought to the job site, and the job is usually completed in a few days or a week. This means that her tools have to be moved often from one distant location to another. And we do mean distant. Many of the folks interested in photovoltaics made the same mistake we did, wanting to live a low-impact lifestyle but trying to do it way out in the sticks where no bus dares to tread. So a perennial roadblock was how to maintain Rebekah's career of spreading solar electricity in our area while trying to be as minimally car-dependent as possible.

Since we had three cars (yes, that's right, we had three cars), we knew we had to get rid of at least two of

FIG. 11.1. **Sustainable transportation is not possible with the continued hegemony of the automobile.** Cartoon by Kirk Anderson

them, and those two had to be the two fossil-fuel burners: a '98 Chevy S-10 pickup and a '95 Toyota Tercel. The last, a '77 Mercedes 300D (diesel), might be a keeper, the problem being that even though it could be run on biodiesel, it got about 25 mpg compared with the Tercel's 47 mpg. The Mercedes had seen relatively light duty; we'd purchased it a while back as we experimented with locally available biodiesel and drove it only on weekends.

The question became: do we keep the Mercedes, fit it out with a rack and even perhaps a hitch, and make it Rebekah's main commuting car, or do we sell it as well and think about purchasing a new vehicle for her job? Since Stephen is working nearby and his jobs generally last for much longer, it's not difficult to take all the necessary tools over to the job site and leave them there some evening, having any larger items required delivered by the hardware store or sawmill, and then commuting daily by foot or bike.

But what about for Rebekah? Quite honestly, it was quite difficult to give up the trusty little Tercel. Comparatively, it sipped gas, sometimes achieving 49 mpg, even with over 200,000 miles; it was extremely reliable and initially cost about as much as the two replacement batteries we would have theoretically needed if we'd been driving a Prius the last dozen years ($3,600 each dealer-installed, every 100,000 miles). But every time at the gas pump, the heartache would return. Who died for us to fill up this time? It had to go.

We test-drove an electric car, the Bleecker ZX40. It's a neighborhood electric vehicle (NEV), or what Rebekah refers to as a glorified golf cart. Stephen's reply: what's wrong with a glorified golf cart? Well, the price for starters. It was around $16,000 and its speed was limited to 25 mph. Actually 25 mph would work for most of our in-town driving, and if we just needed a little something to go to the grocery store or over to a friend's on a cold, rainy night (and, oh yeah, if we made a lot more money), it might have been perfect. One problem, however, was that the volt meter didn't work, telling us how much charge was left in the battery. This is equivalent to test-driving a gas car at a dealer with the fuel gauge not working. Rebekah, who

FIG. 11.2. **Yes, we know, it's a car. Given our budget, this was the best choice among many, many bad ones to serve part of our current transportation needs. Until a hybrid/biodiesel car cooperative opens up in the neighborhood, we'll be stuck owning and driving this 1977 orange Mercedes 300D on used veggie oil. For now, the shackles remain.**

deals with volt meters and batteries all the time, was especially unimpressed. If this part was already broken, how long would the thing work? Nobody knows yet, and we won't be the ones to tell you, at least not from our own personal experience.

Next we thought about selling the Mercedes and getting a newer, more reliable diesel that would run on biodiesel. We have a local biofuels co-op (Piedmont Biofuels) that makes most of their biodiesel from locally available waste products. Currently, they're using chicken guts, since central North Carolina has lots of chicken farms, and virgin soybean oil. While we're supportive of our biofuels co-op and the local model they are trying to create, nevertheless, running our car off industrial meat detritus and GMO Roundup-Ready virgin soybeans does not make us feel all warm and fuzzy inside. The argument is often made that at least the soybeans support local farmers, but in fact the large agricultural concerns like Archer Daniels Midland and their fossilized brethren are by far the primary beneficiaries, and these are not folks we're particularly interested in supporting. As is often the case, the question with transportation becomes: how much are we willing to compromise ourselves to maintain our excessive mobility?

Another concern was that the new diesels available for sale were slim pickings, especially for our price range, which was $20,000 max. All the new diesel trucks are bigger than our house and cost about as much, so they were out of the question. A year-or-two-old Volkswagen Golf TDI with a rack was a possibility, or even a newish Beetle TDI, but the cars have some reliability issues and seem to be expensive to repair. Older Volkswagen models were available, although not locally and oftentimes at steep prices. Even though these vehicles got better gas mileage than our Mercedes, it didn't seem to make much sense to sell the Mercedes and still have to pay several thousand dollars extra for an almost equally old car. We were beginning to realize that despite the hundreds of models of cars out there, almost none of them are diesels. When it comes down to it, despite the untold number of different car models, there really isn't a real range of choices. In countries that actually understand some of the harm cars and gasoline create, gas is higher priced and smaller car models are available. In Japan, there's a virtual mini-car craze going on, and of course in Europe, the Smart Car has been around for years. Finally, the Smart Car has arrived stateside. Hopefully this is a harbinger of a wider range of different vehicle sizes here.

So for the lack of options as much as anything else we decided to keep the '77 Mercedes and have it converted to run on used fryer oil. Several things worked in our favor. We already had the car. Our friend Luc lived right up the block and did conversions using the Elsbett kit, a nifty German company's invention that allows for use of the original tank with any combination of veggie oil, biodiesel, and standard diesel. Also, being in the city meant we were near lots of restaurants that were potential sources of used oil. While obviously not everyone can do this (there are many more people than restaurants), it's still a relatively untapped resource locally.

Two other considerations tipped us over the edge. The first was that, as is the case for most major appliances, about half the energy consumed over the lifetime of a car is used in its initial production. Since the median age for a car is 17 years, any use past that age is essentially energy-production-free. Consider a hypothetical SUV named the Ford Explosion that gets 12 mpg. In reality, when its embodied production energy is considered, it gets more like 6 mpg over the course of its 17 years, since half the energy went into its creation. If it operates beyond this, we can finally consider its mpg to be 12. Keeping the vehicle running displaces the expenditure of additional energy in the production of another vehicle. Of course, if it is retired before the 17 years, then its lifetime mpg is less than 6 mpg, since the totality of the embodied production energy did not get used.

Our Mercedes is way past its median life span, so the real miles per gallon including embodied energy is closer to 25. That's about equivalent to a new Volkswagen Golf TDI that gets around 50 mpg. And our burnt-orange Mercedes is a lot cooler looking than those new Golfs. One of the big questions now is, do we get to tag on another theoretical 25 mpg if our '77 300D makes it past 34 years? (Hey, that's only three away!)

This is the energy economy inherent in using products for as long as possible, even though they might not be the most energy efficient. Making something new, even if it's quite energy efficient in its operation, still takes a lot of energy, and this is a concept that gets short shrift in discussions about appliance and vehicle efficiency, probably because our society thinks it can solve almost every problem by going shopping. Generally, it is not worth retiring a vehicle or appliance early (i.e., before it is too costly to repair) unless the new product you are purchasing is *more than* twice as efficient than what you are replacing.

We both have older thin-tire bikes that ride well and are our main source of in-town mobility. Incredibly, we got Rebekah's bike from some lost soul who was tossing his bike in the dump. In our land of plenty, it's not difficult to come up with a good bike for cheap. Here in Durham, we're blessed with the Durham Bike Co-op, a group of enthusiasts who are dedicated to taking old bikes and getting them back out on the road as well as helping cyclists learn how to maintain their

Biofuels: Better Off To Fill Your Tank Or Your Tummy?

No area is more ripe for conservation than our mobility. We use as much fossil energy for our transportation needs as for almost all aspects of our home.[1] It's not hard to figure out why when we take a look at the average car on the road, typically a 3,000-pound vehicle toting around 150 pounds of cargo. With this as our baseline, at best we're looking at 5 percent efficiency, with 95 percent of the energy going to moving the weight of the vehicle as opposed to the cargo. Unfortunately, based on government figures,[2] only about 15 percent of the fuel burned in a gasoline engine goes to move the car down the road, much of the rest being lost to heat produced by the motor and friction from tires. So we're already at less than 1 percent efficiency, without taking into account refining and transportation losses of the original fuel. Less than 1 percent

isn't quite zero, but it's damn close! Simply put, there's no way such a system of mobility could ever be sustainable for all our transportation needs, no matter if the fuel comes from soybeans or switchgrass or pools of dead dinosaurs and ferns buried under the earth.

As an example of the automobile's inefficiency, say your car is powered by biodiesel derived from soybeans rather than diesel fuel. The 41 pounds of soybeans it took to make the gallon of biodiesel[3] would propel the car about 30 miles. If instead you were on a 15-pound bicycle, you would burn about 500 Kcal/hour at 15 mph. Of the 158,670 Kcal in the 41 pounds of soybeans you would expend 30 percent in metabolism, leaving you with 111,069 Kcal to push your bike down the road. This would keep you going for 222 hours and take you 3,332 miles, or all the way across the country and then some. From this biofuel source, the bicycle ends up being over 100 times more efficient than the automobile. See figure 11.3.

own bikes. Every Sunday you can take your bike over there and for some volunteer work they'll let you use their facilities and generously share their knowledge of how to keep your wheels spinning. Many localities have similar bicycle recycling programs, some run by the local government. Check with your municipality for some potentially cheap wheels.

First and foremost, before the Mercedes and bicycle, we use our legs to propel ourselves forward in one of the most efficient and highly developed organisms known to the world, the human body. We walk.

THE OPTIONS

Like cooking without fossil fuels, you may find that having a few transport options depending on the situation will provide needed flexibility. While a bicycle might be the best option for the short trip during the

day, taking the bus or using a car for the occasional shopping trip on a cold, damp, and dark December evening can be worth a great deal. But before you decide to sell your car and buy a scooter, you have to know the options and how well they work. In America, where many people think the right to a car is enshrined in the Constitution, this topic is clouded by obfuscation and outright propaganda from dozens of groups with conflicting agendas. Hopefully by taking a closer look at the options and their relative efficiencies we can clear up the decision-making process a little bit.

The bicycle and the car are the two extremes of our mobility options. Obviously, a car is not a bicycle nor vice versa. In some situations we want them to do very different things. But much of the time we are asking them to do exactly the same thing: move our bodies from one point to the next. We are not advocating everyone bicycling everywhere all the time. However, coming up with a system of carbon-free mobility that

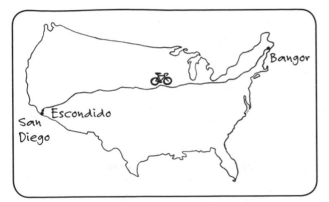

FIG. 11.3. **Using biofuels to power our bicycles rather than our vehicles can mean a hundredfold increase in efficiency. In this example, soybeans converted to biodiesel in a car instead of human energy on a bike would leave the motorist stranded in Escondido, just 30 miles north of San Diego. The bicyclist, on the other hand, takes those same calories and makes it 3,332 miles all the way to Bangor, Maine.**

does not include the bicycle seems either excessively constrained or downright impossible. That said, let's look at the other options and how they fare in getting the job done.

(We're much indebted to James Strickland's excellent Web site [http://strickland.ca/efficiency.html] for discovering many of these sources and compiling much of this information.)

By its nature, mobility requires lots of energy. Forget about all the other wasteful aspects of a highly mobile life like eating out or the portable electronics that we drop, break, or lose. Instead, concentrate on the vast amount of energy it takes just getting around through the course of the day, about nine barrels of oil or its equivalent every year (or 378 gallons),[4] with many folks using much more than this. We need to first take a long, hard look at what the advantages and disadvantages are of all this racing hither and yon. Is our life really better driving out to the suburbs every day just to eat dinner and then go to bed? Might it not be much more efficient AND lead to a much better life if instead we lived near where we worked, we had much more free time and money, and we could go out hiking or canoeing in the country on the weekend? Looking at table 11.1, we find that by far the most

efficient methods of transportation are self-propelled. Obviously, these have a more limited range. But is it really worth expending 50 times as much energy to drive 12 miles to work every day instead of moving closer to work and biking for 5 miles (each method taking about a half hour)?

BIOFUELS

There has been much talk lately of biofuels coming to save the day from the twin scourges of peak fossil energy and global climate disruption. In order to talk frankly about this subject we have to take a look at the energy return on energy invested (EROEI) or net energy of these fuels compared with what our automobilized, industrialized society was built on. First, take note that a car operating on biodiesel is less efficient at accomplishing its goal of moving a body down the road than the progenitor of the biofueled transportation options, the horse. We seem to have forgotten that all transport (and all work, for that matter) was biofueled in the not-so-distant past. And we shouldn't be surprised that a horse (or a human) that has evolved over millennia (and weighs less) should be better at its job than a car.

So what is the energy return on ethanol and biodiesel? That is, for a calorie of input, how much do we get in return? It takes a certain amount of energy to grow these crops, most of it from fossil fuels, and we need to know if the fuel we end up with is worth more energy-wise than the fuel we started with. How much of the sun's energy were we able to catch and store during the year we were growing these crops? By much reckoning, the 350 gallons of ethanol we get from an acre of (genetically modified, Roundup-Ready) corn does not exceed, at least not by much, the energy (Btu) equivalent of the 230 gallons of gasoline in total (tractors, fertilizers, pesticides, et cetera) it took to grow it, refine it, and ship it. The story for sugar beets or cane is perhaps better, but not by much, and here in the United States, that's not what we're using.

For biodiesel, the story is better, with (genetically modified, Roundup-Ready) soybeans returning

TABLE 11.1 Daily Transportation Options and Their Efficiencies

	Avg. Passenger Miles/1,000 Kcal	Avg. MPH Urban	Avg. MPH Hwy.	Fossil-fuel Free?	Pros	Cons
Average Car[5]	0.6	25	45	Absolutely not!	Readily available, good for hauling larger items.	Killing the planet.
Compact Car[6]	1.2	25	45	No.	Better than regular car, good at hauling medium-sized items.	Still major cause of global climate disruption.
Hybrid Car[7]	1.4	25	45	Limited use of plug-in model could potentially come close.	Better than regular car, good at hauling medium-sized items.	Twice as expensive as compact for almost no benefit if run primarily on gasoline; costly; expensive to maintain.
Diesel Car[8]	0.9	25	45	Biodiesel potentially if used very sparingly.	Diesel engine more efficient; biodiesel has greater net energy return than ethanol.	New models are expensive; used models unreliable or hard to come by.
Horse[8]	2.7	10	15	Yes, if not fed fossil grains.	Beautiful, fun, good companions, manure great for garden.	Stupid laws restrict highway use, extra care required, exposed to the weather.
Walking[10] (5)	23	3	3	Absolutely!	Healthy, free, entertaining.	Slow, exposed to the weather, very hard to haul large items.
Electric Car[11] (6) (Neighborhood Electric Vehicle)	2.3	25	25	Potentially with renewable electric system.	Compact, can move up to four persons or smaller hauls.	Limited availability, and testing, expensive, slow, battery replacement required after a few years.
Bus[12] (7)	5.6	20	45	Potentially with biodiesel.	No maintenance, inexpensive.	Limited availability, scheduling conflicts, difficult for hauling large items.
Light Rail[13] (8)	6.9	25	45	Potentially with biodiesel or renewable electric system.	No maintenance, inexpensive.	Very limited availability depending on location, scheduling conflicts, difficult for hauling large items.
Bicycle[14] (9)	30	10	15	Yes!	Very inexpensive personal transportation.	Exposed to weather, difficult for hauling large items.
Electric-Assist Bike[15] (10)	20	15	15	Potentially with renewable electric system.	Inexpensive personal transportation, assures constant speed	More expensive than regular bike, limited range.
Gas Scooter[16] (11)	2.4	25	35	No.	Much cheaper and more efficient than car.	Exposed to weather, difficult for hauling large items, noisy and polluting two-stroke engine.

*In most places the public transportation options will be running on fossil fuels, but don't take this as a reason not to use them. They are often the most efficient use of these fuels. Comparison of transportation efficiencies courtesy of James Strickland.

FIG. 11.4. **A lush primeval tropical forest in Indonesia, home to myriad species including the threatened orangutan.** Photo by Longgena Ginting

energy somewhere in the neighborhood of between two or four to one (depending on the source), somewhere around 60 gallons net per acre. Since biodiesel is one and a half times as energy dense as ethanol and soybeans use fewer inputs than corn, the energy return ends up being significantly better. But our automobile planet was built on energy returns from fossil fuels that were much, much greater than this. In the early days of the oil industry, it was not uncommon to find a field containing 100 million barrels of oil after drilling a few holes in the ground. The energy return multiple was in the thousands or even millions in some cases, leaving prodigious quantities of excess energy that allowed for the creation of roads crisscrossing the planet and the hundreds of millions of cars that drive on them. By current measures, the net energy from fossil-fuel extraction is between 10 and 20, or about an order of magnitude (ten times) what we're getting from ethanol and biodiesel. Attempting to maintain

our excessively mobile culture using biofuels almost ensures the conversion of all remaining forest to farms for liquid fuel production. Using a gallon of biodiesel a day means having six acres of land permanently dedicated to your mobility needs. There are currently about 3.2 billion acres of arable land worldwide, or about ½ acre per person,[17] so even if you ate nothing you would be using about a dozen times more than the sustainable and equitable level of farmland. A complete transition to biofuels without altering our current transportation infrastructure would mean not just our cars consuming all the available farmland but also a rapine despoiling of the last great forests on the planet. It would mean nothing less than the end of nature and the mass starvation of the dispossessed.

What is ultimately more important than what you are driving is how much you are driving. Any reduction helps, even if it's eliminating only one trip a week. Is there a sustainable level of driving, or do we have

FIG. 11.5. **An Indonesian forest clear-cut in preparation for another palm oil plantation to feed the world's starving automobiles. Bicycles are a biofueled alternative that are 100 times more efficient at moving our bodies around.**

Courtesy Borneo Orangutan Survival International/Rita Sastrawan

to think about eventually abandoning the car altogether? With our half-acre of land, how many gallons of renewable fuel could be produced for your benefit and still leave you with something to eat? Because most agriculture uses fossil fuels and not renewable ones, the numbers quickly become conflated and confused. The acreage numbers are understated because the amount of land it would take to fuel the tractors and the trucks is not included. Nevertheless, it's illuminating to note that our current system of fossil-fuel-subsidized agriculture requires approximately around half an acre of land to feed each person, leaving no equitable distribution of land left over for our thirsty cars.

John Jeavons details a more sustainable approach in his book, *How to Grow More Vegetables*. His alternative, biointensive gardening, produces 100 percent of the required calories for a vegan diet on 3,200 square feet, or less than 1/10th of an acre. For argument's

sake we'll take this best-case scenario, which leaves us roughly 4/10ths of an acre each left over for sustainably raising biofuels. At around 60 gallons an acre for an actually positive net energy fuel like biodiesel from soy, this yields roughly 25 gallons of fuel. This is if the remaining acreage is used in its totality for biofuels and not other things like clothing fibers or dairy and meat production. For a biofueled car of average economy, this produces an annual mobility of around 500 miles, or about a mile and one-third a day.

The point of all this is that the automobile culture as it exists today cannot continue, biofueled or not, with any sense of social and environmental justice. Even cars with doubled efficiency of 40 mpg give us a meager less than three miles a day from our half-acre, and these not-quite-three miles are dairy-less and naked. More satisfaction would likely be achieved if one biked instead of drove and had clothing and the occasional milkshake.

Of course, one does not take a culture that has been built around the automobile and turn it on its head in one fell swoop. Nor does one need to, as long as reductions are consistent and ongoing. While it is important to make a commitment to weaning ourselves from fossil fuels, staking everything on a silver bullet like biofuels will not solve our problems. But that does not mean that they cannot be *part* of the solution.

For example, it could be the case that people could have access to a car when they needed one and we did not use any fossil fuels nor destroy the planet. Instead of each of us owning a car individually, we would all be members of car cooperatives, using these vehicles sparingly when we *really* needed them. Instead of a conventional car, it would instead be a plug-in hybrid ultracompact, say of Smart Car size, running on biodiesel and solar, wind, and wave power. Combined with mass transit for the majority of our mobility needs, our half-gallon of biodiesel a week then might actually get us 100 miles or more. The massive inefficiencies that can be overcome in our current vehicle fleet, combined with advances in renewable electricity, would make a transition to such a society feasible in a few decades or less, *if* we have the motivation and political will.

PUBLIC TRANSPORTATION

Biofuels also start to make sense with public transportation, especially locally sourced biofuels. Generally, riding public transportation is an order of magnitude more efficient than using liquid fuels in a conventional personal vehicle. With public transportation, while you'll still be using fossil fuels to get around, regardless of the type of fuel you'll be using way less of it. And getting your mass transit provider to use more renewable energy may simply be a matter of tapping into the political will of the ridership and demanding that it happen.

It is currently the case that many communities in the United States have meager public-transportation options, and even these meager options are often sorely neglected. And the dominance of the automo-

bile has led to a general sprawl that makes light rail increasingly difficult to implement because of its high fixed and operating costs. Although light rail is more popular in people's imaginations than buses, the fact is that buses do a much better job of using the existing road infrastructure to create a viable mass-transit option. Where communities were built around existing rail infrastructure, maintaining and expanding this infrastructure should be paramount. Yet most often in America this is not the case.

With buses, a kind of chicken-and-egg problem has developed, where no one wants to ride because of the poor quality, and no community wants to improve the quality of its bus service because no one is riding. Breaking this impasse will take some work, most of it in changing people's car-centric mentality and rehabilitating the image of the bus. As Lynn Sloman points out in her book, *Car Sick*, for shorter trips (two miles or less), the bicycle and the bus take roughly the same amount of time on average as driving when door-to-door numbers are used. Yet people instinctively grab the car keys as they go out the door and not the bus schedule or the bike lock, even though many trips fall within this range.

When surveyed, many people give the fact that they are unaware of the routes and/or times as the primary reason for driving instead of taking the bus. Oftentimes the actual bus times and routes would have been sufficient for them to have taken the bus, given their stated waiting times and walking distances in the survey. As an individual, then, becoming informed of the routes and times of your nearest buses is the quickest way to begin reducing your dependence on the automobile. Lynn Slomann estimates that, on average, 40 percent of car trips could instead be accommodated by mass transit already in operation and get folks to their destination on time.

The next 40 percent of trips are ones that could be accommodated by busing with improvements. This means more frequent service, more routes, cleaner buses, waiting areas protected from the weather, bike racks on buses and at bus stands, and so on. If you and others in your community start to break the impasse by riding more for the easy 40 percent, this next 40 percent will most likely start to take care of itself. Increased ridership will produce the motivation for those in charge to improve the service and increase the number of routes. By being a pioneer in this area and riding the bus when feasible, you can help break your community's dependence on the automobile.

The last 20 percent of trips, as Sloman points out, are more intractable. These are the emergency trips, the trips to haul large items, and the trips to out-of-the-way places that might not ever be feasibly served by public transit. At this point, however, car sharing and car co-ops become extremely practical. Some communities have car co-ops already, and you could always start one with neighbors and friends (www.cooperativeauto.net is a network of established Canadian co-ops). Flexcar and Zipcar are two private companies that operate car sharing in a handful of states already, and it may be possible to get enough folks together to convince one of them to open a local branch. One of the great things about car co-ops is the reduction in the amount of cars on the road, sometimes by up to 90 percent, which means much less parking is required. Those parking lots can be converted to parks or whatever other needs the local community has.

With fewer people driving in the future, grocery and other stores will likely offer delivery services as they do in places like New York and San Francisco. The money saved from abandoning the costly car, which a recent study by the American Public Transportation Association (2007) put at over $6,200 a year, can be spent on things like solar panels and hot-water heaters. New hybrid buses could run on locally produced biodiesel, as could the ultracompact cars at the car cooperative. Bicycling and walking are always biofueled. The evil hegemony of the automobile and its twin sister, oil, would slowly fade from memory.

THE HORSE

Allow us a moment of indulgence. Although it is extremely unlikely to be adopted anytime soon on a large scale, we would like readers to consider the beneficial aspects of public transportation powered by the original biofueled vehicle, the horse and cart. This combination is perfectly capable of maintaining the average urban traffic speed of 8 mph. Teams of horses are capable of pulling bus-size vehicles full of passengers, especially on streetcar tracks that produce much less resistance than rubber tires.

Horses are complicated creatures, capable of turning inedible hay into efficient work. Even with a single rider, they go five times farther per given amount of energy than a motorist alone in a car. And instead of producing toxic belches of particulates from their tailpipes, the waste from these biofueled wonders is perfectly balanced (in carbon:nitrogen terms) organic fertilizer that can be put directly on most vegetables and orchards. Horse manure also has the potential to greatly enhance biogas production from home or neighborhood biodigesters, while still making an excellent, nitrogen-rich amendment to area gardens.

A truly enlightened neighborhood in an enlightened city might have an open area for the stabling of horses mixed with general recreation. The stable would have a facility for the collection of not only horse but also human and other animal manure, which would be anaerobically digested to produce cooking gas for the neighborhood. This effluent would be sold to local gardeners as a safe and effective organic fertilizer. The horses would be rotated in shifts with horses from other neighborhoods for pulling trolleys for public transportation. Individual horses (or horse and carriages) could be rented for trips that involved hauling or trips out to the country.

HYBRID ELECTRIC VEHICLES

Hybrid technology has the potential to enhance the efficiency of buses and trains. This development is genuinely exciting in this regard. For cars, the story is more complex. The Honda Insight, for example, gets a seemingly impressive 60 mpg, and the Toyota Prius gets a decent 45 mpg. But straight internal-combustion cars with similar carrying capacities, such as the Smart Car and the Toyota Tercel or Geo Metro, are much simpler machines that get nearly the equivalent miles per gallon. A doubling of complexity has led to a doubling of price, with little apparent benefit. While the jury is still out, we suggest people research the actual benefits (and costs) of choosing a hybrid over a conventional car extremely carefully if they are considering purchasing one. It not obvious at all that hybrid cars are a good thing.

ELECTRIC VEHICLES

Electric vehicles are making a limited resurgence. Their efficiency gains come primarily from being smaller, but also because electric on-demand engines often perform better than constantly running internal-combustion engines, and because energy that would be lost to heat from braking can be recaptured by the electric motor and stored again in the battery.

A few smaller companies are converting existing gasoline models or importing new electric models from China. These are called neighborhood electric vehicles (NEVs). Their speed is limited. Some get up to 35 mph, others go no faster than 25 mph. Powering one of these using photovoltaics or other renewable energy is a possibility, and the idea of making all the juice you needed to fuel your car at home is certainly tantalizing. Generally speaking, these vehicles cost in the $12,000–18,000 range new. Many of these models are new or difficult to obtain, and testing has been spotty. The Idaho National Laboratory has done some testing, and their Web site is a great place to start your research if you are interested in NEVs (see resources). We highly recommend setting up a test drive with a dealer before committing yourself to a purchase, as driving a NEV is substantially different from driving a traditional internal-combustion car.

Generally speaking, a full-size, full-speed electric car such as the EV-1, made by GM in the early 2000s but then shamefully crushed into oblivion after California abandoned its Zero Emission Vehicle (ZEV) program, gets around 3 miles per kWh. Smaller neighborhood electric vehicles, of which Global Electric Motors (GEM) is the largest seller, typically get close to 6 miles per kWh. Depending on the model and the city and state regulations, these vehicles are limited to 25 to 35 mph. They weigh in at around 1,000 pounds, battery included, and come in two- or four-passenger models.

So what does this mean for powering these vehicles using renewable energy? One of the main reasons to consider an electric vehicle is because the potential exists to run it off a solar array on one's roof. Instead of using food to biofuel one's vehicle, the blank space on one's roof, assuming it is large enough and south-facing (and you've got a few spare pennies), can be covered with photovoltaics and produce enough power for a limited amount of battery-powered mobility (how much depends on the number of miles you'll be averaging per day, and for solar power your average insolation). As an example, if you planned on going a dozen miles a day in a NEV, you would use at least 2 kWhs, or more in stop-and-go traffic. On average, then, your NEV would require 400 additional watts of installed solar panels if you receive an insolation in the range of five hours. At an average installation price of $10/watt, that adds about $4,000 to the initial expense. Failing to fully charge your car batteries regularly could severely shorten their life, a significant expense. If your solar system is off-grid, it would be wise to have more installed capacity to ensure they were fully recharged.

One of the great things about electric vehicles is the potential, in places with time-of-use electricity rates, to charge up overnight when utility costs are generally at their lowest. A grid-tied PV system could sell its solar electricity during the day for the highest possible price and buy it back at the lower overnight rate to recharge the NEV. The fly in the ointment here is the quality and reliability of the current crop of NEVs, as well as their relatively high price. Because of the limited testing and the slew of new models that have recently become available, going the electric-vehicle route will make you something of a pioneer, with all the risks (and potential glory) that this implies.

When will a full-speed, highway-approved electric vehicle be available again? There is a huge amount of buzz in the electric car world at the moment, with major players like Mitsubishi in Japan and Bolloré and Pininfarina in Europe planning on widespread releases no later than 2010. In the United States, Chevy won't commit to a date for its Volt, so we'll have to ignore that development. The most promising development as of this writing appears to be two independent manufacturers, both based out of California. Aptera (www .aptera.com) has a three-wheeled space-age-looking two-seater that should be available by 2009. Miles Automotive Group (www.milesev.com) hopes to have a more conventional-looking sedan on the road by 2010. If you're in the market, it's worth checking in with these folks to see what's up.

ELECTRIFICATION OF TRANSPORT

Worth mentioning is using neighborhood light rail such as streetcars for public transportation. If it is powered by electricity, then substantial efficiency gains could be won compared with the use of liquid-fueled public transport or electric cars that require large batteries. Most towns established before World War II had electric streetcars that provided the majority of their citizens' mobility. Since the most efficient forms of renewable energy produce electricity, such as hydroelectric, wind, and solar, using these technologies to power our mobility needs instead of turning crops into liquid fuels makes loads of sense.

For a detailed discussion of this very interesting topic, read Alan S. Drake's "Electrification of Transportation as a Response to Peaking of World Oil Production," which can be found at www.lightrailnow .org/features/f_lrt_2005–02.htm.

BICYCLES

The bicycle is the only vehicle that, efficiency-wise, is an improvement on our natural way of getting

FIG. 11.6. **The modern streetcar is an efficient, quiet, stylish, and potentially pollution-free method of mass transit. Using electricity for our mass-transit options can mean using locally produced renewable electricity. By using mass transit instead of vehicles, the same amount of passenger miles can be achieved with only around 10 percent of the required energy.** Courtesy LTK Engineering Services

around, walking (actually, we suspect that skateboards fall in this category as well, but we couldn't find any studies to back it up). In many regards, bicycling is the *only* alternative mode of transport worth talking about. Measured against the bicycle, everything else is a failure.

The most important aspect of using a bicycle as a primary transportation option is not so much the bike itself, although old clunkers make riding tedious, but the accessories. These things help alleviate the three main problems with bike riding: safety, exposure to weather, and hauling stuff like kids, groceries, or your pooch. Reflectors, LED blinking safety lights in front and back (powered by rechargeable batteries), a bright safety vest or other bright clothing, and a helmet are all *required* safety features. They are not optional. If you ride every day, at some point in your life some SUV-driving fool, eating a doughnut, smoking a cigarette, and talking on his or her cell phone, is going to come barreling down on you and send you diving into the bushes. Reducing the chances of this happening with lights, reflectors, and vest, and *always* wearing a helmet for when the dive does happen, will make sure you outlive that SUV-driving fool by many decades.

Rain jacket, rain pants, and helmet cover, all in bright colors, will make it so you don't mind venturing out even when the weather is against you. A good pair of very warm gloves in addition to your other winter clothing will make sure you don't get in a wreck trying to stuff one of your hands into your pants pocket some frosty morning.

For keeping all this stuff handy and for hauling other smallish items, the minimum should be a rack over the back tire, capable of carrying a saddlebag on each side. Don't skimp on this simple addition, or you'll find yourself weaving down the road, possibly into a passing truck, clutching a dangling plastic bag with some needed item in one hand and steering with the other. A removable weatherproof saddlebag makes short trips to most stores feasible. A permanent basket

FIG. 11.7. **Rebekah's Schwinn, recently saved from being tossed in the dump by a fellow in a tie-dyed T-shirt who had obviously gone over to the dark side. Used bikes are easy to come by in urban settings. Sustainable, carbon-free living without some transport done by bicycle is almost unimaginable.**

in back or on the handlebars is another, not as weatherproof option.

For more serious hauls, or for toting the kids or the dog around town, consider a trailer. While items like trailers at several hundred dollars or more can seem pricey, remember that this is what the average person spends on his or her car *every month*! Don't be a grinch about souping up your renewable transportation options or your chains to fossil transport will continue to grow ever shorter.

These bicycle accessories are extremely important. They are what make riding a bike on a daily basis practical, safe, and comfortable as well as fun. You wouldn't ride around in a car that didn't have headlights, a seatbelt, a roof, or a trunk, so why skimp on your bicycle? If you're hoping to get daily use out of your bike, you'll need to soup it up.

ELECTRIC BICYCLES

Electric-assist bikes make sense for people who are commuting long distances (10 or more miles daily), who need to get where they're going a little quicker, and/or who are not in quite as good shape as they once were. This is far and away the best mode of motorized transport in terms of efficiency. Electric bikes and their cousins, a group of vehicles referred to as light electric vehicles (LEVs), some of which are pedal-assisted and some that aren't, require just a few hundred watts to charge and provide enough boost to maintain a 12–25 mph average speed. The higher the maintained speed, the less efficient they are and the lower the range, but many quality electric bikes get between 25 and 40 miles on a charge.

Generally speaking, everything that applies to normal bicycles applies to LEVs as well. Safety accessories, weather-protective clothing, and a rack or two with saddlebags greatly increases their practicality. They can be moderately heavy; the motor and battery add between 15 and 20 extra pounds, which makes them a little bit more of a pain when they need to be manually moved, into a car, for instance, or up onto a storage rack at home.

FIG. 11.8. **Tom Ed's electric bike with collapsible trailer. We watched as Tom Ed filled this puppy with groceries and band equipment and then powered up a steep hill at 15 mph without breaking a sweat. Amazing!**

From communicating with LEV owners and researching on the Web, we found that the you-get-what-you-pay-for mantra seems to hold especially true. Try to take a test ride of the model you are considering before making the plunge. This can be hard to do currently, as most bike shops don't stock any. Finding an owner locally may be your best bet. Check bike clubs and Listservs near you. Most owners seem particularly fond of talking about their bikes, in a positive or negative light.

WALKING

Walking should be everyone's default option for getting where they're going. Walking is second only to bicycling in its efficiency at getting us where we want to go. In a classic 12-year study published by the *New England Journal of Medicine* in 1998, men who walked 2 miles or more a day reduced their mortality rates by almost half compared with those who walked less than 1 mile. Walking 2 to 3 miles has been shown to alleviate back pain and aid in digestion, among myriad other health benefits. It's the way we were meant to get around. If you find it is impossible to incorporate walking into your daily activities, it probably means you're living too far away from where you work, shop, and play and are violating the first pillar of reducing your fossil-energy consumption.

LONG-DISTANCE TRAVEL

Fossil-fuel-free travel is not an easy thing to achieve. The extra miles require a lot of energy, and there's

TABLE 11.2 Long-distance Transportation Options and Their Efficiencies				
	Avg. Passenger Miles / 1,000 Kcal	Fossil-fuel Free?	Pros	Cons
Passenger Jet[18]	1.5	No chance!	Fast	Pollution in upper atmosphere especially damaging
Car, Single Occupancy	0.7	No	Convenient	Killing the planet
Car, Double Occupancy	1.4	No	Better than riding alone	Still bad
Car, Quintuple Occupancy	3.5	Potentially with biodiesel	Best use of automobile	Have to find four other folks traveling at same time
Bus (Diesel)	4.9	Potentially with biodiesel	Comfortable, convenient for urban dwellers	Primary bus company, Greyhound, has notoriously bad service
Rail (Diesel-Electric)	5.7	Potentially with biodiesel or renewable electric systems	Comfortable, convenient for urban dwellers	Spotty service, frequent delays mostly due to no dedicated passenger rail track
Bicycle	30	Absolutely!	Experience the country, great for health, etc.	Quite slow, exposed to elements, etc.
Freighter*[19]	9.9	Potentially with biodiesel or biodiesel-sail hybrids	Unique experience, time for reflection, reading, painting, etc.	Slow, spotty, service only along major trade routes, can be expensive

*For passenger jet, bus, and rail, 70 percent occupancy was assumed. For the freighter number, the comparison was based on a comparison of the efficiencies of rail cargo versus barge cargo as no numbers for passenger barges could be found. This may overstate the efficiency of passenger boats, as cargo can be packed much more tightly than human cargo. Nevertheless, under the same conditions (cargo transport), boats performed better than rail, and the rail cargo number was used as a baseline. Comparison of transportation efficiencies courtesy of James Strickland.

again a wide discrepancy in the options. Table 11.2 summarizes the basic ones.

The winner in terms of efficiency is, of course, the bicycle. Again, the bicycle is the only transportation option that is an improvement over our natural mode of transport, whether it's a trip of one mile or one thousand. All other modes gain speed and convenience by sacrifices in energy efficiency.

Surprisingly, airplanes are equivalent to a double-occupancy vehicle, although this doesn't take into account the extra driving to airports. While this may at first seem like an argument for flying, the fact that planes cover so much ground in so little time means folks travel many more miles more quickly. Thus, the increase in quantity negates the modest improvement over the single-occupied car.

It also appears to be the case that the contrails of jets in the upper atmosphere behave like cirrus clouds, allowing sunlight to pass into the atmosphere but trapping the radiation in the lower levels from leaving.[20] How much this exacerbates global climate disruption is still up for debate. Even so, on a mile-by-mile basis

it's probably better than the worst option, driving alone, but not by much. The problem is that the speed of flying means people travel much more than they would if they didn't fly. And while some argue that flying is more efficient because it gets you from point A to point B in a more direct line, the opposite may be true as passengers often go well out of their way during layovers. Getting to and from airports to city centers also consumes plenty of energy. At some point, if we want the planet to keep living we're going to need to give up flying as a frustrating, energy-intensive, and globe-homogenizing activity.

Again, buses and rail are nearly an order of magnitude more efficient than the car. Enough said.

Travel by freighter is a little-explored option that many folks don't know about. Many routes are offered, although they are currently more expensive than traveling by air (because they take longer and room and board are provided). Small groups of people (usually less than a dozen) are booked in rooms on cargo boats that ply the world's main trade routes. The accommodations are comfortable and meals are provided. The passengers are left to entertain themselves. It takes about 9 days to cross the Atlantic and 25 to cross the Pacific. Rates are typically $75–125/day/person. See the resources section for more information.

OUR STORY—TRAVEL

We've been a lot of places. Between high school and now (in our early thirties), we've visited the continental United States, parts of Canada, Mexico (twice), Guatemala, Honduras, Peru, Brazil, Spain, Morocco, Mali, Japan, India (twice), and Nepal. Visiting these places taught us a tremendous amount, from the people we met and the amazing things we saw. But as we learned more about global climate disruption and the exacerbating effects flying has on this planet-destroying problem, we took a long, hard look at this mode of travel.

Only 5 percent of the world's population has ever flown, and it was our hope to never have to engage in this activity again. When you tell your friends and family that you will never fly again, they look at you like you just fell out of a truck on the way to the loony bin, half sympathetic, but half afraid. Why would you impose such a hardship on yourself? they ask. Being unable to be anywhere in the country in half a day is just no longer conceivable.

It's an old adage, but it rings true, that getting there is half the fun. Our previous travels have taught us that much. And besides killing the planet, flying just isn't glamorous anymore but is cramped, delayed, and draining. Half of what used to make a vacation a great time to recoup from the excesses of work and catch up on one's other interests and hobbies was a long, slow ride there. Every aspect of flying makes this impossible.

All travel does not cease with the elimination of the airplane. Its hegemony has existed for only a scant four decades or so. Instead of lots of fast vacations that spend tremendous quantities of energy, we should make our vacations slow and earthbound and take the extra time to catch up on our reading and relation-ships. As others have coined it, we're part of the slow-movement movement.

Except when it comes to work, unfortunately. While Stephen has managed to stay out of those energy-wasteful, hurtling tin cans, Rebekah has not been so lucky. As a teacher for Solar Energy International, she attends occasional weeklong, far-flung workshops for training folks in photovoltaic installations. While promoting renewable energy by expending large quantities of fossil fuels is not ideal, it's a compromise we've both accepted. Hopefully, teaching 30 people how to install solar systems will save more fossil fuels from being burned in the long run than the one plane trip used.

URBAN PLANNING

You may be thinking it's too late for any discussion of urban planning. We've thrown in our lot with the automobile and we'll just have to sink or swim with that decision. The problem, of course, is that cars are very heavy and sink very fast.

Society is ever in flux, and even though we must either wean ourselves from fossil fuels to keep the planet from burning or be forcibly removed from that malevolent teat through depletion, we will not simply watch as everything rots (or tries to, at least, since so much of it is made of nonbiodegradable plastic). In many cases, especially with the vast suburban tracts around many of our cities, we need to use our dynamism to make the most of a bad situation.

Can the situation be rectified? If so, we need to figure out in which direction we want to head. To a large extent, much of the problem is one of regulation and zoning. The dominance of the automobile has created a society that measures access to necessities—shopping, work, and play—in the minutes driven in an automobile rather than the historical norm of in minutes by foot. Almost always it's the case that when you ask someone how far away something is they will answer with something like, "Oh, about 10 minutes." Implicit in this answer is that the route is traveled by car. This assumption has allowed neighborhoods developed since the autonomy of the automobile to gauge access to conveniences in miles rather than in yards.

The first reaction to the intertwining problems of global climate disruption and peak fossil energy, then, should be to extirpate the assumption, deeply embedded in almost all of our psyches, that the car is the default mode of transportation. It will immediately follow that all the zoning laws that enshrine that mentality must go. They will need to be rewritten to allow neighborhoods to have a mix of activities on each block: retail, entertainment, restaurants, small farms and manufacturing, childcare, et cetera. If the zoning entanglements that stipulate that retail must all be in this square mile, housing in this other square mile, and work in this other square mile are removed, then individuals, working on their own initiative, will begin disassembling the car-dependent culture that many of us inhabit without the mass razing of tract homes or the destruction of the freeways. Instead, the car culture will be disassembled by reconfiguring our existing infrastructure to provide these amenities closer to our homes, where they are needed and wanted.

Ultimately, we need to focus on (re)creating cities and towns where having an automobile is not a necessity and where our streets give priority to walking, biking, and mass transit before the car. We need to get our political leaders to join us in this effort as soon as possible, so send that e-mail or make that phone call right now. We have seen over the course of the past 60 years that once the necessity of the car is established, it feeds on itself. Once you have a car, why would you not use it? The answer now, of course, is obvious: the destruction of the planet and our enslavement to a diminishing supply of energy owned and managed by other nations, many of whom are not particularly fond of us (oftentimes with good reason). The answers to car dependency are relatively straightforward if not exactly easy.

We need denser populations that can be effectively served by mass transit. Urban dwellers typically use less than half the energy of their suburban counterparts.[21] Creating denser populations means rehabbing

The Woonerf, or Living Street

A movement that originated in the Netherlands is picking up steam all over Europe and is finally posting a few beachheads on the other side of the Atlantic. This is the idea of the Woonerf, or Living Street, as it is loosely translated from the Dutch. The idea is to take streets away from the sole domain of vehicles, especially residential streets, and return them to multiuse functions, such as hanging out, playing stickball, basking in the sunshine, concessions, et cetera.

Urban dwellers in North America often feel confined to their homes because the outside world is literally ruled by the automobile. The air is foul and speeding cars are one misstep away from running over you or your children. The answer lies in multiuse spaces where the car is slowed to the speed of a pedestrian, primarily by planters and other obstructions that take what was once a straight street and make it curved. In the process the size of the road is reduced, sometimes by making it one-way, leaving room for outdoor patios and other playspace. Our desire for this ideal landscape had a malignant and counterproductive growth in America called the suburban cul-de-sac, but the Dutch and others achieve these multiuse spaces in dense urban settings, giving the residents of the neighborhoods plenty of space for outdoor play and recreation just outside their door. Higher speeds for motorized traffic are limited to main thoroughfares. Most streets in America are plenty broad enough for this application and are ripe for being reclaimed for many uses beyond driving. Learn more about it and start freeing your street from the hegemony of the car by turning your neighborhood into a Living Street.

the existing housing in our cities to be carbon free, filling in the empty spaces with low-energy housing and shops, and massively upgrading our bicycling and bus infrastructure, including in the longer term dedicated covered bikeways and the redevelopment of light-rail streetcars. Rather than abandon the tract housing on the periphery, we should deregulate its zoning and, where necessary, move isolated homes onto lots further in town. Beyond this are the farms and forests that should supply us not only with our food, fiber, and fuel but also the wildlands that provide us with recreation and our fellow earth-dwellers with a place to call home. Many of the people that will inhabit the rezoned and reconfigured ring of tract homes will find work either in their neighborhoods or in the farms and manufacturing facilities that are already sprouting up again around our cities. They will have the opportunity and the space for large gardens and orchards and other small manufacturing businesses that can serve the urban population. The business professionals, many of whom now occupy these suburban tract homes, will need to either move into the city where they once lived or telecommute if possible, working and shopping in their existing neighborhoods.

These are all changes that can happen relatively quickly, in less than a decade if we so will it. We must rehab our existing infrastructure rather than trying to start from scratch, as this latter option is far too energy intensive to be achieved this late in the day. While in the ideal we would have used our one-time fossil-fuel bounty to have developed a socially and environmentally just, renewable-energy-powered civilization once we realized the inherent limitations of our earth's sources and sinks some three or four decades ago, we must now content ourselves with working with what we've got.

Hopefully, the brief survey of transportation and urban planning options we've outlined here can convince you such a transformation is not only possible but also desirable. It will, without a doubt, be a huge amount of work. The alternative of killing off much of the planet and allowing the wonderful achievements of our civilization to collapse and die should be a pretty good motivator. And if there's one thing the past century has proven, it's that we know how to get some work done! We just need to refocus our effort on building a sustainable society in harmony with the millions of other species on the globe. Success is achievable, but not without the requisite effort. Time to get cracking!

RESOURCES

Books

Alvord, Katie. 2000. *Divorce Your Car! Ending the Love Affair with the Automobile*. Gabriola Island, BC: New Society Publishers.

Balish, Chris. 2006. *How to Live Well without Owning a Car: Save Money, Breathe Easier, and Get More Mileage Out of Life*. Berkeley, CA: Ten Speed Press. Great practical advice on how to rid your life of these planet-killing behemoths.

Morris, Douglas. 2005. *It's a Sprawl World After All*. Gabriola Island, BC: New Society Publishers. How sprawl and car culture isolate us as individuals and ruin communities.

Sloman, Lynn. 2006. *Car Sick: Solutions for Our Car-Addicted Culture*. Devon, England, UK: Green Books. Excellent policy ideas for reconfiguring our cities to be bicycle and mass-transit friendly.

DVDs

Who Killed the Electric Car? 2006. GM's latest crime, exposed.

Internet

Community Solution. Besides hosting annual conferences on peak oil and how to mitigate it, Community Solution puts out informative quarterly newsletters called *New Solutions* analyzing energy use in our daily lives. www.communitysolution.org

Critical Mass. The unofficial site of this non-organization, a monthly bicycle ride to raise awareness of bicyclists in over 200

North American cities. Great place to meet knowledgeable cyclists and show your support for bicycling. www.critical-mass.org

Dynamic Cities Project. "Nonprofit creating energy transition strategies as a proactive response to peak oil and climate change." www.dynamic cities.squarespace.com/home

Electric-Bikes.com. Great overview of electric biking options. www.electric-bikes.com

Internet Guide to Freighter Travel. Comprehensive introduction with great links to passenger-carrying freighters. www.geocities.com /freighterman.geo/mainmenu.html

Low Fly Pledge. Commit in writing to giving up this ridiculous activity. http://lowflyzone.org

National Association of Rail Passengers. www.narprail .org

National Biodiesel Board. www.biodiesel.org

Piedmont Biofuels. One of the earliest, and best, biodiesel co-ops. A model for locally manufactured biodiesel. www.biofuels.coop

Ridesharing. Someone's probably already going where you want to go. Find them here. www.erideshare .com

Magazines

Carbusters Magazine. www.carbusters.org

Endnotes

1. Community Solution Newsletter *New Solutions #11: The Energy Impact of Buildings.* January, 2007. Yellow Springs, OH. See www.communitysolution.org.
2. U.S. Department of Energy. www.fueleconomy.gov.
3. Biofuel Conversion Factors: www.fapri.missouri .edu/outreach/publications/2006/biofuelconversions .pdf.
4. Community Solution Newsletter *New Solutions #11: The Energy Impact of Buildings.* January, 2007. Yellow Springs, OH. See www.communitysolution.org.
5. U.S. Department of Energy. www.fueleconomy.gov.
6. U.S. Department of Energy. www.fueleconomy.gov.
7. U.S. Department of Energy. www.fueleconomy.gov.
8. U.S. Department of Energy. www.fueleconomy.gov.
9. Susan Evans Garlinghouse, "A formula for energy expenditure." www.shady-acres.com/susan/energy .shtml.
10. Figure based on 3.5 mph, 150-pound person expending 0.035 cal./lb./mile.
11. Advance Vehicle Testing Activity—Idaho National Lab. See http://avt.inl.gov.
12. National Renewable Energy Lab. "Demonstration of Caterpillar C-10 Dual-Fuel Engines in MCI 102DL3 Commuter Buses." www.nrel.gov
13. Colorado Railcar Company. Ft. Lupton, CO. See www.coloradorailcar.com.
14. Figure based on 15 mph, 150-pound person, 15-pound bicycle, expending 0.05 cal./lb./mile.
15. Figure based on comparison of watt usage of a typical electric bike and the calorie consumption for bicycle riding.
16. Green Consumer Guide. See www.greenconsumer guide.com/scoot.html.
17. United Nations Food and Agriculture Organization. www.fao.org.
18. Jet Blue Annual Report 2004.
19. "Energy Use in Freight Transportation," Congressional Budget Office, February, 1982.
20. Michael Shirber. "Longer Airline Flights Proposed to Combat Global Warming." *Live Science*, January 26, 2005. www.livescience.com.
21. Jonathan Norman, Heather MacClean, and Christopher Kennedy. "Comparing Low and High Residential Density: Life-Cycle Analysis of Energy Use and Greenhouse Gas Emissions." *Journal of Urban Planning and Development,* 132 (1): 10–21. http://64.106.229.11/jetblue2004.

Conclusion

Fossil fuels waited like buried treasure for millions of years until humanity had the technological capacity to exploit them. They allowed for the creation and use of countless gadgets and laborsaving devices and the proliferation of the automobile. First we marveled at these objects, then we bought them and used them with wonder, then we took them for granted, and then we became dependent on them for everything. For our food and mobility, our health and entertainment, even our very own identities. We became what we bought and what we had, a commodity among heaps and piles of other commodities.

It's fall in the year 2007 as we write this, and the sun is setting on these stranded pools and piles of long-ago sunlight. Like rich, spoiled children who have gorged themselves on an excessive inheritance, we have no idea what to do now that we are faced with the fact of our wealth's inherent destructive properties and vanishing existence. To live on our annual income of energy seems impossible without binges of Jet Skis, airplanes, SUVs, candy bars, video games, and all the rest. How will we ever survive without them?

The junkie in the gutter has asked himself that same question many, many times. But the realities of our situation are unavoidable. The ice caps are melting at a rate faster than anyone expected, imperiling thousands of species as well as towns and villages around the globe. Oil production has stagnated for several years even as prices reach record highs, and a near-term peak seems all but certain. What's more, as oil and other fossil fuels run out, we're turning to dirtier forms to make up the shortfall. Tar sands are difficult to exploit, and huge amounts of energy (and water) must be expended to extract them. We burn coal of lower quality every year. Facts like these mean that even if we behave exactly as we did the year before, we will contribute more CO_2 into the atmosphere every year.

"What can I do?" you ask. The problem seems so overwhelming that action is pointless. But we can't forget that the problem is the cumulative result of our individual actions. If Americans would only just put their electronics on power strips and turn these off when not in use, eliminating phantom loads, we could save enough electricity to power the continent of Australia.[1] A little bit of extra effort and we've got one continent taken care of.

As to what a life is like without fossil fuels, we can tell you. We won't claim that no fossil fuels are ever burned for our benefit (a goodly amount were burned to make the book you're holding in your hands, for instance), but we do go about our daily lives without using them. We have hot water and electricity, and we cook, and use our computer, our washing machine, and our stereo. When we walk outside we're greeted with hundreds of different species of plants and flowers that are visited by bumblebees, hummingbirds, and butterflies. We live a short walk or bike ride from our friends and our favorite hangouts. We save over $10,000 every year because we have few bills and, more importantly, only one car. This means we can work less and drive less and spend more time sipping homebrew with neighbors or reading books on our green roof. Much of our food is grown either in our yard or by friends who live nearby in the countryside. When we do want to work, we have more than enough of it, because interest in renewable energy is exploding. There's a lot of solar-water panels and solar air heaters that need installing out there, and a little job security never hurt anyone. All in all, it's hardly the apocalypse lots of folks talk about when they imagine the oil running out.

Tar sands open pit mining in northeastern Alberta, Canada. Once the home of boreal forest, a quarter of the province of Alberta is being threatened with tar sands development. Every time you put gasoline in your car, this wasteland gets a little bigger. Lindsay Telfer, Sierra Club Canada

When our children have become grandparents, more than likely they will not be using fossil fuels and their derivatives in very many aspects of their lives. Not only are fossil fuels finite in quantity and being depleted at an accelerating rate, but the harm their use entails to this planet that sustains us all is now undeniable even by half-wits and madmen.

We are now presented with a choice, a choice that is likely unprecedented by any species in the history of earth, because of its scale but also because of our cognitive ability to understand the problem and change our behavior. We can attempt to continue on with our lives as they are now for as long as possible, doing whatever it takes to feed our habits of growing consumption of the earth's limited resources until we are forcibly made to stop by disruption and exhaustion of the supplies this requires. Or we can choose to live within our annual budget of energy and materials, as every other species on the planet does. We won't be living in hollowed-out logs like many of the animals of the forest, however, as our own story can testify to. Our intelligence and dexterity will allow us to use our more limited budget as effectively as possible, with lives as comfortable as the ones we live now.

Two generations may seem like a long time, an era that will never come. We are now in the darkest hour, when our dependence on fossil fuels is almost absolute. Ignoring the goal of a carbon-free civilization and

Electronics often consume three times as much power when off as when on, because of the standby function. How many of these West Virginia mountaintops were laid to waste just to keep all our electronics sitting idly by?

Courtesy Ohio Valley Environmental Coalition

carrying on as before seems like the easier choice. In the short term, no doubt, this is true. But two generations is about the same amount of time it takes for an acorn to sprout and grow into an oak tree in a clearing in the woods. When the seedling first pokes its head through the leaves, imagine if its first response on learning that it had to grow 100 feet tall to reach the canopy was, "Aw, screw it, that's too far. I give up!" Just because we have only begun to grow our renewable energy economy and convert our lives to carbon freedom is not any reason to feel despair. It's not anything we can do in a year, probably not even in a decade. But in a year we'll be a little bit farther along, and in a decade we'll be able to imagine what it will feel like to reach the top.

The time for debate has ended. We must decide one way or the other, by inaction and acceptance of the status quo, or by grabbing our toolbox and getting busy. The need for making our homes and our lives carbon free is well understood and of the utmost importance. Indeed, even the means of making our homes and lives carbon free have already been discovered. Both the problem and the solution have been identified. Now it is only a matter of learning and implementing and, once you have done this, to teach others.

We won't lie to you. Getting to a carbon-free existence will require a hell of a lot of blood, sweat, and tears. Once there, it'll require a little more attention

Our carbon free home, summer 2007.

and involvement than our previous ignorant and fossilized existence. Like every long journey, it's one you have to take a step at a time. One thing is for sure: if you don't do anything, you won't get anywhere! Good luck!

Endnote

1. Schwartz, Joe. "Finding the Phantoms: Eliminate Standby Energy Losses." *Home Power* magazine. 117: 64–67.

Index

green
press
INITIATIVE

The Chelsea Green Publishing Company is committed to preserving ancient forests and natural resources. We elected to print this title on 30% postconsumer recycled paper, processed chlorine-free. As a result, for this printing, we have saved:

40 Trees (40' tall and 6-8" diameter)
14,493 Gallons of Wastewater
28 million BTU's Total Energy
1,861 Pounds of Solid Waste
3,492 Pounds of Greenhouse Gases

Chelsea Green Publishing made this paper choice because we and our printer, Thomson-Shore, Inc., are members of the Green Press Initiative, a nonprofit program dedicated to supporting authors, publishers, and suppliers in their efforts to reduce their use of fiber obtained from endangered forests. For more information, visit: www.greenpressinitiative.org.

Environmental impact estimates were made using the Environmental Defense Paper Calculator. For more information visit: www.papercalculator.org.